MUSIC IN THE BAROQUE

Western Music in Context: A Norton History

Walter Frisch SERIES EDITOR

Music in the Medieval West, by Margot Fassler

Music in the Renaissance, by Richard Freedman

Music in the Baroque, by Wendy Heller

Music in the Eighteenth Century, by John Rice

Music in the Nineteenth Century, by Walter Frisch

Music in the Twentieth and Twenty-First Centuries, by Joseph Auner

MUSIC IN THE BAROQUE

Wendy Heller

Princeton University

W. W. NORTON AND COMPANY

NEW YORK • LONDON

W. W. Norton & Company has been independent since its founding in 1923, when William Warder Norton and Mary D. Herter Norton first published lectures delivered at the People's Institute, the adult education division of New York City's Cooper Union. The firm soon expanded its program beyond the Institute, publishing books by celebrated academics from America and abroad. By midcentury, the two major pillars of Norton's publishing program—trade books and college texts—were firmly established. In the 1950s, the Norton family transferred control of the company to its employees, and today—with a staff of four hundred and a comparable number of trade, college, and professional titles published each year—W. W. Norton & Company stands as the largest and oldest publishing house owned wholly by its employees.

Editor: Maribeth Payne
Associate Editor: Justin Hoffman
Editorial Assistant: Michael Fauver
Developmental Editor: Harry Haskell
Manuscript Editor: Jodi Beder
Project Editor: Jack Borrebach
Electronic Media Editor: Steve Hoge
Marketing Manager, Music: Amy Parkin
Production Manager: Ashley Horna
Photo Editor: Stephanie Romeo
Permissions Manager: Megan Jackson
Text Design: Jillian Burr
Composition: Jouve International—Brattleboro, VT
Manufacturing: Quad/Graphics—Fairfield, PA

A catalogue record is available from the Library of Congress

ISBN: 978-0-393-92917-1

W. W. Norton & Company, Inc., 500 Fifth Avenue, New York, NY 10110-0017
wwnorton.com

W. W. Norton & Company Ltd., Castle House, 75/76 Wells Street, London W1T 3QT

2 3 4 5 6 7 8 9 0

For my father, Professor Gerald S. Heller, who taught me about teaching
And my students, past, present, and future

CONTENTS IN BRIEF

Contents		ix
Anthology Repertoire		xii
Series Editor's Preface		xv
Author's Preface		xvii
CHAPTER 1	Baroque Music in Early Modern Europe	1
PART I	**Musical Expression and Innovation**	
CHAPTER 2	Ancients and Moderns	20
CHAPTER 3	Theatrical Baroque	39
CHAPTER 4	The Art and Craft of Instrumental Music in the Early Seventeenth Century	56
CHAPTER 5	Music in Civic and Religious Ritual	75
PART II	**Musical Institutions**	
CHAPTER 6	Opera in Venice and Beyond	95
CHAPTER 7	Power and Pleasure at the Court of Louis XIV	112
CHAPTER 8	Music in Seventeenth-Century England	130
CHAPTER 9	Music and Education	148
CHAPTER 10	Academies, Salons, and Music Societies	163

PART III   **Musical Synthesis in the Capitals of Europe**

CHAPTER 11   Rome in the Age of the Arcadian Academy   184

CHAPTER 12   Parisians and Their Music in the Eighteenth Century   201

CHAPTER 13   Music in City, Court, and Church in the Holy Roman Empire   218

CHAPTER 14   The London of Handel and Hogarth   235

CHAPTER 15   Postlude and Prelude: Bach and the Baroque   252

GLOSSARY   Al

ENDNOTES   Al0

CREDITS   Al4

INDEX   Al6

CONTENTS

Anthology Repertoire   xii

Series Editor's Preface   xv

Author's Preface   xvii

CHAPTER 1   **Baroque Music in Early Modern Europe**   1
Defining "Baroque" **3** • Humanism and Beyond **6** • Political and Religious
Conflict **10** • Toward the Enlightenment **13** • Baroque Music and Style **14** •
For Further Reading 16

PART I   Musical Expression and Innovation

CHAPTER 2   **Ancients and Moderns**   20
Theory and Practice in the Age of Humanism **21** • Inventing Opera **22** •
Dramatizing the Madrigal: *Il pastor fido* **28** • Moving the Passions with
Song **30** • From Performance to Print and Back Again **34** •
For Further Reading 37

CHAPTER 3   **Theatrical Baroque**   39
Monteverdi's Mantua **40** • Opera in Italy and Beyond **46** • Other Varieties
of Musical Theater **48** • Exoticism **52** • *For Further Reading 55*

CHAPTER 4   **The Art and Craft of Instrumental Music in
                   the Early Seventeenth Century**   56
The Practical Musician **58** • Building Instruments for Sight and Sound **59** •
Patrons, Audiences, and Performers **61** • Music, Rhetoric, and National
Styles **63** • Genre and Style in Seventeenth-Century Instrumental
Music **65** • *For Further Reading 73*

CHAPTER 5   **Music in Civic and Religious Ritual**   75
Music, Faith, and Ideology **76** • Religious Diversity and Stylistic
Pluralism **79** • Music and Paraliturgical Practices **88** •
For Further Reading 92

PART II   Musical Institutions

CHAPTER 6   **Opera in Venice and Beyond**   95
Opera and the Venetian Republic **96** • The Venetian Opera Industry **97** •
The Anatomy of an Opera: Monteverdi's *L'incoronazione di Poppea* **98** •
Staging Venetian Opera **104** • Cavalli's *Giasone* **106** • Beyond *Giasone* and
Venice **108** • Operatic Conventions in the Late Seventeenth Century **109** •
For Further Reading 110

CHAPTER 7   **Power and Pleasure at the Court of Louis XIV**   112
Centralization of the Arts under Bourbon Rule **114** • What Is So French about
French Music? **116** • Staging the Monarchy **121** • The Burlesque as a Mirror
of the Court: The *Comédie-Ballet* **123** • The Tragic Ideal **124** • The Power of
the Sorceress: From *Armide* to *Médée* **126** • *For Further Reading 129*

CHAPTER 8   **Music in Seventeenth-Century England**   130
Music in the Jacobean and Caroline Ages **131** • Music for the Church of
England **135** • The Interregnum **136** • John Playford: Music Publishing from
the Interregnum to the Restoration **137** • Music during the Restoration **141** •
Henry Purcell **142** • *For Further Reading 146*

CHAPTER 9   **Music and Education**   148
Choirboys **149** • Learning to Sing **152** • Convents **154** • Orphans and
Foundlings **158** • *For Further Reading 162*

CHAPTER 10   **Academies, Salons, and Music Societies**   163
Singing at the Italian Academies **164** • Women Patrons: The Salons **170** •
Professionalism: The Accademia Filarmonica of Bologna **173** • Musical
Entrepreneurs and the Rise of Public Concerts **176** • *For Further
Reading 179*

PART III Musical Synthesis in the Capitals of Europe

CHAPTER 11 **Rome in the Age of the Arcadian Academy**   184
Patrons and Composers in Eighteenth-Century Rome **185** • Alternatives to
Opera **188** • The Arcadian Academy **191** • Opera and the Arcadians **195** •
Corelli and the Cult of Instrumental Music **196** • *For Further Reading 200*

CHAPTER 12 **Parisians and Their Music in the Eighteenth Century**   201
Resisting the Monarchy: The Politics of the Italian Style **202** • Pleasures
in Paris **204** • François Couperin and *Les goûts réunis* **208** • The French
Cantata **212** • Paris during the Regency **213** • *For Further Reading 217*

CHAPTER 13 **Music in City, Court, and Church in the Holy
                Roman Empire**   218
A Domestic Music Scene in North Germany **219** • Buxtehude in Lübeck **221** •
Public Concerts in Hamburg and Lübeck **224** • Heinrich Biber in
Salzburg **226** • Vienna and the Imperial Style **230** • *For Further Reading 233*

CHAPTER 14 **The London of Handel and Hogarth**   235
Commerce and Politics in Eighteenth-Century London **237** • Italian Music in
London **240** • Oratorio and the Apotheosis of Handel **248** • *For Further
Reading 251*

CHAPTER 15 **Postlude and Prelude: Bach and the Baroque**   252
The Road to Leipzig **254** • Music in Leipzig **255** • Music for the
Church **257** • The Coffeehouse Composer **263** • Beyond Genre: The
Universal Bach **264** • *For Further Reading 271*

Glossary   A1
Endnotes   A10
Credits   A14
Index   A16

ANTHOLOGY REPERTOIRE

1. Claudio Monteverdi: Fifth Book of Madrigals: *O Mirtillo*
2. Giulio Caccini: *Le nuove musiche: Dovrò dunque morire*
3. John Dowland: *Second Book of Songs or Ayres: Flow, my Tears*
4. Claudio Monteverdi: *L'Orfeo*, Act 2: *Tu se' morta* and *Ahi, caso acerbo*
5. Claudio Monteverdi: *Madrigali guerrieri et amorosi: Lamento della ninfa*
6. Girolamo Frescobaldi: *Toccate e partite d'intavolatura di cimbalo*, Book 1: Toccata No. 2
7. Dario Castello: *Sonate concertate in stil moderno*, Book 2: Sonata No. 2
8. Johann Jacob Froberger: *Libro quarto di toccate, ricercari, capricci, allemande, gigue, courante, sarabande:* Suite in C Major, FbWV 612
9. Claudio Monteverdi: *Vespro della Beata Virgine: Duo Seraphim*
10. Heinrich Schütz: *Symphoniae sacrae*, Book 1: *Fili mi, Absalon*, SWV 269
11. Giacomo Carissimi: *Jephte: Plorate colles*
12. Francesco Cavalli: *Giasone*, Act 3, scene 21: *Infelice, ch'ascolto?*
13. Jean-Baptiste Lully: *Armide*, Act 5, scene 5: *Le perfide Renaud me fuit*
14. Henry Purcell: *King Arthur*, Act 3: *What ho!* and *What power art thou*
15. Antonio Vivaldi: Concerto for Viola d'amore and Lute, RV 540: Movement 1, Allegro
16. Barbara Strozzi: *Cantate, arietta*, Op. 3: *Begli occhi*
17. Arcangelo Corelli: Violin Sonata in A Major, Op. 5, No. 9
18. François Couperin: *Pièces de clavecin:* Order 3, *La ténébreuse,* and Order 6, *Les moissonneurs*
19. Jean-Philippe Rameau: *Platée*, Act 2, scene 3: *A l'aspect de ce nuage*
20. Dieterich Buxtehude: *Membra Jesu nostri*, BuxWV 75: *Ad cor: Vulnerasti cor meum*

21. Georg Philipp Telemann: *Ouverture burlesque de Quixotte,* TWV 55: G10

22. Heinrich Ignaz Franz Biber: *Mystery* Sonatas: *Crucifixion* Sonata

23. George Frideric Handel: *Rinaldo,* HWV 7a: Act 1, scenes 6, 7, and 9

24. George Frideric Handel: *Saul,* HWV 53: Act 1, scene 3

25. Johann Sebastian Bach: *St. John Passion,* BWV 245: Part 2, Nos. 27–32

26. Johann Sebastian Bach: *The Art of Fugue,* BWV 1080: Contrapuncti 1 and 7

Western Music in Context: A Norton History starts from the premise that music consists of far more than the notes on a page or the sound heard on a recording. Music is a product of its time and place, of the people and institutions that bring it into being.

Many music history texts focus on musical style and on individual composers. These approaches have been a valuable part of writing about music since the beginnings of modern scholarship in the later nineteenth century. But in the past few decades, scholars have widened their scope in imaginative and illuminating ways to explore the cultural, social, intellectual, and historical contexts for music. This new perspective is reflected in the volumes of Western Music in Context. Among the themes treated across the series are:

- The ways in which music has been commissioned, created, and consumed in public and private spheres
- The role of technology in the creation and transmission of music, from the advent of notation to the digital age
- The role of women as composers, performers, and patrons
- The relationships between music and national or ethnic identity
- The training and education of musicians in both private and institutional settings

All of these topics—and more—animate the pages of Western Music in Context. Written in an engaging style by recognized experts, the series paints vivid pictures of moments, activities, locales, works, and individuals:

- A fourth-century eyewitness report on musical practices in the Holy Land, from a European nun on a pilgrimage
- A lavish wedding at the court of Savoy in the mid-fifteenth century, with music by Guillaume DuFay

- Broadside ballads sung on the streets of London or pasted onto walls, and enjoyed by people from all levels of society
- A choral Magnificat performed at a church in colonial Brazil in the 1770s, accompanied by an organ sent by ship and mule from Portugal
- The barely literate impresario Domenico Barbaia making a tidy fortune at Italian opera houses by simultaneously managing gambling tables and promoting Gioachino Rossini
- A "radio teaching piece" from 1930 by Kurt Weill celebrating the transatlantic flight of Charles Lindbergh

Each volume of Western Music in Context is accompanied by a concise anthology of carefully chosen works. The anthologies offer representative examples of a wide variety of musical genres, styles, and national traditions. Included are excerpts from well-known works like Aaron Copland's *Billy the Kid*, as well as lesser-known gems like Ignacio de Jerusalem's *Matins for the Virgin of Guadalupe*. Commentaries within the anthologies not only provide concise analyses of every work from both formal and stylistic points of view, but also address issues of sources and performance practice.

StudySpace, Norton's online resource for students, features links to recordings of anthology selections that can be streamed from the Naxos Music Library (individual or institutional subscription required), as well as the option to purchase and download recordings from Amazon and iTunes. In addition, students can purchase access to, and instructors can request a free DVD of, the Norton Opera Sampler, which features over two hours of video excerpts from fourteen Metropolitan Opera productions. Finally, for readers wanting to do further research or find more specialized books, articles, or web-based resources, StudySpace offers lists of further readings that supplement those at the end of each chapter in the texts.

Because the books of the Western Music in Context series are relatively compact and reasonably priced, instructors and students might use one or more volumes in a single semester, or several across an academic year. Instructors have the flexibility to supplement the books and the accompanying anthologies with other resources, including Norton Critical Scores and *Strunk's Source Readings in Music History*, as well as other readings, illustrations, scores, films, and recordings.

The contextual approach to music history offers limitless possibilities: an instructor, student, or general reader can extend the context as widely as he or she wishes. Well before the advent of the World Wide Web, the renowned anthropologist Clifford Geertz likened culture to a spider's web of interconnected meanings that humans have spun. Music has been a vital part of such webs throughout the history of the West. Western Music in Context has as its goal to highlight such connections and to invite the instructors and students to continue that exploration on their own.

-Walter Frisch
Columbia University

AUTHOR'S PREFACE

Of all the periods in Western music history, the one conventionally known as the Baroque—stretching from the end of the sixteenth century to the middle of the eighteenth—is perhaps the most full of contradictions. Musicians sought to break with the immediate past, but found inspiration for their innovations in the ancient world. The courts of absolute monarchs flourished, producing expensive and luxurious music, while a growing population of middle-class consumers gained access to musical pleasures. The music of the seventeenth and early eighteenth centuries was also shaped by a series of disastrous wars—the Thirty Years' War, the English Civil War, and the War of the Spanish Succession—yet it benefited from periods of economic growth and political stability. Even as Baroque musicians developed distinctive national styles, increased mobility and circulation of printed music created an international market.

Another apparent contradiction is that the best-known heroes of the musical Baroque—Handel, Bach, Telemann, and Vivaldi—were born only at the end of the period, in the final decades of the seventeenth century, and flourished as the new galant style, considered by John Rice in *Music in the Eighteenth Century*, was capturing the imagination of listeners. We will not neglect these figures; but to focus on their lives and music or to see the works of earlier composers as mere antecedents strips away much of the richness and complexity of Baroque music-making. We consider not only the music that is commercially successful today, but also what was popular in the seventeenth and early eighteenth centuries, examining why and how it moved listeners and incited controversies. In telling compelling stories, we incorporate new scholarship and place politics, visual art, social history, economics, and more at the center of the narrative.

The tripartite division of *Music in the Baroque* corresponds to the conventional view of an early, middle, and late Baroque. However, each section approaches the repertory with a set of questions different from those encountered in most narratives. Part I considers the host of musical innovations and stylistic variety that characterized the first half of the century and contextualizes them in the political and economic crises of the era: the ways in which the ancients inspired the moderns (Chapter 2), the use of theatrical music in the major European courts (Chapter 3), the new expressivity of the instrumental music (Chapter 4), and the role of music in religious and civic ritual (Chapter 5). In Part II, we turn to the various institutions that produced music in the seventeenth and early eighteenth centuries, including public theaters of Venice (chapter 6), governments and commercial sectors of France and England (Chapters 7 and 8), as well as choir schools, convents, academies, salons, and music societies (Chapters 9 and 10), topics rarely covered in textbooks.

Part III examines music in a selected group of cities in the late seventeenth and early eighteenth centuries: the Rome of Handel and Scarlatti (Chapter 11), the pleasures of Paris as the power of Louis XIV waned (Chapter 12), and the diverse music making in the Holy Roman Empire, moving from the "free imperial" cities of Hamburg and Lübeck, to Salzburg, and finally Vienna, the court of the Habsburg emperor (Chapter 13). Chapter 14 focuses on the complexities of Handel's London, while our final chapter, "Postlude and Prelude," devoted to J. S. Bach, reflects both the historical reality of Bach's unique position in relation to musicians of the time and the special role his music has played in the life of musicians and music scholarship in the years since his death.

Music in the Baroque takes account of the most recent scholarly research and perspectives, with minimal endnotes and references to interrupt the narrative. A short list of readings at the end of each chapter points the student to some of this more specialized literature; an expanded bibliography is available on StudySpace, Norton's online resource for students. Quotations from primary sources, many drawn from *Strunk's Source Readings in Music History*, introduce readers to the eloquent voices of the past. For those who wish to explore these sources in more detail, page references to both the single-volume and the seven-volume editions of *Strunk* appear in parentheses after quotations from this text. Bibliographic information for other source readings appears in endnotes.

The text is also sparing in its use of musical examples and analytical remarks. For those who want to delve deeper into individual works, twenty-six musical scores, each with detailed commentary, are included in the accompanying *Anthology for Music in the Baroque*. Links to recordings of anthology repertoire are available on StudySpace.

ACKNOWLEDGMENTS

I owe an enormous debt of gratitude to the many colleagues, students, and friends without whom this book would never have been completed.

One of the privileges of tackling this project was having the opportunity to delve into the writings of my colleagues and friends, particularly those from the Society for the Study of Seventeenth-Century Music and the American Handel Society. I am grateful not only for their support but also for their brilliant work, which was an inspiration throughout this project. This book could capture but a glimmer of the richness and complexity of their scholarship. I extend special thanks to a number of friends and colleagues who read drafts, shared ideas, and listened patiently as I rehearsed the various challenges that this undertaking necessarily entailed: Susan Boynton, Jennifer Williams Brown, Donald Burrows, Michael Burden, Eric Chafe, Seth Coluzzi, Gabriel Crouch, Rebecca Cypess, Jayson Dobney, Christine Getz, Beth Glixon, Jonathan Glixon, Catherine Gordon-Seifert, Ruth HaCohen, Kelley Harness, Rebecca Harris-Warrick, Robert Holzer, Roger Freitas, Jeffrey Kurtzman, Ellen Harris, Berta Joncus, Kathryn Lowerre, Kimberlyn Montford, Ellen Rosand, Lois Rosow, Alexander Silbiger, Louise Stein, Ruth Tatlow, Andrew Weaver, Barbara White, Nancy Wilson, Amanda Eubanks Winkler, and Patrick Wood. Margaret Murata provided me with the wonderful example from a Pasqualini cantata included in Chapter 10, and her thoughtful selections and translations in her revision of the Baroque volume of *Strunk's Source Readings in Music History* were a pleasure to weave into the narrative.

I would like to express gratitude as well to generous colleagues who read various versions of the manuscript for W. W. Norton, including not only anonymous readers but also Gregory Barnett, Georgia Cowart, Markus Rathey, Andrew Dell'Antonio, and especially Mark Kroll, who went far beyond the call of duty and read numerous drafts, testing chapters with his students and improving all aspects of the texts with his keen editorial eye and musical insights. My thanks as well to Richard Freedman, Hendrick Schulze, David Kasunic, and Danill Zavlunov, who tested chapters in the classroom, providing valuable feedback and encouragement. I am also enormously grateful to my friend John Burkhalter, who brought his deep knowledge of Baroque music to bear in his reading of the proofs.

A huge debt of gratitude goes as well to my teammates on this project: Margot Fassler, Richard Freedman, John Rice, Joseph Auner, and especially our editor, Walter Frisch, who has been unfailingly encouraging and positive. It is truly an honor to be part of such a distinguished group of colleagues, and I salute their creativity, friendship, and sense of humor. Maribeth Payne has patiently supported this project with her enthusiasm and wisdom since its outset, even as deadlines came and went. My special thanks to Harry Haskell, who spent an unforgettable summer editing the text and anthology, saving me from innumerable errors. Thanks also to Jodi Beder, Jack Borrebach, Michael Fauver, Ariella Foss, Justin Hoffman, Debra Nichols, Megan Jackson, and Stephanie Romeo.

I am particularly grateful to my undergraduate and graduate students over the years, who have inspired me in countless ways. I thank first several generations of

Princeton students in Music 234 (Music in the Baroque), who taught me so much. Saraswathi Shukla first took the course as a young teenager, grew up during the book's gestation, and spent much of her senior year at Princeton hunting down examples and images, proofreading and copyediting, and providing much-needed companionship and humor. Nicholas Lockey, who finished an entire dissertation in the shadow of this project, has been a perennial source of support and sage advice. Nick prepared many of the musical examples and reductions, provided an invaluable sounding board at critical junctures, and read the entire manuscript several times over. Christa Pehl, Emily Snow, and Reba Wissner all assisted me in the early stages of the project, and Jamie Greenberg, James Steichen, and Micaela Baranello offered helpful comments on chapter drafts. I also owe a special debt to my current and former graduate students, from whom I have learned so much, especially those who call the Baroque period their home: Marisa Biaggi, Michele Cabrini, Ireri Chavez, Valeria De Lucca, Susan Lewis Hammond, Nicholas Lockey, Maria Purciello, Stephanie Tcharos, and Aliyah Shanti. They will no doubt see the legacy of their research in these pages.

I would also like to acknowledge the support of my colleagues and staff in the Music Department at Princeton University, where I have had the privilege of spending the majority of my academic career. I am grateful as well to the Metropolitan Museum of Art, and the Department of Musical Instruments, for their generosity during my year as the Sylvan Coleman and Pamela C. Coleman Memorial Fellow. Michael Burden graciously hosted me at New College, Oxford, where I wrote the first few chapters.

Finally, my gratitude to my family and loved ones for their encouragement and understanding for the countless times the project took me away from them: the Hellers (my brother, Allen, his wife, Beth, and my nephews, David, and his wife Arianne, Richard, and Stephen); my dear friend Kim Scown; my beloved "second mother" Barbara Sparti, whose recent loss I mourn even as I write these words; and especially my husband, Jack Hill, whose patience and confidence in me have been a source of comfort and strength.

MUSIC IN THE BAROQUE

CHAPTER ONE

Baroque Music in Early Modern Europe

In 1607, in the northern Italian city of Mantua, the opera *L'Orfeo* (Orpheus) by Claudio Monteverdi (1567–1643) was presented for a small audience gathered at the Ducal Palace, the residence of the ruling Gonzaga family. Opera—a drama that was entirely sung—was still a novelty, a point underscored by the fact that the first character to sing in the prologue was the female personification of Music, who praised the glorious deeds of illustrious heroes and the art of music itself.

Female figures were often used in paintings, statues, and illustrated books with didactic verses, known as emblem books, to represent the muses or allegorical concepts, as in the painting *Allegory of Music* by Laurent de La Hyre (1649; Fig. 1.1) in which a beautiful woman is shown tuning her theorbo, a long-necked lute. In *L'Orfeo*, however, Music could be both seen and heard. In the second strophe of her aria, she proudly introduces herself to the audience, flaunting her power (Ex. 1.1).

> I am Music, who in sweet accents
> can calm each troubled heart,
> and now with noble anger, now with love,
> can kindle the most frigid minds.

Figure 1.1: *Laurent de La Hyre,* Allegory of Music *(1649)*

Example 1.1: *Claudio Monteverdi, "Io la musica son," from* L'Orfeo *(1607), Prologue*

I am Music, who with sweet accents, knows how to calm each troubled heart

On the surface, Music's boasting seems excessive. The first measure, after all, has nothing but a series of repeated notes, and the bland melodic line, chopped up into one-measure units, is in a decidedly narrow range, without any ornaments or virtuosic display. The bass part—a single line with primarily whole and half notes—likewise seems unpromising. But if we consider the vocal part in relation to the text, Monteverdi's choices make more sense. Note, for instance, the tender way in which Music invokes her "sweet accents" in measure 2: after a beat's rest, the vocal line ascends a minor third, gently leaning onto the dotted quarter on the word "dolci" (sweet), touching on the upper D, only to fall luxuriously on the whole-note B♭ before descending a half step to A in a kind of sigh.

The music and words are so closely matched that it almost seems as if Music is spontaneously addressing the audience in declamatory song. What makes that possible, however, is the special nature of the accompaniment. The single line in the bass clef provides only a hint of the varied sounds that could be produced by the (one or more) instruments usually referred to as the basso continuo. This could include keyboard instruments (such as a harpsichord or organ), plucked instruments (such as harps, lutes, or theorbos, the latter shown in Fig. 1.1), bowed instruments (such as the cello or the fretted members of the viol family— most notably the bass viol played "da gamba" or between the legs and the larger violone, a relative of the double bass) or even the low double reed winds (such as dulcians the forerunners of the bassoon) or brass instruments (such as sackbuts and trombones). Used in varying combinations, the instruments of the basso continuo provided a colorful cushion of supporting harmonies, giving the singer the freedom to declaim the text in an expressive and rhythmically flexible manner. (See Chapter 2 for further discussion of basso continuo; we will take a closer look at Monteverdi's opera in Chapter 3.)

How was it that Music—who perhaps spoke for Monteverdi himself—could so boldly claim to calm the "troubled heart" and inspire emotions as varied as anger, love, and devotion? What do we know of the musicians who possessed such skills or the listeners whose passions were kindled, even those with the most "frigid minds"? This book will grapple with such questions, focusing on music of the seventeenth century and the first half of the eighteenth, which was likely written, performed, and heard with these goals in mind. Music historians have traditionally used the birth of opera on the Italian peninsula around 1600 to signify the end of the Renaissance and the beginning of a new era, often described by the word "Baroque," that concluded with the death of Johann Sebastian Bach and George Frideric Handel in 1750 and 1759 respectively. We will adhere to this basic framework, while recognizing that the aesthetic values and stylistic habits of any given time period are rarely uniform and that history inevitably resists our attempts to divide it into tidy categories.

In this chapter we consider the music of this era from two perspectives: first, in relation to the notion of "Baroque," a term borrowed from the visual arts and applied somewhat imprecisely to music; second, as part of the cultural, social, and political life of Europe in the so-called early modern era, a term adopted by many scholars to acknowledge the unifying features in the long period stretching from the waning of the Middle Ages around 1400 to the establishment of an industrialized society in the late eighteenth century. We will explore not only what the term *Baroque* means, but how the music that has long been described as Baroque can be understood in relation to other intellectual, social, and scientific trends.

DEFINING "BAROQUE"

One of the thorniest problems in defining Baroque art, music, or literature arises from the term's negative connotations. Originally used by jewelers to describe irregularly shaped pearls, the adjective "Baroque" was adopted by critics and historians to distinguish the florid architecture of the eighteenth century from the more classically based (and thus, in their eyes, superior) building style of the previous centuries. The influential nineteenth-century Swiss historian Jacob Burckhardt likened the entire Baroque to a "corrupt dialect" of the Renaissance language. Indeed, English-speaking tourists who consulted the 1877 edition of *Baedeker's Central Italy and Rome*, the most authoritative guidebook of the day, learned that the Baroque Era was merely a "degenerate" Renaissance.

The first appearances of the word *Baroque* in relation to music were equally derogatory. In 1734, an anonymous writer to the French periodical *Le Mercure galant* invoked the term to condemn the "babbling" and compositional innovations in the operas of Jean-Philippe Rameau, as opposed to those of his predecessor Jean-Baptiste Lully. Jean-Jacques Rousseau's musical dictionary of 1768 defines Baroque music as that in which "harmony is confused, charged with modulations and dissonances, in which the melody is harsh and little natural, the intonation difficult, and the movement constrained."

Only in the late nineteenth century did the term *Baroque* begin to lose some of its negative associations and come to be used as a relatively neutral label for the general style and aesthetics of seventeenth-century art and architecture. The Swiss art historian Heinrich Wölfflin described Renaissance art as rational, controlled, and harmoniously balanced, whereas Baroque art was emotional, theatrical, and characterized by movement and the play of light and shadow. The German musicologist Curt Sachs, also trained as an art historian, was the first to apply to music the period labels most familiar from the visual arts. He and other music historians expanded the time frame for Baroque music so that it included not only the seventeenth century, but also music of the eighteenth century by composers such as Bach and Handel, whose works were of primary concern to the founders of the discipline of musicology in the late 1800s.

Two works of sculpture, one by the Renaissance master Michelangelo Buonarotti and the other by the seventeenth-century sculptor Gian Lorenzo Bernini, illustrate differences between Renaissance and Baroque styles in the visual arts that are relevant to our consideration of music. Michelangelo's *David* shows the harmonious balance of the human body—an idealized David that is both realistic and more perfect than any natural specimen. The hero's emotional state is of less importance than the sheer beauty of his body, and although we know that he will soon aim the fatal slingshot at the giant Goliath, he is, for the moment, quite still (Fig. 1.2).

Bernini's virtuosic *Apollo and Daphne* depicts the god's pursuit of the chaste nymph and her miraculous escape from his advances as she is transformed into a laurel tree (Fig. 1.3). Bernini captures the wonder of the human body not only as it is, but also as it might be in an unstable, fantastic, and magical world. The ornamentation and intricate detail blur the line between what is real and what is not. Are those Daphne's limbs or the trunks of a tree? Is her head adorned with long, flowing hair or with leaves? The relationship between the two figures and

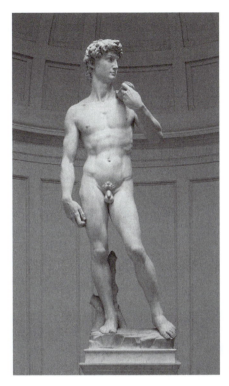

Figure 1.2: *Michelangelo Buonarotti,* David *(1501–04)*

Figure 1.3: *Gian Lorenzo Bernini,* Apollo and Daphne *(1622–24)*

Figure 1.4: *Gian Lorenzo Bernini,*
Ecstasy of Saint Teresa *(1645–52)*

the intensity of their facial expressions also tell us a good deal about what they are feeling.

Another sculpture by Bernini, *Ecstasy of Saint Teresa* (Fig. 1.4), shows how profound religious experiences inspired drama, movement, and passionate emotional expression, as we will see in Chapter 5. Bernini captures the intensely physical nature of the nun's mystical encounter with the Angel; what Teresa described in her autobiography as sweet and excessive pain is reflected in her swooning body and transfixed expression. While there is no exact correspondence between the visual arts and music, the comparison between Michelangelo and Bernini underscores some of the features that we will find in Baroque music—theatricality, virtuosity, and passion.

HUMANISM AND BEYOND

This desire to go beyond traditional modes of expression may well be part of a general tendency among scientists, philosophers, poets, and musicians in the seventeenth century to question long-standing assumptions. As Richard Freedman shows in *Music in the Renaissance*, educated men (and some women) of the Renaissance had devoted considerable attention to exploring the philosophy, science, and aesthetics of the ancient Greeks and Romans and reconciling their discoveries with their Christian beliefs. This intellectual movement, known as humanism, continued to transform ways of thinking about history, philosophy, and science throughout the early modern period. By the sixteenth and early seventeenth centuries people in all spheres of life had begun to explore how the knowledge and values of antiquity and modernity could coexist. Were there not modern poets, painters, and scientists who equaled or even surpassed the ancients? Was it possible to learn from the ancients—glean their wisdom—while still prizing innovation and looking at the world with optimism and hope for the future?

LITERATURE

The battle between the ancients and moderns was particularly fierce in the realm of literature. On the one hand, sixteenth- and seventeenth-century authors were deeply committed to translating and commenting on the works of Greek and Latin writers. Numerous works of Homer, Virgil, Ovid, and Euripides were translated into the vernacular and widely published. On the other hand, commentators also embraced the Christian epics of Renaissance writers, such as Ludovico Ariosto's *Orlando furioso* (Mad Orlando) and Torquato Tasso's *Gerusalemme liberata* (Jerusalem Liberated), which told of Christian knights and the Crusades. Both would inspire numerous operas and ballets in the Baroque era.

Many of the arguments about ancient and modern theater concerned the authority of Aristotle, who had established a set of fundamental rules concerning ancient tragedy and poetry. Yet, even while citing the so-called Aristotelian unities, whereby a play must consist of a single action, be set in a single location, and take place within a 24-hour period, poets often contradicted these rules in their plays and operas, making conventional apologies and explaining their transgressions as attempts to appeal to the fickle tastes of their audiences. Baroque opera would also be influenced by popular pastoral plays, in which nymphs, shepherds, gods, and goddesses loved, suffered, and cavorted in ways that entirely ignored the ancient rules. In fact, the battle between the ancients and moderns would play a vital role throughout the history of opera.

ASTRONOMY AND ASTROLOGY

Even as astrology retained enormous importance in early modern society—and kings and popes based crucial political decisions on the advice of trusted astrologers—that society was transformed by important discoveries in the realms of astronomy and physics by such figures as Galileo Galilei, Johannes Kepler, and Isaac Newton.

Scientists sought not only to understand the workings of the universe, but also to verify theories with their own eyes, sometimes putting religion and science at odds. When Galileo invented the telescope in 1609, he was able to see for himself that the sun rather than the earth was at the center of the solar system. Skepticism still abounded. His colleague and rival Cesare Cremonini refused even to look through the instrument, and in 1633 Galileo was tried and condemned for heresy by the Inquisition. He ultimately recanted, with the following words: "I must altogether abandon the false opinion that the sun is the center of the world and immovable, and that the earth is not the center of the world."

BIOLOGY AND SEXUALITY

Biological scientists were also interested in looking beneath the skin to see what went on inside the human body. The same era that nurtured the birth of opera saw the opening of anatomical "theaters" in which doctors, medical students, and—in some instances—the public had an opportunity to observe the dissection of an animal or human.

Despite the increased understanding of human anatomy, views about medicine inherited from the ancients persisted. Many doctors practiced according to the theory of the humors, whereby the body was governed by a balance of yellow bile, black bile, blood, and phlegm, which corresponded to the four elements of fire, earth, air, and water. In order to achieve health and happiness one needed a proper balance of these elements. There were also basic misconceptions about the differences between male and female bodies. Women—who were thought to be colder and moister than men—were viewed as innately weak, passive, and lacking in ability to think or reason. Aristotle and the Greek physician Galen had taught that female bodies were imperfect "inverted" versions of male bodies; their genitals remained inside their body because they had insufficient heat. The so-called "one-sex" model of the human body—whereby women's genitalia were just like those of men, but upside down—led to all kinds of misunderstandings about reproduction and sexuality. It was incorrectly assumed, for instance, that women—like men—had to have a sexual climax in order for conception to occur. Moreover, this flexible notion about male and female bodies meant that many believed that it was actually possible for men to turn into women and women to turn into men.

Attitudes about sexual preference and homosexuality were also quite different in the early modern period than they are now. Same-sex desire was prevalent in any number of communities that included musicians, artists, and their patrons, particularly among groups that prided themselves on being free from conventional moral strictures. However, in the early modern period, men and women did not define themselves as gay or lesbian, regardless of whether they occasionally or exclusively had sexual relationships with members of the same sex. Since same-sex activities were illegal, men and women typically kept their practices secret in order to avoid prosecution.

All of these factors influenced the production of music. If women had to be aroused in order to conceive, then nude paintings and even erotic music and poetry might actually help a noble couple produce an heir—though in some instances expressions of desire may well have been intended for someone of the same sex. Because silence was regarded as the most appropriate virtue for a woman, many regarded the female singer as a dangerous presence. This was particularly true in the churches throughout Europe, where boys and men did the public singing. In this context we can better understand not only the use of falsettists but also the continued popularity of the castrati, the male singers who were castrated in their youth so that they might maintain a high-pitched voice after puberty. While castrati were first used in church in the late sixteenth century, they would garner praise on the opera stage well into the nineteenth century. (The role of Music in Monteverdi's *L'Orfeo*, like the other female roles in the opera, was sung by a castrato.) Although the very idea of a castrato or a male falsettist may seem peculiar to us, seeing and hearing a woman sing in church would have been just as strange, even shocking, to early modern listeners. (Nun musicians, as we will see in Chapter 9, sang behind a grating so they would be heard but not seen.) Finally, the perceived close relationship between male and female bodies provided musicians and listeners with a whole range of expressive possibilities that could be exploited to great effect on and off the stage. In order to appreciate fully some of the oddities of Baroque musical theater—the numerous plots featuring cross-dressing and gender ambiguity, when a male character might sing a love duet with another man disguised as a woman, and in which boys, women, and men so often sang in the same vocal register—an understanding of the complexities of early modern sexuality is essential.

TECHNOLOGY

A number of technological advances in the seventeenth century had a profound impact on the production and distribution of music. The art of violin making reached its apex in northern Italy, with makers such as Amati and Guarneri achieving in their instruments a sweet, penetrating sound that challenged the supremacy of the human voice. The Baroque period also witnessed important innovations in keyboard instruments. Working in Florence around 1700, Bartolomeo Cristofori invented the fortepiano, the predecessor of our modern piano, in which a hammer striking the strings (rather than plucking, as in the harpsichord) could bring forth sounds that were both *forte* and *piano* (loud and soft), depending upon how hard the key was pressed. At the same time, composers and players took advantage of the experiments in harpsichord design and the expanded pedal boards and new tone colors of the magnificent organs in northern Europe.

Technology also played an important role in the theater. Engineers and designers such as Giacomo Torelli developed machinery capable of creating dazzling special effects. Borrowing techniques from shipbuilders, theater designers used a complex system of pulleys and ropes that made it possible for a group of stagehands to change the set from a royal palace to a garden instantaneously, imitate the sounds of a thunderstorm, or allow gods and goddesses to float down magically from the heavens on clouds. The elaborate fireworks that were the climax of so many court entertainments were also perfected during this time.

POLITICAL AND RELIGIOUS CONFLICT

The emotional power of Baroque music may well reflect not only changing artistic tastes but also broader historical trends and forces. Europe in the 1600s was divided not only by language and customs, but also by religious differences, which had become acute in the aftermath of the sixteenth-century Protestant Reformation. Protestants held sway in England and much of northern Europe, including Holland, Sweden, and Denmark. Protestant communities also abounded in some of the German-speaking principalities within the predominantly Catholic Holy Roman Empire, the collection of northern European states that were nominally governed by the Habsburg ruler of the Austrian Empire (known as the Holy Roman Emperor).

The Catholic cause was championed by both the Spanish and Austrian branches of the Habsburg family, as well as by the kingdom of France and the numerous city-states that dotted the Italian peninsula. This shared faith, however, did not necessarily engender political unity; the independent Italian city-states were often caught in the power struggles between France and the Habsburgs in Spain and Austria.

On the Italian peninsula, the sense of cultural unity resulting from a common history, language, and religion was undermined by differences in artistic tastes, economic circumstances, and political interests. The duchy of Mantua in Lombardy, where *L'Orfeo* was premiered under the patronage of the Gonzaga family, was a vibrant center of Italian musical culture in the late sixteenth and early seventeenth centuries. Spain wielded its power in the duchy of Milan, Genoa, and the Papal States (Rome and its environs); the kingdom of Naples, which included Sicily and Sardinia, was directly under Spanish rule until the early eighteenth century. French influence was predominant in the duchies of Parma (ruled by the Farnese family), Savoy and Piedmont, and Tuscany (ruled by the Medici family in Florence). Florence, as we will see in Chapter 2, was a major center for the development of the new musical style.

The Republic of Venice adroitly maintained its independence from both Spain and France, but frequently found itself in conflict with Asiatic powers, particularly the Ottoman Empire. The apparent threat from the East, which fueled European anxieties and fantasies throughout much of the century, was epitomized by the Turkish army's unsuccessful siege of Vienna in 1683 (see Chapter 13). At the same time, Westerners became increasingly fascinated with foreign and exotic lands, as European powers established colonies in Asia, Africa, and the Americas.

The volatility of the relationships between these diverse political entities was apparent in the many wars and disputes that broke out in the first half of the 1600s. Numerous lives were sacrificed in the effort to resolve differences within the Catholic Church and between the various Protestant sects, including the Anglicans in England, the Lutherans and Calvinists in Holland and Germany, and the Puritans who fled to America for religious freedom and founded early colonies there. Many suffered because of religious intolerance. In the Holy Roman Empire, the conversion of a prince from Catholicism to Protestantism (or vice versa) could force an entire community to change its practices or suffer the consequences. Although the Peace of Augsburg (1598) promoted religious coexistence by allowing German princes to choose their religious affiliation, it did not prevent the Thirty Years' War from wreaking havoc in so much of central Europe between 1618 and 1648.

In England, "recusant" Catholics practiced their faith in secret and were kept under close surveillance by the Crown for signs of treasonous activities. The religious and political conflicts that plagued the reign of King James I intensified when Charles I came to power in 1625, culminating in a civil war and the execution of the king in 1649. The religious conflicts between Anglican Britain and Catholic Ireland, so intense during this period, would continue into the late twentieth century. During the period known as the Interregnum (1649–60), Oliver Cromwell (and later his son) led the Commonwealth government until the monarchy was reconstituted in 1660 under Charles II, who was crowned king on April 23, 1661. In France, by contrast, it was the non-Catholic Huguenots who were persecuted and exiled. France was also beset by tensions with Spain and bouts of internal political unrest. (When Louis XIV came of age in 1661, he initiated a long period of stability.) Even the city of Naples had its own revolution in 1647, when a fisherman named Masaniello led a vigorous protest against Spanish rule, an event that would be dramatized in operas and plays in the late seventeenth and eighteenth centuries.

THE POLITICS OF MUSIC

Music played a vital role in defining both national and religious identity during the Baroque. Because music was such an integral element in worship, changes in religious beliefs and liturgy impacted musical practices. The introduction of new musical styles incited considerable discussion among both Catholic and Protestant theologians as to whether music enhanced faith or induced the vulnerable listener to sin. Martin Luther, the architect of the Protestant Reformation in German-speaking lands, maintained that elaborate music was a gift from God and an essential element of worship, thereby inspiring some of the greatest sacred masterworks of the early sixteenth century (see SR 55:361–62; 4/20:83–84). Calvinists, on the other hand, emphasized private devotion over formal ritual and therefore rejected the ornate music favored by the Lutherans and Catholics (see SR 57:364–67; 4/22:86–89).

Catholics, too, began to reconsider the theological implications of their own styles of music. At the series of ecclesiastical conferences known as the Council of Trent (1545–63), Church authorities voiced a preference for simple polyphony that did not obscure the text (see SR 61:374–76; 4/24:90–94). Yet by the early seventeenth century many felt that the faithful would be brought closer to God by reveling in the sensory stimulation provided by the expressive vocal and instrumental music that had become fashionable in the secular sphere. Thus, as we will see in Chapter 5, Catholics and Protestants may have disagreed on theological and political issues, but they also shared a rich musical culture.

As an expression of political and national identity, music was also frequently used by ruling families or the absolute monarchs of the age to shape a nation's cultural and political life. Some of the most lavish performances of the period were commissioned by monarchs, nobles, and religious leaders to celebrate marriages, births, coronations, and military victories. At the court of Louis XIV, the arts not only provided pleasure for the king and his courtiers, but were also used to extol the superiority of French taste throughout Europe—a strategy emulated by other European monarchs (see Chapter 7).

In Venice, both opera and opulent religious music expressed the city's pride in its republican form of government (see Chapter 6). At the Habsburg court in Vienna, Ferdinand II and his successors, Ferdinand III and Leopold I, used art and music to further their pro-Catholic agenda, realizing that music could sometimes succeed where the sword failed (see Chapter 5).

Reflecting this growing sense of national identity, the various "national styles" of composition became so well codified during this period that composers could learn to "speak" another musical style in much the same way that they learned a language (see Chapter 4). The French composer François Couperin wrote a set of works called *Les nations* (The Nations, 1726) in which he self-consciously demonstrated his ability to write in both the Italian and French styles initially publishing the daring Italian-style works under a pseudonym. In 1735 Bach published his *Italian Concerto* and *French Overture* together in one volume. Significantly, neither composer ever left the country of his birth. Italian and French styles, and the musicians who mastered them, became commodities that could be imported or exported by a discerning patron. Such was the case in Vienna, where Italian music and performers had the upper hand for much of the Baroque period. Many musicians also traveled extensively, acquiring and sharing new musical styles. George Frideric Handel left his native Saxony at an early age to study in Italy, and ultimately became a naturalized citizen of England.

Musical delights could also be sampled by the many visitors who traveled from one European center to another as tourists, diplomats, or even spies, as evidenced by the enthusiastic descriptions in their diaries. In 1608 the Englishman Thomas Coryat praised the ravishing music he heard in Venice, which could "stupefy" strangers who had never heard the like. Upon visiting Rome in 1644, the Englishman John Evelyn was equally taken by the fireworks and music-making in the streets in honor of the new pope, Innocent X. The musically sophisticated traveler thus returned home with a host of new ideas, and perhaps a printed score tucked away in a suitcase.

In the course of the century, Europeans became increasingly aware that they were no longer at the center of the universe. Exploration and expanding trade routes stimulated travel to the Americas, Africa, and Asia, while in Europe many had the opportunity to brush shoulders with exotic foreigners. In Venice, the Egyptians, Greeks, Turks, and Moors who could frequently be seen on the streets of that cosmopolitan city were also represented in opera. The firsthand reports of missionaries and explorers about ceremonies performed by indigenous populations on the American and Asian continents also inspired theatrical entertainments in which "native" practices were imaginatively reinvented for the pleasure of European audiences.

TOWARD THE ENLIGHTENMENT

While the first half of the seventeenth century was marked by a number of wars and crises, the later seventeenth century was a time of growing prosperity. The spread of music-making from the courts and chapels into salons, taverns, private homes, and public theaters laid the foundation for what would ultimately become a broad-based middle-class musical culture. By publishing their music, composers gained wider audiences and opened up new venues for performance, sometimes without the benefits (or restrictions) of royal or ecclesiastical patronage.

As the rate of literacy increased, there was a greater desire to organize knowledge and make it readily accessible. The first dictionaries and encyclopedias were compiled in the early modern period; indeed, as John Rice points out in the volume that follows this one in the Western Music in Context series, the 1700s would come to be known as the Encyclopedic Century. Nobles assembled private museums that featured natural specimens and ancient artifacts, circulating drawings of their prized possessions in printed volumes. Music in both manuscript and print was a commodity that could be catalogued, gathered into libraries, and classified into genres. The French philosopher René Descartes (1596–1650) had profoundly influenced thinking across the arts by classifying human passions, while eighteenth-century writers about music organized emotions (then referred to as "affections") into divisions based on categories used in rhetoric, expanding on ideas espoused in antiquity by Aristotle and Quintilian.

All of these developments fed the great intellectual and cultural movement known as the Enlightenment. This term is used to describe new ways of thinking about knowledge, power, and the innate rights and privileges of human beings that emerged in the late seventeenth century, stimulating the kind of thinking that inspired the American and French revolutions. While our consideration of music will end before these tumultuous events occur, many of the ideals that motivated the revolutionaries in both the Old and New Worlds were developed and circulated much earlier, influencing music and musicians in unexpected ways.

BAROQUE MUSIC AND STYLE

We have briefly considered some of the primary historical forces that shaped musical culture in the seventeenth and early eighteenth centuries. Music, however, like the other arts, is not only subject to the influence of contemporary events. It is also an independent entity, regulated by its own internal logic, rules, and aesthetic premises. Placing a piece of music or art in its social, economic, or cultural context does not tell us what makes it beautiful or exceptional, nor does it necessarily explain why a musician or painter chose one technique over another or gravitated toward new styles.

Although Baroque musicians did not use the same techniques and materials as Bernini and his fellow artists, their expressive goals—drama, passion, and virtuosity—were in many respects the same. The seventeenth century might be called the era of the soloist, as represented by the allegorical figure of Music discussed at the outset of this chapter. This was the period in which the sixteenth century's burgeoning interest in individual virtuosity blossomed fully. Singers were expected to astound and move audiences with plaintive laments or fiery displays in operas, oratorios (sacred dramas), and cantatas (vocal chamber works). The increased emphasis on instruments not only led to the invention of a plethora of new genres, but motivated composers to explore colors and styles derived from combining voices and instruments in new ways. An important feature of Baroque music is the use of *stile concertato* (concertato style), in which two or more groups of instruments or voices interact and compete with another. This is a feature of the Baroque instrumental concerto (see Chapter 10), in which a soloist or group of instruments is set in relief against an entire orchestra.

This is also the era in which counterpoint—the art of combining independent musical voices in a coherent and pleasing manner—was forever altered. For sixteenth-century composers the rules of counterpoint were of paramount importance, while their seventeenth-century counterparts were emboldened to break the rules and experiment with unconventional dissonances in the interest of dramatic expression. By the end of this period many composers—Bach in particular—brought contrapuntal music to new levels of complexity and expressivity.

Harmony—the chords or vertical sonorities that underpin music—also began to change, although in a manner that was by no means systematic. Composers began to use what is often referred to as "common practice tonality"—that is, music based primarily on major and minor scales and the chords derived from them. One of the controversial issues in this period for modern scholars concerns the methods of describing and analyzing music that conforms neither to the system of the church modes (which had been used to organize music by melodic and tonal types in the Middle Ages and Renaissance) nor to modern tonal practice. Are the church modes still part of the Baroque composer's toolbox, or do they merely reflect an inherited reverence for the Church and the legacy of the ancients? Particularly in the first half of the seventeenth century, old and new practices sit side by side: some of the most expressive compositions of the period are ones in which composers use a tonal language that may seem eccentric by "modern" standards.

Baroque music also sounds unusual to modern ears because of the use of different tuning systems. This is a period in which the methods used for tuning instruments with fixed string or pipe lengths (as in the harpsichord and organ) or fret placement (as in the lute, viol, and guitar) varied widely. Listeners today are accustomed to equal temperament, the system in which all twelve semitones are exactly the same size. However, this is just one of numerous methods used to compensate for a basic acoustical anomaly first described by the Greek philosopher and mathematician Pythagoras (of "Pythagorean theorem" fame). When Pythagoras tuned a circle of fifths (C, G, D, A, E, B, F♯, C♯, G♯, D♯, A♯, E♯, and B♯) in perfectly pure intonation, he may well have been surprised to discover that the final B♯ was not the same pitch as C♮, but differed by what is now termed "one Pythagorean comma." The entire history of tuning can be briefly summarized as a series of attempts to distribute or "temper" that comma or error to avoid unpleasant, out-of-tune sonorities.

Seventeenth-century composers addressed this issue by writing music in the keys that were the most in tune, that is, key areas closest to C, and shifting the "Pythagorean error" to rarely used keys such as B♭ minor or B major. This allowed them to approximate the purity of just intonation, while occasionally exploiting the expressive potential of exotic sonorities in the more distant key areas. In seventeenth-century France, for instance, the key of F♯ minor (and later the even more rarely used F♯ major) sounded so harsh and out of tune that it was dubbed the *ton de la chèvre* (the key of the goat).

Composers from the first half of the eighteenth century, eager to expand their tonal palettes to include more-distant keys, experimented with new ways to distribute the Pythagorean error. The prime example is Johann Sebastian Bach's *Well-Tempered Clavier*, which he wrote to demonstrate that one could indeed devise an unequal temperament that allowed performer and composer to use all 24 keys, without sacrificing the characteristics and affects associated with each individual tonality.

You may notice that the musical works discussed in the later chapters of this book are considerably longer than those at the beginning. Throughout the seventeenth and early eighteenth centuries, many vocal and instrumental works began to consist of small movements linked together, and contrasting key areas were often used to set off sections of single movements. As composers learned to spin out musical ideas with elaborate melismas (groups of notes sung to a single syllable) or intricate counterpoint, gravitating to one or another key area, they extended the listener's musical journey, and pleasure, over a longer span of time.

Whether writing vocal or instrumental works for the Ducal Palace in Mantua, a Roman church, the Imperial Theater in Vienna, a German coffeehouse, a Parisian salon, or a London pleasure garden, seventeenth- and eighteenth-century musicians invented a myriad of ways to capture the attention of their listeners, to inspire, seduce, and even overwhelm them with sensory stimulation. Sometimes the goal was to arouse religious fervor, patriotic duty, or love for a monarch. At other times the aim was simply to amaze with virtuosic improvisation and a dazzling show of bravura, or to provide entertainment for the skilled amateur at home, in the neighborhood tavern, or in the town square. If there is a unity in this period that can be understood as "Baroque," it may well come from a universal embrace of variety.

FOR FURTHER READING

Bianconi, Lorenzo, *Music in the Seventeenth Century,* trans. David Bryant (Cambridge: Cambridge University Press, 1987)

Coelho, Victor, ed., *Music and Science in the Age of Galileo* (Dordrecht, NL: Kluwer, 1992)

Eck, Caroline van, and Stijn Bussels, eds., *Theatricality in Early Modern Art and Architecture* (Chichester, UK: Wiley-Blackwell, 2011)

Hill, John Walter, *Baroque Music: Music in Western Europe, 1580–1750* (New York: W. W. Norton, 2005)

Laqueur, Thomas, *Making Sex: Bodies and Gender from the Greeks to Freud* (Cambridge, MA: Harvard University Press, 1990)

Minor, Vernon Hyde, *Baroque and Rococo: Art and Culture* (New York: Abrams, 1999)

Munck, Thomas, *Seventeenth-Century Europe: State, Conflict and the Social Order in Europe, 1598–1700* (Basingstoke, UK: Macmillan, 1990)

Skrine, Peter, *The Baroque: Literature and Culture in Seventeenth-Century Europe* (London: Methuen, 1978)

PART I

Musical Expression and Innovation

On February 17, 1600, the Italian philosopher and scientist Giordano Bruno was burned at the stake in the center of the Campo dei Fiori in Rome. Accused of heresy in 1576 on account of his unconventional theological views, Bruno spent much of the subsequent years traveling in Europe, lecturing, and publishing his works, many of which were banned by the Roman Catholic Church. Immediately upon his return to Italy, Bruno was imprisoned, tried, convicted, and—after failing to recant—sentenced to death. He came to represent the cause of religious and intellectual freedom during a time in which politics, the state, and knowledge were still under the sway of religious ideologies. Today, a statue of Bruno in Dominican garb looks out disdainfully on the fruit vendors, flower stalls, shoppers, and tourists that fill the colorful Campo dei Fiori each day.

The tragic story of Giordano Bruno is perhaps a curious place to begin our study of music in the Baroque; nonetheless, his tale dramatizes many of the conflicts and crises that were to influence thinking in the first half of the seventeenth century. Historians of the early modern period have generally seen the seventeenth century—particularly the first half—as a time of crisis, not only in Europe, but also in much of the rest of the world, including Asia and the Americas. We might view Europe as undergoing a sort of slow burn in the first half of the century that, by midcentury, emits potentially lethal sparks.

Some scholars see these crises as emerging from natural phenomena, in particular a deterioration of the weather that had a negative effect on crop production, causing famine, shifts of population from rural to urban areas, poverty, and political instability. Recurring epidemics of bubonic plague lowered the population in many cities and exacerbated social and economic crises. Countless lives were lost in conflicts such as the Thirty Years' War (1618–1648) and the English Civil War (1642–1651), generated in no small part by religious strife. Meanwhile, many governments, pressed to fund expensive wars or wanting to invest in artistic projects that enhanced their image, began to tax their citizens more aggressively. Thus, ironically, the very process that ultimately caused social discontent in so much of Europe also provided financial support for music and art.

A time of crisis it was, to be sure; but it was also a time of enormous creativity and innovation, in which—as we will see in Chapters 2–5—musicians found a host of new means of expressing the intense passions that were so great a part of the lives of men and women during the Baroque. In fact, certain features of early-seventeenth-century music seem to resonate with, reflect, and even exult in the political strife of the era. This is an age in which composers delighted in unexpected and shocking dissonances, breaking the rules of counterpoint and harmony; in which Protestants and Catholics alike embraced colossal choral works, producing walls of sound that overwhelmed and seduced listeners; and in which individual soloists—singers or instrumentalists—garnered previously unknown glory. We might even wonder if the Baroque passion for the concertato style, in which groups of instruments and voices are pitted against one another, in some respects reflects the competitive spirit of the age.

Indeed, it is all too easy to let the sheer luxury and spectacle of Baroque music distract us from the complexity of the underlying social and political processes. In fact, music could confirm alliances, entertain diplomats, incite political dissension, inspire soldiers on the battlefield, and mitigate religious differences. Even in those instances in which the production of music was far removed from political strife or social unrest, providing a background for everyday activities, the very multiplicity of musical styles provoked disputes between those who advocated change and those who preferred older styles and the traditional values with which they were associated.

It is difficult to know whether these debates were symptoms of a troubled age—a reflection of the anxiety that seeped from life into the realm of music—or whether such disputes were part of a regular cycle of aesthetic shifts in which the history of music abounds. What we do know, however, is that in the first half of the seventeenth century musicians adopted new expressive techniques in order to move more deeply the passions of their listeners, inspiring a burst of creativity. This was an extraordinarily vital moment in the history of music.

CHAPTER TWO

Ancients and Moderns

Around the year 1590, a Florentine teenager named Rafaello Cavalcanti jotted down a collection of songs and accompaniments for the lute. Though he was a wealthy nobleman rather than a professional musician, his manuscript has much to tell us about music and society in seventeenth-century Italy. Like other young men with close ties to the Medici, Florence's ruling family, Cavalcanti had plenty of leisure time to learn the skills appropriate to a well-educated courtier of his social class, including dexterity with weapons, dancing, painting, and the ability to engage in graceful and erudite conversation.

Musical talent was also highly valued in the noble circles in which Cavalcanti traveled. He likely participated in casual musical sessions, collecting and exchanging songs, trying out new techniques, and capitalizing on family connections and social networks in the pursuit of artistic novelty and adventure. From Cavalcanti's manuscript and others like it, we learn something about the musical tastes and preferences of these young aristocratic musicians. Their repertory included arrangements for voice and lute of popular polyphonic works; standard bass lines for variations that could be used by lute players to accompany other instrumentalists, singers, and dancers; and new songs conceived specifically for singer and lutenist. The direct and personal style of communication between singer and listener in the performance of lute songs captured the imagination of the exuberant Florentine youth culture at the turn of the seventeenth century.

Cavalcanti's manuscript also tells us something about the state of the musical marketplace in the late 1500s. Since printers were just beginning to publish solo songs (we will consider some English lute songs printed at the turn of the seventeenth century later), Cavalcanti and his friends were constrained to make handwritten copies of the music they enjoyed playing together. They did so using a style of notation popular among lutenists: a system we refer to as tablature. Used for a variety of keyboard and string instruments, tablature provided a pictorial representation of the strings or keys on the instruments, instructing the players exactly where to place their fingers, and when and where they should be moved to form a new sonority.

This chapter explores some of the music that so enraptured the musicians of Cavalcanti's generation. We begin in the northern Italian city of Florence, where new musical styles provided much of the creative fuel for entertainments at the Medici court. We then consider the ways in which similar preoccupations about music's expressive power influenced the madrigal, the most popular secular polyphonic vocal genre of the Renaissance, inspiring composers such as Claudio Monteverdi to break with old traditions and rules in favor of a new musical aesthetic. Finally, we trace the fortunes of solo songs as they entertained cardinals and nobles in Rome and entered the marketplace in printed volumes to be enjoyed by both professionals and amateurs as far away as London.

THEORY AND PRACTICE IN THE AGE OF HUMANISM

In his *Dialogo della musica antica, et della moderna* (Dialogue on Ancient and Modern Music), published in 1581, Vincenzo Galilei (late 1520s–1591), father of the astronomer Galileo Galilei, praises the superior abilities of the ancient singer. Unlike his own contemporaries, the ancient singer, Galileo imagined, would have "diligently" considered the age, sex, and character of the person depicted in the poem. He would then have expressed these conceptions in tone "with the accents and gestures, the quantity and quality of sound, and the rhythm appropriate to that action and to such a person" (SR 72:466; 3/37:188).

Galilei's comments on ancient musicians may seem irrelevant to a study of artistic innovation. In the early decades of the seventeenth century, after all, musical modernity was in fashion. The composer and singer Giulio Caccini (1551–1618), named his first printed collection of solo songs *Le nuove musiche* (The New Musical Works, 1602) in an unabashed attempt to promote himself as a purveyor of the hottest styles, while the Venetian wind player Dario Castello entitled one of his first collections of instrumental music *Sonate concertate in stil moderno* (Concerted Sonatas in Modern Style, 1621).

Galilei was one in a long line of musicians who, like other humanists, looked to the writings of the ancients for wisdom and inspiration. Since the study of music had traditionally been regarded as a branch of mathematics, medieval and Renaissance musicians had based their studies of music on the writings of Pythagoras, whose experiments with tuning we considered in Chapter 1. Pythagoras described the numerical ratios that represent our basic intervals, such as 2:1 (the octave) and 3:2 (the fifth), believing (as did Plato) that such sonorities were earthly manifestations of planetary vibrations—the so-called harmonies of the spheres. In the sixteenth century, the influential Neo-Platonic philosopher Marsilio Ficino recast this notion in Christian terms, maintaining that music was an essential link between the human and heavenly realms that could bring men and women closer to God (see SR 64:385–89; 3/29:107–11). Musical theater using Neo-Platonic imagery would prove particularly useful for rulers throughout the early modern period, who sought to demonstrate that their power was ordained by God.

By the late sixteenth century musicians and listeners were becoming increasingly interested in music's power to incite extreme emotional states of the sort that had been engendered by ancient Greek tragedy. As they began to consider music as a branch of rhetoric rather than mathematics, they looked to the writings of Plato's student Aristotle. Was it possible for music to inspire the same violent emotions that might lead to the catharsis (emotional cleansing) described by Aristotle? And if so, why did music no longer seem capable of soothing wild beasts or rousing warriors on the battlefield, as the ancients had so eloquently described? Thus, paradoxically, for musicians such as Monteverdi, Galilei, Caccini, and Castello, the modernity they so prized was inspired by encounters with the ancients and the desire to harness music's power to new expressive ends.

Such inquiries necessarily presented practical problems. Should composers continue to adhere to the strict rules of counterpoint established by such theoretical masters as Gioseffo Zarlino that underlay the sonic splendor of the Renaissance mass and motet? Or, in the interest of heightening the emotional content of their music, might they be freer with dissonance and voice-leading in order to give more weight to text expression—like the ancient musician described by Galilei? As more emphasis was placed on the emotional response of the listener, producers of music looked for new ways to exploit music's awakening power to persuade, astonish, and influence audiences. In so doing, they not only discovered innovative ways to make music expressive, but also changed music's role in society.

INVENTING OPERA

Florence was at the epicenter of this musical revolution in the late sixteenth century. Two important patrons—Giovanni de' Bardi, count of Vernio, and the nobleman Jacopo Corsi—sponsored meetings at their palaces for those interested in discussing and experimenting with music and poetry. Often referred to as academies, such gatherings brought together talented noblemen, poets, and musicians. In addition to Vincenzo Galilei, the Florentine circle included three musicians who would compete for primacy in the new arena of opera: Giulio Caccini, his younger colleague Jacopo Peri (1561–1633), and the Roman dancer, choreographer, and composer Emilio de' Cavalieri (1550–1602). Poets were deemed no less important; the most famous who frequented these academies were Ottavio Rinuccini (1562–1621) and Gabriello Chiabrera (1552–1638).

BARDI'S CAMERATA

The earliest academy, later dubbed the Camerata (Chamber) by Caccini, met at Count Bardi's home for almost 20 years, from approximately 1573 to 1592. More than 40 years later, Bardi's son Piero would boast about his father's "delightful and continual academy from which vice and in particular every kind of gaming were absent." In it, some young nobles of Florence (such as Cavalcanti) passed their time "not only in pursuit of music, but also in discussing and receiving instruction in poetry, astrology, and other sciences which by turns lent value to this pleasant conversation" (SR 81:523; 4/1:15).

Francesco de' Medici, the grand duke of Tuscany, had hired Bardi, who was also an accomplished musician, to oversee court entertainments. Along with Cavalieri, he was one of the primary creative forces behind one of the most spectacular musical-theatrical events of the late sixteenth century: the lavish *intermedi* or musical interludes performed between the acts of the play *La pellegrina* (The Pilgrim) that was staged to celebrate the wedding of Francesco's younger brother (and successor) Ferdinando to Christine of Lorraine in 1589. Here the connection to Neo-Platonic philosophy and music theory is unmistakable: the first *intermedio*, aptly called "Harmony of the Spheres," opened with the renowned soprano Vittoria Archilei personifying Harmony, much like the representation of Music in the prologue to *L'Orfeo*. Unlike Music, however, Harmony descended from the heavens on a cloud machine, singing in praise of the bride and groom (Fig. 2.1).

An excerpt from the final section of Archilei's aria shows how Neo-Platonic imagery, classical mythology, and the power of the human voice could be used to flatter nobles. In a highly ornamented passage over a simple chordal accompaniment (Ex. 2.1), Harmony compares Christine to the goddess Minerva and Ferdinando to Hercules (also known as Alcide). Such dazzling virtuosity not only invoked the supernatural powers of the gods, but also provided an aural equivalent of magical stage effects.

EXPERIMENTS WITH SOLO SINGING

For Galilei and other musicians in Bardi's circle, solo singing was the key that unlocked the secrets of ancient music's expressivity. To better understand this, Bardi encouraged Galilei to correspond with Girolamo Mei (1519–1594), one of

Figure 2.1: *Agostino Carracci, First Intermedio for* La pellegrina *(Harmony of the Spheres) (1592), after a drawing by Andrea Boscoli, after an original sketch by Bernardo Buontalenti*

the first scholars of his era to study Greek music theory in the original sources (see SR 76:485–95; 3/41:207–17). Influenced by Mei, Galilei condemned the popular polyphonic masses and motets of his contemporaries that were, in his words, "the mortal enemy" of the ancient music he sought to re-create. "For its sole aim is to delight the ear, while ancient music is to induce in another the same passion that one feels oneself" (SR 72:465; 3/37:187). He deplored the frequent use of text painting or "madrigalisms" (so called because they were frequently used in madrigals), such as a melodic leap upward to indicate the heavens.

Galilei's solution, later explored successfully by his colleagues Peri and Caccini, was a style of song in which a solo singer declaimed the poetry in a speechlike but essentially lyrical fashion in the manner of La Musica (see Chapter 1). The composer provided only a vocal line and bass line. The implied harmonies were then filled out or "realized" by keyboard, harp, lute, or another continuo instrument in a manner that greatly enhanced the expressive power of the singer. (We will discuss the basso continuo in more detail later.)

Scholars have traditionally used the term *monody* to describe a wide range of music for one or more solo voices and continuo composed before 1630, although this term was not used in the seventeenth century. Early-seventeenth-century musicians described these compositions vividly using such terms as *stile rappresentativo* (dramatic style), *cantar recitando* (reciting in song), referring to a tuneful style of singing, and *stile recitativo* (recitative style), referring to more

Example 2.1: *Emilio de' Cavalieri, "Dalle più alte sfere," from* La pellegrina *(1589), First Intermedio, mm. 38–40*

As you, new Minerva, and brave Alcides . . .

speechlike recitation. Since such terms were used somewhat inconsistently, for our purposes we should simply note that Baroque composers used varying degrees of speechlike or tuneful vocal writing, depending upon their tastes, the dramatic situations, and the kind of poetry they were setting.

On one end of the stylistic spectrum is the type of singing usually referred to as recitative—that is, recitation akin to speech. Largely syllabic, driven by the rhythms of the text, and usually in some kind of blank verse (called *versi sciolti* in Italian), recitative is used in dramatic music (operas, cantatas, and oratorios) when characters speak to one another or impart important information to the listener. Recitative that is accompanied only by continuo would later be referred to as *secco*, or dry, recitative. Beginning in the late seventeenth century, for highly dramatic situations composers sometimes added an entire orchestra to accompany or punctuate the recitative; this is referred to as *recitativo accompagnato* (accompanied recitative).

On the other end of the spectrum is the aria. This is a setting of a poetic text in which musical considerations, rather than the text, dominate. Arias—as opposed to recitative—thus tend to be reflective rather than narrative. We also find examples in between these two extremes: lyrical recitative that is less syllabic and more melodic is often referred to as arioso. While in the first half of the seventeenth century, Italian composers often shifted between aria and recitative style in a very fluid manner, by the third quarter of the century the two styles would become clearly differentiated. (French recitative, which we consider in Chapter 7, is quite distinctive and in fact much closer to aria.)

All of this was still in the future in 1592, when Bardi departed for Rome and experiments with the new style of solo singing intensified under the leadership of Corsi. Believing (mistakenly) that Greek drama had been sung in its entirety, Corsi and his followers proposed to create a modern equivalent. Their work culminated in another entertainment for the Medici family: a drama that was entirely sung. We have come to call this opera (which means "work" in Italian), though in the Baroque it was often called by such titles as *favola in musica* (fable in music) or, by the mid-seventeenth century, simply *dramma per musica* (drama through music). *Euridice* (Eurydice), with music by Peri and poetry by Rinuccini, was performed in October 1600 as part of the festivities for the wedding of Marie de' Medici and Henry IV of France. It was the first of numerous operas that presented the popular mythological tale of the musician Orpheus, who descends to the underworld in order to rescue his dead bride Eurydice, using his music to charm the god Pluto.

In his preface to the printed score of the opera (1601), Peri provides a precise explanation of his debt to the ancients: "I judged that the ancient Greeks and Romans (who, according to the opinions of many, sang their tragedies throughout on the stage) used a harmony which, going beyond that of ordinary speech, fell so short of the melody of song that it assumed an intermediate form." Peri goes on to say that the singer could intone words in such a way that harmony "can be founded upon them," reciting through subsequent words until arriving on the next consonance. In order to express grief, joy, and similar states, Peri writes, "I made the bass move in time to these, now faster, now slower, according to the emotions" (SR 107:659–60; 4/27:152).

We see how effective this strategy can be in scene 2 of *Euridice*, a pivotal moment in the opera, as the nymph Daphne recounts in *stile recitativo* the sudden death of her companion Eurydice from a snake bite, singing: "Alas, from terror and pity my heart freezes in my breast" (Ex. 2.2). The flexible rhythms and the sudden alternation of G-minor and G-major chords, resulting in the unexpected juxtaposition of flat and sharp sonorities, match Daphne's volatile emotions. Her initial cry, for instance, in which she sustains the first syllable for a full three beats before descending a minor third, is halfway between a prolonged sigh and a scream. The unexpected G-major sonority in the next measure inspires a quickening of

Example 2.2: *Jacopo Peri, "Lassa! che di spavento," from* Euridice *(1600), scene 2, mm. 214–19, 229–30*

Alas, from terror and pity . . . oh, woe

the rhythm to eighth notes representing her terror. The contrasting notion of pity in measures 217–218 brings back G minor and a deliberate quarter-note ascent to the sustained B♭, leading to a less anguished half-step sigh as the vocal line comes to rest on a D-major sonority in measure 219. Her anguish reaches a climax several measures later with the cry "ohimé" (oh, woe). The sense of shock is heightened here as Daphne sustains the B♭ in measure 229 over the E and G♯ in measure 230 before "resolving" to the E-major sonority in the second half of the measure.

Corsi regarded the performance of *Euridice* as a great triumph; several months later he would commission a statue of Orpheus from the Florentine sculptor Cristoforo Stati commemorating the event (Fig. 2.2). For the musicians, however, the invention of opera was marked by rivalry. Caccini composed his own setting of *Euridice* that was actually published prior to Peri's. Seven years later, the same tale would provide the basis of Claudio Monteverdi's seminal first opera *L'Orfeo* (see Chapter 3), introduced, as we saw in Chapter 1, by the tuneful aria sung by Music.

Influenced by Peri's setting, Monteverdi's *L'Orfeo* would be regarded by many as the first masterwork in the genre. Meanwhile, Cavalieri, who would grumble that he was never given sufficient credit for his accomplishments, had already staked his claim in the field of musical theater. His *Rappresentazione di anima et di corpo* (Representation of the Soul and the Body), a sacred allegorical drama, had been presented in Rome before an audience of 35 cardinals in February

Figure 2.2: *Cristoforo Stati (Cristofano da Braciano), Orpheus (1600), carved for Jacopo Corsi for the Palazzo Corsi, Florence*

1600, some ten months before the first performance of *Euridice*. Historians have tended to idealize the pioneering spirit and collaborative efforts of the first producers of opera, yet it is apparent that competition and self-promotion played no small part in the creative process.

DRAMATIZING THE MADRIGAL: *IL PASTOR FIDO*

While Galilei, Rinuccini, Caccini, and Peri were experimenting with opera and monody, composers of polyphonic madrigals were exploring ways to heighten the expressivity of this popular genre that had so captivated sixteenth-century Italian musicians and listeners. In some respects the madrigal offered even more room for stylistic innovation than solo song. The use of multiple voices created the opportunity for textural variety and contrasts of timbre, and unconventional voice-leading procedures could make text-driven dissonances all the more effective.

A number of forces fueled experiments in the madrigal. First, the discerning patrons in the northern Italian courts, such as the Gonzagas in Mantua and the Este family in Ferrara, sought out the best poets, composers, and musicians to produce sophisticated music for their own consumption. Second, music printers took advantage of the popularity of the genre to publish hundreds of madrigal collections in sets of partbooks (each singer sang from a booklet containing only his or her own part). Thus the madrigal became one of the chief genres by which a composer established his or her reputation. Finally, composers delighted in setting the passionate or at times frivolous poetry of the new generation of poets, matching this heightened poetic expression with innovative and musical devices that were deemed controversial by some critics.

Some of the disputes concerning madrigals had their roots in the realm of literature, where, as we noted in Chapter 1, poets and critics also argued about the relative merits of the ancients and moderns. One such debate erupted in the 1590s, ignited by the pastoral play *Il pastor fido* (The Faithful Shepherd, 1589), by Battista Guarini, court poet for the Este family in Ferrara. Pastoral plays were set in the idyllic, fictional realm of Arcadia, where shepherds and nymphs enjoyed and lamented both unrequited and requited love, and where the occasional appearance of a beastly satyr provided a frisson of danger. What was so controversial about *Il pastor fido* was that it was a tragicomedy, a hybrid genre for which there was no model in antiquity. In response to the objections of some conservative commentators, Guarini and his supporters argued that the new genre was more true to life than pure tragedy or comedy, and thus more pleasurable.

Composers were fascinated by the joy, despair, and fury expressed by Guarini's characters Silvius, Myrtillus, and the beautiful Amaryllis, and by the evocative language used to convey their emotions. Consider the fervor with which Myrtillus berates his beloved in Act 1: "Cruel Amaryllis, you who even with the name to love [*amare* means "to love" in Italian], alas, teach bitterness." Guarini's poetry, playing on the harsh initial consonant of the word "cruda" (cruel), vividly contrasts the notions of bitterness and love. Of the many settings of this monologue, Monteverdi's "Cruda Amarilli" in his Fifth Book of Madrigals (1605) is particularly striking for its use of unresolved dissonances to capture the nymph's harshness. Note the effect of the descending sixteenth notes in measure 12 that mark the poet's description of Amaryllis's bitterness, followed by the intense exclamation "ahi" underscored by the clash between the high A in the soprano and the G in the bass in measure 13. (Ex. 2.3).

Amaryllis's response in the next madrigal in Monteverdi's collection, "O Mirtillo" (see Anthology 1), is no less intense. The nymph contemplates Myrtillus's condemnations of her ostensible cruelty with burning dissonances that illustrate Myrtillus's own harshness and the pain Amaryllis herself suffers from not being permitted to reveal her love.

THE ARTUSI—MONTEVERDI CONTROVERSY

Monteverdi's rule-breaking settings of texts from Guarini's *Il pastor fido* generated a debate that raged for a dozen years, from 1598 to 1610. Usually referred to as the "Artusi–Monteverdi controversy," this published exchange was instigated by the Bolognese theorist Giovanni Maria Artusi (1540–1613), who apparently heard some selections from Monteverdi's Fifth Book in November 1598—some seven years before their publication—at the home of a musical amateur in Ferrara.

The crux of the disagreement seems to concern musical aesthetics: on what basis does one judge a musical composition? For Artusi, there was an objective standard that could be applied to all works: composers should follow the rules of counterpoint to avoid inappropriate use of dissonance and what he referred to as the mixing of modes—that is, beginning in one tonal area and traveling to other, more distant regions. "If the purpose can be obtained by observing the precepts

Example 2.3: *Claudio Monteverdi, "Cruda Amarilli," from the Fifth Book of Madrigals (1605), mm. 9–14*

Who with your own name, alas, [teach] to love [bitterly] . . .

and good rules handed down by the theorists and followed by all the experts, what reason is there to go beyond the bounds to seek out new extravagances?" Artusi asks (SR 82:533; 4/2:25). He regards the new style of madrigals as "artificial," since it disobeys the laws of nature and is thus dangerous to the listener, reserving some of his sharpest criticism for Monteverdi's "Cruda Amarilli" and "O Mirtillo."

Monteverdi's first response came in the form of a letter included in the preface to his Fifth Book of Madrigals. Reminding his readers that he is far too occupied in his position at the Mantuan court to respond to Artusi's criticisms of "minor portions" of his madrigals, Monteverdi claims to be in the process of writing his own treatise, *The Second Practice, or The Perfection of Modern Music.* He emphasizes that the "modern" manner of composition opens up a new way of thinking about music that appeals to both reason and the senses. To buttress his case, he begins his volume with the very two madrigals that particularly offended Artusi, "Cruda Amarilli" and "O Mirtillo."

Monteverdi never published the promised treatise, however the most detailed defense of the composer was provided by his brother Giulio Cesare, who penned the preface to Claudio's next publication, *Scherzi musicali* (Musical Jests, 1607). Here Giulio Cesare articulates the basic principle of his brother Claudio's *seconda prattica* (second practice), namely, "it has been his intention to make the words the mistress of the music" (SR 83:538; 4/3:30). This he contrasts with the *prima prattica* (first practice), represented by the polyphonic style of the Renaissance, that "turns on the perfection of the harmony, that is, the one that considers the harmony not commanded, but commanding, and not the servant, but the mistress of the words" (SR 83:539–40; 4/3:31–32).

Historians have focused on this pivotal exchange, often casting Monteverdi as the forward-looking hero and the knowledgeable Artusi as a cantankerous conservative. Yet, as some scholars have suggested, their musical argument may reflect other concerns. Artusi, a staunch supporter of the pope, may well have disapproved not only of the modal mixture but also of the somewhat secular musical tastes of the northern Italian courts, while Monteverdi's own defense might even have been inspired by his fear of papal censure for breaking with traditional contrapuntal rules. In defending himself, however, Monteverdi was the first to articulate clearly the notion of a *seconda prattica*, thus boldly laying claim to a *stile moderno* (modern style) that was already flourishing by this time. Regardless of the motivations, the echoes of these battles between words and music, rules and freedom, would reverberate for centuries.

MOVING THE PASSIONS WITH SONG

In the preface to *Le nuove musiche*, Giulio Caccini reminisces about his youthful experiences in Bardi's Florentine Camerata with the "foremost musicians, intellectuals, poets, and philosophers of the city." He credits them with

encouraging him to avoid music in which the words were difficult to understand and to "follow that style praised by Plato and the other philosophers
who maintained music to be nothing other than rhythmic speech with pitch
added" (SR 100:608; 4/20:100). We have already considered the theoretical
speculations on music in the groups led by Bardi and Corsi; now let us examine more closely the solo song and Caccini's claims for originality. What was
so new about *Le nuove musiche*?

As we saw in our discussion of Rafaello Cavalcanti above, solo songs were
already popular in Italy and elsewhere before the publication of Caccini's collection, and within a short time thereafter they would be an important part of the
musical life of aristocrats throughout Europe. In his *Discorso sopra la musica de'
suoi tempi* (Discourse on the Music of His Times, 1628), the Roman collector and
well-traveled nobleman Vincenzo Giustiniani noted "that the fashion and manner of singing changes from time to time according to the tastes of the noblemen
and princes who delight in it, just as happens in styles of dress, whose fashions
are always changing according to things introduced at important courts" (SR
54:356; 3/19:78).

In Rome, Giustiniani would have heard music at the homes of cardinals
such as Francesco Maria del Monte and Alessandro Peretti Montalto, the latter
of whom, according to Giustiniani, played "the cembalo [harpsichord] excellently" and sang "in a sweet and affecting manner" (SR 54:355; 3/19:77). Such
patrons provided musicians and artists not only with financial support and
professional connections, but also with lodging, so that they would always be
available to provide entertainment as needed. A gathering at Montalto's house
might have included performances by young castrati who, having sung in the
papal choir by day, entertained the cardinal and his friends by night. Paintings
such as Caravaggio's *The Musicians*, commissioned by Montalto, likely decorated
the room in which these performances were held and provide a vivid picture of
the musical activities that took place under noble patronage.

Performances in Montalto's house also included women singers such as
Vittoria Archilei, who sang the opening number in the Florentine *intermedi*
of 1589. The soprano Adriana Basile (1580–1640), a favorite among the Roman
elite, reportedly knew more than 300 songs in Italian and Spanish by memory.
Her daughter, the singer Leonora Baroni (1611–1670), whose patron and lover was
no less a figure than Cardinal Antonio Barberini, nephew of Pope Urban VIII,
was also celebrated in Roman circles in verse, engravings, and paintings. The
fact that Baroni appears in a painting chastely attired, with a dress covering
her from the floor to her collarbone, shows some of the strategies that female
singers and their patrons sought to counteract the perennial associations of
female singing with lascivious behavior. A half-naked cupid in the painting—
who holds a broken bow—hints at the desire that the chaste Baroni nonetheless
inspired.

Many of the most successful singers of Baroni's day found ingenious ways to circumvent the inevitable aspersions on their reputation; nonetheless, the new emphasis on music's power to arouse both men and women put sexual desire in the foreground of many performance situations.

DESIRE, PLEASURE, AND LAMENT

Regardless of the setting, or of the gender or status of the singer and audience, most solo songs or monodies dealt with love in its various forms. Caccini's "Dovrò dunque morire" (Must I thus die; see Anthology 2), which circulated in lute books such as Cavalcanti's at least 20 years before its publication in *Le nuove musiche* in 1602, uses poignant dissonances, descending melodic lines, sigh motives, and ornamentation (much of which was not notated but was to be added according to Caccini's instructions in the preface) to capture the anguish of the unrequited lover. (See Chapter 9 for a discussion of some of Caccini's ornaments.) Listeners may have been particularly captivated by the double entendre in the question "Must I thus die before I see you again?" The desperate poet is pleading with his lover to grant him the metaphorical death of sexual fulfillment before he suffers actual biological death.

If serious monodies such as "Dovrò dunque morire" highlighted the complexities of love and desire, lighthearted canzonettas such as Caccini's "Amor ch'attendi" (Love, what are you waiting for?; Ex. 2.4) are unambiguously joyful. Like other canzonettas, "Amor ch'attendi" is a dancelike strophic song, with each of the six verses set to the same music. The canzonetta has none of the tonal shifts, rhythmic freedom, and dissonance suitable for tragic situations or unrequited love. The focus is on a cheerful regularity (four-measure phrases) and rhythmic vitality, generated by the accentual pattern of the canzonetta poetry. The mood is heightened by the addition of an instrumental refrain or ritornello between the strophes that could be varied with each repetition. "Amor ch'attendi" is dominated by a six-beat rhythmic pattern, indicated with brackets and labeled motive "**a**" in the example. (In the third repetition, labeled

Example 2.4: *Giulio Caccini, "Amor ch'attendi," from* Le nuove musiche e nuova maniera di scriverle *(1614), mm. 1–8*

Love, what are you waiting for? Hurry, why not take your arrows . . . ?

"**al**," the second and third quarter notes are subdivided, the shorter note values energizing the drive to the cadence in m. 8.)

Caccini claimed that everyone wrote canzonettas and that they were particularly apt for "relieving depression." In addition to publishing a set of them in his aforementioned *Scherzi musicali*, Monteverdi included several in his opera *L'Orfeo* (see Chapter 3) as an expression of joy.

Composers also elicited the opposite affective response from their listeners with monodic laments, musical settings of the dramatic monologues recited by heroes and heroines in epic poetry that in ancient times reportedly moved listeners to tears. Sigismondo d'India (1582–1629) crafted a number of laments that trace the shifting emotions of a lover in despair. "Infelice Didone" (Unhappy Dido) depicts the episode from Virgil's *Aeneid* in which the Queen of Carthage uses the *stile recitativo* of Peri and his colleagues (Ex. 2.5) to bemoan her fate after being abandoned by Aeneas. In her despair, Dido cries out with a series of rhetorical questions: "Where are you going, cruel one? Why do you leave me alone? Why do you flee from me? What are you doing, my heart? Why deny me, alas, a final farewell?" D'India represents her increasing anguish by setting each question a whole or half step higher than the previous one, her halting melodic line broken up by rests, passing from the initial G-minor sonority to G major and C major, landing on an A-major sonority.

LUTE SONGS IN ENGLAND

By the late sixteenth century, the English, too, had become enamored of solo songs and their direct and intimate mode of music-making, stimulated in part by contact with Italian models. Lute songs were sung in private homes, in noble

Example 2.5: *Sigismondo d'India, "Infelice Didone" from* Le musiche, *Book 5 (1623), mm. 13–18*

Where are you going, cruel one? Why do you leave me alone? Why do you flee from me? What are you doing, my heart? Why deny me, alas, a final farewell?

residences, and at court, and were also featured on the stage. As in Italy, English publishers took advantage of the lute song's popularity, printing over 36 different collections between 1597 and 1622.

One of the greatest song composers was John Dowland (1563–1626), who, after failing to gain an appointment as lutenist to Queen Elizabeth I, traveled to Venice, Padua, Ferrara, and Florence on his way to landing a position at the court of Christian IV of Denmark. Dowland based his best-known song, "Flow, my tears," published in his *Second Booke of Songs or Ayres* (1600), on a previously written pavan (a slow dance in duple meter) for solo lute known as *Lachrimae* (Tears). The melodic line is permeated by a single motive, a stepwise descending tetrachord (four-note scale segment) first heard in the opening measure that not only captures the poet's sorrow but also represented the motion of the tears as they fall from the eyes (see Anthology 3). Descending tetrachords were often used by seventeenth and eighteenth century composers not only in the melody, as in "Flow, my tears," but also in the bass as an ostinato (repeated pattern), also called a ground bass. When placed in the minor mode, a ground bass with a descending tetrachord was often associated with sorrow and lament, an effect that was sometimes enhanced with the addition of chromatic passing tones.

The song "Flow, my tears," and the many instrumental variations on that same theme by Dowland and others, became closely identified with Dowland's reportedly depressive nature and can be understood as part of a general preoccupation with melancholy in the early modern period. But lute songs also had a humorous side, as illustrated by Tobias Hume's (ca. 1579–1645) "Tobacco is like love," in which the poet compares the craving for tobacco to unfulfilled sexual desire.

The fact that women were among the major consumers of lute songs led some to associate music in general, and lute songs in particular, with corrupt, effeminate, foreign influences. Several English commentators charged that the musical devices used in songs written in the Italian style had a potentially dangerous, feminizing effect on listeners; they described the poignant dissonances and chromaticisms that characterized the genre as "wanton" or "whorish." Nonetheless, the musical skills of the many noblewomen who performed lute songs were readily acknowledged and praised, indicating that in England, as in Italy, a substantial number of women as well as men received vocal training.

FROM PERFORMANCE TO PRINT AND BACK AGAIN

The printing of volumes by composers such as Dowland and Caccini preserved a performance tradition and packaged it into standardized, commercially available versions that, at least theoretically, could be re-created anywhere by musicians with appropriate training. Printed music made it possible for

Dowland to build his reputation in England while working at the Danish court, and for Caccini to gain renown as a singer and teacher outside of his native Florence. The lute tablature used by Dowland and his contemporaries in the printed editions of lute songs showed the accompaniment with absolute precision; there was no question as to what notes should be played for the inner voices, and while aspects of the rhythm could be improvised, the player was still constrained to follow the singer and the rhythms of the text. The design of the page also tells us something about varying performance practices: the song could be sung either as a solo or as a duet, as the part for the additional voice was printed on the side, so it could be read by somebody standing or sitting nearby (Fig. 2.3).

Caccini, who complained that his songs had been "tattered and torn by singers," used his edition of *Le nuove musiche* to amplify the notation with written guidelines that tell singers what ornaments to use and where to put them. None of this is intended to be rigid: he advocates a style of singing characterized by "a certain noble *sprezzatura*," by which he means a kind of negligence or graceful disregard of rules for the sake of expressivity (SR 100:608; 4/20:100). Caccini provides singers with exercises to train their throat muscles to articulate pitches cleanly, clearly, and accurately. He also includes several arias that presumably record the specific ornamentation used by singers during the Florentine wedding in 1600. The volume thus provides valuable information about performance practices that would otherwise be elusive in an age in which electronic recording was not possible.

BASSO CONTINUO

Caccini was among the first to employ the system of notation now known as figured bass, which would dominate much of the Baroque period. The composer provided a single bass line with numbers added above or below the staff for the instruments of the basso continuo group, which we considered briefly in Chapter 1. Players of chordal instruments, such as lute, organ, harpsichord, harp, and guitar, read the "figures" and "realized" the required harmony. The use of figured bass was convenient for printers as well as for knowledgeable players who were sufficiently fluent in the style to interpret the figures. Continuo players had enormous freedom in accompanying singers or solo instruments: they could reinforce the sentiments of the text or affect of a piece by determining the texture, choosing the number of notes for any chord, and adjusting dynamics, arpeggiation, and rhythmic accent in a way that was dramatically compelling and full of variety.

Since the instruments were not specified—the bass line, for instance, could be reinforced by viols, cellos, or low winds and brass instruments—the musical effect of the basso continuo was far richer and more expressive than it appeared

Figure 2.3: *John Dowland, "Flow, my tears," for voice and lute (with lute tablature) and optional second vocal part for bass on the side, from the* Second Booke of Songs or Ayres *(London, 1600)*

to be on the printed page. This innovative mode of notation, in conjunction with new expressive goals, made it possible for musicians of the early seventeenth century to realize their imagined notion of how ancient music sounded, albeit with techniques that were unmistakably modern.

By the beginning of the seventeenth century all the requisite elements for compelling musical theater were in place. Composers, willing to bend or even break the rules of counterpoint, enticed the ear with evocative dissonances that matched the impassioned tone of contemporary poetry. The basso continuo provided support for the virtuosic singer or player, thus enhancing their expressive power. Technological advances in stagecraft and machinery made possible instantaneous scene changes and other special effects. Dance, so vital to the training of the Renaissance courtier, played a central role in many theatrical genres, providing an appropriate way for nobles to join in court performances. Military training meshed with musical theater, as mock naval battles, tournaments, and equestrian ballets became all the rage, often capped off by fireworks displays. Music, in partnership with its sister arts, was part of a total sensory experience that entertained courtiers, enlivened Carnival festivities, lent variety to plays in public theaters, and accompanied improvised performances by traveling troupes of actors and comedians on streets and in public squares. The theatrical age had begun.

FOR FURTHER READING

Brosius, Amy, "'Il Suon, Lo Sguardo, Il Canto': The Function of Portraits of Mid-Seventeenth-Century *Virtuose* in Rome," *Italian Studies* 63 (2008): 17–39

Carter, Tim, *Music in Late Renaissance and Early Baroque Italy* (Portland, OR: Amadeus Press, 1992)

Coelho, Victor, "The Players of Florentine Monody in Context and in History, and a Newly Recognized Source for *Le nuove musiche*," *Journal of Seventeenth-Century Music* 9 (2003): www.sscm-jscm.org/v9/no1/coelho.html

Gerbino, Giuseppe, *Music and the Myth of Arcadia in Renaissance Italy* (Cambridge: Cambridge University Press, 2009)

Hill, John Walter, *Roman Monody, Cantata, and Opera from the Circles around Cardinal Montalto* (2 vols., Oxford: Clarendon Press; New York: Oxford University Press, 1997)

Holman, Peter, *Dowland: Lachrimae (1604)* (Cambridge: Cambridge University Press, 1999)

Monson, Craig, "Songs of Shakespeare's England," in *The World of Baroque Music: New Perspectives*, ed. George B. Stauffer (Bloomington: Indiana University Press, 2007)

Murata, Margaret, "Image and Eloquence: Popular Song," *Cambridge History of Seventeenth-Century Music*, ed. Tim Carter and John Butt (Cambridge: Cambridge University Press, 2006)

Ossi, Massimo, *Divining the Oracle: Monteverdi's Seconda Prattica* (Chicago: University of Chicago Press, 2003)

CHAPTER THREE

Theatrical Baroque

All great diversions are dangerous for a Christian life, but among all those the world has invented none is to be so feared as that given by theater: it creates a representation so natural and so subtle of human passions that it excites and engenders them in our heart.

—Blaise Pascal, *Pensées* (1655–62)

Whether or not the French philosopher Pascal was specifically thinking of opera or musical theater when he penned these remarks, they reflect both the enthusiasm and the anxiety that many felt as theater—with or without music—became increasingly integral to everyday life for many nobles in seventeenth-century Europe.

In this chapter we consider opera and other varieties of musical theater in the Italian peninsula and beyond. We begin at the Gonzaga court, where Monteverdi and his colleagues capitalized on the Florentine innovations discussed in Chapter 2, producing not only opera but also plays adorned with extravagant *intermedi*, *balli* (ballets), tournaments with music, and other such spectacles. From there we travel to England, Spain, and France, where opera had yet to take hold, and consider the masques, comedies, and court ballets that not only entertained monarchs and courtiers, but sometimes even featured them as performers.

MONTEVERDI'S MANTUA

When Monteverdi entered the service of Duke Vincenzo Gonzaga in Mantua around 1590, he joined a court that placed a high value on musical excellence. The duke was known for his extravagance, and, following the family tradition of artistic patronage, dedicated considerable resources to supporting the best poets, artists, and musicians. His decision to hire Monteverdi (who served the Gonzagas until the duke's death in 1612) attests to his musical intuition. The family did not always treat the composer particularly well, as we learn from Monteverdi's letters. Nonetheless, Monteverdi dedicated his Fifth Book of Madrigals to Duke Vincenzo, noting the "singular favor" his music had found at court.

Elaborate entertainments were one way in which Vincenzo demonstrated his cultural sophistication and competed with other Italian city-states such as Ferrara and Florence. Among his most impressive undertakings was a performance in 1598 of Guarini's *Il pastor fido* (see Chapter 2), the pastoral play that inspired so many madrigal composers and incited controversy because of its anticlassical mixture of tragedy and comedy. The Gonzaga court welcomed the best-known companies of traveling actors that toured the Italian peninsula and Europe, such as I Fedeli (The Faithful Ones), led by Giovanni Andreini and featuring his wife Virginia Ramponi, whose performance in Monteverdi's *Arianna* at the 1608 Gonzaga wedding we consider later. The Gonzagas also enjoyed performances by troupes of Jewish actors and musicians who had special permission to leave the Ghetto (the area of Mantua in which the Jews were compelled to live) in order to perform, and who had long benefited from favorable treatment under the duke. (We'll meet one of these musicians, Salamone Rossi, in Chapter 5.) The combination of originality and spectacular public display created a fertile environment for the development of all kinds of music, both sacred and secular.

A VOYAGE TO THE UNDERWORLD: *L'ORFEO*

On February 23, 1607, a Mantuan gentleman named Carlo Magni wrote to his brother about the splendor of one of the comedies presented during Carnival, the period between Christmas and Lent that was traditionally given over to masquerades, parades, and other entertainments. However, Magni particularly looked forward to a serious play that was to be staged in one of the apartments of the Ducal Palace, sponsored by Francesco Gonzaga, son of Duke Vincenzo. "It should be most unusual," he wrote, since "all the actors are to sing their parts. . . . No doubt I will be driven to attend out of sheer curiosity, unless I am prevented from getting in by lack of space."

Magni's letter captures the eager anticipation that nobles must have felt in contemplating the cornucopia of theatrical and other pleasures that awaited them prior to the arrival of Lent and the enforced sobriety of the Easter season.

The comedy he attended was probably presented by the Jewish actors of Mantua, but the singular event that piqued Magni's interest was that play in which "all the actors are to sing their parts"—in other words, opera.

Magni credits only the sponsorship of Francesco Gonzaga. However, we now know that the letter refers to the first performance of *L'Orfeo*, with music by Monteverdi and libretto by Alessandro Striggio the Younger. It was produced under the auspices of a Mantuan literary academy, the Accademia degli Invaghiti (Academy of the Lovestruck), on the evening of February 24, 1607. The event was sufficiently novel to attract the attention of Francesco's father, Duke Vincenzo, who attended the rehearsals and the premiere, and subsequently ordered a repeat performance on March 1 "for the ladies of the city."

Long regarded as the first great opera, *L'Orfeo* is the also the earliest opera to be performed with any frequency in the twentieth and twenty-first centuries. Although no detailed descriptions of the first performance have come down to us, we do have the printed version of Striggio's libretto of 1607. Monteverdi's score, published two years later, also provides invaluable information about performing his opera, including an extensive list of instruments and precise instructions as to when they should be used.

Monteverdi's choice of opera subject was not entirely original. The story of the musician Orpheus, also used by Jacopo Peri and Ottavio Rinuccini for the Florentine performance of *Euridice* in 1600 (see Chapter 2), was one of the best-known tales told by the Roman poet Ovid in his *Metamorphoses* and would prove to be one of most enduring myths in music, art, and literature. Perhaps because it was presented for an academy meeting rather than a wedding, the version of the story presented by Striggio and Monteverdi is somewhat less celebratory than the tale presented for the Florentine wedding in 1600. Whereas Rinuccini's hero succeeds—not only does his playing and singing win over Pluto, but he manages to bring his bride out of Hades without incident—in Monteverdi's opera Orpheus fails to heed Pluto's warning not to turn back and gaze upon his bride. As a result, she is snatched away and returned to the underworld, leaving the hero to lament yet again. Thus, self-control failed where music had succeeded.

Striggio's libretto as published in 1607, soon after the premiere, follows Ovid's violent version quite faithfully: Orpheus, in the aftermath of losing his wife, condemns all womankind and is ripped to shreds by the Bacchantes, the wild female followers of Bacchus, the god of wine. However, the published score of 1609 provides a somewhat more uplifting *lieto fine* (happy ending), rife with Christian overtones: Apollo descends to earth and escorts Orpheus to the heavens, where he can gaze on Eurydice in the stars.

Like Orpheus, Monteverdi may well have regarded the opera as a test of music's power. He uses nearly all the available styles of vocal music and a host of instrumental colors to dramatize the antithesis between Orpheus's joy at his marriage to Eurydice and his sorrow at losing his beloved twice to the underworld. Orpheus's wedding in Act 1 is celebrated with exuberant madrigals and canzonettas, while the sorrowful choruses and monologues in *stile recitativo* reflect the hero's despair over his bride's death in Act 2. The mood changes are reflected in the choice of instruments so carefully prescribed in the score: the celebratory choruses of nymphs and shepherds in the bright pastoral realm of Act 1 are accompanied by violins, theorbos or *chittaroni*, harpsichords, harps, and recorders, while for gloomy Hades in Act 4 Pluto and the spirits of the underworld sing to a regal (a nasty, nasal-sounding organ), trombones, and a bass viol.

The most shocking shift between happiness and despair occurs in Act 2, through the juxtaposition of the two distinctive styles of solo song that we explored in Chapter 2: the canzonetta and the lament monologue. With its playful syncopations and dancelike rhythms, Orpheus's joyful canzonetta "Vi ricorda, o boschi ombrosi" (Recall, O shady woods) perfectly captures the musician's joy upon his marriage and memories of his lonely life before he met Eurydice (Ex. 3.1).

As one of the shepherds responds appreciatively, singing cheerfully in C major, the festive mood is interrupted by the arrival of the messenger Sylvia (La Messaggiera). The sense of impending doom is signaled by an abrupt tonal shift: the bass moves unexpectedly up a half step from C to C♯, which underpins a shocking A-major sonority. Sylvia, with the words "Ahi, caso acerbo" (Ah, bitter fate), enters with a sustained high E for four beats, the bitterness reflected in her falling E-major triad, as she holds a G♯ against the A in the bass before resolving (Ex. 3.2).

As in Greek tragedy, the most horrific events are merely described rather than presented on the stage. Thus, the audience listens along with Orpheus to Sylvia's stirring *stile recitativo* description of the demise of Eurydice. Orpheus responds with the lament "Tu se' morta" (You are dead), in which he resolves

Example 3.1: *Claudio Monteverdi, "Vi ricorda, o boschi ombrosi" from* L'Orfeo *(1607), Act 2, mm. 1–3 (vocal line only)*

Recall, O shady woods . . .

Example 3.2: *Claudio Monteverdi, "Ahi, caso acerbo" from* L'Orfeo *(1607), Act 2*

Ah, bitter fate . . .

to retrieve his beloved from the underworld. The chorus echoes Sylvia's woeful announcement and concludes the act with appropriate tragic grandeur: Orpheus's wedding is thus transformed into a funeral (see Anthology 4).

The two endings of *L'Orfeo*—the tragic one in the first version of the libretto and the joyous one in the score—leave us with a mystery. Might Monteverdi and Striggio have presented the tragic, violent ending for the Mantuan literary academy, crafting one in which the hero is rescued from the Baccantes for subsequent public performance? And if so, what kind of music would Monteverdi have initially written for the death of Orpheus? Regardless, in giving voice to the sorrow of the legendary hero, the new genre of opera performed the ultimate metamorphosis by bringing the ancient world to life.

LAMENTING AT THE MANTUAN WEDDING

Later that same year (1607) when Duke Vincenzo was planning to celebrate his son Francesco's marriage to Margherita of Savoy in May of 1608, Monteverdi was among the musicians enlisted to create the entertainments for the wedding. Although only some of the music survives from the festivities, we know a good deal about them from the detailed description provided by Federico Follino, the Gonzagas' court publicist. The lavish celebration began with the entrance of the bride into the city on May 24, 1608, and continued as follows:

> May 27: The guests spend the day and evening at the Palazzo del Tè, the Gonzaga villa on an island just outside the center of Mantua. A play is presented in the afternoon.
>
> May 28: Monteverdi's *Arianna* (Ariadne), with poetry by Rinuccini, is presented in a temporary theater that reportedly holds between four and six thousand spectators.
>
> May 29: The wedding guests enjoy a sumptuous banquet and a hunting expedition, followed by a sung mass and yet another banquet, and a subsequent trip to see a play presented by Giovanni Andreini's company.
>
> May 31: A mock naval battle, accompanied by music and followed by fireworks, is presented on the lake, having been postponed from the previous day because of weather.
>
> June 2: The wedding guests attend the central performance of the week: the play *Idropica* by Battista Guarini, with elaborate *intermedi* penned by the poet Girolamo Chiabrera and music by a group of composers associated with Mantua, including Claudio Monteverdi, Salamone Rossi, Giovanni Gastoldi, Marco da Gagliano, and Giulio Cesare Monteverdi. The performance reportedly begins two hours before sunset and ends at 5 a.m.
>
> June 4: A tournament is staged in the courtyard, reportedly for 15,000 spectators, followed by a performance of Monteverdi's *Mascherata dell'ingrate*

(Masquerade of the Ungrateful Women), a sung *ballo* or dance with dramatic action, with poetry by Rinuccini.

June 5: Following a mass celebrating the feast of Corpus Domini and some festive jousting, another *ballo* titled *Il sacrificio d'Ifigenia* (The Sacrifice of Iphigenia), with poetry by Striggio and music by Gagliano, is presented, followed by yet another sumptuous concluding banquet.

The wedding guests thus had the opportunity to witness in close succession several genres of musical theater: opera, a play with musical *intermedi*, and a sung *ballo*. The festivities were nonetheless unified ideologically, emphasizing the glory of Mantua, its prosperity, and the anticipated bliss and fertility of the newlywed couple. Most of the tales dramatized for the Mantuan wedding entertainments dealt with familiar myths involving amorous unions between gods and nymphs that, although somewhat violent by our standards, were fully compatible with contemporary ideas about marriage. In the first *intermedio* for Guarini's *Idropica*, the underworld god Pluto abducts the nymph Proserpina, entering the stage on a chariot drawn by actors disguised as "two of the blackest horses" and followed by "horrid and monstrous spirits" who burst through the earth amid flames. The story ends with the wedding of Proserpina and Pluto. In the next *intermedio,* a lament is sung by the nymph Europa, who, according to the myth recounted by Ovid, was raped by the god Jupiter in the guise of a bull.

The most famous lament heard at the wedding festivities was from Monteverdi's opera *L'Arianna* (1608). Described by the librettist Rinuccini as a "tragedia" (tragedy), *L'Arianna* dramatizes another myth that would prove popular in the history of opera: the tale of the Cretan princess Ariadne. Having been abandoned on the island of Dia by Theseus, she is rescued by Bacchus, the god of wine, who grants her immortality. Unfortunately, all that survives of Monteverdi's opera is the lament that Ariadne sings to the fishermen and her companion Dorilla upon discovering that Theseus has abandoned her. Follino tells us that the scene was acted by Virginia Ramponi with "so much emotion and in so piteous a way that no one hearing it was left unmoved, there was not one lady who did not shed some little tear at her beautiful plaint."

In Rinuccini's monologue, Ariadne expresses an extraordinary range of emotions, which Monteverdi set with great flexibility and spontaneity. In the famous depressive opening of the lament, Ariadne expresses her desire for death—"Lasciatemi morire" (Let me die)—in a series of failed attempts to ascend melodically. She begins with a mere half step, sustaining the dissonant B♭ against the A in the bass, only to sink lower for the mention of death. She then attempts a chromatic ascent, pushing through the B♮, C, and C♯ to the D, only to plunge down the octave in despair, as if an unseen force were pulling her downward (Ex. 3.3).

Ariadne's suicidal anguish is transformed into anger as she imagines herself, once a princess, food for wild animals on the island. Monteverdi depicts her

Example 3.3: *Claudio Monteverdi, Ariadne's Lament from* L'Arianna *(1608), mm. 1–6*

Let me die

Example 3.4: *Claudio Monteverdi, Ariadne's Lament from* L'Arianna *(1608), mm. 43–54*

She who left her homeland and kingdom for you, and who, on these shores, will even leave her bare bones as for wild and pitiless beasts, O Theseus . . .

volatile emotions with rapid repetitions of short note values (Ex. 3.4)—what he would later describe in the preface to his *Madrigali guerrieri et amorosi* (Warlike and Loving Madrigals, 1638) as *stile concitato*, or agitated style (SR 109:665–67; 4/29:157–59). At the end of the monologue, Monteverdi's heroine—unlike the Ariadne of mythology—apologizes for cursing Theseus, claiming that it was her tongue that spoke, not her heart. Thus, like so many opera heroines, she expresses herself with extraordinarily eloquence, but ultimately conforms to early modern notions of female virtue that prized silence and obedience.

In keeping with the spirit of the wedding celebration, *L'Arianna* does not end unhappily, even if the lament did bring tears to the eyes of the viewers. In the depths of Ariadne's despair, Bacchus arrives with his noisy band of satyrs and bacchantes, riding a tiger-driven chariot. The opera concludes, as does the myth, with the celebration of their marriage as the abandoned Ariadne takes her place among the immortals. However, since the music for this joyous scene is lost, as with the first ending of *L'Orfeo*, we can only imagine how Monteverdi might have set it.

Another of Monteverdi's celebrated laments, the *Lamento della ninfa* (Lament of the Nymph; see Anthology 5), provides an intriguing comparison with that of Ariadne. It was published in his *Madrigali guerrieri et amorosi*, a collection of what is usually called concerted madrigals, scored for voices and instruments (including basso continuo), which allowed for even greater contrasts in texture and sonority than those scored for vocal ensemble alone.

Monteverdi uses a special musical technique for the anonymous nymph (who, like Ariadne, is lamenting her abandonment by a lover): he underpins the entire composition with a repeated bass line called an *ostinato* or ground bass using a minor descending tetrachord on the pitches A, G, F, E. The hypnotic repetitions of the bass line reflect the nymph's obsession, while at the same time creating piquant dissonances with the vocal line. Like Ariadne, whose lament was witnessed by Dorilla and the fishermen, the nymph is not alone: she is accompanied by a trio of male singers who both introduce and conclude the monologue with brief madrigals that comment throughout the lament, somewhat ironically, on her tragic situation.

The presence of the male voyeurs in the *Lamento della ninfa* raises an important question about laments: Why would those planning a wedding celebration place so many obviously unhappy women in the spotlight? In fact, there could not have been a more fortuitous intersection between gender ideology, humanism, and innovations in musical style than the early-seventeenth-century female lament. In a period in which chastity and silence were considered paramount virtues for women, such unfeminine outbursts in highly dramatic musical language contradicted accepted standards of behavior. Yet they also made for pleasurable musical experiences. Moreover, since virtually all of these tales ended happily (at least from the male perspective), the tears that might have been inspired by the passionate musical outpourings of gifted young singers were ultimately transformed into joy, as the heroine—like the bride—willingly accepted her divine or royal spouse and marriage bed.

The necessity of encouraging women to give in to their lovers was made explicit in the penultimate theatrical event of the Gonzaga wedding festival: Monteverdi's *Mascherata dell'ingrate*, later published as the *Ballo delle ingrate* in his *Madrigali guerrieri et amorosi*. The *ballo* is danced at the mouth of Hades—a deep, fiery cavern with what Follino describes as "countless monsters of the inferno so horrible and frightening"—where Pluto has imprisoned all women who resist the power of love. Despite the pleadings of the goddess Venus and a final lament sung by Ramponi as an ungrateful soul, the obstinate women are ultimately swallowed by the flames—an unforgettable lesson for any mortal bride.

OPERA IN ITALY AND BEYOND

Whether inspired by the success of *L'Orfeo* and *L'Arianna* or simply intrigued by the novelty of sung drama, a variety of patrons on the Italian peninsula adopted the genre to suit their varying political, social, and artistic needs. The virtuous hermit Saint Alexis, who refuses all earthly pleasures (including the seductive music of the devil), came to the Roman stage in 1632 in *Sant'Alessio*.

With music by Stefano Landi (1587–1639) and a libretto by Giulio Rospigliosi, the future Pope Clement X, *Sant'Alessio* is one of a number of operas sponsored by the Barberini, the family of Pope Urban VIII (elected in 1623). The Barberini, who patronized no less a sculptor and architect than Gian Lorenzo Bernini, sponsored a number of great architectural projects that brought glory to Rome and the papacy.

In Florence, where Duchess Christine of Lorraine and Archduchess Maria Magdalen (a tireless opera patron) ruled on behalf of the young Prince Ferdinando de' Medici, many of the operas presented powerful female characters. One such work is *La liberazione di Ruggiero dall'isola d'Alcina* (The Liberation of Ruggiero from Alcina's Island, 1625), by Francesca Caccini, daugher of Giulio Caccini (see Chapter 2), who was renowned at the Florentine court for her talents as a singer and composer. The first operatic entertainment composed by a woman, *La liberazione* was presented during Carnival for the visiting Prince Władysław of Poland, who Maria Magdalen hoped would marry her daughter. Based on episodes from the sixteenth-century epic poem *Orlando furioso* by Ludovico Ariosto, *La liberazione* boasted two powerful female sorceresses: the beautiful Alcina, who holds the hero Ruggiero captive on her magic island, and the clever Melissa, who urges him to leave Alcina's sensual realm and pursue his noble destiny. Ruggiero ultimately escapes with the aid of Melissa, which enrages Alcina. She not only calls upon her monsters to seek vengeance on her behalf, but in fact turns into a monster before escaping on the back of a dragon as her enchanted island explodes into flames. Alcina may have represented one kind of dangerous female power; but the good Melissa, who frees not only Ruggiero but a host of women that were turned into plants, provides a positive image of female rule.

During the early decades of the seventeenth century, Italian opera began to capture the attention of rulers north of the Alps. It may have been Francesca Caccini's opera that later inspired King Władysław IV to produce nine Italian operas in Warsaw between 1633 and 1648, all on librettos by Virgilio Puccitelli, a castrato who served as secretary to the Polish court. Elector Johann Georg I of Dresden took another approach: he commissioned Martin Optiz to create a German translation of Ottavio Rinuccini's first opera libretto, *La Dafne*; the music by Heinrich Schütz (see Chapter 5) is lost.

It is perhaps paradoxical that some of the most lavish performances of Italian operas were staged for dynastic celebrations in northern European courts where German was the principal language. One example is the trilogy of musical theater works produced at the Bavarian court in Munich in 1662 celebrating the birth of Maximilian II Emanuel, the son of Elector Ferdinand Maria and his Italian wife, Henrietta Adelaide of Savoy. It included a conventional opera; a tournament featuring mock battles, floats, and processions with musical interludes; and a final "drama di fuoco"—an opera presented out of doors featuring fireworks in which yet another female sorceress—this time Medea—flies away on a magic dragon, as her palace (and the entire set) appears to burst into flames (Fig. 3.1).

Figure 3.1: *Pietro Paolo Bissari,* Medea vendicativa *(Munich, 1662), final scene*

OTHER VARIETIES OF MUSICAL THEATER

In countries with a rich tradition of spoken drama, such as Spain, France, and England, there was less initial interest either in adapting Italian opera or in creating an entirely sung drama in the native language. Music did feature in many plays of the period, including those by William Shakespeare and Lope de Vega, but it was rarely central to the dramatic action and was unlikely to have been heard to best advantage in open-air theaters like London's Globe. More-sophisticated music was probably heard in the plays presented by boy actors drawn from the best London choirs, such as those of the Chapel Royal and St. Paul's Cathedral during the reigns of Elizabeth I and James I, which attracted an elite audience.

Musical theater could also be seen and heard on the streets of many cities. In Parisian "medicine shows," for instance, so-called charlatans (or imposters) presented performances to help sell "magic" elixirs guaranteed to cure any illness. The most famous charlatan was Antoine Girard, known as Tabarin, who promoted his products by singing, accompanied by a hurdy-gurdy (a rustic stringed instrument in which the sound is produced by a wheel rubbing against the strings, controlled by a crank) and both the small and large members of the viol family.

At royal courts, non-operatic entertainments such as masques (see below), ballets, processions, and mock tournaments provided an opportunity for nobles to participate and even star in their own performances. More than mere diversions, these were rituals of great importance for representing the power and legitimacy of the monarchy, the harmonious rapport between ruler and subjects, and the superiority of their own courts to other, presumably less civilized societies.

THE ENGLISH MASQUE

In the first half of the seventeenth century, the masque became the standard entertainment for holidays and special dynastic events at the English court; its unique mixture of singing, dialogue, dancing, and spectacle would influence musical theater in England well into the next century. Popular during the reigns of James I (r. 1603–25) and Charles I (r. 1625–49), masques were supported enthusiastically by the royal spouses, the Danish Queen Anne and the French-born Henrietta Maria respectively. They typically opened with an "antimasque" of a comic, grotesque, or exotic character, usually featuring professional dancers. The antimasque gave way to the elegant main masque, performed by both courtiers and professionals, and the entertainment culminated in revels, in which everyone danced into the wee hours of the morning. The progression was thus from disorder to order: bizarre, strange, or foreign characters were transformed miraculously into an affirmation of an idyllic court life, and at the end royalty, courtiers, and spectators commingled.

We know a great deal about masques from printed texts, which included spoken dialogue, lyrics, descriptions of the action, and dedications to the nobles—but relatively little of the music survives. *The Masque of Queens* (1609), produced by the creative team of poet Ben Jonson and architect and stage designer Inigo Jones, exploited the English fascination with witches on the stage best known today from Shakespeare's *Macbeth*. Eleven witches (played by professional male actors), with such names as Suspicion, Malice, Rage, Impudence, and Slander, danced to "hollow and infernal music," making a "confused noise" and "strange fantastic motions of their heads and bodies." At the climax of the antimasque, loud music was heard "as if many instruments had given one blast." The witches vanished entirely, giving way to the masque proper: "a glorious and magnificent building, featuring the House of Fame." Inside were 11 Amazon warrior queens, played by Queen Anne and her ladies in waiting, who were praised for their virtue, courage, and loyalty to their husbands.

Contrasting musical styles accentuated the difference between the antimasque and masque characters: the witches danced and sang with shifting meters and erratic bodily movements, accompanied by raucous wind instruments, whereas the warrior queens, supported by large groups of lutes and strings, were controlled and dignified. Alfonso Ferrabosco's (ca. 1575–1628) setting of "So beautie on the waters stood" from *The Masque of Beauty* (1608; Fig. 3.2), presented here in its published version for voice and lute, evokes the grandeur and elegance that was associated with Queen Anne and her attendants. After lingering on low G for two beats, the melody ascends stepwise by deliberate quarter notes in the first phrase, then teases the listener with a bold skip of a minor seventh to F in measure 3 as the name of Love is invoked. (We will have more to say about another of Queen Anne's masques later.)

Figure 3.2: *Alfonso Ferrabosco, "So beautie on the waters stood," for voice and lute, from* Ayres *(London, 1609), sung in* The Masque of Beauty *(1608)*

MUSICAL THEATER AT THE FRENCH COURT

French theatrical tastes in the seventeenth and early eighteenth centuries were shaped by several factors: their interest in ballet, a respect for the principles of classical tragedy, centralization resulting from the king's granting of a monopoly to a single director or company, and a highly ambivalent attitude toward visiting Italian singers, musicians, and actors. As we will see in Chapter 7, this insularity would lead the French later in the seventeenth century to develop a distinct style of opera.

At the French court, the primary form of musical theater was the *ballet de cour*, or court ballet, a spectacle that included elaborate vocal music, stage machinery, costumes, and masks, as well as dances. It was performed by professionals and male nobles, and was usually arranged into a series of scenes called *entrées*. Court ballets first became popular in the late sixteenth century, encouraged in part by Catherine de' Medici and Marie de' Medici, the wives of Henry II and Henry IV, respectively, who introduced many aspects of Italian music at the French court. As with Italian musical theater, the ballets were inspired by classical mythology, epic poetry, and pastoral plays from the Renaissance. The participation of nobles in ballets also conveyed important political messages, particularly when Louis XIII and later Louis XIV (renowned for his skill as a dancer) appeared in carefully selected roles.

The performance in 1617 of *La délivrance de Renaud* (The Deliverance of Renaud) in the *grande salle* of the Louvre (now the famed art museum, but then the Parisian palace that housed the French court) featured the 18-year-old Louis XIII at a particularly auspicious political moment: Marie de' Medici's power over her royal son had been severely curtailed by the king's advisor, Charles d'Albert, the duke of Luynes. The music was by court composer Pierre Guédron (1570–1620) and the poetry was by Etienne Durand, who would be executed a year later for conspiring with the queen against her son. The plot of *Renaud* was drawn from *Gerusalemme liberata*, Torquato Tasso's epic poem about the liberation of Jerusalem by the Christian hero Godfrey of Boulogne. The ballet presents a series of entrées and songs about the Christian knight Renaud who, much like Ruggiero in Francesca Caccini's opera (see above), is held prisoner by an evil sorceress, named Armida in Tasso's epic. (Might she have been intended to represent Marie de' Medici?) The duke of Luynes, reputed to be a better dancer than political advisor, played the role of Renaud.

Louis XIII's appearances in *La délivrance de Renaud* were carefully designed to demonstrate his transformation into a hero. He was first seen in Armida's garden, outfitted in a demon costume with artificial flames constructed out of enamel "made more brilliant" by the reflection of the "innumerable torches" in the hall. Later he assumed the identity of Godfrey of Boulogne. Political power was also demonstrated by the splendor of the production. Five scene changes were accomplished with the latest in Italian stage machinery. The ensemble (including "extras") reportedly consisted of 92 voices and 45 instruments. Louis, who would soon lead battles in the name of Catholicism on behalf of his own country, could not have created a stronger public acknowledgment of his readiness to rule. The *ballet de cour* would become an even more powerful tool of the monarchy during the reign of Louis XIV (see Chapter 7).

COMEDY, MASQUE, AND SPECTACLE IN SPAIN

Musical theater on the Iberian peninsula was also largely independent from the rest of Europe, employing dramatic conventions, characters, popular songs, and dances that were distinctively Spanish. This is particularly notable in the music used in the popular *comedias nuevas*, or new-style comedies, presented in the public theaters by Lope de Vega and his contemporaries. The music in *comedias nuevas*, as in most spoken theater, functioned very differently than in Italian opera. The authors, seeking to represent the complexities and richness of contemporary Spanish life, rejected the classicizing tendencies that had shaped the birth of Italian opera. Music was included only when a character was called upon by the drama to sing or dance, to provide appropriate sound color for stock theatrical situations, or as background for a change of scenery (where it helped to drown out the sound of the stage machinery).

Under Philip III (r. 1598–1621) and the stern Queen Margaret, the preferred form of court entertainment was the dignified ball or *saraos*, which gave the king ample opportunity to show off his dancing skills. Special occasions, such as the birth of the future Philip IV in 1605, inspired elaborate spectacles, including *mascaras* (masques), ornate floats, mock tournaments, or exhibitions featuring the renowned Spanish horses who were trained to execute complex choreographies. Both Philip III and his successor hosted *particulares*, private performances of comedies by professional companies, which allowed the royals to see the latest dramas without having to venture out into the public theaters. Plays on chivalric or heroic topics, using professional court musicians, were performed throughout this period, but particularly flourished under Philip IV's patronage (r. 1621–40).

EXOTICISM

One of the most intriguing features in all of these entertainments is the attempt to incorporate elements of foreign and exotic cultures. The fascination with the exotic was inspired in no small part by early modern explorers of the East and the Americas. Richard Ligon's history of Barbados (1657), for instance, includes descriptions of the unusual rhythms used by African slaves in their drumming. "The drum, all men know, has but one tone; and therefore variety of tunes have little to do in this musick, and yet so strangely they vary their time, as 'tis a pleasure to the most curious ears. . . ." If only they used a similar variety in melody, he mourns, "they would do wonders in that art" (SR 118:714; 4/38:206).

The fascination with exoticism continued well into the eighteenth century. Writing from the Ottoman Empire in the early eighteenth century, Lady Mary Wortley Montagu (1689–1762) described the music and dance she saw at a harem, where she was welcomed by "2 black eunuchs" and some 20 "fair maids," four of which played airs on instruments that resembled lutes and guitars, accompanied by singing and dance, different than anything she had ever seen before. "Nothing could be more artful or proper to raise certain ideas, the tunes so soft, the motions so languishing, accompanied with pauses and dying eyes, half falling back and then recovering themselves in so artful a manner that I am very positive the coldest and most rigid prude upon earth could not have look'd upon them without thinking of something not to be spoke of" (SR 119:718; 4/39:210).

Lady Mary was not the only one to get a delicious thrill from her exposure to the music and culture of exotic climes. It would be some time before the sounds of Asia or the Americas were absorbed by composers. However, in the seventeenth century we find a number of operas, spectacle plays, masques, and court ballets representing Gypsies, Muslims, Africans, or Native Americans in ways that might be regarded as objectionable today but were readily accepted in early modern Europe. In *The Masque of Blackness* (1605), for example, Queen Anne and the other English court ladies danced as the daughters of Niger wearing blackface makeup (Fig. 3.3).

Figure 3.3: *Inigo Jones,* Masquer: A Daughter of Niger *(ca. 1605), from* The Masque of Blackness

The Masque of Flowers (1614) was one of several that featured Native American characters. The antimasque stages a contest between the jovial satyr Silenus (companion to the wine god Bacchus) and the Native American god Kawasha, in which Silenus tries to get Kawasha drunk. The French likewise included exotic elements in works such as the *Ballet du Prince de la Chine* (Ballet of the Prince of China, 1601) and the *Ballet des Moscovites* (Ballet of the Muscovites, 1623). Debates concerning national and religious identity and state policy were also played out in court entertainments. In 1617 the duke of Lerma attempted to secure Philip III's favor with *The Masque of the Expulsion of the Moriscos,* which used song, dance, and spectacle to justify the expulsion of 350,000 Spaniards of Muslim descent from the Iberian peninsula—a policy designed by the duke himself. The music and text do not survive, however witnesses described an entertainment in which the Moors were presented as a threat to the purity of Spain's Christian society, with appropriately decadent music, dance, and costumes. Despite this effort, the duke lost his influential position with the king the following year.

The entertainments we have discussed in this chapter represent a small sample of the wide range of musical theater that could be found in every corner of Europe in the first half of the seventeenth century. Regardless of the remarkable variety of musical styles, languages, genres, and social customs, all of these works illustrate the close relationship between politics and art in this period, as well as the complex ways in which patrons used pleasure as a tool to enhance their reputations, solve political disputes, or simply impress visitors.

Scholars disagree about how to interpret some of these entertainments. Was the transformation of the antimasque into the masque a suppression of dissent or a welcome opportunity for subversive thinking? What are the implications of having Louis XIII dance the role of one of Armida's demons? Did the representation of foreign cultures on the stage express imperial ambitions, anxiety, or merely a fascination with the exotic? Perhaps we are better off assuming that these works were multivalent, imparting diverse meanings to different viewers.

In the context of these collaborative efforts, it is notable that the composer, usually the hero in music history textbooks, often turns out not to be the most prominent figure. Even Monteverdi was overworked and neglected by his employers, and much of his theatrical music was lost. Nonetheless, the surviving images, descriptions, and music provide us with a glimpse of the marvelous marriages of sight and sound that were enjoyed by the most privileged spectators of this era.

FOR FURTHER READING

Carter, Tim, *Monteverdi's Musical Theatre* (New Haven and London: Yale University Press, 2002)

Cusick, Suzanne, *Francesca Caccini at the Medici Court: Music and Circulation of Power* (Chicago: University of Chicago Press, 2009)

Harness, Kelley, *Echoes of Women's Voices: Music, Art, and Female Patronage in Early Modern Florence* (Chicago: University of Chicago Press, 2006)

MacNeil, Anne, *Music and Women of the Commedia dell'Arte in the Late Sixteenth Century* (Oxford: Oxford University Press, 2003)

Pirrotta, Nino, "Early Opera and Aria," in Nino Pirrotta and Elena Povoledo, *Music and Theater from Poliziano to Monteverdi*, trans. Karen Eales (Cambridge: Cambridge University Press, 1982)

Powell, John, *Music and Theater in France, 1600–1680* (Oxford: Oxford University Press, 2000)

Ravelhofer, Barbara, *The Early Stuart Masque: Dance, Costume, and Music* (Oxford: Oxford University Press, 2006)

Stein, Louise, *Songs of Mortals, Dialogues of the Gods: Music and Theatre in Seventeenth-Century Spain* (Oxford: Oxford University Press, 1993)

Van Orden, Kate, *Music, Discipline, and Arms in Early Modern France* (Chicago: University of Chicago Press, 2005)

Walls, Peter, *Music in the English Courtly Masque, 1604–1640* (Oxford: Oxford University Press, 1996)

CHAPTER FOUR

The Art and Craft of Instrumental Music in the Early Seventeenth Century

In Act 3 of Monteverdi's *L'Orfeo*, when the hero sings the virtuosic aria "Possente spirto" (Powerful spirit), his aim is to persuade the boatman Charon (Caronte) to escort him across the river Styx to the underworld, where his beloved Eurydice languishes. The printed score of the opera hints at the kind of sonic splendor Monteverdi imagined for this moment: it includes both plain and embellished versions of the aria, the latter designed to showcase the talents of the first Orfeo, the tenor Francesco Rasi. As Orpheus praises Charon, his highly ornamented appeal is echoed first by one and then by another violin (Fig. 4.1).

The effect is magical. On the one hand, the violins heighten Orpheus's rhetorical power and demonstrate his legendary musical prowess. On the other hand, the wordless echo effect calls attention to the cavernous space of the underworld. The first strophe features violins echoing each of his utterances (and playing a brief ritornello at the conclusion), while in each of the subsequent strophes Orpheus is imitated by a different pair of instruments, each with a unique timbre: the mellow sounds of the violins are heard in strophe 1, the brilliant *cornetti* (curved wind instruments with a conical bore) in strophe 2, and the celestial sounds of harps in strophe 3.

Figure 4.1: *Orpheus echoed by violins in Claudio Monteverdi's* L'Orfeo, *Act 3 ("Possente spirto"), facsimile of 1609 score (Monteverdi indicates that Orpheus should sing only one of the two parts to the sound of the* chitarrone *[theorbo] and* organo di legno *[organ with wooden pipes])*

That Orpheus both sings and plays for Charon is symptomatic of changing attitudes toward instrumental music and recognition that instruments, like the voice, had the expressive power to move the passions of listeners. In the early decades of the seventeenth century, patrons devoted increasing resources to training and supporting instrumentalists; builders developed new techniques for constructing instruments; and composers disseminated instrumental music and instructions books in print to enthusiastic consumers of music, including both amateurs and professionals. By 1638 the French viol player André Maugars, on a visit to Rome, wrote with astonishment about the high regard Italians had for excellent instrumental playing. He observed "that one man can produce by himself more beautiful inventions than four voices together, and that it [instrumental music] has charms and liberties that vocal music does not have." The age of the virtuoso instrumentalist, begun in the sixteenth century, was now well underway.

In this chapter we consider how instrumentalists of the early seventeenth century were influenced and challenged by the virtuosity and expressivity of singers; the contexts in which their music was heard; their patrons and audiences; and the compositional strategies they used to produce the "beautiful inventions" and "charms and liberties" that Maugars extols.

THE PRACTICAL MUSICIAN

The vast majority of instrumentalists who made their living at music were not star solo performers but rather employees of a court, city, or church, serving the same practical functions as their counterparts from earlier periods. Courts typically kept a group of wind players on hand for public functions, since their loud instruments could be easily heard in large banquet halls, outdoor festivals, on barges, or on the streets. As many as 35 wind players were employed by the French court in its Grande Écurie (literally, Great Stable) for such occasions, occupying the same status as blacksmiths, fencing instructors, stable boys, and coachmen.

Wind and brass players were also employed by towns and villages. The *Stadtpfeifern* (city wind players) in German-speaking lands, town *waites* in England, and *piffari* in Italy played a variety of wind instruments, serving as night watchmen, human alarm clocks, and even weathermen; they could also perform for town festivals and supplement their income with engagements in taverns and private homes. Brass instruments had long been used for communications on the battlefield, but were also heard in church or at special feasts and victory celebrations. They were ideal for the grand processions that were integral to civic and religious life in much of Europe (see Chapter 5).

Softer instruments, such as lutes, viols, members of the violin family, and keyboard instruments (harpsichords, chamber organs, virginals) were favored indoors, and were suitable for the "private music" that entertained nobles. They were also used frequently and to great effect in church, accompanying solo voices or choirs, or enhancing an important moment in the service or liturgy. By the second quarter of the century wind and brass instruments also appeared alongside recorders, flutes, and violins in chamber music settings.

Instruments also grew to be among the prized possessions for families of successful merchants and entrepreneurs, the growing middle class that would become enthusiastic consumers of music throughout the era. Many paintings from the period provide us with invaluable evidence about otherwise undocumented musical activities in the home. Jan Olis's *A Musical Party* (1633; Fig. 4.2), for example, captures a Dutch family in the act of playing chamber music at home—in this case using a *broken* (also called *mixed*) consort of viola da gamba, flute, violin, and lute.

Musicians were a necessity for another important activity: dancing. We have already considered the centrality of dance in court entertainments, in which both professionals and courtiers participated. While almost any instrument could be used to accompany dancers, many dance masters favored a miniature violin called a *pochette* (French for "pocket") or kit, which could be used while teaching in noble households, accompanying social dancing, or choreographing ballet for the theater.

BUILDING INSTRUMENTS FOR SIGHT AND SOUND

In 1620, German composer and theorist Michael Praetorius (1571–1621) published an illustrated guide entitled *Theatrum instrumentorum* (Theater of Instruments). Replete with drawings and discussions of "all musical instruments old and new, foreign, barbarian, primitive, and obscure, as well as native, artistic, pleasant and familiar," Praetorius's book demonstrates the increased interest in and knowledge about instruments and instrument construction in the seventeenth century. During these years, players and instrument builders enjoyed close, mutually beneficial relationships: the burgeoning skills of players

Figure 4.2: *Jan Olis,* A Musical Party *(1633)*

inspired builders to make changes in construction that allowed musicians to play higher or lower, to achieve a greater range of dynamics and timbres, and to execute difficult passages with greater ease and facility. This, in turn, encouraged both players and composers to experiment with new styles and techniques.

Instrument building was both a family business and a regional phenomenon, driven in many instances by the availability of natural resources. Northern Italy was the center for the construction of the violin family—violins, violas, cellos, and basses—in no small part because of the excellent wood available in the area. From the late sixteenth through the eighteenth centuries, members of the Amati, Guarneri, and Stradivari families established Cremona, the birthplace of Monteverdi, as the foremost center for violin making. Their instruments are still prized above all others. In France, various branches of the Philidor and Hotteterre families became particularly well known for the construction and refinement of woodwind instruments: recorders (known then as flutes) which ranged from the tiny sopranino to the bass recorder, transverse flutes (played sideways like modern flutes, but made of wood), and reed instruments such as the oboe and bassoon. Another popular instrument wind instrument in France was the musette, a refined version of the bagpipe often associated with the pastoral games of the nobility. By the second quarter of the seventeenth century France was also an important center for lute making.

The availability of metals facilitated the construction of both brass instruments and organs in Germany. In Nuremberg, where nearby copper and silver deposits had transformed the prosperous city into a major center for the manufacture of weapons, armor, stoves, and other objects, Johann Wilhelm Haas and his descendants crafted trumpets, horns, and trombones. The firm established by the German organ builder Arp Schnitger was responsible for some of the largest organs of the day. While some of the 170 organs built by Schnitger's studio stayed in northern Germany, many were exported to such faraway lands as Russia and Brazil. The visual and sonic magnificence of Schnitger's organs is exemplified by the modern organ at the Örgryte New Church in Gothenberg, Sweden, completed in 2000 (Fig. 4.3). Modeled on several of Schnitger's surviving instruments, this splendid organ was made with the same materials and methods used in the seventeenth and eighteenth centuries, including the traditional technique for casting pipe metal on sand.

Instrument builders banded together in guilds, or associations of craftsmen, many of which traced their roots to the early Middle Ages. When the Guild of Trumpet Makers in Nuremberg broke away from the Guild of Coppersmiths in the sixteenth century, it became one of the first professional guilds specifically intended for instrument makers. These groups often had long lists of rules and restrictions concerning sales, apprenticeship, and construction materials and techniques, all intended to protect the members of the guild and further their interests. The Nuremberg guild even prohibited its members from marrying outsiders, lest they give their secrets away to other families. The Guild of Saint Luke in the Flemish city of Antwerp was one of several in which

Figure 4.3: *Modern organ modeled on Arp Schnitger instruments in Örgryte New Church, Gothenberg, Sweden*

keyboard builders, such as the famed Ruckers studio, joined together with other artisans, including engravers, printers, painters, and sculptors. The beautifully painted lids on many harpsichords underscore both the importance of the contact between painters and instrument builders and the considerable investment nobles made in transforming their instruments into artworks worthy of display.

PATRONS, AUDIENCES, AND PERFORMERS

An important factor in the rise of instrumental music and the changing status of players was a subtle but definitive reconfiguration of the relationships between performers, patrons, and listeners. Music-making was one of many "performances" that Renaissance courtiers used to display their refinement, sophistication, and largesse. However, in the seventeenth century—particularly in Italy, where composers were writing increasingly difficult music—nobles put aside performance for connoisseurship, treating music as a commodity that could be collected and displayed, much like paintings or ancient sculpture. Composer-performers responded to their attentive listeners by exploring still further the virtuosic and expressive potential of their instruments, which now required the skills of professional players, while also demanding more of audiences. In short, listening became an art in itself.

One way for a noble to demonstrate mastery of this new "art," as well as his or her prestige and taste, was by sponsoring fine music in the home or palace. This involved not only hiring the best players, but also commissioning builders to construct instruments that were beautiful to behold. The inventories of cardinals Francesco and Antonio Barberini and their brother Taddeo, the three nephews of Pope Urban VIII, give a sense of the quantity and quality of the instruments needed to serve the household's musical establishment and the kind of listening that such patrons encouraged. Cardinal Antonio owned as many as ten harpsichords of different sizes, along with organs and small spinets, many of which were decorated with the Barberini family symbol, the bee. The harpsichord likely owned by the Roman nobleman Lorenzo Colonna is a particularly dramatic example of a luxurious instrument: a golden mermaid, a symbol of the powerful Colonna family, sits beneath the main body of the harpsichord (Fig. 4.4).

To satisfy listeners' expanding appetite for technical display, many musicians began to fashion careers in which their reputations rested on their abilities on a single instrument or family of instruments. The Brescian violinist Biagio Marini (1594–1663) was the best known member of a family of musicians. He published works for various instrumental combinations, but is most remembered as one of several composers of his generation to extensively exploit the unique aspects of the violin. The international fame of Girolamo Frescobaldi (1583–1643) rested not only on his astonishing keyboard virtuosity, but also on the wide dissemination of his music through printed editions. These must certainly have reached Johann Jacob Froberger (1616–1667) in his native Stuttgart, for he made the long trip to Rome to study with Frescobaldi. Froberger subsequently became court organist in Vienna and brought much of what he learned on his travels throughout Europe to such cities as Paris, London, and Amsterdam.

The degree to which instrumental performers and composers could achieve success depended largely on the tastes of their patrons and the economic and

Figure 4.4: *Seventeenth-century Italian harpsichord, likely owned by the Colonna family*

artistic conditions under which they worked. Political squabbles and wars could have a devastating effect. Numerous musicians lost their posts or indeed their lives during the English Civil War of 1642–51 (see Chapter 8). Working conditions for musicians were so deplorable that one commentator noted that the local fiddlers were "ready to hang themselves in their strings for a pastime, for want of other employment."

Even when musicians had a steady salary and position, the often arbitrary whims of patrons meant that they had to avail themselves of every opportunity to earn a living wage, supplementing their income with outside employment. Frescobaldi was able to spend his whole life in Rome, finding work in that city's countless churches (including a high post at St. Peter's) and gaining support from several noble families. Many of his colleagues, however, led itinerant lives. Marini, who began his career at Saint Mark's Cathedral in Venice under Monteverdi, subsequently found employment in Brescia, Parma, and Milan, and spent a substantial portion of his professional life in the German court at Neuberg an der Donau. Orlando Gibbons (1583–1625) was one of several English composers who served as a Gentleman (musician) of the Chapel Royal and moonlighted by playing the organ at Westminster Abbey.

The keyboard composer and virtuoso John Bull (ca. 1562/63–1628) would seem to have had a most secure position: in addition to serving as the first professor of music at Gresham College in the City of London, he was a member of the household of Prince Henry (the son of James I) and taught keyboard to Henry's younger sister, Elizabeth Stuart. However, an accusation of adultery forced Bull to leave England for Amsterdam, where he studied with the organist Jan Pieterszoon Sweelinck (1562–1621) before completing his career as an organist in Brussels. Sweelinck, on the other hand, spent his entire career in Amsterdam as organist at its famous Oude Kerk (Old Church). One of Europe's richest cities during the first half of the seventeenth century, Amsterdam, a major center for book and music publishing, was celebrated for its intellectual freedom, tolerance of Jews and foreigners, and the enormous commercial success its residents reaped from international trade and shipbuilding. Sweelinck enjoyed the admiration and support of the city's many wealthy middle- and upper-class music lovers, who became eager patrons of the arts.

MUSIC, RHETORIC, AND NATIONAL STYLES

One of the challenges embraced by composers and instrumentalists in the seventeenth century was to embody the principles of the new expressive style in their works, even when the music lacked a text. Frescobaldi posits one solution for keyboard players: in a letter that prefaces the second edition of his *Toccate e partite d'intavolatura di cimbalo* (Toccatas and Partits Scored for Harpsichord, Book 1, 1616), he tells players not to play strictly in time, but rather to imitate the singers of modern madrigals, playing languidly or quickly as singers must do in order to match the meaning of the words. Marin Mersenne, in his *Harmonie universelle* (Universal Harmony) of 1636, extols the power of the viol, which he thought could "imitate the voice in all its modulations, and even in its accents most significant of sadness and joy."

Johann Mattheson, writing toward the end of the Baroque, describes instrumental music as the daughter of vocal music. As the mother, vocal music must thus direct "the daughter to conform to her motherly precepts as best as possible." Thus, Mattheson continues, "we can easily perceive which instrumental melodies are true daughters and which are produced as if out of wedlock, according to how they take after the mother, or deviate from type." Like Mersenne, Mattheson emphasizes the expressive power of instrumental music, which may be without words but cannot be without the affections—that is, without emotions such as happiness, grief, tenderness, joy, or seriousness—since "the true goal of all melody can only be a type of diversion of the hearing through which the passions of the soul are stirred" (SR 116:697–98; 4/36:189–90).

Like vocal music, instrumental music—which could invoke notions about the harmony of the spheres, as we saw in Chapter 2—played an important role in the spiritual realm. In an age in which Protestant and Catholic preachers were stirring congregations with impassioned orations, an instrumental composition could be a sermon without words. Thomas Mace, in *Musick's Monument* (1676), waxes poetic about the experience of playing viol consorts accompanied by organ, which he described as "many Pathetical Stories, Rhetorical and Sublime Discourses, Subtle and Accute Argumentations." These were so subtle and agreeable to the "Inward, Secret, and Intellectual Faculties of the Soul and Mind" that there were no words in language sufficient to describe them.

Part of the way music "spoke" to listeners in the seventeenth and eighteenth centuries was through different styles, often reflecting local preferences. In many instances, these styles were integral to the growing sense of national identity that we discussed in Chapter 1. As noted in Chapter 2, Vincenzo Giustiniani observed that musical habits shifted in the same way as did fashions for clothing at court. Athanasius Kircher, a Jesuit scholar in Rome who wrote extensively about music, proposed that the "difference in musical style of the different nations does not come from anywhere else except either from the spirit of the place and natural tendency, or from custom maintained by long-standing habit." Thus, the Germans are "born under a frozen sky and acquire a temperament that is serious, strong, constant, solid, and toilsome, to which qualities their music conforms," while the French have a temperament that is "cheerful, lively, and innocent of restraint." Kircher saves his greatest praise for the Italians, who having appointed themselves to "the first place in music from the beginning," benefit from a "temperate clime" and use "all styles appropriately and with the best judgment, and were truly born for music" (SR 117:709–10; 4/37:201–2).

In some instances, the tastes of a particular patron could have a strong impact on the musical preferences of an entire nation. The French interest in dance was no doubt heightened by the pleasure that Louis XIII and Louis XIV took both in dancing themselves and in supporting the art. Yet, as we will see in Chapter 7, the French developed a unique style, linked to special features of the French language and the manners and attitudes of courtiers, which retained its identity outside the country's borders.

Local tastes were also shaped by the types of instruments constructed in a given region. Italian skill with the violin family contrasts with the French preference for the lute and wind instruments, while the Germans lavished much of their attention on brass instruments and organ. As a result, by midcentury the Italians had developed a set of techniques for violin playing that imitated and even exceeded the virtuosity of their renowned singers. French lutenists invented a characteristic manner of playing, using arpeggiations that provided a suggestion of more-complex contrapuntal texture, called *style luthé* (lute style), but referred to by modern scholars as *style brisé*, or broken style (see Chapter 7). German organists, playing on instruments with an expanded pedal board, exploited the contrapuntal potential of their instruments.

Styles were not necessarily confined by geographical borders or national identity. The group of *24 Violons du roi* (24 violins of the king) established at the French court by Louis XIII (see Chapter 7) garnered such fame that Charles II of England, having heard them while in exile, started his own violin band. As we will see in Chapter 13, many German-speaking courts imported aspects of French and Italian culture along with the musical styles. In addition to cultivating a taste for French decorative arts, music, and dance, the Munich court was one of several in the Holy Roman Empire that used French for noble conversation. In Vienna, where Italian music dominated for most of this period, the Italian language was used for diplomatic exchanges.

Politics—in particular, dynastic weddings—also influenced the transmission of music. The entire history of ballet in France might have followed a very different course had not Henry II of France married Catherine de' Medici, who brought Italian dancing masters to France. In Vienna, Ferdinand II's enthusiasm for Italian music was likely stimulated by his marriage to Eleonora Gonzaga of Mantua, who also patronized Italian music and musicians at the Habsburg court. For audiences and musicians, playing and listening to music from a different country was thus much like learning a new language or even setting off to explore an exotic land.

GENRE AND STYLE IN SEVENTEENTH-CENTURY INSTRUMENTAL MUSIC

One of the most fascinating—and at times daunting—aspects of instrumental music in the seventeenth and eighteenth centuries is the proliferation of genres. Dozens of names were applied to Baroque instrumental compositions, with enormous ambiguity and overlap in the ways compositions were labeled. The problem of categorization of genres and styles preoccupied a number of seventeenth-century writers. The Roman musician Marco Scacchi, who served as *maestro di cappella* (chapel master) to the king of Poland, devised a set of categories that largely reflected where music was performed at major European courts—in the chapel, theater, or in private settings (chamber). However, the place in which a work was performed may not tell us anything about what it sounded like: dance music could be heard in both chamber and theater, and highly contrapuntal or improvisational solo music might be designed for the connoisseur at court or as part of the liturgy at church. In his *Musurgia universalis* (1650), Kircher tried to solve the problem by considering both style and function: his list includes church style (*stylus ecclesiasticus*), canonic style (*stylus canonicus*), fantastic style (*stylus phantasticus*), madrigal style (*stylus madrigalus*), melismatic style (*stylus melismaticus*), and dance style (*stylus hyporchematicus*).

The numerous printing firms in such cities as Venice, Antwerp, Amsterdam, Nuremberg, and London also played a role in classifying music, creating collections designed for a certain type of buyer (amateur or professional), a specific instrument (virginal, viol, theorbo), or a given number of players, often implying something about their intended purpose (church or chamber). Some collections had something for everyone. Biagio Marini's landmark 1626 collection, expansively entitled *Sonatas, Symphonies, Canzonas, Passamezzzi, Balletti, Correnti, Galliards, and Ritornelli for 1, 2, 3, 4, 5 Voices and Every Sort of Instruments*, included both abstract instrumental compositions and popular dances. We can better understand such stylistic diversity by considering a few of the basic types of instrumental writing in the first half of the seventeenth century, which would influence composition throughout the Baroque period.

FANTASY AND CRAFT

Numerous instrumental works from the seventeenth century can be categorized loosely under the heading of "fantasy and craft." Writing in the late 1500s, Thomas Morley placed the fantasy among the most esteemed types of composition: "In this may more art be shown than in any other music, because the composer is tied to nothing but that he may add, diminish, and alter at his pleasure" (SR 75:481; 3/40:203). Kircher considered his fantastic style to be "the most free and unrestrained method of composing; it is bound to nothing, neither to words nor to a melodic subject." Yet he also tells us that "it was instituted to display genius and to teach the hidden design of harmony and the ingenious composition of harmonic phrases and fugues."

In these accounts the composer's imagination could manifest itself in two seemingly opposite ways. On the one hand were works written in a free, quasi-improvisatory style in which the composer might indulge in sudden changes of affect, texture, tempo, or dynamics, or in bursts of virtuosity; on the other were those that displayed the composer's command over contrapuntal techniques, in particular the use of strict imitation. Frescobaldi's Toccata No. 2 (see Anthology 6), with its abrupt rhythmic and textural contrasts, has a spontaneous feeling that exemplifies the fantastic style. The chords in the opening measure, for instance, were likely used as the basis of improvisation; the florid passage in measure 6 hints at the kind of virtuosity for which Frescobaldi was renowned. Yet his "craft" is manifest in the exchange of motives between the left and right hands in measures 2–5 (Ex. 4.1).

Contrapuntal expertise is foremost in Sweelinck's *Fantasia chromatica*: it achieves a somber, introspective tone through its exploration of the chromatic descending tetrachord (that is, a tetrachord with chromatic passing tones), which is imitated and combined with contrasting melodic and rhythmic ideas. The learned *stile antico* (ancient style) invoked with the long note values and imitative texture in the opening (Ex. 4.2) ultimately gives way to the unrestrained virtuosic display associated with the *stile moderno* (modern style), as shown in the concluding measures (Ex. 4.3).

Pyrotechnics, rhythmic contrasts, and sudden changes in affect were equally effective in compositions for strings, brass, and wind instruments, in which the instruments—accompanied by basso continuo—could surpass singers in terms of range and speed. The Venetian wind player Dario Castello (fl. first half of the seventeenth century) was among the instrumentalists to apply the *stile moderno* to an instrumental idiom. The contrasting sections in his Sonata No. 2 from *Sonate concertate in stil moderno . . . libro secondo* (Concerted Sonatas in Modern Style, Book 2, 1629; see Anthology 7) encompass a broad range of affects

Example 4.1: *Girolamo Frescobaldi, Toccata No. 2 from* Toccate e partite d'intavolatura di cimbalo, *Book 1 (1615), mm. 1–6*

Example 4.2: *Jan Pieterszoon Sweelinck,* Fantasia chromatica, *mm. 1–6*

Example 4.3: *Jan Pieterszoon Sweelinck,* Fantasia chromatica, *mm. 194–197*

and techniques, requiring considerable virtuosity regardless of whether a violin or wind instrument is playing the treble line. Castello even calls for special effects—in this instance a tremolo, which could be created either with the bow (on a violin) or with the breath and tongue (on a wind instrument).

As is apparent from these examples, a hallmark of "fantasy and craft" pieces is the variety of names they are given, which only sometimes indicate the style or the instruments for which they are intended. Toccatas (from the Italian verb "to touch") are typically flashy, virtuosic keyboard pieces in which the player's "touch" is on display, whereas fantasias, which may be more or less contrapuntal, are written for all types of instruments. Some genres, such as the imitative ricercar (from the Italian verb "to look for") and the canzona ("song"), have roots in the imitative practices of Renaissance vocal music, as do the Spanish tientos and Portuguese tentos, the predominant keyboard genres on the Iberian peninsula. The term sonata (from the Italian "to sound") was so ubiquitous that it could be applied to almost any type of piece written for instrumental ensemble or solo instrument with continuo. Some preludes served as introductions, as their name suggests, while others were freestanding compositions.

Louis Couperin's Suite in A minor provides an intriguing example of the ambiguity of genre names and the improvisatory nature of the fantasia style (Fig. 4.5). Couperin (ca. 1626–1661) was foremost among several mid-seventeenth-century French composers who wrote "unmeasured preludes"—preludes or sections of preludes in whole notes, without barlines or rhythms, in

Example 4.4: *Johann Jacob Froberger, Toccata No. 1 in A minor, FbWV 101 (1649), mm. 1–3*

Figure 4.5: *Louis Couperin*, Prélude de M^r. Couperin à l'imitation de M^r. Froberger en a mi la

which the pitches are connected by multiple slur lines whose meaning has still not been completely determined.

Entitled "Prélude . . . à l'imitation de Mr Froberger," the beginning of Couperin's prelude is in essence a whole-note version of the opening measures of Froberger's Toccata No. 1 in A minor, which Couperin might have heard Froberger play during his Paris sojourn in 1652. These two pieces, using the same pitches but notated very differently, not only remind us that the labels "toccata" and "prelude" are at best fluid, but provide valuable insights into the performance practices in these genres. Despite its traditional notation, the opening measures of Froberger's toccata may well have been performed with more rhythmic freedom than the score would suggest at first glance (Ex. 4.4). This raises the distinct possibility that all works of this type, regardless of the notation, were played in a quasi-improvisational style.

DANCING FOR THE EARS

Another category of instrumental music emerged from the realm of dance, where players and listeners had a rather different set of priorities. Instead of spontaneity and quasi-improvisatory freedom, music for dance required regularity and predictability: symmetrical phrases, standard formal structures, and consistent rhythmic patterns, tempos, and moods to accommodate the steps of one dance or another.

By 1617, however, the German composer Johann Hermann Schein (1586–1630) was describing a new kind of instrumental dance music that was suited "more for the ears" than "for the feet." Attracted by the sonic ideal associated with the dance, composers sought to capture the distinctive rhythmic qualities, tempos, moods, and characters of popular dances such as the pavan, a slow processional dance in duple meter, and the lively galliard, with its characteristic hemiola rhythmic patterns. Both of these are found alongside fantasia-style pieces in numerous collections of instrumental music, such as the *Fitzwilliam Virginal Book*, an important English keyboard manuscript from the early 1600s.

Composers of "dances for the ears" achieved contrast not by abrupt juxtapositions within a given movement, as in the fantasy style, but rather by grouping different dances together in sets that highlighted their differences. Froberger, who acquired a knowledge of international dance styles during his travels, was among the first to codify the sequence of dances that is typically called the suite. His Suite in C Major, FbWV 612 (see Anthology 8) begins with a fantasia-style instrumental lament on the death of the young Ferdinand IV (which we will consider in the section on character pieces below) and includes three popular French dances: a gigue (a lively dance in compound meter), a courante (literally, "running"—usually in triple meter with rapid steps), and a sarabande (a slow dance, thought to be of Spanish origin, with a characteristic accent on the second beat). By the third quarter of the century, suites would take on the standard format of allemande-courante-sarabande-gigue, with the occasional addition of minuets, bourrées, passepieds, and other dances. These were played by every type of instrument or combination imaginable: keyboard and plucked instruments, solo instruments with continuo, consorts of viols or violin bands, and ensembles of two treble instruments and basso continuo, a combination that later served as the standard ensemble for trio sonatas (see Chapter 10).

GROUNDS AND VARIATIONS

One of the best ways for instrumentalists to demonstrate their skill and imagination was in sets of variations. Composers would choose a theme—a familiar sacred or secular tune, or a distinctive melodic fragment—and repeat it, altering one or more elements with each iteration. This might involve the addition of ornamentation or changes in tempo, meter, rhythmic style, or texture; the melody might move from one to another voice or shift between major and minor. Numerous instrumental compositions were also based on repeated bass patterns or harmonic progressions derived from popular songs and dances such as the *folia* (literally, "madness"), *romanesca, bergamesca, ruggiero,* and the ever popular chaconne (ciaccona) and passacaille (passacaglia). What made these ground basses appealing for both vocal and instrumental music was the special combination of predictability and novelty that could be achieved through continual variations over a stable rhythmic and harmonic pattern.

We have already considered the special power of this technique in vocal music, in particular the laments with descending tetrachords (see Chapter 3 and Anthology 5). The passacaglia, with its stepwise pattern that gave rise to suspensions and dissonances, was particularly good for creating a mournful affect. Tarquinio Merula's (1594–1665) Ciaccona from *Canzoni overo sonate concertate per chiesa e camera, a 2–3, libro terzo* (Canzonas or Concerted Sonatas for Church and Chamber, for 2–3 Voices, Book 3, 1637) illustrates one of the popular bass patterns for the lively chaconne that was used as a basis for variations in both vocal and instrumental works (Ex. 4.5). A treatise by Christopher Simpson, an English viola da gamba player, instructs beginning instrumentalists on how

Example 4.5: *Tarquinio Merula, Ciaccona from* Canzoni overo sonate concertate, *Book 3 (1637), mm. 1–6*

to improvise over a ground bass using divisions (melodic lines with longer notes subdivided into smaller note values). "Variety," he emphasizes, "it is which chiefly pleaseth," since "the best division in the world, still continued, would become tedious to the hearer" (SR 104:636; 4/24:128).

CHARACTER PIECES

Character pieces, which express extramusical ideas, represent another important category of Baroque instrumental music. These are individual movements, some of which are part of sonatas or suites, that depict people, animals, emotions, moods, or real or mythological settings. In his *Affetti musicali* (Musical Affects, 1617), for example, Biagio Marini included a number of works named for friends and acquaintances. Instruments were also used to mimic natural sounds or create sound effects. Battle pieces that imitated the sounds of war were always popular, with repeated chords and *stile concitato* effects evoking gunfire, drum rolls, and clashing swords. Carlo Farina's (ca. 1604–1639) *Capriccio stravagante* (Extravagant Caprices) uses the unique qualities of string instruments to produce a number of bizarre or "extravagant" effects, including animal sounds such as a cat's meow.

A special category of instrumental pieces with extramusical associations includes works intended to mourn the death of a specific individual. Unlike the operatic or theatrical laments we encountered in Chapter 3, in which the protagonist expresses his or her own despair, wordless instrumental *tombeaux* or *lamenti* were intended to convey the personality of the deceased as well as the emotions of those who were left behind. The first movement of Froberger's C-Major Suite FbWV 612, which we considered above in the section on dance suites, is a lament composed on the death of the young Ferdinand IV, whose father, Ferdinand III, was one of Froberger's frequent dedicatees. The composer expresses his faith in the afterlife both sonically and visually: a rising three-octave C-major scale in the final measure disappears into a cluster of radiant clouds that is drawn on the manuscript, confirming the ascension of the young boy's soul into heaven (Fig. 4.6).

When Michael Praetorius published his *Theatrum instrumentorum*, he could scarcely have imagined all the ways in which instrumental music would transform and enrich the lives of men and women over the course of the seventeenth century. Through the efforts of players, patrons, printers, and instrument builders, audiences discovered how music without words could speak a variety of languages with astounding power and eloquence, even surpassing the ability of the most gifted orators. It is thus perhaps not surprising that Michel de Saint Lambert, in *Les principes du clavecin* (Principles of the Harpsichord, 1702), not only acknowledges that a "piece of music resembles a piece of rhetoric," but

Figure 4.6: *The second page of Johann Jacob Froberger's manuscript* Lamento sopra la dolorosa perdita della Real M. di Ferdinando IV Re de Romani

claims that it is actually "rhetoric that resembles a piece of music since harmony, number, measure, and the other similar things which a skilful orator observes in the composition of his works belong more naturally to music than rhetoric." In other words, all the things that a great speaker does to move listeners are in fact properties of music.

It is this dimension of music that was harnessed so effectively in the service of civic and religious ritual in the seventeenth century. As we will see in Chapter 5, the rhetorical power of music was particularly vital in the sacred realm, as composers tapped new styles and genres and enlisted the skills of both singers and instrumentalists to compete for the hearts and minds of their listeners. The theological battles that caused so much dissent and destruction in seventeenth-century Europe also fueled the composition of new and exciting musical works in a variety of Baroque styles that both inspired the faithful and empowered rulers.

FOR FURTHER READING

Carter, Stewart, ed., *A Performer's Guide to Seventeenth-Century Music,* expanded and revised Jeffery Kite-Powell (Bloomington: Indiana University Press, 2012)

Collins, Paul, *The Stylus Fantasticus and Free Keyboard Music of the North German Baroque* (Aldershot, UK, and Burlington, VT: Ashgate, 2005)

Cunningham, John Patrick, *The Consort Music of William Lawes, 1602–1645* (Woodbridge, UK, and Rochester, NY: Boydell Press, 2010)

Dell'Antonio, Andrew, *Listening as Spiritual Practice in Early Modern Italy* (Berkeley: University of California Press, 2011)

Hammond, Frederick, *Frescobaldi* (Cambridge, MA: Harvard University Press, 1983)

Kroll, Mark. *Playing the Harpsichord Expressively* (Lanham, MD: Scarecrow Press, 2004)

Silbiger, Alexander, "Fantasy and Craft: The Solo Instrumentalist," in John Butt and Tim Carter, eds., *Cambridge History of Seventeenth-Century Music* (Cambridge: Cambridge University Press, 2005)

Silbiger, Alexander, ed., *Keyboard Music before 1700*, 2nd ed. (New York and London: Routledge, 2004)

CHAPTER FIVE

Music in Civic and Religious Ritual

For seventeenth-century men and women who were neither professional musicians nor patrons of the arts, rituals associated with worship and state ceremony provided the most regular exposure to music. Indeed, music in praise of God and in the service of faith was omnipresent. Sacred music was not only heard as part of the liturgy (religious services) and for special devotions in churches, monasteries and convents, confraternities (charitable religious for non-noble lay people), and schools (usually run by religious authorities); it was also an integral part of ceremonies, processions, and celebrations in royal palaces, town squares, on rivers and canals, and even battlefields—where civic and religious elements commingled.

These rituals and the music that accompanied them were vital to the formation of religious identity in seventeenth-century Europe. In a society in which church and state were for the most part inseparable and a monarch's authority was viewed as divinely ordained, both blasphemy and treason were capital offenses. Thus religion—and the manner of worship—were of central importance in all aspects of daily life.

In this chapter, we explore how the prolonged tension between old and new musical styles intersected with the profession of faith in the aftermath of the Reformation. We first examine how religious ideologies shaped musical practices, and then consider the multiplicity of musical styles heard and sung by worshippers in the Baroque as manifest in Claudio Monteverdi's *Vespers* of 1610 and the music of northern European Lutheran composers such as Johann Hermann Schein and Heinrich Schütz. After examining Salamone Rossi's settings of Jewish liturgical texts in Hebrew, we investigate the role of music in practices that historians describe as paraliturgical—special devotions, processions, and sacred music dramas—where we see the full ramifications of Baroque theatricality in the realm of faith.

MUSIC, FAITH, AND IDEOLOGY

By the early decades of the seventeenth century, the words and deeds that had led to the Protestant Reformation were almost 100 years old; nonetheless, the impact of the break with the Catholic Church led by Martin Luther (1483–1546), John Calvin (1509–1564), and King Henry VIII (1491–1547) continued to be felt. This was a period in which many rulers and their subjects had to choose their preferred brand of Christianity, and these decisions led directly to such conflicts as the Thirty Years' War (1618–48) and the English Civil War (1642–51).

Although significant theological differences separated the various Protestant sects, all grappled with the question of which Catholic traditions should be maintained and which should be expunged. Indeed, many of the basic theological principles of the Reformation necessitated major changes in long-standing liturgical and musical practices. The Protestant belief that Christians could pray directly to God (without the intercession of priests, the Virgin Mary, or the saints) had any number of consequences. Not only were many churches stripped bare of statues and paintings of the Virgin and other decorations deemed too Catholic, but prayers and feast days were abolished, along with sumptuous rituals: processions with robed priests, candles, incense, and—in some cases—accompanying music. Since priests were not used as intercessors in prayer, many Protestants placed emphasis on congregational singing (rather than professional music-making) as an expression of the individual believer's faith in God. The fact that cloistered life was antithetical to Protestant beliefs, moreover, meant that numerous convents and monasteries were disbanded and destroyed, their treasures, lands, and holdings confiscated. Protestants also eliminated the chanting of the Divine Office, the daily services that had been sung by monks and nuns since the Middle Ages.

Protestant groups may have agreed with one another in their anti-Catholic sentiments. Nonetheless, there were profound differences in their views about the proper role of music in worship. Unlike Anglicans (members of the Church of England) or Lutherans, many reformed sects such as Calvinists (in Northern Europe) and Puritans (in England and the Massachusetts Bay Colony) zealously opposed elaborate vocal polyphony and instrumental music (including that of the organ). Instead, they favored hymn tunes and metrical versions of psalms that could easily be sung by congregations. *The Bay Psalm Book*, published in

Massachusetts Bay in 1640—the first book of any kind to be printed in the North American colonies—reflected the musical preferences of the first generation of American Puritans, many of whom emigrated in order to separate themselves from the Church of England. The rejection of the organ in the liturgy by Calvinists and Puritans did not necessarily mean that the organ was never played. In the Calvinist city of Amsterdam, for instance, where the churches contained many fine organs, the prohibition against using the instrument for services led to the development of solo organ recitals. Thus, between 1581 and 1621 citizens and visitors to Amsterdam had the opportunity to hear daily recitals played at the Oude Kerk (Old Church) by no less an organist and composer than Jan Pieterszoon Sweelinck, whom we discussed in Chapter 4.

By the early seventeenth century, Lutherans, who also emphasized congregational participation, had developed a vast repertory of German hymns called chorales, with relatively simple melodies and narrow vocal ranges appropriate for congregational singing. A typical example is the cheerful Christmas chorale "Vom Himmel hoch, da komm ich her" (From Heaven above to Earth I come here; Fig. 5.1), one of the many chorales that would be also be employed as a cantus

Figure 5.1: *A Children's Song for Christmas for the Baby Jesus from Chapter 2 of the Gospel According to Saint Luke [by] Dr. Martin Luther ("Vom Himmel hoch, da komm ich her"),* Geystliche Lieder welche von Frommen Christen *(Leipzig: Valentin Babst, 1545)*

firmus or as the basis of variations in vocal and instrumental compositions by Lutheran composers, as we will see below with Johann Hermann Schein.

At the same time, Luther's belief that music played a vital role in expressing faith and banishing the devil led him and his followers to nurture music in their worship services, placing high value on both congregational singing and elaborate music-making by professionals. Since Lutherans continued to use many elements of the Catholic liturgy, including the Ordinary of the Mass (Kyrie, Gloria, Credo, Sanctus, and Agnus Dei) and the Vespers (the evening service), their liturgy often included music originally composed for and by Catholics. The widespread practice of making *contrafacta* (Latin for "counterfeits"), whereby the text of one musical composition replaced another, meant that musicians could easily transform a work written for a Catholic service into one suitable for Protestants. Despite the objections of a group of Lutherans known as Pietists, who voiced some objections to the use of the florid, Italian style for the liturgy, by the late seventeenth century even the most Italianate music had found its way into Lutheran religious works, such as sacred cantatas (multimovement vocal works), oratorios (unstaged dramatic works on sacred topics), and Passions (representations of the trial and death of Jesus).

As we will see in Chapter 8, the situation was particularly complex in Britain. The English monarchy, which headed the Church of England, continued to support a splendid musical liturgy in such establishments as the Chapel Royal and London's two major cathedrals, Westminster Abbey and St. Paul's Cathedral. The substitution of English chant and anthems for Latin plainsong and motets, however, was not enough to quell persistent anxieties about the threat of Catholicism. Indeed, the composition and performance of Latin sacred music had political overtones and could even be regarded as treasonous. This attitude was to have a profound effect on the careers of recusant Catholics such as William Byrd (ca. 1540–1623).

For its part, the Catholic Church viewed the sensory stimulation of music, art, and architecture as powerful tools with which to resist the Reformation, even as the ecclesiastical judicial system set up to fight heresy, the Inquisition, gained traction. During the meetings of the Council of Trent in the sixteenth century, as Catholics sought to defend their faith against the Reformation, some wished to simplify the complex polyphony that impeded the intelligibility of the text. Paradoxically, the new styles of solo singing that we tend to associate with secular music also served the goals of the Church. By the early seventeenth century, as the papacy invested enormous resources in enhancing the beauty of St. Peter's Basilica and the Vatican, Catholics embraced the stylistic innovations of Baroque music as a means of heightening spirituality, devotional intensity, and piety.

In their desire to enhance intelligibility and accessibility, Catholics even gravitated to the vernacular for many devotional works, as apparent in the proliferation of Italian sacred madrigals, sacred concertos (discussed below), and cantatas, as well as the Portuguese and Spanish villancicos (popular religious songs) that spread throughout the Iberian peninsula and New Spain.

As Protestants and Catholics competed with one another for the hearts and minds of the faithful, music was often the victor.

RELIGIOUS DIVERSITY AND STYLISTIC PLURALISM

It may well be an accident of history that so many conflicts involving religious diversity and tolerance erupted at a time of stylistic pluralism in devotional and liturgical music. As a result of the relative conservatism of ecclesiastical institutions and the longevity of liturgical practices, the styles that had been the backbone of sacred music in the sixteenth century—monophonic chant and imitative polyphony—continued to thrive. At the same time, composers of sacred music and their listeners enthusiastically embraced new musical styles for worship, such as small-scale sacred concertos (and later cantatas) for one or more soloists with continuo. (These were sometimes supplemented with additional instruments referred to as "obbligato," which meant that they were necessary for the performance.) These took advantage of all the expressive qualities explored by Caccini in *Le nuove musiche*—free treatment of dissonance, sensitive text setting, and virtuosity.

SACRED CONCERTO

Lodovico Viadana's (ca. 1560–1627) exceedingly popular *Concerti ecclesiastici a una, a due, a tre e a quattro voci* (Ecclesiastical Concertos for One, Two, Three, and Four Voices; 1602), published the same year as *Le nuove musiche*, was the first sacred collection to include a basso continuo part; it would be reprinted and imitated throughout Europe. Viadana explained in his preface that his goal was to supply suitable compositions for singers who, wishing to sing with the organ, would otherwise be forced to modify motets intended for many more parts. He endeavored to compose sacred concertos for a single voice or various combinations that were "singable and coherent," to provide, when appropriate, "convenient opportunities for ornaments and passagework," and to take "pains that the words should be so well disposed beneath the notes that . . . it should be possible for them to be clearly understood by the hearers, provided that they are delivered distinctly by the singers" (SR 101:618–19; 4/21:110–11).

The word *concerto* is most often associated with instrumental works in which one or more instruments interact or "concert" with an orchestral ensemble. (In Chapter 1 we introduced the term *concertato style*, which describes works in which two or more distinct groups of voices or instruments work together or collaborate.) However, in the seventeenth century, the term *concerto* was also used to describe some sacred compositions for voices and instruments. These are usually settings of scripture (in prose rather than poetry) in which the vocal parts are relatively independent and thus "concerted" with the continuo. (To further complicate the issue, these works are sometimes referred to simply as motets, while later in the century multimovement vocal works that included musical settings of poetic texts, or arias, were usually called cantatas.) Small-scale sacred concertos were a good alternative for institutions that did not have the financial resources to maintain large musical ensembles. Consider, for example, the dire situation at the Dresden court in 1641. During the Thirty Years' War, the Lutheran composer Heinrich Schütz (1585–1672), who had recently composed two sets of *Kleine geistliche Concerte* (Short Spiritual Concertos), compared himself to a doctor treating a terminally ill patient, as his employer could no longer finance the performance of the large-ensemble works that Schütz had learned to compose in Venice.

COLOSSAL BAROQUE

The style that Schütz mourned, known as the "colossal Baroque," developed in Venice in the late sixteenth century and often involved the use of multiple choirs of voices and instruments—so-called *cori spezzati* (separated choruses). Some of these grand works were composed specifically for the special layout and acoustic properties of the magnificent Basilica of St. Mark, where Giovanni Gabrieli (ca. 1554/57–1621) served as *maestro di cappella*. The separate walls of sound produced by *cori spezzati* created an extraordinary effect inside the giant Venetian church (Fig. 5.2).

Many of the most novel compositions of the period, by both Catholic and Protestant composers, derived much of their drama and splendor from the juxtaposition of solo and colossal elements within a single work. The grand sonic

Figure 5.2: *Gabriele Bella,* Presentation of the Doge to the Population *(eighteenth century), showing the interior of St. Mark's Cathedral in Venice*

effects created by the multiple choruses using concertato style could thus be contrasted with virtuosic solo singing, satisfying Catholic, Lutheran, and Anglican sensibilities. We thus find these stylistic features in English verse anthems, French motets, villancicos from the Iberian peninsula and in the New World, and throughout German-speaking northern Europe. At the Habsburg court in Vienna, the composer Giovanni Valentini (1582/83–1649) described his efforts to "invent a new way of combining trumpets with voices and instruments" in his *Messa, Magnificat et Jubilate Deo* (1621) for seven choirs and trumpets, a massive work (no longer extant) written to celebrate the Catholic emperor Ferdinand II's early victories in the Thirty Years' War. Much the same style was used for Protestant celebrations in Dresden by Schütz and an entire establishment of Italian-born Catholic musicians supported by Elector Johann Georg II.

MONTEVERDI'S *VESPERS* OF 1610

Examples of all of these styles are found in what is arguably the most magnificent collection of sacred music published during the entire seventeenth century, Claudio Monteverdi's *Vespro della Beata Vergine* (Vespers of the Blessed Virgin, 1610). The complete title of the volume hints at the range of music contained therein: "For the Most Holy Virgin, a Mass for Six Voices suitable for church choirs, and Vespers to be performed by diverse forces (together with some motets) suitable for chapels or the chambers of princes."

Dedicated to Pope Paul V, the collection was published at a critical moment in Monteverdi's career. Exhausted by the demands of producing theatrical music for the Gonzaga family in the aftermath of the 1608 wedding celebrations (see Chapter 3), Monteverdi wanted to show his versatility as a composer of sacred music with the aim of securing a position at a top ecclesiastical institution. After failing to win a post in Rome, he was appointed *maestro di cappella* at St. Mark's Basilica in Venice in October 1613 (arriving there after an ill-fated journey in which he, his son, and a maid were robbed at gunpoint by a group of three bandits).

Monteverdi's prospective employers in Venice must surely have been impressed with the breadth of styles included in the *Vespro della Beata Vergine* and the originality of his approach. First, he demonstrates his mastery of the *prima prattica* in the six-voice *Missa in illo tempore* (Mass "In That Time") that prefaces the collection. Based on a motet by the Renaissance composer Nicholas Gombert, the work might have been a response to Giovanni Maria Artusi's criticisms (see Chapter 2), demonstrating Monteverdi's ability to follow the rules of counterpoint when it suited his purpose.

In his choral settings of psalms conventionally used for the Vespers service, Monteverdi avails himself of the old-fashioned technique of employing an underlying melody known as a cantus firmus, drawn from plainchant; however, everything else in these movements is bold and innovative. In the opening movement, a setting of the traditional versicle (short biblical verse) "Deus in adjutorium meum intende" (God, come to my assistance) and response "Domine ad adjuvandum me" (O Lord, make haste to help), the plainchant is harmonized by the double chorus, which declaims the text on a D-major sonority—a style of chant recitation known as *falso-bordone*. Monteverdi further enriches the texture and the dramatic effect by adding another layer: he superimposes upon the harmonized chant the same instrumental toccata for brass and winds that he had used to open the opera *L'Orfeo* just three years previously (see Chapter 3). The effect is electrifying: by subtle revoicings of a single chord, Monteverdi creates an iridescent wall of sound. He then injects a suggestion of playfulness to the movement with a brief, triple-meter dancelike ritornello, which later becomes a tender choral refrain on the word "alleluia."

Likewise, Monteverdi's setting of "Laudate pueri" (Praise the Lord, O children; Psalm 112) contains an astounding variety of textures in a single movement: homophony (all the voices move at the same pace), concertato style (highlighting the double chorus), imitative counterpoint, and virtuosic vocal writing, with frequent shifts between duple and triple time. Example 5.1 shows

Example 5.1: *Claudio Monteverdi, "Laudate pueri" from* Vespro della Beata Vergine *(1610), mm. 12–17*

Praise the name of the Lord. Blessed be the name of the Lord.

an excerpt from the end of the first portion of the psalm, in which Monteverdi shifts from the rich sonorities of the eight-voice chorus to a brilliant duet for two sopranos singing parallel thirds, accompanied by plainchant in longer note values (see Tenor 2, bottom stave) and supported by continuo.

Monteverdi's most unusual move in the *Vespers*, however, is to eliminate the usual antiphons (responses) sung after the psalms in a Marian (relating to the Virgin Mary) Vespers service and replace them with sacred concertos for one to three voices and continuo that are entirely in the modern style. "Duo Seraphim" (Two Seraphim), for three tenors, dramatizes the cries of the celestial seraphim with unearthly suspensions, exquisitely painful dissonances, and some of the most virtuosic writing in any sacred music of the period. It begins as an intimate duet; in the second part of the motet, a third tenor is added, thus completing the image of the trinity (see Anthology 9).

Where "Duo Seraphim" invokes the ethereal and infinite heavens, "Nigra sum" (I am dark), for solo voice and continuo, is decidedly worldly. This is one of several sacred concertos in the *Vespers* that set poetry from the Old Testament book known as the Song of Songs, much of which is frankly erotic. Although the poems make no specific mention of God, the Song of Songs was often used to represent allegorically the various aspects of religious devotion or a mystical union with God. In "Nigra sum," the first voice we hear is that of the "dark and lovely daughter of Jerusalem." She tells of the king who loved her and brought her to his chamber, saying, "Arise, my love, and come, already the winter is past." In setting these provocative words, Monteverdi explores the imitative potential of the word "surge" (arise): an elaborate melisma extending a full octave and a fifth is followed by a series of ascending passages in which the voice imitates the bass line in a seductive dance in the subsequent passage (Ex. 5.2). There could be no better demonstration of the porous boundaries between sacred and secular that were so intrinsic to Baroque music and art.

PRINTED MUSIC FOR PROTESTANT SERVICES

Some of the stylistic variety that is displayed in Monteverdi's *Vespers* also characterizes the music composed and published by Protestant musicians. Indeed, Protestants not only had a practical need for music to accompany worship services, but

Example 5.2: *Claudio Monteverdi, "Nigra sum" from* Vespro della Beata Vergine *(1610), mm. 14–17*

Arise, arise

also used printing as a means of establishing their own distinct religious identity. We have already noted the numerous publications of metrical psalms in both English and German, such as the *Bay Psalm Book*. Publications by and for Lutheran church musicians included not only collections of the chorale tunes set to German texts that were the backbone of Lutheran worship, but also Latin motets and sacred concertos, which were adapted from Italian models as necessary.

We see another example of the way the Italian sacred concerto was appropriated by Lutherans in Johann Hermann Schein's "Vom Himmel hoch, da komm ich her," published in a collection entitled *Opella nova* (New Triflings, 1618). Schein (1586–1630) was among the first to combine the newly imported style of solo singing with Lutheran chorales, marrying the Italian sacred concerto and the contrapuntal ingenuity associated with northern European composers. There are three compositional layers to this work. The basso continuo provides harmonic drive and support, the tenor presents an unadorned version of the chorale melody in half notes (mm. 14–16), while the two sopranos use a fragment of the chorale as the basis of an imitative duet (Ex. 5.3).

Heinrich Schütz was one of many Germanic composers who acquired his experience with Italian music directly, as noted above. He first studied with Giovanni Gabrieli in Venice between 1609 and 1612. In a memorandum about his career addressed to the elector of Saxony, Schütz describes how Gabrieli, on his deathbed, bequeathed to him one of his rings out of "special affection" (SR 86:557–61; 4/6:49–53). At the height of the Thirty Years' War, in 1629, he persuaded his employers in Dresden to let him return to Venice to study with Monteverdi.

Whereas Monteverdi exploited multiple styles within a single collection, Schütz published 14 volumes of (primarily) sacred music between 1611 and 1671, devoting individual volumes or sets of volumes to a single style or genre. He translated the expressive elements of the Italian style into a distinctly northern European idiom, masterfully deploying unusual combinations of voices and

Example 5.3: *Johann Hermann Schein, "Vom Himmel hoch, da komm ich her" from* Opella nova *(1618), mm. 14–17*

I bring to you good news

instruments to create novel sonorities. His willingness to use unconventional tonal relationships to achieve special effects is apparent in his setting for double chorus of Psalm 84, verses 1–2, "Wie lieblich sind deine Wohnungen" (How lovely is thy dwelling place), from *Psalmen Davids* (Psalms of David, 1619). This joyful psalm, which Brahms would later use in *Ein deutsches Requiem* (A German Requiem, 1868; see Walter Frisch, *Music in the Nineteenth Century*), expresses the longing of the earthly soul for the beauty of God's kingdom.

Schütz's novel scoring captures the psalm's emphasis on the antithesis between the earthly and heavenly realms. Rather than dividing his two choruses into equal complements of soprano, alto, tenor, and bass, as Monteverdi did in the *Vespro della Beata Vergine* (see Ex. 5.1), Schütz restricts the first chorus to high voices (sopranos, altos, and tenors) and the second to lower voices (two tenors and two basses). Thus, many of the *stile concitato* effects are achieved through the contrast of high and low—heaven and earth—as is apparent in the opening measures (Ex. 5.4). The first chorus sings the words "Wie lieblich" on a series of three whole-note chords. While the move from C major to F major is absolutely typical, the subsequent shift up a third to A major creates a shimmer that seems to shine a light toward the heavens. The effect is intensified further in the next three measures as the series of chords is transposed up a fifth.

Among Schütz's most expressive compositions is the Latin motet "Fili mi, Absalon" (My son, Absalom), published in the first volume of his *Symphoniae sacrae*, SWV 269 (Sacred Symphonies, 1629). The text of this lament—sung by King David upon learning of the death of his son—is taken from the Old Testament book of Samuel (II: 18:33). Again scoring is of critical importance in the expression of the text. Schütz uses a solo bass and four trombones to create a haunting, somber tone that, as we recall from Monteverdi's *L'Orfeo*, was associated with death and the afterlife (see Anthology 10).

SALAMONE ROSSI AND THE JEWISH LITURGY

One of the most unusual publications of seventeenth-century sacred music comes from the Jewish composer Salamone Rossi (1570–ca. 1630), whom we met briefly in our consideration of music and theater in the Gonzaga court at Mantua (see Chapter 3). Rossi, an accomplished violinist, published several volumes

Example 5.4: *Heinrich Schütz, "Wie lieblich sind deine Wohnungen," SWV 29, from* Psalmen Davids, *Op. 2 (1619), mm. 1–3*

How lovely . . .

of secular vocal and instrumental music. However, in publishing two volumes of
Jewish liturgical music in Hebrew, *Hashirim asher leSholomo* (The Songs of Solomon, 1622–23), Rossi challenged centuries of Jewish liturgical practices.

Jewish services were conducted entirely in Hebrew, using chant that was
transmitted orally. Biblical passages were chanted according to a system known
as cantillation, whereby signs included with Hebrew letters indicated the musical motives that should be intoned, which underscored the syntax and accentual patterns of the text. The basic melodic patterns that were used differed
depending upon whether the passage was in prose or poetry, the time of year,
the liturgical occasion, and the location of the Jewish community. (Ashkenazic
Jews, from Eastern Europe, for instance, had a substantially different musical
tradition than native Italian Jews or the Sephardic Jews who came to Italy from
Spain and Portugal after the expulsion from the Iberian peninsula.) Jewish
tradition also forbade the use of instruments in the synagogue. (This was a sign
of the continued mourning of the Jews in the aftermath of the destruction of
the Second Temple in Jerusalem in the first century CE by the Romans.)

Rossi's settings of liturgical Hebrew texts for three, four, and five voices
are conservative in their use of dissonance, and the largely homophonic vocal
settings made the text easy to understand, an important principle both for
traditional Jewish practice and for the new style of liturgical music. Rossi
sometimes uses melismatic writing as an ornament on important syllables and
cadential passages, or simply to heighten the intensity of words with special
spiritual significance. This latter is the case for the Barekhú (Blessed; Ex. 5.5),
a dramatic prayer in which the worshippers together bless God, signaling the
beginning of a major portion of the service. All three voices are woven together
in a delicate counterpoint, with hints of imitation, that nonetheless has a
chant-like, introspective quality.

One of the challenges that Rossi faced in publishing his compositions was
deciding how to arrange the printed page, since Hebrew, unlike music, is traditionally read from right to left. The solution, as shown in Figure 5.3 (which
reproduces the cantus [top] part of the Barekhú), was to present the music moving from left to right, with the Hebrew text moving from right to left. One consequence of this is that in some instances, as in Barekhú in Example 5.5, we can
only make an educated guess as to the correct text underlay.

Example 5.5: *Salamone Rossi, "Barekhú" from* Hashirim asher leSholomo (*The Songs
of Solomon) (1622–23), mm. 1–4*

Blessed . . .

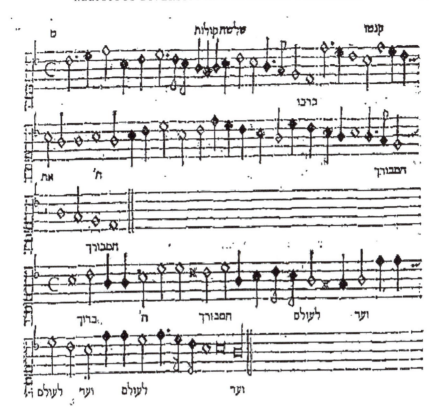

Figure 5.3: *Page from* Barekhú *cantus partbook, showing music from left to right and Hebrew from right to left. Salamone Rossi,* Hashirim asher leSholomo *(Venice, 1622–1623)*

Rossi's publications raise a number of questions. Were the works ever used in the liturgy, and if so, how did synagogue authorities and worshippers react to them? We learn something about these questions from the comments in the printed preface to the volume by Venetian rabbi Leon Modena, who, in addition to preaching in synagogues, writing, and teaching, was a musician and cantor (service leader) in the Italian Synagogue in Venice. Modena, taking up the task of defending Rossi from detractors who accused him of borrowing music from the Christians, accused the Christians of stealing music from the ancient Hebrews. Rossi's work thus simply returned to Jewish music the glory that had been lost. Rabbinic authorities would debate these issues for centuries. It is also not clear whether there were other composers of Jewish music writing in the contemporary style whose works are not preserved in print. Perhaps most critical is the question of identity: did Rossi compose his Hebrew settings in an attempt to mitigate the differences between Jews and non-Jews in a predominantly Christian society? Indeed, it is telling that the English traveler Thomas Coryat, whose praise of Venetian music we considered in Chapter 1, noted that the service leader or cantor sang "not with a sober, distinct, and orderly reading, but by an exceeding loud yaling [yelling], undecent roaring, as it were a beast bellowing of it forth." The question of music's role in Jewish identity and the expression of anti-Semitism—and the supposed contrast between orderly Christian music and chaotic Jewish music—became particularly pronounced in Northern and Eastern Europe where the often simultaneous, seemingly disorderly chanting of Ashkenazic Jews was described by Christian observers as cacophonous, barbaric, and even uncivilized. (By the third quarter of the eighteenth century, music historian Charles Burney would compare the sounds of an Ashkenazi synagogue in Amsterdam to that of buzzing bees.) By publishing Jewish liturgical music that conformed to contemporary styles, Rossi thus made a rare public statement about Jewish cultural identity.

MUSIC AND PARALITURGICAL PRACTICES

Much of the sacred music heard in the seventeenth century was intended not for traditional services, but for paraliturgical ceremonies. Indeed, it is often in paraliturgical events that we see the most blurring between church and state, sacred and secular. In processions, for example, religious pageantry escapes from the confines of the church and spills out onto the piazzas, streets, rivers, and canals, imbuing civic spaces with religious significance.

In the Republic of Venice, one of the most striking settings for a procession was just outside St. Mark's Basilica. Adjacent to the Ducal Palace, the home of the doge (the elected leader of Venice) and the seat of republican government, the cathedral's Byzantine mosaics and five distinctive domes presided proudly over Piazza San Marco. Figure 5.4 shows the procession that occurred in 1610 for the Feast of Corpus Christi, one of more than 80 that Venetians might have witnessed over the course of the year.

During these processions, which took place both inside and outside of churches, retinues of gondolas or makeshift bridges made of boats often provided a way for the faithful to cross the canals or the lagoon. One of Venice's most important celebrations, known as the Sensa, took place on Ascension Day, when the doge, accompanied by the nobility and members of the Senate, went out into the lagoon in a golden barge in order to toss into the water a ceremonial ring symbolizing Venice's marriage to and domination of the sea. The music that accompanied these outdoor celebrations was, by all accounts, loud. Designed to impress the observer, it might include gunshots, artillery or mortar fire, and fireworks, reminding attendees that divine power and military might were closely allied. The special ceremonies involving the doge featured the famous six long silver trumpets that were reportedly given to the city by Pope Alexander III in the twelfth century.

Processions were also used to seek divine intervention in time of war. In March 1645, during the waning years of the Thirty Years' War, Ferdinand III,

Figure 5.4:
Procession in
Piazza San Marco,
*from Giacomo
Franco,* Abiti
d'uomini e donne
veneziani *(Venice,
1610)*

the Holy Roman Emperor, led a procession at the Habsburg court in honor of
the Virgin Mary as the enemy armies approached Vienna. While the court's best
musicians played and sang works that we can only imagine, the emperor, his
wife, the bishop of Vienna, and members of all the city's religious orders carried a wooden statue of the Virgin through the streets, placing it at St. Stephen's
Cathedral, where it was displayed for a week.

In this instance, the procession served not only military but also theological objectives: Ferdinand III, in contradiction to Church dogma of the time,
supported the doctrine of the Immaculate Conception, which stated that Mary,
although conceived by human parents, was herself free of original sin. The
emperor took this opportunity to pray to Mary, promising to establish the Feast
of the Immaculate Conception throughout his realm should victory be forth-
coming. Thus, at a moment in which the Austrian people were no doubt fear-
ful and weary after decades of war, the procession reaffirmed the power, piety,
and longevity of the Habsburg dynasty, even as it celebrated and advanced
Ferdinand's religious program.

Processions and other outdoor ceremonies could also have a more insidious,
even threatening influence on peoples who were excluded from the mainstream
by reason of religion, race, or nationality. This was the case, for instance, in
the biconfessional (both Protestant and Catholic) city of Augsburg, Germany,
where Catholic processions, with music and associated pageantry, provided an

unwelcome or even threatening reminder of the relatively marginal status of the city's Protestants. Melchior Volcius, the pastor of St. Anna's, the Protestant church in Augsburg, condemned the "special, nightly procession with great pomp and apparatus" held yearly on Good Friday by Catholics. Among the objectionable elements were the "histories of Christ's passion, with painted and pasted pictures and idols." Volcius condemned those who followed Christ's example by flagellating themselves until they bled. Protestants also complained that the processions deliberately traversed their neighborhoods. The Jesuit preacher Conrad Vetter, known for his pro-Catholic writings and oratory, defended the Catholic position by extolling the quality of the music performed at the Feast of the Ascension: the singing of choirs and the ringing of bells would have made Volcius's heart "leap in his breast."

The almost militant nature of these paraliturgical processions can be seen in the ceremonies established by missionaries in the American and Asian colonies, where the adoption of local customs, music, dance, and costumes for processions helped make Christianity more palatable to the indigent populations. For example, the processions of the Corpus Christi festival at the cathedral in Cuzco, the former Inka capital in Peru, mixed the customary European practices with the dances, music, and costumes of the indigenous people, thus staging the triumph of Christianity over local spiritual practices.

THEATRICAL DEVOTION

Many faiths include some form of sacred musical theater among their paraliturgical ceremonies. The practice of dramatizing stories from the Old Testament or presenting Passion plays dates back to medieval times (as Margot Fassler describes in *Music in the Medieval West*). This was in many respects an ideal way to educate illiterate congregants, for whom it may have been the only means of learning scripture, as well as to inspire highly educated students and teachers in universities.

We have already considered in Chapter 3 some of the sacred operas performed at the papal court during the papacy of Urban VIII. The merging of theater and religion was particularly important in special performances at Roman confraternities, religious orders (groups of nuns or monks in which members take vows), and schools. Religious plays, including those with music, would become an integral feature of the educational programs at numerous schools and colleges established by religious orders and missionaries in Europe, Asia, and the Americas. This includes in particular the Jesuits (Society of Jesus), a religious order founded in the 1530s by Ignatius Loyola and Francis Xavier. The Jesuits emphasized the study of classical philosophy, literature, science, art, and music. By participating in student plays (often with music), young priests gained valuable skills in oratory that would be useful to them in the pulpit. In 1622 the Jesuits celebrated the canonization of their two founders with the performance of a Latin opera entitled *Apotheosis sive consecratio SS. Ignatii et Francisci Xaverii* (Deification or Consecration of St. Ignatius and St. Francis Xavier) by Giovanni Kapsberger.

Sacred dramas were also an important part of the program initiated in late-sixteenth-century Rome by Filippo Neri, later canonized as St. Philip. Neri gathered together priests and laymen for informal prayer, spiritual discussions, and music outside the church in a separate building called an "oratory." Known as the Oratorians, Neri's society gave its name to one of the most important sacred musical genres of the Baroque: the oratorio.

The term *oratorio* referred to music on a religious topic in which singers assumed the roles of protagonists. Oratorios used the familiar forms of aria and recitative, albeit without the elaborate staging, sets, and costumes associated with opera. The French viol player André Maugars has given us a first-hand description of a sung spiritual play that took place in 1639. Each singer, he tells us, "represented a personage of the story and expressed perfectly the force of the words." After a sermon, there was a recitation of the Gospel of the day or the Passion, in which the singers impersonated the characters identified by the Evangelist. "I could not praise enough that *musique récitatif*," Maugars added; "it is necessary to have heard it on the spot to judge well its merits."

Such descriptions apply to an "oratorio" composed somewhat less than a decade later: *Jephte* by Giacomo Carissimi (1605–1674). The libretto, drawn from a passage in the Old Testament book of Judges (11: 1–40), tells the tale of the warrior Jephtha, who promised that if God made him victorious in his campaign with the Israelites against the Ammonites, he would sacrifice the first person he saw upon his return. *Jephte* dramatizes the critical moment when the protagonist is met by his daughter, singing and dancing in celebration of the victory, and is therefore obliged to condemn her to death in order to keep his vow. The dignified lament sung by the warrior's daughter in the final section of *Jephte*, in which unexpected chromatic intrusions reveal her inner sorrow, followed by the empathetic response of the chorus of Israelites, provides a moving conclusion to this extraordinary work (see Anthology 11).

The Latin oratorios of Carissimi would not become the standard of the genre; while they were marvelous works and historically significant, in all probability they were heard by a relatively limited audience. By the third quarter of the century, as we will see in Chapter 11, the Italian oratorio, so similar to opera, became popular as the ideal Lenten entertainment. Like opera, it spread from Italy to many German-speaking territories. During the 1660s, the Viennese, for instance, regularly performed the *sepulcro* (sepulcher), a brief Italian musical dramatization of the Passion, often including scenery and costumes. Another relative of the Italian oratorio was the Lutheran *historia*, a biblical story set to music. The most popular topics were drawn from the Gospels, in particular the recitation of the Passion, which continued to be an integral part of Holy Week services in the

Catholic Church. Typically, the soloists took the roles of various characters (Mary, Jesus, Peter, Pontius Pilate), while the Evangelist narrated in recitative. We will consider Bach's setting of the *St. John Passion* as an example of this in Chapter 15.

The stylistic innovations of the seventeenth century may have been nurtured in the realm of profane or secular music; however, their broadest impact was in the world of sacred music, as Europeans of all social classes and religious persuasions were inevitably touched by rituals involving music, whether in churches or synagogues, at court, on the streets, or in private devotions in their homes. Worshippers were certainly the beneficiaries, for, compared to their sixteenth-century forebears—who heard either chant or Renaissance polyphony during services—congregants in the early Baroque had the privilege of hearing a far broader range of styles and sounds: colossal polychoral works, intimate sacred concertos, and stirring oratorios in which even biblical characters had the power to move the emotions with song. Authorities may not always have agreed about what music was best for the faithful, but in an age in which religious strife abounded, they knew well how to harness music's power to inspire awe, piety, and religious zeal in their listeners.

FOR FURTHER READING

Baker, Geoffrey, "Music at Corpus Christi in Colonial Cuzco," *Early Music* 32 (2004): 355–67

Fisher, Alexander, *Music and Religious Identity in Counter Reformation Augsburg* (Aldershot, UK, and Burlington, VT: Ashgate, 2004)

Frandsen, Mary, *Crossing Confessional Boundaries: The Patronage of Italian Sacred Music in Seventeenth-Century Dresden* (New York and Oxford: Oxford University Press, 2006)

Kurtzman, Jeffrey, *The Monteverdi Vespers of 1610: Music, Context, and Performance* (New York and Oxford: Oxford University Press, 1999)

Kurtzman, Jeffrey, and Linda Maria Koldau, "*Trombe, Trombe d'argento, Trombe squarciate, Tromboni*, and *Pifferi* in Venetian Processions and Ceremonies of the Sixteenth and Seventeenth Centuries," *Journal of the Society for Seventeenth-Century Music* 8 (2002): www.sscm-jscm.org/v8/no1/kurtzman.html

Varwig, Bettina, *Histories of Heinrich Schütz* (Cambridge: Cambridge University Press, 2011)

Weaver, Andrew H., *Sacred Music as Public Image for Holy Roman Emperor Ferdinand III: Representing the Counter-Reformation Monarch at the End of the Thirty Years' War* (Aldershot, UK, and Burlington, VT: Ashgate, 2004)

PART II

Musical Institutions

From the Carnival of Venice to the salons of the social elite in Paris and the amateur music societies in London, music in the seventeenth century was sponsored by a variety of institutions, each with its own clientele, aesthetic concerns, and economic realities. Part of the richness of musical life in the 1600s is directly attributable to the diversity in these institutions. Now that we have a better sense of the different types of music and their functions during the seventeenth century, we can pose a different set of questions: Who paid for music and why? What are the central musical institutions that fostered musical performance and whom did they serve? How did young musicians learn music and what impact might their education have had on their subsequent careers? How did musicians who were not connected to court or the church find an outlet for musical expression?

We begin in Chapter 6 with the development of the commercial opera industry in Venice. Although opera was invented in the courts of northern Italy, as we saw in Chapter 3, it was in the Venetian Republic that the conventions of the genre and the mechanisms for financing public opera would be established—shaped by another quintessentially Venetian institution, Carnival. From Venetian opera we learn how the new genre functioned and flourished in "La Serenissima" (The Most Serene Republic), and examine the basic principles of the commercial opera business that were established there. Although risky as a financial investment, Venetian-style opera would nevertheless be adopted and flourish in numerous other cities and courts. It was embraced by audiences, investors, and patrons, some of whom were absolute monarchs who saw in the genre an opportunity for self-promotion.

In Chapters 7 and 8 we turn to the kingdoms of France and England, whose national institutions nurtured systems of artistic production that were in some respects different from the rest of Europe. The French court was unique in fostering an insular and highly individualized style of music that became identified entirely with the king and the state. In England, on the other hand, the temporary dissolution of the monarchy after the Civil War forever marked that country's court and religious institutions, and provided an impetus for one of the most vibrant commercial markets for music in all of Europe.

In Chapters 9 and 10, we abandon a strictly chronological approach to consider the schools, orphanages, convents, academies, salons, and music societies of the seventeenth and eighteenth centuries. A study of these institutions, rarely given their due in surveys of the period, provides a broader understanding of the day-to-day circumstances in which musicians thrived, exploring how nuns and courtesans might publish music, how an orphan might have the opportunity to become an accomplished virtuoso, and how all sorts of academies and salons stimulated both practical and theoretical experimentation in music. Our protagonists are men and women of every age and from a range of social classes: rulers and courtiers, choirboys and choirmasters, as well as ordinary citizens, both amateurs and professionals. All of them found new ways to create, perform, and enjoy music that had long been the exclusive property of nobles.

CHAPTER SIX

Opera in Venice and Beyond

After a trip to Venice in 1645, the English traveler and diarist John Evelyn penned a vivid description of an evening at the opera, one of the most "magnificent and expensive diversions the wit of men can invent." He lauded the excellent vocalists and instrumentalists, noting the reputation of the Roman singer Anna Renzi as the best female soprano. He mentioned an unnamed eunuch (castrato) who in his view was superior to Renzi, as well as an "incomparable" bass from Genoa. He was also fascinated by the visual spectacle, including 13 scene changes "painted and contrived with no less art of perspective," lauding the flying machines with their "wonderful motions," all of which "held us by the Eyes and Ears til two in the morning."

Opera may have been invented in the self-consciously humanistic atmosphere fostered by the northern Italian courts (see Chapter 3), but it was in Venice that it became a commercial enterprise, gaining characteristics that would shape the genre over the next several hundred years. In this chapter, we explore how the special nature of the Republic of Venice, the allure of the city's singular beauty, and the many pleasures afforded by Carnival shaped and nurtured opera. Over the course of the seventeenth century, the style of commercial opera that first flourished in Venice spread to every city on the Italian peninsula and beyond. The skills of the Italian poets, singers, composers, choreographers, and designers who knew how to produce Italian opera became a precious commodity in many of Europe's most powerful courts.

OPERA AND THE VENETIAN REPUBLIC

The unique features of Venetian opera and the industry that developed around it were in large part a result of Venice's republican form of government. Unlike the absolute monarchies that dominated the rest of Europe, Venice was essentially an oligarchy. A Senate and various councils consisting of the nobility (from which women were excluded) ruled the Republic of Venice. Laws carefully regulated the reach of the doge, the elected ruler, whose power was largely symbolic.

Foreigners and natives alike extolled La Serenissima for the special beauty of the watery city that had developed atop structural pilings in a lagoon off the Adriatic Sea. The evocative canals and enviable maritime position that allowed Venice to gain so much power both in the Mediterranean and the East also made it a crossroads for trade and travel. During Carnival, the period after Christmas when Catholics traditionally indulged in pleasures (fireworks, ballets, gambling, masquerades) before the sobriety of Lent, Venice became one of Europe's most popular destinations.

All of this had a profound effect on musical theater. While in most court cities, artistic patronage was largely concentrated in the hands of a single patron or family, Venice's political system fostered an artistic milieu funded by noble families and investors. Financial investment in opera, like many other activities in the city, was motivated both by the ever-elusive hope of monetary gain (opera was usually unprofitable) and by the quest for a less tangible commodity: prestige. Thus competition was an important element in Venetian opera from its inception.

Venetian opera was also shaped by the somewhat libertine intellectual leanings of the Venetian nobles and citizens who were involved in its production. The first Venetian opera theater opened in 1637, only 34 years after the end of the Interdict, when the pope had briefly excommunicated the entire Republic on account of Venice's defiance of papal authority. Although firm in their Catholicism, many Venetians who grew up during this period were particularly eager to declare their independence from Rome and the stifling effects of the Inquisition. The Accademia degli Incogniti (Academy of the Unknown Ones), founded in the 1630s by the Venetian nobleman Giovanni Francesco Loredano, became the center of intellectual and literary activities both for native Venetians and for the many poets, artists, and freethinkers who were drawn to the liberties afforded by the Most Serene Republic. In addition to publishing poems and discourses, many of which were banned by the Church, some Incogniti penned opera librettos, using the new genre to promote their pride in Venice's beauty and special freedoms. (In Chapter 10, we will sample some of the pleasures enjoyed by the Venetian academies, in particular the music of the singer-composer Barbara Strozzi.)

Finally, Venice was home to one of Europe's most famous Carnivals, where opera became the featured entertainment. This topsy-turvy world, in which servants and masters traded identities, and courtesans roamed the streets or floated down the city's canals with masked lovers even more freely than usual, flowed onto the stage in Venice, much to the delight of onlookers such as Evelyn (Fig. 6.1).

Figure 6.1: Venetian Masque in Piazza Santo Stefano during Carnival, *from Giacomo Franco,* Abiti d'uomini e donne veneziani *(Venice, 1610)*

THE VENETIAN OPERA INDUSTRY

Public opera first took hold in Venice during the Carnival of 1637, when a traveling troupe of professional musicians and actors presented the opera *L'Andromeda* at the Teatro S. Cassiano, the first of several comedy theaters to be retrofitted for opera under the auspices of Venetian patricians. Venice had thus found its signature entertainment, which would display the city's many fine musicians, poets, and artists to the entire world. By 1660 Venice could boast five opera theaters spread throughout the *sestieri*, or six city districts. In 1678, with the opening of the luxurious Teatro S. Giovanni Grisostomo, one of several run by the Grimani family, there were nine functioning theaters in Venice, although on average only four new operas were produced a year. Competition was the name of the game, simultaneously resulting in innovation and in the development of a set of stable dramatic and musical conventions that would shape Italian opera throughout the seventeenth and early eighteenth century.

Since no single patron supported Venetian opera, producers solved the problem of financial backing by involving an eclectic group of supporters, each of whom played a different role. The opera theaters usually had an owner, an

impresario who rented the theater building from the owner, individual investors or companies who put up the money, guarantors who pledged to cover the
loan in case of problems, and cashiers who managed the payments and receipts.
Noble protectors functioned more like conventional patrons in lending their
names and therefore their prestige to the undertaking, and in using their power
to negotiate with other nobles who served as patrons for singers. The impresario
took charge of the production from both the practical and creative ends, often
choosing singers, composers, librettists, designers, and choreographers.

Unlike the duke of Mantua, who did not have to worry about ticket sales for the
operas performed for the wedding of his son in 1608 (see Chapter 3), the producers of Venetian opera were deeply concerned about raising capital from investors
at the beginning of the season in order to pay for costumes, scenery, and singers. Additional income was generated by ticket sales, the sale and rental of boxes,
or *palchi,* and even the rental of seats. The system of boxes was essential to the
"public" nature of Venetian opera. Placed on different levels, boxes made it possible for the theater to accommodate spectators from different social classes who
might not care to mingle with one another. A private box, decorated and fur-
nished, enabled noble spectators to entertain select visitors, converse, eat supper, or play cards at the opera. Indeed, boxes were so prized that in one instance
an owner actually stabbed the theater superintendent several times for letting a
well-known Venetian noble sit in his private box without permission.

Although many went to the opera to see and to be seen, artistic merit also
mattered. A less popular opera ran the risk of incurring a financial loss, which
would reflect poorly both on the theater owner and on Venice itself. Opera
may have been "public" in that anyone who could afford it was eligible to buy a
ticket. But the most influential members of the audience were the investors and
patrons, and the nobles and foreign dignitaries to whom printed librettos were
so often dedicated.

THE ANATOMY OF AN OPERA: MONTEVERDI'S *L'INCORONAZIONE DI POPPEA*

How was a Venetian opera put together, and what was it about this particular style
that would take so much of Europe by storm? We can explore these questions
by considering one of the two surviving Venetian operas by the elderly Claudio
Monteverdi: *L'incoronazione di Poppea* (The Coronation of Poppaea), composed at
the end of his life in 1643 (and perhaps finished by one or more of his younger
students). Unlike the mythologically based operas we have considered, *Poppea*
is based on a lurid episode in Roman history, when Emperor Nero (37–68 CE)
(or Nerone in the opera) rejected his wife, Octavia (Ottavia), to marry his high-
born mistress, Poppaea Sabina (Poppea), against the objections of his tutor, the
philosopher Seneca.

THE IMPRESARIO AND THE SINGERS

The first step in planning an opera production was for the impresario to choose the creative artists: the librettist, composer, scenographer, and choreographer, some of whom may have been regular employees at a given theater. Very early in the process—perhaps even before the season was fully planned—the impresario would hire the principal singers, which was probably the most expensive and complex part of the planning. Although impresarios had available to them some local singers, such as the men who sang at St. Mark's Basilica, in order to hire the best singers they needed to cast a wider net and send out agents with good ears to scout the best prospects.

Casting in Venice followed certain conventions: the major female characters were always sung by women, while the male heroic characters (such as Emperor Nero) were usually played by castrati. This contrasted with Rome, where the influence of the Church often prevented women from singing in public. The emphasis on high voices would remain a characteristic of Italian opera throughout the seventeenth century. Tenors were usually not heroes in this period; instead they played comic characters (sometimes in female dress). Basses sang the roles of kings and older characters. In Monteverdi's *Poppea*, the philosopher Seneca was cast as a bass, the soprano Anna di Valeria is thought to have sung the role of Poppaea, and Anna Renzi, who two years later would earn John Evelyn's praise, received acclaim as Empress Octavia.

We can see something of how the business worked from the 1644 contract that Renzi signed with the impresario Geronimo Lappoli at the Teatro Novissimo (Newest Theater), in which she agrees to sing in one or more operas that season (SR 89:569–71; 4/9:61–63). A clause allows for a reduction of her wages by half if she is ill and cannot perform. Should the opera be canceled for reasons beyond her control, however, she will still be paid in full. The contract provides Renzi with a box for the season, and all her costumes. Lest she worry about the theater going bankrupt, it also stipulates that a local resident, in this case a Jewish physician, will guarantee her fee.

THE LIBRETTIST

In seventeenth-century Venice, the librettist was perhaps the most important member of the dramaturgical team. He took responsibility for deciding how the drama should be presented: what episodes in myth or history would be used, the alterations that needed to be made for theatrical purposes, how the material should be distributed over the usual three-act scheme (some of the first Venetian librettists followed classical precedents and wrote five-act operas), and what would be included in the prologue. As a result, he usually received top billing. During opera's formative years in Venice, poets penned librettos as a hobby. Many were professional lawyers or diplomats, or nobles who had no need of employment beyond the various jobs they performed in service to the Venetian government. In the case of *Poppea*, the librettist was Giovanni Francesco Busenello, a lawyer of the citizen class (the class that included Venetians who were not noble but who ranked above commoners). He was also an amateur poet and a member of the Accademia degli Incogniti who had already proved his skill by writing two librettos set by Monteverdi's young student Francesco Cavalli (whose opera *Giasone* we consider below).

It may well have been Busenello, in consultation with Monteverdi, who made the unusual decision to write an opera based not on mythology, but instead on an episode in Roman history in which none of the characters behaves in a particularly admirable way. The first-century Roman historian Tacitus is responsible for the most famous rendition of this story. Over the course of the opera Poppaea persuades Nero to banish his wife (the historical Octavia was killed by Nero), marry her, and crown her as empress. When Seneca objects to the marriage, Nero orders his suicide. Even the wronged characters—Poppea's husband, Otho (Othone), and Nero's wife, Octavia—make decisions that are morally suspect. Octavia manipulates Otho into disguising himself as a woman to sneak into the garden and attempt to murder Poppaea. (He is prevented from doing so by the appearance of Love, who defends Poppaea.) Like most seventeenth-century operas, the opera ends happily—at least for Nero and Poppaea, who sing a sensuous love duet at the end. However, since Nero marries his mistress, banishes his wife, and calls for the suicide of the virtuous Seneca, this is a work in which it is fair to say that virtue is not rewarded and vice is not punished.

Busenello and Monteverdi may have had a good reason for choosing this unconventional topic. During this period several of Busenello's colleagues in the Accademia degli Incogniti had published satirical novels focusing on the sexual and political misconduct of figures from imperial Rome. The badly behaved Romans served Venetian republican interests, since the Roman Empire offered an excellent example of the questionable moral values of a monarchy. Both libretto and music encapsulate the Academy's fascination with moral ambiguity and its preoccupation (as expressed in the writings of other Incogniti) with the allure and danger of female power and sexuality.

In adapting the historical narrative for the stage, Busenello made a number of changes that both conformed to Venetian operatic convention and called attention to the amorality of the protagonists. First, he invented several new characters: these include a young woman named Drusilla who is in love with Poppaea's husband Otho, two elderly nurses (one for Poppaea and one for Octavia), and a couple of young servants who sing a highly erotic love duet. Busenello distorted history so that the suicide of the great philosopher Seneca takes place in the center of the opera, rather than several years *after* the real-life Octavia was murdered and Poppaea was made empress. Also in keeping with operatic convention, Busenello included a prologue with allegorical figures, in which Love triumphs over Virtue and Fortune.

In consultation with the impresario and designers, Busenello, like other librettists, determined the settings and set changes for the various scenes, and provided descriptions of these along with basic stage directions. Since the poetic meter usually determined the placement of the arias and recitatives, the poet decided not only what words should be sung by the individual characters, but what style of singing should be used. A strophic text with a regular rhythm and rhyme scheme typically suggested an aria, while blank verse (*versi sciolti*) indicated that the passage should be set in recitative. One of the prime differences between Monteverdi's first opera, *L'Orfeo*, and a Venetian opera such as *Poppea* was the greater concentration in the latter on solo singing (principally lyrical recitative and brief arias). Since some dramatic moments were better suited to song than recitative, Italian librettists throughout the century developed conventions for certain types of arias (laments, vengeance arias, love duets, comic tirades against women, mad scenes, lullabies) and the appropriate situations in which they should be sung.

THE COMPOSER

None of Monteverdi's surviving letters provides details about the composition of his Venetian operas, but evidence concerning the collaboration between Busenello and Monteverdi can be derived by comparing the composer's actual settings to the poetic cues provided by the librettist. These reveal that Monteverdi—more than any of his contemporaries—took control of the lyrical flow of the opera. He often "recomposed" the poetry, turning text intended for arias into recitatives and vice versa. In Monteverdi's Venetian operas—and to some degree those of his contemporaries—characters often shift rapidly back and forth between speechlike recitatives and lyrical arias. The lyrical moments, usually in triple meter and featuring an expansion of a single phrase through word repetitions or more-virtuosic vocal writing, convey a spontaneous expression of emotions, or are calculated rhetorical gambits designed to seduce or persuade a given character.

One such example occurs in Act 1, scene 3 of *Poppea*, as Nero tries to leave his mistress after a night of lovemaking. Poppaea, eager for Nero to discard his wife and make her empress, uses lyrical recitative, generously laden with sensuous chromatic inflections, as she tries to extract from him a commitment not only to return to her bed but also to acknowledge their relationship officially. When he fails to succumb to her entreaties, Poppaea presents him with a sly ultimatum: "Sir," she sings modestly, "you always see me, but you don't really see me, for as long as you keep me hidden in your heart, you will not be able to gaze upon my eyes." In other words, Poppaea tells Nero that if he continues to keep her hidden—that is, if he does not acknowledge her publicly—he will no longer have the pleasure of seeing or sleeping with her.

Despite the fact that Busenello's poetry called for a continuation of recitative, Monteverdi sets this passage in aria style (Ex. 6.1). The chromaticism and languor vanish, and Poppaea sings in a diatonic C major over a bass that moves in quarter

Example 6.1: *Claudio Monteverdi, "Signor, sempre mi vedi" from* L'incoronazione di Poppea *(1643), Act 1, scene 3, mm. 94–98*

Sir, you always see me, but you don't really see me

notes. After a deferential musical bow on the word "Signor," she slips into a jaunty rhythm with little bursts of coloratura (fast, florid passagework) as she provocatively repeats the most important words of her ultimatum, "sempre mi vedi" (you always see me)—almost like a musical striptease. The implied threat is unmistakable as she lingers coyly on the half-note G on the word "anzi" (but) in measure 98.

The aria style is one of the rhetorical tools that Poppaea uses to seduce the emperor. Nero's wife, Octavia, on the other hand, who is represented as being less desirable, sings in angular recitative throughout almost the entire opera, breaking into triple meter only once as she furiously imagines Nero in the arms of his mistress. Anna Renzi, reputed to have been a superb singing actress, nonetheless earned considerable acclaim for her portrayal of Octavia, moving audiences to tears despite—or perhaps because of—the less opulent vocal style.

Poppea also includes ensemble singing, in which Monteverdi deftly incorporates the compositional styles employed in his collections of concerted madrigals, such as the *Madrigali guerrieri et amorosi* (see Chapter 3). In representing the moments before Seneca's suicide in Act 2, scene 3, for example, a trio of his faithful followers (*familiari*) plead with the philosopher not to end his life in an imitative passage featuring ascending chromatic scales, in which none of the semitones properly resolves (Ex. 6.2).

The vocal virtuosity associated with the madrigals comes to the fore in the highly sensuous duet sung by Nero and his companion Lucan (Lucano) in Act 2, scene 6: they celebrate the death of Seneca by interweaving their ornate melodic lines over a ground bass—again a descending tetrachord. The unmistakable eroticism in their duet may well reflect the sexual freedom championed by the Accademia degli Incogniti and a certain tolerance for same-sex desire apparent in some of their more controversial writings. Crossed-out sections in one of the surviving manuscripts of the opera suggest that the duet might even have been censored at some point.

The exquisite concluding duet that portrays Nero and Poppaea exulting in their passion, which scholars speculate might have been composed by one

Example 6.2: *Claudio Monteverdi, "Non morir, Seneca" from* L'incoronazione di Poppea *(1643), Act 2, scene 3*

Do not die, Seneca

Example 6.3: *Claudio Monteverdi, "Pur ti miro" from* L'incoronazione di Poppea *(1643), Act 3, scene 8, mm. 14–18*

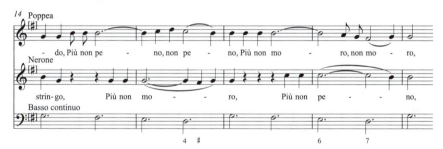

No more suffering, no more death . . .

of Monteverdi's younger contempororaries, is perhaps the most unsettling moment in the opera. Since a castrato played Nero, the two voices sing in the same register, melding in a manner that might seem at first to erase gender differences for twenty-first-century listeners, but is in fact remarkably sensual. As in the *Lamento della ninfa* (see Anthology 5), we find a descending tetrachord ground bass. Here, however, it does not indicate sorrow or lament; rather, as in the Nero–Lucan duet, the constant repetition creates erotic tension, which in this duet becomes particularly acute with the searing minor-second dissonance on the words "peno" (suffering) and "moro" (death) in measures 16–17 (Ex. 6.3).

The listener is left with a dilemma: Are we to rejoice in the happy ending, despite the death of Seneca and the banishment of Octavia? Or does the opera convey an implicit judgment in light of the historical fact that the pregnant Poppaea would later die from a kick in the abdomen by an enraged Nero? Regardless, this morally ambivalent libretto inspired some of Monteverdi's most remarkable music.

STAGING VENETIAN OPERA

As we recall from Evelyn's comments, Baroque opera was a treat for both eye and ear. An important part of the production process involved visual spectacle, requiring the skills of choreographers, set designers, machinists, and painters. Although, as far as we know, there were no dances in *Poppea*, the majority of the operas that Venetian audiences saw included elaborate *balli*, usually at the ends of the first and second acts. The influence of one of the period's great Italian dancing masters, Giovanni Battista Balbi, resulted in the widespread inclusion of *balli* featuring satyrs and nymphs, dancers in animal costumes, and statues, as well as exotic Turks, Native Americans, and Moors. Italians favored an athletic, pantomimic style of dance rather than the courtly dances and complex footwork popular in France (see Chapter 7). An illustration of a Dance of the Four Turks from Gregorio Lambranzi's *Neue und curieuse teatralische Tantz-Schul* (New and Curious Theatrical Dancing School, 1716) hints at the inventive nature of the theatrical dance in Venetian opera (Fig. 6.2).

The marvelous set designs and changes that Evelyn praised so highly were also an Italian invention. Venetian audiences in the 1640s were particularly fortunate to have at their disposal a set designer and inventor of stage machinery named Giacomo Torelli. He and his colleagues made advances on a system of scene construction and perspective that had been developed earlier in the century. We have a glimpse of the splendor from Torelli's set design for Act 3, scene 3 of *Venere gelosa* (Jealous Venus, 1643), presented the same year as *Poppea*, with music by Francesco Sacrati and libretto by Nicolò Bartolini, which inspired the painting reproduced on the cover of this book. It consisted of several pairs of

Figure 6.2: *Dance of the Four Turks, from Gregorio Lambranzi,* Neue und curieuse theatralische Tantz-Schul *(Nuremberg, 1716)*

painted flats—in this case the columns that decorate the courtyard—each pro-
gressively smaller and placed closer to one another on a raked, or slanted, stage.
The decreasing size of the flats created a sense of depth, and the spectator's eye
was drawn to the painted backdrops that completed the scene. Here, the audience had the illusion of being able to see deep into the interior of the palace. The
spectacle was enhanced by the sudden appearance of Jupiter, who descended on
a cloud machine that seemed, according to one contemporary description, to
imitate the "breadth of the heavenly gyrations," thus lending greater majesty
to the god.

The challenge was to change scenes quickly and (if possible) with relatively
little noise. This was accomplished by placing each flat in a wooden track cut
into the stage floor, enabling the flats to be moved from underneath the stage
through a system of ropes and pulleys. One way to shift the flats simultaneously
was to attach them to carriages (which were under the stage and thus invisible to
the audience). Torelli invented a system whereby the entire mechanism could be
moved by releasing counterweights hung above or to the side of the stage. One
spectator marveled at the speed at which a 15-year-old boy was able to transform
a maritime scene into a courtyard with loggias, bronze statues, and a triumphal
arch by simply releasing a single counterweight.

One of the few theaters in which a similar mechanism survives is the
Drottningholm Court Theater near Stockholm. The stage set shown in Figure 6.3

Figure 6.3: *Stage of Drottningholm Court Theater, near Stockholm*

shows a royal court similar to the one pictured in Torelli's painting, in which we can see how the series of flats, decreasing in height, creates the impression of a columned room. The wooden curves visible behind the columns at the rear of the stage are part of a wave machine that, when cranked, creates a surprisingly realistic imitation of the ocean.

CAVALLI'S *GIASONE*

After Monteverdi's death in 1643, Venetian opera continued to flourish in the hands of the younger generation of composers, the most important of whom was Francesco Cavalli (1602–1676), who likely studied with the elder master. Cavalli composed his first Venetian opera, *Le nozze di Teti e di Peleo* (The Marriage of Thetis and Peleus, 1639), for the Teatro S. Cassiano within two years of the first public opera performance in that theater. He would dominate Venetian opera for the next three decades, composing some 41 works, of which 27 have survived.

Cavalli's most popular opera was *Giasone* (Jason, 1649). As is often the case in Venetian operas, the libretto by Giacinto Cicognini provides a somewhat humorous, even antiheroic look at a well-known figure in mythology: *Giasone* (Jason), the captain of the Argonauts, who is on a quest to retrieve the Golden Fleece. In the opera, he is pursued by two powerful women linked to him in the mythological sources: Queen Hypsipyle of Lemnos (Isifile in the opera) and the sorceress Medea, best known for killing her own children in the ancient Greek tragedy of the same name by Euripides. A comic stuttering servant and a bawdy nurse complete the none-too-serious picture.

Giasone and other midcentury Venetian operas by Cavalli and his colleagues led to the codification of many features that would be adopted elsewhere in Italy and Europe. Compared with *Poppea*, for example, *Giasone* displays a much sharper division between aria and recitative. (We will have more to say about this tendency below.) Cavalli is more apt than Monteverdi to follow the cues of the poet, though he often inflects a line of recitative with a lyric quality to heighten the impact of individual words. *Giasone* contains a broad range of conventional aria types, from high tragedy to low comedy, infused with the lush melodies that flowed with apparent ease from Cavalli's pen.

Cavalli's innate lyricism is apparent in Act 1, scene 2. Although Jason has been charged with the heroic quest of retrieving the Golden Fleece, he has been enjoying a yearlong dalliance with Medea. Since he visits her only at night, he claims not to know her true identity and indeed never to have seen her face, despite the fact that she has borne him a pair of twins. The audience's first glimpse of the hero shows him lying in bed, complaining of exhaustion after having spent the night making love. Note the lilting triple meter, the gentle alternation between even and dotted rhythms, and the conjunct, descending vocal line, echoed indolently by a pair of violins (Ex. 6.4). In the second phrase, when we would expect the aria to be gathering steam, Jason sings a sustained A on the word "fermate" (stop), demonstrating his lack of energy just at the point when heroic action is called for.

Jason's lazy sensuality contrasts markedly with Medea's powerful music in her incantation scene, where she calls upon the spirits of the underworld to support the hero in his quest. She casts the spell by repeating the same note over a series of E-minor chords in a hypnotic rhythm that is derived from the unusual accents in her poetry. (Each line ends with the accent on the third-to-last syllable, rather than on the penultimate one, a pattern often associated with supernatural or rustic characters.) Medea's magical powers are also manifest in her aggressive ascent into the upper register on an E-minor triad (Ex. 6.5).

Jason's heroism is further undercut in the final scene of the opera, when he must face his former lover after having tried to have her murdered. Hypsipyle, with her two children at her side, confronts Jason in a lengthy monologue

Example 6.4: *Francesco Cavalli, "Delitie e contenti" from* Giasone *(1649), Act 1, scene 2, mm. 1–6*

Delights and pleasures that ravish my soul . . . stop

Example 6.5: *Francesco Cavalli, "Dell'antro magico" from* Giasone *(1649), Act 1, scene 14, mm. 4–5*

Of this magic cavern, creaking hinges . . .

charged with melodramatic intensity (see Anthology 12). After begging him to kill her in an angry recitative, she shifts abruptly to a moving lament-style aria as she pleads with the onlookers to see that her children are properly cared for. Utterly shamed by Isifile's eloquence, Jason gives in, leaving Medea to her former lover, King Aegeus (Egeo). The reunited couples then enjoy the customary happy ending.

BEYOND *GIASONE* AND VENICE

Giasone proved to be one of the most popular operas of the seventeenth century: in an era in which novelty was prized and operas were rarely adopted for subsequent seasons, there were 13 separate revivals of *Giasone* between 1650 and 1685 in Ancona, Bologna, Brescia, Ferrara, Florence, Milan, Naples, Perugia, Piacenza, Rome, Vicenza, and Viterbo. The 1671 Roman performance included some new music (and updating of the old) by Alessandro Stradella (1639–1682) and was presented with the title *Il novello Giasone* (The New Jason), one of a number of Venetian operas presented at Rome's first public opera theater, the Tordinona (see Chapter 10).

The revivals of Cavalli's *Giasone* are only one manifestation of the popularity of Venetian-style opera in Europe during the second half of the seventeenth century. Through the efforts of Giulio Mazzarini (whom we will meet in Chapter 7 as Cardinal Mazarin, the virtual ruler of France before Louis XIV came of age), a few Venetian operas made it to Paris in the 1640s. Mazarin would in fact bring Cavalli to Paris to compose an opera for the marriage of Louis XIV, which proved to be a decidedly unpleasant experience for the composer.

Venetian opera was heard in Naples as early as 1650, when the Spanish viceroy, the count of Oñate, hired the choreographer and director Giovanni Balbi and his troupe to perform Cavalli operas at a temporary outdoor theater at the royal palace, with some performances open to a ticket-buying public. Subsequent viceroys supported opera in Naples, most notably the marquis del Carpio, Gaspar de Haro y Guzmán. Drawing on his experience as producer of Spanish opera and *zarzuela* (a form of musical theater with both sung and spoken dialogue) in Madrid, he installed Alessandro Scarlatti (see Chapter 11) as both *maestro di cappella* and opera composer in Naples.

It is curious that a genre developed in public theaters in a decidedly antimonarchical context became the darling of so many absolutist princes north of the Alps. Two of Cavalli's successors, Pietro Andrea Ziani (1616–1684) and Carlo Pallavicino (ca. 1630–1688), for instance, were hired by Elector Johann Georg II to write operas for the opening of his new theater in Dresden in 1666–67. Vienna attracted a number of experienced Venetian composers and librettists who were in search of more stable employment. Antonio Draghi (ca. 1634–1700), who began his career as a singer on the Venetian opera stage, served as both librettist and composer for the Habsburg court.

By the mid- to late seventeenth century, the numerous professionals required for the production of Venetian-style opera (composers, poets, choreographers, designers, singers, and instrumentalists) traveled between one opera center and another, bringing entire operas or favorite arias with them in their suitcases and altering them as necessary to suit the tastes of different audiences. *La Semirami* by Antonio Cesti (1623–1669), first performed in Vienna in 1667 in honor of the empress's birthday, extolled the virtue and power of the Assyrian queen Semiramide, who, according to ancient sources, switched identities with her effeminate son to go to war in his place while he stayed at court impersonating her. The libretto then traveled to Venice, where the Venetian Matteo Noris carefully edited the text for "Venetian use" by highlighting the sexual appetites of the queen and the potential for same-sex desire that was only implicit in the Viennese version and was so welcome in the Carnival city.

OPERATIC CONVENTIONS IN THE LATE SEVENTEENTH CENTURY

Even as Venetian-style opera spread across Europe, the genre itself became increasingly regularized by both dramatic and musical conventions. Librettists continued to embrace often complex and carnivalesque plots in which cross-dressed lovers, comic servants, extravagant spectacle, and high drama happily coexisted. Poets supplied composers with an increasing number of aria texts, which gave the singers an opportunity to display their considerable skills. For the French nobleman Saint-Didier, arias were the chief attraction. While criticizing the poetry (for not following classical rules) and the dancers (who seemed to wear "lead in their shoes"), he notes that the "charms of their voices do make amends for all imperfections." After expressing some amazement at the cost of the singers, he observes that the "airs are languishing and touching" and that the small orchestra, composed of lutes, theorbos, and harpsichords, keeps "time to the voices, with the greatest exactness imaginable" (SR 91:576; 4/11:68).

By the third quarter of the century, the aria itself had become more standardized. The incipient separation between aria and recitative that we see in Cavalli's operas was now clear-cut, and arias in the *da capo* (from the head or top) form permeated all of the dramatic vocal genres—opera, cantata, and oratorio. In a da capo aria, the text and music are divided into two parts. The first, or **A**, section of the poem, set in the tonic key, is usually longer than the second, and the vocal phrases are typically set off with introductory, medial, and concluding repeated passages called *ritornelli*. The second, or **B**, section, in a contrasting key, is typically briefer and often forgoes the ritornello altogether. After the cadence of the **B** section, the singer and orchestra return to the top (*capo*) of the aria and repeat the entire **A** section, with ornaments added by the singer. While these early da capo arias are far briefer than those by later composers such as

George Frideric Handel (see Chapter 14 and Anthology 23), the dramatic rhythm created by the alternation of da capo arias and recitatives became the standard for Italian operas, oratorios, and cantatas well into the eighteenth century.

By the last decade of the seventeenth century, however, it was an open question whether these well-established conventions were truly beneficial to the genre. The most extravagant praise and damning condemnation of Venetian opera came in 1690 from a single critic, Giovanni Crescimbeni, whose involvement with the Roman Arcadian Academy we will consider in Chapter 11. After praising *Giasone* as "the first and most perfect drama," he proceeded to criticize the same opera for "having brought about the end of acting, and consequently, of true and good comedy and tragedy." In particular, Crescimbeni deplored the fashionable mixing of comic and serious modes, the juxtaposition of heroes with buffoons and servants, the use of poetry more suited to short arias than to noble speech, and the multiplicity of brief arias. "The overwhelming impropriety of having characters speak in song," he noted, "removed from compositions the power to move the affections." Crescimbeni may have admired *Giasone*, perhaps even thought of it as a guilty pleasure, but he recognized that many of its features were precisely those that he and his colleagues would seek to reform in the eighteenth century.

Had opera really deteriorated, or did Crescimbeni's comments betoken a changing aesthetic and a different set of values that came to dominate in the late 1600s? The mixture of comedy and tragedy that some critics found so problematic was common in many seventeenth-century plays, including those of Shakespeare. In fact, it is precisely this mix of high and low elements and the concomitant delight in gender ambiguity that may have fueled the revival of Venetian opera in the late twentieth and twenty-first centuries. As we will see, not every librettist, composer, and critic would follow Crescimbeni's lead. Handel, for instance, who revised a number of Venetian librettos for his London operas, would retain some of the incongruities that disturbed Crescimbeni and his colleagues. Despite repeated efforts in subsequent centuries to reform opera, the genre would be forever marked by Venice and its Carnival.

FOR FURTHER READING

Carter, Tim, "Re-Reading Poppea: Some Thoughts on Music and Meaning in Monteverdi's Last Opera," *Journal of the Royal Musical Association*, 122 (1997): 173–204

Glixon, Beth L., and Jonathan E. Glixon, *Inventing the Business of Opera: The Impresario and His World in Seventeenth-Century Venice* (Oxford and New York: Oxford University Press, 2005)

Heller, Wendy, *Emblems of Eloquence: Opera and Women's Voices in Seventeenth-Century Venetian Opera* (Berkeley and Los Angeles: University of California Press, 2003)

Heller, Wendy, "Tacitus Incognito: Opera as History in *L'incoronazione di Poppea,*" *Journal of the American Musicological Society* 52 (1999): 39–96

Martin, John Jeffries, and Dennis Romano, eds., *Venice Reconsidered: The History and Civilization of an Italian City-State, 1297–1797* (Baltimore: Johns Hopkins University Press, 2002)

Rosand, Ellen, *Monteverdi's Last Operas: A Venetian Trilogy* (Berkeley and Los Angeles: University of California Press, 2007)

Rosand, Ellen, *Opera in Seventeenth-Century Venice: The Creation of a Genre* (Berkeley and Los Angeles: University of California Press, 1991)

Rosand, Ellen, ed., *Cavalli's Operas on the Modern Stage: Manuscript, Edition, Production* (Aldershot, UK: Ashgate, 2013)

Louise Stein, "A Viceroy Behind the Scenes: Opera, Production, Politics, and Financing in 1680s Naples," in *Structures of Feeling in Seventeenth-Century Cultural Expression* (Toronto: University of Toronto Press, 2013)

CHAPTER SEVEN

Power and Pleasure at the Court of Louis XIV

In the final entrée of *Ballet de la nuit* (Ballet of the Night, 1653), the 15-year-old Louis XIV delighted audiences by dancing the role of the Sun who chases away the darkness (Fig. 7.1). Still under the regency of his mother, Anne of Austria, the young king—who had inherited the French throne at age five—had been encouraged by Cardinal Mazarin, the Italian-born chief minister, to take part in court entertainments. His much-lauded performance in *Ballet de la nuit* was an artistic success, both for the future "Sun King" and for a relatively unknown Florentine composer and dancer who had won his favor, Giovanni Battista Lulli, better known as Jean-Baptiste Lully (1632–1687). The ballet also conveyed a potent political message: here was a ruler with the power to triumph over the forces of darkness. Indeed, after the death of Mazarin in 1661, Louis XIV astounded his mother and his advisors by refusing to appoint a chief minister so that he might rule the empire himself.

A comparison of the 1653 drawing with a painting executed by Hyacinthe Rigaud in 1701, 14 years before the king's death (Fig. 7.2), sheds light on Louis XIV's reign and his special relationship with dance and music. Draped in royal garb, his sword visible at his side, and gazing boldly at the viewer, Louis is a man in charge. His face, with a slightly sagging chin, shows signs of aging; his legs, however, recall the lithe boy who had triumphed in *Ballet de la nuit*, reminding

Figure 7.1: Louis XIV as Apollo, *from* Ballet de la nuit *(French, ca. 1653)*

Figure 7.2: *Hyacinthe Rigaud,* Louis XIV, King of France *(1701)*

the viewer that both arms and arts were an essential facet of the king's persona, and of the identity of France both at home and abroad.

In this chapter we consider music in the era of Louis XIV and the close rapport between politics, absolute authority, and spectacle in seventeenth-century France. We begin with a discussion of the musical institutions and centralization of the arts that were so critical to Louis IV's long reign (1643–1715). We then look at some uniquely French genres and styles of music, focusing on the works of Lully, and at the somewhat insular way in which the French sought—often unsuccessfully—to resist the Italian style that dominated so much of Europe. As we will see, the results of the king's unified cultural program were mixed: on the one hand, the king used music and art to control and manipulate his courtiers; on the other hand, the very arts that he nurtured provided a means for the aristocracy to counter the propaganda of the monarchy.

CENTRALIZATION OF THE ARTS
UNDER BOURBON RULE

By the time Louis XIV ascended to the throne in 1643, the process of centralizing the arts and sciences begun under his father, Louis XIII, and Mazarin's predecessor, Cardinal Richelieu, was well underway. As in other royal courts in Europe, the musicians of the royal household were organized into performing ensembles that served different functions. Chamber musicians (known as the *musique de la chambre*), provided secular and devotional music for the court and included a small group of singers (with boys singing soprano), lutes, harpsichords, flutes, and viols. Louis XIII had maintained a group of violinists to accompany *ballets de cour* and social dancing. French violinists would in fact gain prestige over the course of the seventeenth century: new laws for the musicians' guild established by Guillaume Dumanoir in 1658, for instance, provided professional protection for those designated as masters (SR 93:581–4; 4/13:73–76). Lully would take advantage of their skills, utilizing 24 *Violons du Roi* (24 Violins of the King), founded by Louis XIII, renowned for their disciplined and elegant playing. (Although the exact numbers varied throughout the century, it included a full complement of string players; the name referred not just to the violin itself, but to all the members of the violin family.) As noted in Chapter 4, the musicians of the Grande Écurie, the riding arena in front of the royal stables, played loud instruments such as trumpets, oboes, and drums for outdoor ceremonial occasions. The musicians of the Chapelle Royale (Royal Chapel) provided music for worship at court.

France differed from other monarchies in the establishment of royal (rather than private) academies to systematize intellectual and artistic life. The Académie Française (French Academy), founded by Richelieu in 1635, concerned itself with all matters relating to the French language. The Académie Royale de Peinture et de Sculpture (Royal Academy of Painting and Sculpture), formed in 1648 on the model of the Accademia di San Luca in Rome, provided professional certification for artists. The early years of Louis XIV's reign saw the establishment of academies in literature, science, architecture, and—most important for our purposes—the Académie de Danse (1661) and the Académie d'Opéra (1669). The latter two merged to create the Académie Royale de Musique, better known as the Opéra, the sole body permitted to perform opera or sung drama in France. Music produced at the Opéra and elsewhere in France was disseminated through music publishing, which was also centralized. In 1553, the Ballard family took over from Pierre Attaignant to become "sole printer to the King of France" for 200 years.

The nationalization of the arts was not merely an administrative convenience; it became an important part of Louis XIV's political program, inspired to some degree by his anxiety about political instability. The young king had been profoundly traumatized by the uprising known as the Fronde, a series of civil wars waged between 1650 and 1653 that forced Louis and his family to flee Paris for a time. By requiring nobles to participate in a lively court life filled with ballets, theater, and social dancing, and to conform to an elaborate social etiquette, Louis sought to reduce their time and inclination for political dissent. If the arts served the further propagandistic purpose of reinforcing the power of the king, as was the case with *Ballet de la nuit,* so much the better.

Similar goals lay behind Louis's decision in the 1660s to begin renovating a former hunting lodge in the town of Versailles, some nine miles southwest of Paris. The location was ideal: situated on a road leading directly to the capital, it was near enough to attract and distract the nobles and keep them under surveillance, yet far enough to insulate them from the temptations of Paris, a perennial hotbed of conspiracies against the monarchy. By the time the entire court moved to the Palace of Versailles in 1682, Louis XIV had created a magnificent realm that would be forever identified with the *ancien régime* (the pre-Revolutionary "old regime").

The symmetry of the palace's magnificent gardens, grottos, and fountains, which took some 40 years to complete, reflected the social order of the court. The Chapelle Royale provided an impressive setting for the performance of the *grands motets* (large motets for double choir and large orchestral forces used to celebrate festivals and grand occasions) and *petits motets* (sacred concertos for solo voices and continuo) sung in praise of God and king. Versailles's celebrated Hall of Mirrors, which would be imitated by other monarchs, allowed the nobles to contemplate their own splendid images. Louis's palace attracted a host of musicians, artists, poets, and connoisseurs. As one of the more egalitarian courts with regard to gender, it also supported some of the period's most creative women, such as the Venetian composer and singer Antonia Bembo and the harpsichordist and composer Elisabeth Jacquet de la Guerre (see Chapter 12).

WHAT IS SO FRENCH ABOUT FRENCH MUSIC?

A common theme in discussions about French Baroque music is its relative insularity and isolation. This is not to say that it was not exported to other countries; as we will see in later chapters, French music was a constant presence at the English court under Charles II (who spent the civil war years in exile at the court of Louis XIV), and Johann Sebastian Bach, Georg Philipp Telemann, and George Frideric Handel were all deeply influenced by the French style. But seventeenth-century France was exceptional in developing a musical style that was perceived throughout Europe as quintessentially French. The creation of a state style in all the arts—one that symbolized the monarchy and could be monitored by the various academies—was integral to the vision of society projected by both Louis XIII and Louis XIV. Even musical institutions that were not directly under the purview of the king, such as churches, colleges, and convents, largely adhered to this aesthetic.

Elegant, refined, and often more subtle than music elsewhere in Europe, French music is difficult to define. In general, it seems to progress through time in a leisurely fashion, as if it were important to linger in the present, rather than to press forward to a point of arrival in the future. It is possible that in the view of the courtiers who played, danced, and sang for Louis XIV, the motoric rhythms, complex polyphony, virtuosity, and chromaticism typical of contemporary Italian and German music did not embody the noble breeding and manners appropriate for the French court. This state style was shaped by several aesthetic and practical factors: the distinctive features of the French language, the importance of dance and bodily discipline, a unique and highly developed system of musical ornamentation, and a fascination with tone colors and sonorities as a means of expression.

LANGUAGE AND SONG

At the core of French Baroque music are the special rhythmic properties of the French language. In setting Italian or German to music, composers followed the accentuation patterns, whereby individual syllables within a given word had a natural stress. Thus, in Italian, the penultimate syllable—where the majority of multisyllable words are accented—would typically be placed on a strong beat. Greek and Latin also had long and short syllables; in setting a Latin text there was little ambiguity as to where accents should be placed. In French, however, stress is not a property of individual words, but instead usually falls on the penultimate or final syllable of an entire verse. In the late sixteenth century, some French humanists tried to address this problem by experimenting with a type of vocal music known as *musique mesurée* (measured music), in which they imitated the rhythms of Greek and Latin poetry.

Interest in *musique mesurée* would quickly fade, although seventeenth-century French composers continued to prefer syllabic settings, avoiding the melismatic writing and virtuosity favored by the Italians. However, in order to insure that the stressed syllables in a given line of poetry landed on a strong beat and received appropriate expressive weight, they crafted melodic lines with irregular phrase lengths and frequent shifts between duple and triple meter.

This high degree of rhythmic plasticity is a feature of the popular French *air de cour* (court air), in particular the *airs sérieux* (serious airs) that became so popular at midcentury both at court and in salons (see Chapter 10). One example is "Par mes chants" (By my songs, Fig. 7.3) by Michel Lambert (ca. 1610–1696), a singer and composer who held the position of *maître de la musique de la chambre du roi* (master of the king's chamber music) and would become Lully's father-in-law. Lambert's willingness to lengthen certain syllables both within measures (as in the word "chants" in m. 3) and across barlines (as in the word "tristes" in m. 5) obscures the sense of meter, creating a languor that corresponds to the overall mournful affect. The phrases are of unequal lengths, and there are constant subtle shifts in pace. In the second system, for instance, the rhythm quickens as the singer contemplates the "douleur qui me presse" (sorrow that oppresses me) in the third system, and the subsequent repetition of the word "douleur" provides a gentle thrust toward the cadence. The shift to triple meter and the upper register at the opening of the **B** section introduces another level of emotional intensity, as the singer laments the cruel weariness that cannot be banished. In a single brief song, the listener experiences a series of highly refined changes in mood. Despair and passion are achieved without the searing dissonances and rhythmic drive that are so essential to works such as Ariadne's lament in Monteverdi's opera (see Chapter 3).

DANCE

Another defining aspect of French style—symmetry, order, and elegance—is reflected in the importance accorded to social and theatrical dancing. The highly stylized nature of French dance required enormous control over the body, which in turn mirrored the order the king sought to maintain at court. Although Louis XIV gave up performing on stage in 1669, he and other nobles participated in quite complex social dances throughout his reign, often dancing with and aspiring to the same level as professionals. According to the Abbé Michel de Pure, a writer and habitué of Parisian salons, these were high standards indeed. Ballet, he notes, "does not consist simply of subtle movements of the feet or of various turns of the body"; it "includes all that a nimble and well-instructed body can accomplish in gesture or action in order to express something without speaking" (SR 110:668; 4/30:160). There was ample opportunity to dance at court. In addition to the court ballets described in Chapter 3, the

Figure 7.3: *Michel Lambert, "Par mes chants" (Ballard, 1689)*

king sponsored informal *jours d'appartements*, evenings in which he would open up his private apartments for visitors to dance, eat, drink, and converse. There were also grand balls in which the social hierarchies that governed so much of French life were carefully choreographed.

It is no coincidence that the French, on direct orders from Louis XIV, were the first to develop a system of notating the social dances that would take Europe by storm. The dance notation invented by Pierre Beauchamps in the 1680s and published by Raoul-Auger Feuillet in 1700 provided detailed instructions on how to execute symmetrical patterns on the ballroom floor in coordination with the music. Beauchamps went so far as to codify in detail not only the movements of the feet, but also the correct positions for the dancers' arms and hands, even down to the correct turn of the elbow.

ORNAMENTATION

Our consideration of dance at the French court sheds light on another important aspect of French music: the unique style of ornamentation designed to demonstrate the performer's finesse in a manner analogous to the graceful movements of a dancer. *Agréments* were used in both vocal and instrumental works. These obligatory embellishments were intrinsic to the music, and one would no more omit them than forget proper court etiquette. (It is telling that the word *agrément* also referred to good manners.) French composers often included a table of *agréments* at the beginning of their volumes to insure that players executed them properly (Fig. 7.4).

We see how integral ornaments are to the French style in an arrangement of a chaconne from Lully's opera *Phaëton* that Jean Henry d'Anglebert (1629–1691) included in his *Pièces de clavessin* (Harpsichord Pieces, 1689). Like the Ciaccona by Tarquinio Merula that we considered in Chapter 4, it contains a series of variations on a brief harmonic pattern. This chaconne, however, features ornaments (mostly *tremblements* or trills) on practically every beat in both the right and left hands, enlivening the rather simple melody (Ex. 7.1).

D'Anglebert also uses the typically French technique of *style brisé* (broken style) or *style luthé* in this and other works. By imitating the arpeggiated texture of lute music in a movement that is essentially written in two parts, D'Anglebert creates the impression of a far richer, multivoiced texture. A player fluent in the French style would also follow the unwritten performance practice known *inégalité* (inequality), according to which rhythms notated as equal values (as in the eighth notes in the left hand in mm. 1 and 4 of Ex. 7.1) are played freely and unevenly, usually in a long-short or strong-weak pattern. Not surprisingly, the composer François Couperin (1686–1733) commented on the difficulty foreigners had in playing French music because it wasn't written the way it was intended to be played.

Figure 7.4: *Ornament table from Jean Henry d'Anglebert,* Pièces de clavessin *(1689)*

Example 7.1: *Jean Henry d'Anglebert,* Chaconne de Phaëton de Mr. De Lully, *from* Pièces de clavessin *(1689), mm. 1–9*

INSTRUMENTAL COLORS

French taste extended to the use of instruments as well. While in the first part of the seventeenth century the lute was extraordinarily popular, the exquisitely sensitive and responsive harpsichords of the period later became the instruments of choice. They allowed skilled players to explore a wider range of expressive dynamics and shadings. With the exception of *grands motets* composed for the Chapelle Royale or military campaigns, the French showed a general preference for quieter instruments—lutes, flutes, recorders, harpsichords, and viols. For similar reasons, they tended to use violins in ensembles or to accompany dance; solo violin music in the "singing" Italian style emerged much later. The viol remained the favorite of French solo string players through much of the century, prized for its human-sounding voice.

FRENCH STYLE IN THE CHURCH

The same aesthetic principles extended to the sacred realm, where—with the exception of the *grands motets* for double choir and orchestra performed at court—a preference for restraint and simplicity nurtured a contemplative, almost mystical style for worship that characterized French sacred music of the Baroque and later periods. The French use of the organ for the liturgy is illustrated in an early work by François Couperin, his *Messe à l'usage ordinaire des paroisses* (Mass for Ordinary Use in the Parishes). The 21 pieces in this set were performed *alternatim*—that is, the organ alternates with the choir during the singing of the various sections of the Mass Ordinary, playing short, wordless responses known as versets, presented in the traditional, somewhat austere *stile antico*.

Couperin's titles, like those of other French organ composers, also included specific instructions regarding registration. Thus, for instance, the *Fugue sur les jeux d'anches* (Fugue on the Reed Stops), a response to the second verse of the Kyrie, is to be played on the brightest, reed stops. The faithful who attended services several times a week could expect to hear not only the same words sung at a given moment in the Mass, but also familiar sonorities that became associated with specific prayers.

STAGING THE MONARCHY

Perhaps the most striking contrast between the arts in seventeenth-century France and the rest of Europe is in the realm of theater and opera. The spoken theater, as we will see below, was particularly vibrant in seventeenth-century France, embracing both the comedies of Molière and the neoclassic tragedies of Racine. Until 1693, when Louis XIV banished the Italian actors, both members of the court and the public enjoyed the performances of the Comédie Italienne, which popularized the commedia dell'arte characters and scenarios for French-speaking audiences.

That France resisted the allure of Venetian-style opera for so long was not for lack of exposure. Cardinal Mazarin, whose interest in Italian opera was both artistic and political, tried but failed to establish the tradition in France. Several Venetian-style operas came to Paris in the 1640s, with stage machinery by Giacomo Torelli and choreography by Giovanni Battista Balbi; in 1647, Mazarin would sponsor the performance of an entirely new Italian opera in Paris—an *Orfeo* by Luigi Rossi, starring the castrato Atto Melani (see Chapter 9).

Mazarin's boldest move—bringing Francesco Cavalli to Paris to compose *Ercole amante* (Hercules in Love) as part of the festivities surrounding the marriage of Louis XIV to Maria Theresa of Spain in 1660—was not a success. Since neither the opera nor the theater was ready in time, Cavalli's *Il Xerse* (Xerxes, 1654) was presented in its place. Audiences praised Lully's interpolated dances, but were less enthusiastic about Cavalli's lengthy opera in a foreign language. By the time *Ercole amante* reached the stage in 1662, Mazarin was dead, as was support for Venetian opera, and Cavalli was eager to return to home. It did not help his cause that Lully had a penchant for interfering and was not supportive of Cavalli's efforts. Paradoxically, in the 1660s Lully, who would all but invent French opera in the 1670s, championed neither Italian opera nor a French alternative, having declared that sung drama was all but impossible in the French language.

There were, however, more fundamental reasons why Italian opera initially failed to take root in Louis XIV's France, while many other courts embraced it. The nobles, many of whom had lost their taste for arms and military discipline under Louis XIII, preferred entertainments that reinforced the pleasurable experiences that were so integral to court life. As Louis XIV became more powerful, pursuing a series of successful military campaigns, he transformed what scholars have described as an "iconography of sovereignty"—a set of symbols that emphasized royal power—into a comprehensive program of propaganda designed to present him as the leader of a great empire. Not surprisingly, foreign music was deemed unequal to the task.

The fact that the various genres of musical theater cultivated during this period accommodated the changing needs of the king and courtiers was due in no small part to the astute management and talents of Lully. Both Lully's experience as a dancer and his ability to assimilate a variety of compositional styles had led to his early success with the *ballet de cour*. One of the most enduring examples of Lully's uncanny ability to judge royal taste is the so-called French overture, which Lully began to include as an orchestral introduction to many of his works. In ternary form, the French overture opens in a stately duple meter with dotted rhythms that radiates a sense of regal splendor. After a lively fugal section, usually in triple meter, it concludes with a return to the slow, majestic style, the meter, and even some of the musical material of the opening. The dignified nature of the overture inspired eighteenth-century composers such as Bach, Telemann, and Handel to begin many of their own works with French overtures.

THE BURLESQUE AS A MIRROR OF THE COURT: THE *COMÉDIE-BALLET*

It would be all too easy to assume that the absolutist regime led by Louis XIV and supported on the musical side by the equally autocratic Lully inspired little or no resistance. That this is not the case is demonstrated by the *comédie-ballet*. Essentially comic plays that included music and dance, *comédies-ballets* were characterized by the use of burlesque, a style of theater in which parody and caricature played a central part. In the 1660s, even as Louis continued to appear in court ballets, Lully, the playwright Molière, and the dancer Pierre Beauchamps produced a series of these hybrid works in which praise and oblique criticism of the monarchy were deftly combined.

In their final collaboration, *Le bourgeois gentilhomme* (The Middle-Class Gentleman, 1670), the three collaborators provided a cynical commentary not only on noble patrons of the arts—including the monarchy—but also on the arts themselves. The protagonist is a newly wealthy middle-class gentleman, Monsieur Jourdain, who attempts to acquire the culture and learning befitting a nobleman by hiring the best musicians, artists, dancers, and tailors. Music becomes the object of parody as Jourdain proves equally inept at singing an *air sérieux* and dancing a minuet. By allowing Jourdain's wife to criticize her husband for attempting this feat at so advanced an age, Molière and Lully may have intended to satirize King Louis, who had recently given up dancing at court.

In the climax of the play, Jourdain, garbed in the popular Turkish attire, believes he is marrying off his daughter to a distinguished Turkish prince, when in fact she is marrying a suitor whom she genuinely loves. The exoticism of the scene recalls the court ballets and English masques that we studied in Chapter 3; yet the entire *comédie-ballet* is a kind of Carnivalesque escapade in which the fool is crowned king. There is little attempt by Lully to actually imitate real or imagined Turkish music, though he did call for the use of the Janissary, a popular instrument among the Ottomans that consisted of a set of bells mounted on a staff. The foreign flavor is also conveyed by the repetition of banal rhythms and through the use of language—a kind of bowdlerized Italian in which the protagonist is addressed as "Giordina."

Le bourgeois gentilhomme was open to interpretation on a number of different levels. Those at court might have seen it as a condemnation of the new middle class, who tried and failed to emulate the nobles. However, since the epilogue takes place in a public theater where different social classes came together, other viewers might have taken it as a criticism of the court and its entertainments. Louis XIV's reaction seems to have been as ambivalent as the work itself: an initial silence (during which time the courtiers must surely have scrambled to guess the king's opinion correctly) followed by apparent approval, a gradual cooling, and finally withdrawal of his support for Molière. Lully astutely took the hint and sought a new genre with which to command the attention of the king and court: *tragédie en musique*, or tragedy in music (referred to in the second half of the eighteenth century as *tragédie lyrique*, lyric tragedy).

THE TRAGIC IDEAL

Arguably, Lully's greatest accomplishment was the invention of something that he himself had once sworn to be impossible: a style of opera suited to the French language. The organist Robert Cambert (ca. 1628–1677) and the poet Pierre Perrin (1620–1675) had already composed several pastoral dramas that were entirely sung in French, having won the initial 12-year royal privilege, or license, to run the Académie d'Opéra in 1669. Their first production was the pastoral opera *Pomone* (Pomona, 1671), usually called the first French opera, from which very little music has survived. Soon after its successful premiere, however, financial troubles landed Perrin in debtor's prison, forcing Cambert to carry on with other collaborators.

For Lully, ever the opportunist, Perrin's misfortune provided an irresistible opportunity. With the support of Louis XIV, he acquired an exclusive hereditary patent on the entire operatic genre and produced his first *tragédie en musique*, *Cadmus et Hermione*, in 1673. Thereafter he composed operas at the rate of roughly one per year, usually premiering them at Versailles and then presenting them in Paris at the Académie Royale de Musique or Opéra. He was fortunate to find a librettist well suited to the task, Philippe Quinault, who penned 11 of Lully's *livrets*, or librettos.

Lully and his previous colleagues had composed numerous musical theater pieces with airs, dances, and choruses. The missing ingredient was the *récit*, or recitative—the "glue" that turned a play with music into sung drama. Lully and Quinault sought to develop a style of declamation closer to the kind heard in the theater. Reportedly, their model was the style of actress Marie Champmeslé, who was known for her performances of neoclassical dramas by Jean Racine.

Regardless of whether this anecdote is true, French neoclassical drama, as represented by the works of Racine and Pierre Corneille, established the ideal for how ancient tragedy should be revived on the French stage that would have a profound influence on the reception of both French and Italian opera for the next 100 years. One immediate impact was on versification in the French *récits*, in particular through Quinault's adoption of Racine's poetic meter—a 12-syllable line called an alexandrine. This can be seen in an example from Act 2, scene 5 of Lully's final tragédie en musique, *Armide* (1686), in which the sorceress Armide is on the verge of killing the sleeping hero Renaud, whom she has enchanted

Example 7.2: *Jean-Baptiste Lully, "Enfin il est en ma puissance" from* Armide (1686), *Act 2, scene 5, mm. 20–27*

(Ex. 7.2). (We will consider *Armide* in more detail below.) The text of her recitative reads:

Enfin, il est en ma puissance,
Ce fatal ennemi, ce superbe vainqueur.
Le charme du sommeil le livre à ma vengeance.
Je vais percer son invincible coeur.

Finally, he is in my power,
this fatal enemy, this magnificent warrior.
The charm of his sleep delivers him to my vengeance.
I will pierce his invincible heart.

Quinault mixes alexandrines (lines 2 and 3) with shorter lines (1 and 4) to vary the rhythmic pace. This required Lully to shift frequently between duple and triple meters so that the rhyming syllables at the end of lines (puis<u>sance</u>, enne<u>mi</u>, vain<u>queur</u>, som<u>meil</u>, and ven<u>geance</u>) fall on the downbeat. The result is a recitative in which the emotional expression is—even more than in the *air sérieux*— in the flexible rhythm of the quite lyrical vocal line, with constantly changing phrase lengths and patterns of accentuation. Armide's struggle between love and hatred is manifest in her repeated and unpredictable ascents into the upper register to high G. When she lands on the lower F in measure 26 for the word "vengeance," for instance, we begin to suspect that she will not have the strength of will to kill Renaud. (Handel's Armida, whom we consider in Chapter 14, suffers the same fate, but uses an entirely different mode of expression.)

The differences between French and Italian operas of this period are particularly evident in their manner of organization. Rather than a series of da capo arias alternating with recitatives, French operas were arranged in what we might describe as a modular fashion. A single scene included a series of "numbers": an air for solo voice might lead directly to a duet, followed by a dance, chorus, or instrumental piece. These modules of varying character and length reflected the rhythm of the drama more flexibly than in Italian opera. Where vocal virtuosity took center stage in Italian opera, that role was taken over by the stylized social dances that featured prominently in the *tragédie en musique*. Lully and his colleagues also highlighted the expressive power of orchestral dances and other numbers that evoked storms, sleep, magic, and the like.

Perhaps the major secret of Lully's success was that his operas could be so easily integrated into Louis XIV's propaganda program. During the years in which France was involved in various wars, Lully and Quinault insured that their works systematically extolled heroism and military victories. The king was praised in encomiastic prologues that likened him to Hercules or other great warriors, while the operas' plots reminded listeners of the necessity of sacrificing love and pleasure for duty.

Moreover, the rhetoric of praise in the *tragédie en musique* was potentially transferable to the sacred realm. Jean Laurent Le Cerf de la Viéville, who presented a passionate defense of French opera over Italian (SR 112:679–82; 4/32:171–74), went so far as to suggest that motets should be modeled on the music that Lully put on the stage in scenes celebrating pagan gods, which would "make Christians pray excellently." Works such as Lully's grand *Te Deum*, composed and performed in honor of military victories and other events involving the royal family, were also part of a rhetoric designed to confirm the king's holiness and his right to lead the French people in battle, regardless of the political or financial costs.

THE POWER OF THE SORCERESS: FROM *ARMIDE* TO *MÉDÉE*

In 1683 Louis XIV's wife Maria Theresa died, and six months later he secretly married Madame de Maintenon. With her encouragement, the king became far less tolerant of secular freedoms at court, particularly the libertine tendencies of some of the musicians and artists in his employ. It was during this period that Louis had a falling out with Lully, who had gotten himself into some sort of scandal involving a male page. In response, the composer sought out other supporters, including the king's only surviving son, the grand dauphin, and the more liberal artistic community that he patronized.

We see hints of the tension between the king and the composer in Lully's *Armide*, considered briefly above. Based on Tasso's epic *Gerusalemme liberata*— the same source that inspired the court ballet *La délivrance de Renaud*, starring Louis XIII (see Chapter 3)—the opera nonetheless seems to underscore less the heroism of the knight Renaud than the power and allure of the enchantress

Figure 7.5: *Jean Berain the Elder,* Mademoiselle Rochois in the Title Role of the Opera Armide by Jean-Baptiste Lully, Italian Composer *(after 1686)*

Armide. In the opera's final scene, Armide struggles between her love for Renaud and her desire for vengeance (see Anthology 13). The opera ends in a flurry of scales, as she destroys her own palace in a burst of fireworks and departs on a flying chariot.

The premiere of *Armide* at the Opéra was a success. The first Armide, the soprano Marie Le Rochois (Fig. 7.5), was praised as having the "air of a queen and of a divinity" and the ability to express all the passions, eclipsing all of those who appeared on the stage with her (SR 90:572; 4/10:64). However, if Lully was trying to appease the king, he failed, as it is doubtful that Louis XIV ever saw this brilliant final opera of the composer he had championed for so many years.

It is perhaps not a coincidence that after the premiere of *Armide* audiences in Paris enjoyed a series of operatic sorceresses, including the splendid *Médée* (Medea, 1693) by Marc-Antoine Charpentier (1643–1704), which also featured Le Rochois in the title role. Charpentier had spent several years in Rome, reportedly studying with Giacomo Carissimi (see Chapter 5), whose influence we can glean not only in Charpentier's output (which includes Latin motets and oratorios) but also in his style.

One would never mistake Charpentier for an Italian composer. His music retains much of the simplicity and directness of communication that is the hallmark of the French style. Moreover, he follows Lully's model in terms of dramaturgy and orchestration, albeit with a somewhat richer harmonic vocabulary that apparently sounded harsh to those accustomed to Lully, and his vocal writing tends to be more melismatic. Nevertheless, his Medea invites comparison not only with Armide—whom French audiences would have associated with Le Rochois—but also with the same character in Cavalli's *Giasone* (see Chapter 6), demonstrating the considerable distance between French and Italian opera at the end of the seventeenth century.

Example 7.3: *Marc-Antoine Charpentier, "Noires filles du Styx" from* Médée *(1693), Act 4, scene 7, mm. 28–33*

Black daughters of the Styx, terrible divinities . . .

Whereas Cavalli and Cicognini treated the tale of Medea and Jason in a humorous fashion, the libretto to *Médée* by Thomas Corneille draws its inspiration directly from Greek tragedy and French neoclassical theater. Thus, as in the play by Euripides, Charpentier's Medée seeks vengeance on Jason for his infidelity by killing their children. Charpentier also gives her an incantation scene, but here—unlike in Cavalli's opera—Medée calls upon the dark forces not to aid Jason but to harm him. A muted five-part string orchestra (one of Lully's innovations) and enriched chords with added ninths and sevenths support her bold declamation, heightening the air of mystery associated with this dark and violent character (Ex. 7.3).

Charpentier's *Médée* had a somewhat mixed reception in Paris, in no small part because of the harmonic richness of his music and the violence of the subject. The *Mercure galant*, a French literary magazine, praised the skill with which the complex tragic play was transformed into an opera, commending the warmth, finesse, and intelligence of Le Rochois's performance, which charmed all of Paris. Paradoxically, while this critic described Charpentier as a disciple of Lully, it was Lully's conservative supporters—the so-called "lullistes"—who would condemn *Médée* for its harsh harmonies and Italianate tendencies. (We will have more to say about the dispute between the "lullistes" and the "ramistes"—the partisans of Jean-Philippe Rameau—in Chapter 12.)

By the final years of his rule, Louis XIV, defeated on the battlefield and in failing health, was no longer the youthful Sun King, a veritable Apollo, who had dazzled contemporaries with his balletic aplomb and military prowess; he had metamorphosed into the elderly man who undoubtedly showed his age even more than in Rigaud's painting (see Fig. 7.1). As his interests shifted away from opera to sacred and chamber music, Paris, with its pleasures, eclipsed the Bourbon court at Versailles and became the new center of French musical life.

Seventeenth-century French musical traditions—and also the glories of Versailles—would live on in the frequent revivals of Lully's works at the Opéra. However, Parisians living in the waning years of the seventeenth century would embrace a new genre, the *opéra-ballet*. As we will see in Chapter 12, the most successful of these new works was André Campra's *Le carnaval de Venise* (Venetian Carnival, 1699). As the new century beckoned, a Carnival in Venice, re-created on the stage of the Paris Opéra, would provide the perfect vehicle for French fantasies about pleasure and delight.

FOR FURTHER READING

Anthony, James R., *French Baroque Music: From Beaujoyeux to Rameau* (Portland, OR: Amadeus, 1997)

Ballet de la Nuit, ed. Michael Burden and Jennifer Thorpe (Hillsdale, NY: Pendragon, 2009)

Cowart, Georgia, *The Triumph of Pleasure: Louis XIV and the Politics of Spectacle* (Chicago: University of Chicago Press, 2008)

Gordon-Seifert, Catherine Elizabeth, *Music and the Language of Love: Seventeenth-Century French Airs* (Bloomington: University of Indiana Press, 2011)

Harris-Warrick, Rebecca, "Ballroom Dancing at the Court of Louis XIV," *Early Music* 14, no. 1 (Feb. 1986): 40–49

Hilton, Wendy, *Dance of Court and Theater: The French Noble Style, 1690–1725* (Princeton, NJ: Princeton Book Company, 1981)

Kroll, Mark, "French Masters," In Robert Marshall, ed., *Eighteenth-Century Keyboard Music,* 2nd ed. (London: Routledge, 2003)

Lully, Jean-Baptiste, *Armide: Tragédie en musique*, score ed. Lois Rosow, livret ed. Jean-Noël Laurenti, in Lully, *Œuvres complètes*, Série III, Opéras, vol. 14 (Hildesheim: Georg Olms Verlag, 2003)

Rosow, Lois, "French Baroque Recitative as a Expression of Tragic Declamation," *Early Music* 11, no. 4 (1983): 468–79

Thomas, Downing A., *Aesthetics of Opera in the Ancien Régime, 1647–1785* (Cambridge: Cambridge University Press, 2002)

CHAPTER EIGHT

Music in Seventeenth-Century England

When the 18-year-old Prince Henry, son of James I, imprudently decided to take a swim in the polluted waters of the Thames River, the course of English history—and English music—was forever changed. The death in 1612 of this much-loved prince from the resulting fever—likely typhoid—inspired a vast outpouring of grief from the royal family and the nation. English musicians mourned in song. John Ward's melancholy madrigal "Weep forth your tears," replete with sigh motives and poignant suspensions, is among a number of melancholy vocal works that specifically invoked Henry's name.

> Since Death has slain
> Prince Henery
> O had he lived, our hopes had still increased,
> But he is dead, and all our joys have ceased.

Even from the depth of their heartache, the royal family and public could scarcely have imagined all the dire consequences that would stem from the death of the prince, who had shown himself to be an astute warrior and politician. Henry's younger brother Charles would inherit the throne in 1625, and then in 1642 would flee London for Oxford in the wake of a brutal civil war;

Charles I would be executed seven years later. For most of the ensuing Interregnum (1649–60), the Puritan Oliver Cromwell (briefly succeeded by his son Richard) ruled as Lord Protector of the republican Commonwealth.

The temporary abolition of the monarchy brought the dissolution of many institutions that supported music. The Church of England was disestablished, its musical liturgy suppressed; many theaters were also closed. Musicians were obliged to search for new venues and sponsorship. Many found patrons among the English nobility who craved entertainment in their country houses or entered the increasingly lively commercial sector. Although the monarchy would be reconstituted in 1660 and Charles would be restored to the throne, music and music-making in England were irrevocably altered by the turmoil of the Civil War period.

In this chapter we trace the impact of these political events on the production and consumption of music in England. We begin by discussing the wealth of sacred and secular music that flourished during the reigns of James I and Charles I—the so-called Jacobean and Caroline ages. We then turn to music during the Civil War and Interregnum, examining the career of the bookseller and printer John Playford, whose publications fueled a vigorous market for domestic music. We also consider the cheaply printed broadside ballads enjoyed by consumers of all classes. The chapter concludes with a discussion of England's distinctive approach to opera, focusing on Henry Purcell's contributions in the realm of musical theater.

MUSIC IN THE JACOBEAN AND CAROLINE AGES

After the death of Queen Elizabeth in 1603, James I ascended to the throne of England, inheriting one of the largest musical establishments in Europe. The Chapel Royal produced liturgical music for the court and included the best English-born musicians, such as William Byrd and Orlando Gibbons. The King's Musick (sometimes called the Royal Musick), the secular branch, was enriched as well by many of the descendants of foreign musicians who had been welcomed to England by Elizabeth I and her predecessors.

Music at court was fashioned not only by where the king might be residing (for indeed the musicians and the entire entourage were mobile, traveling to different palaces with the king), but also by the size and function of the room that he occupied at any given time of the day. Large rooms such as the great hall or presence chamber were used for the masques held on Twelfth Night, Shrove Tuesday, and other special occasions. Diners were entertained by wind bands, which were loud enough to be heard over a noisy banquet, while softer violin bands accompanied dancing. More intimate, esoteric, and experimental music—what is usually referred to as the Private Musick (see below)—was heard in the exclusive settings of the privy chamber, privy apartments, or even the royal bedchamber, to which only the most privileged individuals had access.

Musical life at the English court was enlivened by the number and diversity of venues and patrons, since the wives and children of the king maintained separate households with their own retinues of musicians. Queen Anne of Denmark, the wife of James I whose performance in *The Masque of Queens* we noted in Chapter 3, paid an exceptionally high salary to the Italian lutenist John Maria Lugaro, who served as the groom (a sort of private secretary) of her privy chamber. She also brought to England a number of Danish musicians, establishing lasting cultural connections with the court of Christian IV.

Prince Henry, who sought to model his own court entertainments on those of the Medici, recruited some of the best musicians for his private household, including the brilliant keyboardist John Bull, the viol player Alfonso Ferrabosco, and the composer Angelo Notari. (Charles would employ them after his brother's death.) All of this activity furthered the musical education of Henry's beloved younger sister, Elizabeth Stuart, an accomplished keyboard player who also participated in masques and court performances. Her marriage to Frederick V of the Palatine, just one year after the death of Henry, was marked by the publication of *Parthenia, or the Maydenhead of the first musicke that ever was printed for the Virginalls* (ca. 1612–13). Dedicated to the princess, it was the first anthology of keyboard music printed in England (Fig. 8.1). The importance of this beautiful volume and the occasion is underscored by the use of copper-plate printing, which made it possible to notate complex music with greater accuracy.

Figure 8.1: *Title page of* Parthenia *(London, ca. 1612–13)*

When Charles ascended to the throne in 1625, his already large company of musicians was expanded still further. While there were about 60 musicians in the King's Musick during the reign of James I, there were as many as 85 under Charles I, who in addition to inheriting players from Henry's household, gained a host of French musicians upon his marriage to Henrietta Maria, the sister of Louis XIII of France—including the well-traveled viol player André Maugars. The French musicians also afforded the devout Queen Henrietta Maria, the wife of Charles I, the opportunity to create a Catholic musical establishment at court. The architect Inigo Jones, known for his spectacular sets for the court masques, designed a private chapel for the queen at her residence at Somerset House in London, staffed by Capuchin friars as well as French and English musicians. While this endeared her to British Catholics, it caused no end of political difficulties for her husband, who seems to have lacked his older brother's political instincts.

Indeed, from a political perspective, the reign of Charles I was something of a disaster. He was unable to prevent the Civil War from breaking out and made a number of unwise decisions that ultimately led to his own execution. For better or worse, historians have tended to blame Charles (and Henry's death) for the Civil War. However, Charles made up for whatever he may have lacked as a political and military strategist with his patronage of the arts. Among the painters he favored were Peter Paul Rubens and his student Anthony van Dyck. The former was invited to England in 1629 to help negotiate a peace treaty between England and Spain; that same year Rubens completed his allegorical painting *Minerva Protects Pax from Mars* (also known as *Peace and War*) for Charles I, scarcely anticipating the civil war that would lead to his patron's execution 20 years later.

Charles I is also reputed to have been a competent player of the bass viol, and under his patronage the Private Musick became a locus of musical innovation. The roster of 29 musicians (18 singer-lutenists, 1 harpist, 2 keyboard players, 4 viol players, and 4 violinists) included such leading figures as John Coprario, Orlando Gibbons, and Alfonso Ferrabosco. Charles also hired many of the best players and composers of the younger generation, among them John Jenkins and the Lawes brothers, Henry and William.

The intimate repertory of the Private Musick included not only lute songs and madrigals, but works intended for small ensembles, sometimes called consorts. This was a term used in sixteenth- to eighteenth-century England to refer to any small ensemble, but unless otherwise noted usually refers to instrumental music. Published collections of music for consorts included dances, variations (also called divisions), fantasias, and works based on cantus firmi. Music for viol consorts—that is, ensembles featuring only members of the viol family—were particularly popular in seventeenth-century England, and showed the remarkable range of expression that could be achieved by exploiting the homogenous sonorities of the viols.

Mixed (or broken) consorts, on the other hand, highlighted contrasting sonorities. William Lawes's Consort No. 8 in G Major for harp, violin, bass (division) viol, and theorbo takes full advantage of the contrast between the plucked and bowed strings. The Pavan that precedes the set of variations, with the melodic interplay between violin, division viol, and harp, shows the contrapuntal complexity prized in English consort music. The texture is enriched still further in the first division or variation. The transcription given in Example 8.1 includes the opening of the Pavan (Ex. 8.1a) and two variations on it (Ex. 8.1b). The first variation, shown on the second stave of example 8.1b, proceeds primarily in eighth notes, while the rapid-fire sixteenth notes in the second variation, shown on stave three, provided a challenge for the division viol player. This is precisely the kind of improvisatory skill that Christopher Simpson's influential treatise on the division viol sought to impart (see Chapter 4).

Example 8.1: *William Lawes, excerpts from Consort No. 8 in G Major (before 1645)*

(a) Pavan (mm. 1–6)

(b) First two variations (mm. 1–4)

MUSIC FOR THE CHURCH OF ENGLAND

Sacred music under James I and Charles I was shaped by the political and theological conflicts that had been set into motion by Henry VIII's break with the Catholic Church in 1534. The dissolution of Catholic monasteries and other religious institutions in the sixteenth century disrupted the established mechanisms for maintaining the musical liturgy and producing musicians of high caliber, particularly since criticism of Catholicism often focused on music and liturgical practices that were regarded as too "popish." However, both James I and Charles I followed Queen Elizabeth's example and preserved the high quality of the liturgical music at the Chapel Royal, major cathedrals (such as St. Paul's, Canterbury, and York), and universities (especially Oxford and Cambridge)—despite criticism from Puritan factions.

The Anglican musical liturgy in the early seventeenth century was an amalgam of English and Latin texted music. Parts of the mass continued to be sung in Latin, and some of the most remarkable Latin texted music produced in England during this period was by Catholic recusants who refused to renounce their faith. William Byrd (ca. 1540–1623) was one of several Catholic composers who nonetheless served in the Chapel Royal for both Elizabeth I and James I; his motet *Ave verum corpus* (Hail the True Body) captures the introspective spirituality of the recusant community.

In addition to English chant, seventeenth-century English services were enhanced by a substantial new body of English anthems—choral settings of scripture that was musically sophisticated, yet sufficiently different from the Latin motets and masses associated with the Catholic Church to satisfy Anglican worshippers. In the first half of the century there were two types of anthems. Full anthems, as the name suggests, were for full choir. In verse anthems, such as Orlando Gibbons's "If ye be risen again with Christ," sections for full choir alternated with the so-called verses, scored for one or more soloists and continuo, sometimes supplemented with additional instruments.

In Example 8.2, from one of the anthem's three verse sections, the two sopranos join together for an intricate contrapuntal duet, actively engaging the continuo in dialogue in the manner of a sacred concerto. Despite the high degree of imitation, the mostly syllabic text setting—which eschews the virtuosity and ornamentation that were second nature to the Italians—made the text intelligible, particularly when the same line of scripture was repeated by the full chorus, singing in a

Example 8.2: *Orlando Gibbons, "If ye be risen again with Christ" (before 1625), mm. 12–16*

grand and often homophonic style. Part of the splendid effect of the verse anthems was the contrast between the formality of the full choral sections and the tender intimacy of the verses. In the later seventeenth century, English composers would write symphony anthems for grand royal occasions, which would also include orchestral ritornelli.

THE INTERREGNUM

The Civil War and Interregnum had a profound influence on most aspects of music-making in Britain. When Charles I fled London to Oxford in 1642, members of the King's Musick and the Chapel Royal either accompanied him or were forced to search for scarce work as freelancers. Puritan opposition to the sensory appeal of complex church music had a particularly stifling effect; the suppression of sumptuous organ music and anthems sung at the Chapel Royal, St. Paul's Cathedral, and Westminster Abbey was both a theological and political necessity for Cromwell and his supporters.

As shown by the barrister William Prynne's harsh criticism of theater songs as lascivious and irreligious, many English Puritans viewed music using ornamentation and chromaticism as deceitful, effeminate, and dangerous to masculinity. Thus, although plays continued to be printed and produced in private houses during the Interregnum, public theaters were closed by order of the Commonwealth government in September 1642. Puritan criticism of women who played or sang secular music was particularly harsh, with numerous published tracts condemning such activities as indecent. However, after the restoration of Charles II to the throne, the relaxation of strictures against female performers would make it possible for a new generation of actresses to return to the English stage.

MUSIC AT OXFORD DURING THE INTERREGNUM

The university city of Oxford was one of the beneficiaries of the London exodus, warmly welcoming Charles I, his courtiers, and his musicians. During the four years in which the town served as the king's military headquarters, royal musicians contributed to what was already an active musical life. In the aftermath of the Reformation, the four major Oxford colleges—New College, Magdalen College, Christ College, and St. John's College—had managed to maintain musical establishments for the singing of the mass, providing musical education for choirboys. Oxford's dons and students were notably sympathetic to the Catholic cause, and by the early seventeenth century they had rebuilt a number of organs that had been destroyed during the Reformation. (Many would suffer the same fate during the Interregnum, only to be replaced once more during the Restoration.) Nevertheless, these political upheavals had consequences for Oxford's choirboys. When Charles I decided to store his gunpowder in the cloisters of New College, the boys were forced to move into dark and unpleasant lodgings, about which they complained bitterly.

The exiled royal musicians also benefited from the fact that Oxford was among the first universities to include the study of performance as part of a music curriculum, rather than regarding music solely as a branch of mathematics. This was thanks in part to an endowment established by William Heather, an Oxford-trained musician who had been employed at the Chapel Royal. His gift included funds for a professor to supervise rehearsals as well as for the acquisition of a harpsichord, viols, and partbooks. In this lively atmosphere, the kind of musical experimentation once restricted to court involved a much wider community. University lecture rooms and taverns became part of a network of informal concert venues where admission might even be charged—a practice that would spread throughout England in the latter part of the Baroque, as we will see in Chapters 10 and 14.

JOHN PLAYFORD: MUSIC PUBLISHING FROM THE INTERREGNUM TO THE RESTORATION

In 1659, just a year before the restoration of Charles II to the throne, the printer John Playford (1623–ca. 1687) published *Select Ayres and Dialogues,* a collection of songs for one, two, and three voices accompanied by theorbo or bass viol. The frontispiece (Fig. 8.2) is an allegorical representation of music (not unlike the painting by Laurent de La Hyre that we considered in Chapter 1), printed above a poem intended to explain the allegory.

Together, word and image tell us a good deal about the state of music in the aftermath of the Civil War and Playford's ambitions as a music publisher. Dressed in a fashionable gown, Music is shown holding a theorbo, her mouth half open as if ready to sing. Her breasts are partly exposed, her hair expertly coiffed, her knees spread provocatively, an open songbook on her thigh. The setting is excessively sumptuous, with garlands that seem to touch her hair like an oversized hat, and string and wind instruments decorating the room. The poem, however, refers to the sounds of war—the cannons and drums that have silenced the organ and choirs. In the absence of music in the churches and cathedrals, what Playford promotes here is sensuous, luxurious, and sumptuous music to be enjoyed in the privacy of the home. Indeed, what better way for Playford to advertise his *Ayres* in troubled times than with a provocatively dressed allegorical figure?

Politics may well have been a factor in Playford's decision to specialize in music printing. A member of the trade association for publishers and printers known as the Stationers' Company, Playford began publishing works of

Figure 8.2: *Frontispiece to John Playford's*
Select Ayres and Dialogues for One,
Two, and Three Voices *(1659)*

a political nature in 1647, revealing his sympathies for the royalist cause. By 1651, mounting political pressures seem to have led him into the less controversial area of music printing. From then until his death around 1687, Playford produced some two dozen volumes, each of which underwent multiple printings.

Many of Playford's publications also provided musical instruction, since a more proficient and knowledgeable musical public would be more apt to purchase his books. In the preface to *A Breefe Introduction to the Skill of Musick* (1654), Playford modestly explains how he "made the addition of some necessary plain Rules" in order to help beginners. "The Rules of Arts," he notes in the preface, "ought to be delivered in plaine and brief language, and not with the flowers of Eloquence," a task he felt was suited to his modest literary abilities.

Playford also published volumes for those who wished to master specific instruments. A volume entitled *Musicks Recreation on the lyra viol, being a choice collection of new and excellent lessons for the lyra viol both easie and delightfull for all young practitioners: to which is added some few plain directions as a guide for beginners* (1652), provided instruction on this popular small-sized bass viol. Music for the lyra viol was usually written in tablature, since—like the lute—it was often used as a polyphonic instrument. Unlike the bass viol, the lyra viol used variable tunings, indicated in the tablature, that allowed for tremendous variety in

sonority and resonance. (In Chapter 13 we will consider the influence of different tuning systems in Heinrich Biber's violin music.)

Playford was keenly sensitive to the need to print devotional music that was
acceptable both to Puritans and to those with royalist leanings. One example is
*Mr. William Childs set of Psalms for 3 Voyces, after the Italian way, with a through Basse
cut in Copper,* published by Playford in 1657. William Child (1606–1697) would
become an organist of the Chapel Royal during the Restoration; in this volume,
however, he satisfied both Puritan and Anglican tastes. His psalm settings could
be sung unaccompanied or with basso continuo, in the Italian style. Among the
most important customers of printed collections of psalms were women, who
were not permitted to sing in choirs in England, but nonetheless used the music
for devotional exercises in the home.

Many of Playford's customers sought musical works that were arguably more
pleasurable than edifying. *The English Dancing Master, or plaine and easie rules for
country dancing* (1651), which went through numerous pressings well into the
eighteenth century, brought dance tunes and theatrical songs into the home that
had previously been heard at court or in public theaters.

John Hilton's popular *Catch that Catch Can, or A Choice Collection of Catches,
Rounds, and Canons for 3 or 4 Voyces,* first published by Playford in 1652 and
reprinted numerous times in the subsequent two decades, demonstrates the
widespread demand for lightweight polyphonic songs among people who enjoyed
singing in the casual atmosphere of the home or tavern, as shown on the title
page. (Fig. 8.3). (The collection also includes a set of edifying sacred songs at the
conclusion.) The three-voice catch "Come, come away to the Taverne" (Fig. 8.4), in
which the listener is urged to turn washing day into a holiday, is one of a number

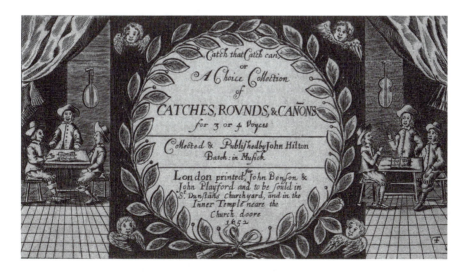

Figure 8.3: *Title page of John Hilton,* Catch that Catch Can *(London: Playford, 1652)*

Figure 8.4: *"Come, come away to the Taverne,"* a catch for three voices from Catch that Catch Can

of drinking songs in the collection. A single line of music is provided; the marking in measure 5 over the word "leave" indicates where the second voice (and later a third) should enter. The engraving that decorates the letter "C" shows an old man with a beard—an allusion to wise Aristotle mentioned in the poem—and a scantily clad woman holding up a washing board.

Several catches feature puns and double entendres that could be quite crude. Although the individual lines in "Here dwells a pretty Mayd" seem quite harmless, the sense changes when all the voices enter and the lines overlap with one another.

> Here dwells a pretty Mayd, whose name is Sis,
> You may come in and kisse;
> Her hole estate is seventeen pence a year,
> You may kisse her, if you come but neare.

BROADSIDE BALLADS

Popular tunes from publications such as Playford's *English Dancing Master* circulated widely on the streets of early modern England in the form of broadside ballads. Single sheets of paper printed on one side, like posters, broadsides were inexpensive to produce and thus a good medium for disseminating advertisements, announcements, and sometimes poems or images. (We will see one in an engraving by William Hogarth in Fig. 14.2.) While broadsides were popular throughout Europe, they were published in particularly large numbers in England and Colonial America.

Broadside ballads typically included an illustration, a poem, and the title of a popular tune to which the poem could be sung. Sold on the street by "ballad mongers" who hawked their wares by singing, they were also pasted on the walls of shops and other public buildings. Men and women of all levels of society purchased broadside ballads.

In addition to containing news of current events, broadside ballads dealt with hunger, adultery, unwanted pregnancies, and other social problems, sometimes in a humorous vein. As indicated on the broadside "Seldome Cleanely," the ballad, which was to be sung to a popular tune called "Upon a Summer's Time," recounted at length the extraordinary frugality of the poet's favorite aunt, who made her puddings fat with the droppings of her nose and saved dish towels by employing her dog's tongue instead.

MUSIC DURING THE RESTORATION

With the coronation of Charles II on April 23, 1661 at Westminster Abbey, a certain degree of normalcy returned for musicians. Indeed, the reinstatement of both sacred and secular music to their former glory was as much a political as an artistic necessity, for music was one means by which the monarchy could increase public confidence in the government and reaffirm the power of the Church of England. After the suppression of the Puritan movement and the reconstitution of the choir of the Chapel Royal, Anglican worship returned in full force, and with it a need for new anthems, chants, and other works for the liturgy, which would be provided by the next generation of composers, including John Blow (1648/49–1708)—about whom we will learn more in Chapter 9—and Henry Purcell (1659–1695).

The fact that Charles II, in the aftermath of his father's execution, spent much of the Interregnum at the court of his cousin Louis XIV was to have a profound influence on both religious and secular music at the English court. Writing in his diary in 1662, John Evelyn, whose commentary on Venetian opera we considered in Chapter 6, applauded the change: "Instead of the antient grave and solemn wind musique accompanying the Organ was introduced a Consort of 24 violins betweene every pause, after the French fantastical, light way." Modeled on the group established by Louis XIII, the English group of 24 violins would participate in the King's Musick as well as join the Chapel Royal for the performance of grand symphony anthems composed by the choir's newly installed gentlemen.

In his *Memoirs of Music* (1728), the nobleman Roger North recalled that during the early years of Charles II's reign, "all musick affected by the *beau-mond* run into the French way." In North's view the "French manner of instrumental musick" did not "make a revolution all at once," but gradually the treble viol went out of favor and the violin was adopted (SR 94:585–86; 4/14:77–78). This trend is reflected in Playford's *Apollo's Banquet: Containing Instructions, and Variety of New*

Tunes, Ayres, Jiggs, and Several New Scotch Tunes for the Treble-Violin (1669), which includes a note on the title page detailing the addition of the "newest French dances, now used at Court and in Dancing-Schools."

After the death of Charles II in February 1685, music at court received somewhat less royal encouragement. Sumptuous sacred music would be composed for the coronations of the Catholic James II in 1685 and the Protestants William III and Mary in 1689, but particularly during the latters' reign (1689–1702), music—both sacred and secular—was far less of a priority. The heyday of the Chapel Royal was over, at least for the seventeenth century (see Chapter 14), and court musicians turned their attention from court to the city of London and its theaters.

HENRY PURCELL

These circumstances provided excellent career opportunities for the young Henry Purcell, who after his voice changed in 1673 became an assistant to the keeper of instruments at court and then composer-in-ordinary to King Charles II. Purcell was also appointed organist of Westminster Abbey in 1679 and of the Chapel Royal in 1682, and by 1685 was sufficiently well situated to write anthems for the coronation of James II. In the realm of instrumental music, Purcell's interest in the contrapuntal techniques and the somewhat retrospective genre of viol consorts is evident in works such as the *Fantasia upon One Note,* ingeniously built upon a cantus firmus consisting of a sustained C in the tenor voice. In addition to the work's textural and rhythmic contrasts, the judicious addition and subtraction of flats (B♭, E♭, and A♭) ultimately create some unexpected tonal adventures, as in measures 10–12 (Ex. 8.3).

Even in the Francophile court of Charles II, the growing influence of the Italian style and the music of Corelli (see Chapter 11) is apparent in Purcell's *Sonnata's of III Parts* (1683), a set of trio sonatas dedicated to the king. In the preface to the score, Purcell is credited with having made "a just imitation of the most fam'd Italian Masters; principally to bring the Seriousness and gravity of that Sort of Musick into vogue, and reputation among our Country-men."

"DRAMATICK OPERA" AND *KING ARTHUR*

Shortly after his triumphant return to London, King Charles II issued patents to two competing dramatic companies, and the English passion for theater was renewed. As with public opera in Venice, the Restoration theater attracted a diverse audience—a lowly merchant might well get a glimpse of the king at a performance. After the stifling morality of the Commonwealth, women of all classes and ranks came to the theater in droves, not only as members of the audience, but as singers, actresses, and playwrights. One of the most famous actresses of the era, Nell Gwyn, became the mistress of Charles II. Musicians

Example 8.3: *Henry Purcell,* Fantasia upon One Note, Z. 745 (1680), mm. 9–13

also found work in London's public theaters. Indeed, music was an integral component of Restoration comedies and tragedies. Instrumental music was heard before the play, as a sort of overture, when the curtain rose, and between the acts. As in masques, songs were prompted by the dramatic action and were often sung by lower-class characters or as part of an onstage "performance."

Some foreign opera, however, was heard in London. Charles II was not much interested in Italian opera, but was an admirer of French music in general and the *tragédies en musique* of Lully in particular. His Master of Musick from 1666–73, the Catalan-born Luis Grabu (fl. 1665–1694), attempted to start a French opera company in London. In 1674 he presented at the Drury Lane Theatre an adaptation of Robert Cambert's *Ariane ou Le Marriage de Bacchus* (Paris, 1659), based on the tale of Ariadne. London audiences also had the opportunity to attend a performance of Lully's first opera, *Cadmus et Hermione,* in 1686. In general, however, the English preferred spoken dialogue to sung recitative, and they disliked the complex plots so favored in French and Italian opera.

The genesis of Purcell's *King Arthur, or The British Worthy* (1691), with poetry by John Dryden, reveals a good deal about the English ambivalence toward sung drama. Dryden had written the text for a musical play named *King Arthur* several years earlier to celebrate the twenty-fifth anniversary of Charles II's ascension to the throne. Rather than focusing on the better-known tale of Lancelot and Guinevere, he chose a patriotic theme that was particularly relevant in the aftermath of the Civil War and Interregnum: the young Arthur's efforts to unify Britain and his battles with the evil Oswald.

Charles II, however, wanted a sung opera in the French style, so Dryden obliged his patron by jettisoning the play and expanding the prologue into a three-act opera, which was then set to music by Grabu. Unfortunately, Charles died before *Albion and Albanius*, as it was called, opened in the theater. The public run was then disrupted by the unexpected arrival of Charles's illegitimate son, the duke of Monmouth, with 4,000 troops and a burning desire for the throne. Monmouth was beheaded later that year, and Dryden and Grabu's opera did not fare much better, holding the stage for a mere six performances.

In the meanwhile, the young Henry Purcell had begun to make a name for himself in the theater with *The Prophetess, or The History of Dioclesian* (1690). Combining spoken dialogue with instrumental and vocal music, *Dioclesian* belonged to a genre that was dubbed "Dramatick opera" by Dryden, but is often referred to today as "semi-opera." Impressed by Purcell's success, Dryden dusted off the poetry for King Arthur, and the two embarked upon a fruitful collaboration.

One of the curious features of *King Arthur*—and other Dramatick or semi-operas—is the fact that the singing and non-singing characters often seem to inhabit two different worlds, while sharing the same stage. In *King Arthur*, for instance, the "royal" characters, such as the king and his beloved Emmeline, who typically set up the drama at the beginnings of the acts, only speak. Song is reserved for Merlin, the other magic characters, and the choruses of shepherds, nymphs, and warriors. Thus, the contrast between spoken dialogue and music becomes a way of shifting between fantasy and normalcy.

The musical design of Purcell's score is extraordinarily varied. Unlike the succession of da capo arias and recitatives of Italian opera, *King Arthur* includes solos, duets, trios, choruses, and instrumental numbers that flow freely into one another once the spoken dialogue, which begins most scenes, is completed. One of Purcell's most ingenious creations is the Frost Scene, in which the Cold Genius ascends from the frozen ground on a rising chromatic line (see Anthology 14). Purcell must have wanted him to sing with a tremulous or shivering voice, as he put mysterious wavy lines over his part in the score. The chorus, too, enters with chattering teeth, "trembling" in the cold. Cupid's aria in response ("'Tis I that have warm'd ye") uses a contrasting lyricism to "defrost" the wintry world. The influence of French opera suffuses the dances, in particular the elegant final chaconne, which inscribes a sense of monarchical majesty onto the work's conclusion.

DIDO AND AENEAS

Given the emphasis placed on entirely sung drama in the rest of Europe, it is perhaps not surprising that Purcell's most famous theatrical work in modern times is his only conventional opera: *Dido and Aeneas*, with a libretto by the poet Nahum Tate. The circumstances concerning its composition and the date of its first performance remain a point of controversy among scholars. All we know for sure is that it was performed in 1689 at a school for girls in Chelsea. Some scholars have hypothesized that it was also performed at court, though there is no definitive documentation to that effect.

Dido and Aeneas is based on an episode from Virgil's epic poem *The Aeneid*, a text that was readily available in English and would have been known to every child who studied Latin. Virgil's tragic tale concerns the unfortunate widow and Carthaginian queen Dido and her love for the Trojan hero Aeneas, who arrives in Carthage in the aftermath of the Trojan War. In the dramatic conclusion of Book 4, when Mercury orders Aeneas to abandon Dido in order to fulfill his destiny as the founder of ancient Rome, Dido concocts an unholy funeral pyre to rid herself of his love, curses Aeneas, and then stabs herself.

The Dido episode—and in particular the final lament in which she kills herself—inspired any number of musical treatments. (See Chapter 2 for Sigismondo d'India's setting of her lament.) Tate and Purcell's opera, however, takes particularly original liberties with the story. Aeneas, the hero of the epic, fades entirely into the background. (One scholar famously described him as a "booby.") The stage is instead commanded by two powerful women—Dido and an evil sorceress (invented by the librettist) who plots the queen's destruction. Perhaps the greatest difference between Purcell's and Virgil's Dido is in the death scene. Purcell's Dido neither curses her former lover nor wields black magic (such tricks are reserved for the sorceress). Instead, she goes to her death with a quiet dignity and a simple request: "When I am laid in earth, may my wrongs create no trouble in thy breast; remember me, but ah, forget my fate."

Dido's justly famous final lament is set over a chromatic descending ground bass (Ex. 8.4). The extraordinary effect of the aria comes not only from the relentless reiteration of this constantly repeating descent by half step, but also from the pattern's odd asymmetry. Whereas ground basses tend to be made up of an even number of measures—usually four, as in Monteverdi's *Lamento della ninfa*—the pattern in Dido's lament is five measures long. Moreover, in the penultimate measure of the ground, Purcell abruptly reverses the steady whole-note and half-note pace that he has established, moving unexpectedly to the D (dominant) on beat 2 (see m.5), as if the bass—like the despairing Dido—cannot quite

Example 8.4: *Henry Purcell, "When I am laid in earth," from* Dido and Aeneas *(ca. 1689), mm. 1–11. (Accompanying string parts omitted.)*

make it to the cadence. As in the *Lamento della ninfa*, the shifting alignment of the bass with the vocal line creates piquant dissonances, vividly depicting Dido's suffering, obsession, and desire for death. The accompanying strings (not shown in the example) enhance the somber mood.

By rejecting the black magic favored by her Virgilian model, Purcell's Dido provides us with a stoic model of female self-sacrifice, a woman who only in death regains her virtue. It is not surprising that almost every music history text produced in the last 100 years includes this remarkable example of Baroque musical style and female eloquence.

England nurtured a vibrant musical life throughout the seventeenth century. Amid political and religious conflicts, the British absorbed elements from continental music and developed their own distinctive musical voice. Introspective viol consorts entertained courtiers and provided pleasure for amateur musicians; rhetorically powerful English anthems gave the Anglican Church much of its musical richness; and English opera, by disdaining the sung drama favored on the Continent, discovered ingenuous new ways to combine music, dance, and poetry.

The publications of John Playford afford a glimpse of the musical activities of all classes of English men and women, while the ever-popular broadside ballads expose the seamier side of life on the streets. As we will see in Chapter 14, the expanding market for music would make London a welcome home to a host of foreign musicians in the early eighteenth century, including no less a figure than Handel, who—remarkably—would turn the British capital into a major center for Italian opera.

FOR FURTHER READING

Austern, Linda Phyllis, "For Musick Is the Handmaid of the Lord: Women, Psalms, and Domestic Music-Making in Early Modern England," in Linda Phyllis Austern, Kari Boyd McBride, and David L. Orvis, eds., *Psalms in the Early Modern World* (Aldershot, UK: Ashgate, 2011)

Burden, Michael, ed., *Woman Scorn'd: Responses to the Dido Myth* (London: Faber and Faber, 1998)

Cunningham, John, *The Consort Music of William Lawes, 1602–1645* (Woodbridge, UK, and Rochester, NY: Boydell Press, 2010)

Eubanks Winkler, Amanda, *O Let Us Howle Some Heavy Note: Music for Witches, Its Melancholic, and the Mad on the Seventeenth-Century English Stage* (Bloomington: Indiana University Press, 2006)

Gouk, Penelope, *Music, Science, and Natural Magic in Seventeenth-Century England* (New Haven: Yale University Press, 1999)

Harley, John, *Orlando Gibbons and the Gibbons Family of Musicians* (Aldershot, UK: Ashgate, 1999)

Heller, Wendy, "'A Present for the Ladies': Ovid, Montaigne, and the Redemption of Virgil's Dido," *Music and Letters* 84 (2003): 189–208

Holman, Peter, *Four and Twenty Fiddlers: The Violin at the English Court, 1600–1690* (Oxford: Oxford University Press, 1993)

Marsh, Christopher, *Music and Society in Early Modern England* (Cambridge: Cambridge University Press, 2010)

Pollack, Janet, "Princess Elizabeth Stuart as Musician and Muse," in Thomasin La May, ed., *Musical Voices of Early Modern Women: Many Headed Melodies* (Aldershot, UK: Ashgate, 2005)

Price, Curtis, *Henry Purcell and the London Stage* (Cambridge: Cambridge University Press, 1984)

Shay, Robert, "Dryden and Purcell's *King Arthur*," in Richard Barber, ed., *King Arthur in Music* (Cambridge: D. S. Brewer, 2002)

CHAPTER NINE

Music and Education

In previous chapters we have encountered a number of musicians who benefited from excellent musical training at an early age. Men of royal descent or noble families, such as Charles I or the lute player Rafaello Cavalcanti, received private instruction in music, dance, and arms that prepared them for life at court and the leisure activities suited to their class and station. Such training was also regarded as appropriate for young, marriageable women, like Princess Elizabeth Stuart, who studied keyboard with the estimable John Bull. Many professional musicians learned their craft through lessons with a local master or a parent. The French harpsichordist François Couperin, for instance, was taught by his father Robert (the younger brother of Louis Couperin). He passed his knowledge on to his daughter Marguerite-Antoinette (1705–ca. 1778), who became the first woman to serve as court musician to the French king (Louis XV) and also taught harpsichord to the king's daughters.

For children from less exalted families and with fewer financial resources, high-quality musical education was provided by a variety of ecclesiastical and charitable institutions: choir schools, universities, orphanages, and convents. The nature of these institutions—and the kind of education they imparted—depended upon a number of factors: the religious affiliation of the school, its location and financial resources, and the age, gender, and economic circumstances of the children.

Despite differences in religious outlook and student populations, these institutions had a common belief in the importance of music in religious education, a vested interest in training boys (and sometimes girls) to produce excellent music, and—in many instances—a willingness to dedicate financial resources to improving the welfare of indigent children. Educational institutions often assumed parental responsibilities, providing room, board, clothing, and supervision for children. In return, the music produced by the students garnered fame and prestige for the institutions, filling church pews and coffers.

In this chapter we consider the education of seventeenth-century children in a variety of such institutions and explore the early experiences of some of the period's most accomplished performers and composers. We begin with choirboys in Italy, England, and Germany before turning to the musical training and compositions of nun musicians in Italy, France, and Spain. The chapter concludes with a consideration of some of the first music conservatories, established in orphanages in Venice and Naples, which by the eighteenth century had become famous for the high quality of the music and musicians they produced.

CHOIRBOYS

The programs set up to educate young choirboys were motivated by the need to create a steady supply of boy sopranos and altos to sing the liturgy, since, except for castrati or those who chose to sing in falsetto, boys were obliged to switch to tenor or bass after their voices changed. Yet while the basic skills needed by choirboys of different faiths were quite similar—the ability to sing chant and polyphony—their backgrounds, experiences, and careers varied considerably.

CATHOLIC CHOIRBOYS: GIOVANNI SANCES AND ATTO MELANI

Giovanni Felice Sances (ca. 1600–1679) was one of many talented choirboys who gained his initial training at the Collegio Germanico (German College), which had been established by the Jesuits to train German-speaking priests in Rome. The college was renowned for the quality of its music both at the school and at the various churches with which it was associated. Under a series of accomplished *maestri di cappella*, including Giacomo Carissimi (see Chapter 5), who served from 1629 to 1674, generations of choir boys or *putti* (literally, little angels), received intensive daily training in the singing of chant (*canto fermo*), *canto figurato* (music in the new style), polyphony, and counterpoint.

In return for room, board, and musical training, Sances and his fellow students were contractually obligated to sing the liturgy—plainchant, motets, and sacred concertos. The breaking of a contract was a serious matter, and financial penalties were imposed in the event that a boy ran away or failed to perform his duties. During Holy Week in 1614, Sances's father was jailed for taking his son out of the Collegio Germanico without permission and failing to pay the substantial fine. Since the 14-year-old Sances had recently distinguished himself by singing in the opera *Amor pudico* (Modest Love) at the palace of one of Rome's music-loving cardinals, his father may have anticipated a more lucrative career for his son outside the college. In any case, the incident seems to have caused Sances no permanent harm; after his voice changed, he went on to considerable success composing and singing in Venice and Padua, and eventually became Kapellmeister at the imperial court in Vienna.

A castrato such as Atto Melani (1626–1714) necessarily followed a somewhat different path, as the decision to have a child emasculated for a singing career often had to be made before musical talent could show itself fully. Atto was one of a number of castrati to emerge from the northern Italian city of Pistoia; three of his seven brothers were castrated, as were two cousins. This was not as radical a decision as it seems to us today, but was viewed by many parents of talented choirboys as a way of giving their sons an opportunity to dedicate their lives to the Church, much like those studying for the priesthood, who also sacrificed a normal family life to serve the Church. Since castrati moved easily within the highest levels of society, Domenico Melani likely viewed castration as a path to success—a way to insure that his children were well educated, made proper social connections, and even attracted patrons.

Atto and his brothers sang in the choir of the Cathedral of San Zeno in Pistoia and, like their counterparts at the Collegio Germanico, studied chant, polyphonic music, and *canto figurato*, and also learned to write counterpoint. Atto's brother Jacopo Melani (1623–1676) had considerable success as a composer in Florence and Rome, as did Alessandro (1639–1703). Atto was a superb singer; he went on to play the title role in Luigi Rossi's *Orfeo* (Paris, 1647) and win the esteem of Louis XIV's mother, Anne of Austria, and the support of Cardinal Mazarin. His talents as a composer are apparent in his 15 extant cantatas. Nonetheless, he spent the latter half of his long life away from music, serving the French court as a diplomat. In his case, his parents' decision to put him on the path to a good musical education and to undergo castration paved the way for upward mobility.

ANGLICAN AND LUTHERAN CHOIRBOYS: JOHN BLOW AND J. S. BACH

English choirboys had a rather different experience as a result of the Civil War and Interregnum (see Chapter 8). When the House of Lords approved the new form of Puritan worship in May 1644, the soldiers quartered in Westminster Abbey smashed the organs, reportedly crying out: "Boyes, we have spoiled your trade; you must go and sing 'Hot pudding pyes'!" Such violence toward musical instruments was not entirely new to the British; when Henry VIII broke from the Catholic Church in the sixteenth century, anti-Catholic sentiment also resulted in the destruction of organs. The sudden need for choirboys and liturgical music in the wake of the Restoration was a boon to the group of talented boys recruited (some forcibly) by Henry Cooke for the reconstituted Chapel Royal choir. The young John Blow (1648/49–1708), who had been an organ scholar in the city of Newark, about 125 miles north of London, was one of these boys.

Cooke was responsible for housing, feeding, and clothing his students, as well as teaching them singing and music theory, often at his own expense. Influenced by the fashions at the court of Charles II, Cooke taught his boys to focus on the violin rather than the viol. Indeed, with fewer services to sing than their Catholic counterparts, English boys had more time for serious study on a variety of instruments, including the violin, which was becoming increasingly popular in Britain. Singing was taught according to the Italian style; indeed, Cooke's students may well have known the English translation of Giulio Caccini's *Le nuove musiche*, published by John Playford.

Encouraged by the king, some of the boys tried their hand at composition. In 1664, John Blow, along with his fellow choirboys William Turner and Pelham Humphrey (Cooke's successor, who trained in France), joined forces to compose "I will always give thanks unto the Lord," subsequently dubbed the "Club Anthem." William Boyce, a composer in the Chapel Royal in the eighteenth century, would later claim that it was "conceived as a memorial of their fraternal esteem and friendship." Humphrey and Turner composed the first and second sections, respectively, while the final section was by Blow.

By the time Blow was in his early twenties, he had obtained appointments as organist at Westminster Abbey and harpsichordist at court. In 1674 he was appointed Master of the Children of the Chapel Royal, in which capacity he had the opportunity to mentor the young Henry Purcell (who is discussed in Chapter 8). Blow expressed his sorrow over the tragic loss of his former pupil at a young age (36) in his *Ode on the Death of Mr Henry Purcell*, published in 1696, the year after Purcell's death, on a text by Purcell's one-time collaborator John Dryden. (Musical odes were often written in honor of specific individuals for special occasions, such as birthdays and funerals.) Scored for two countertenors, a pair of recorders, and continuo, the ode amply demonstrates Blow's contrapuntal skill and his ear for novel sonorities, while the vocal virtuosity invokes the image of no less a musician than Orpheus himself, whom Dryden compares to Purcell.

Lutheran musicians such as Dieterich Buxtehude and Johann Sebastian Bach (whom we will meet again in Chapters 13 and 15, respectively) were taught to regard music as a means of learning about the faith and scripture. As the Lutheran theologian Erasmus Gruber taught in 1673, "the subject and dogma themselves go deeply and more pleasantly into the heart together with the beautiful melodies." Thus, the combination of music and text surpassed what is possible through preaching alone.

Classes in Lutheran Latin schools typically began and ended with the singing of a sacred song, and most instructors had sufficient musical training to provide basic instruction for boys. In Germany, over the course of the seventeenth century, the position of the cantor—which Bach would hold in the city of Leipzig—was increasingly reserved for expert music directors. Cantors chose boys to sing in the elite group known as the *Kantorei*, the members of which earned additional funds by performing for town functions, weddings, and funerals. As cantor and music director at the St. Thomas School in Leipzig, Bach managed to get his regular teaching load reduced so that he could concentrate on the private vocal and instrumental instruction necessary for students to perform his challenging music. (In Leipzig, a strict system of fines for musical errors—whether by accident or mischief—insured that Bach's students toed the line.) All students had seven hours a week of scheduled music classes in addition to their regular studies, and Bach also coached small groups or individuals as necessary.

The darker side of early musical education in Germany (and likely elsewhere) emerges in satirical novels such as those written by Johann Beer (1655–1700). A singer and violinist in Weissenfels (a court in Saxony about 70 miles from Bach's birthplace), Beer was particularly hard on town musicians and cantors, whom he depicted as incompetent or even cruel. One of Beer's fictional cantors, Brutus, is ignorant of both Latin and music, is deaf, and is caught urinating in public while drunk. In another story a cantor beats a talented pupil: "with such a teacher, a boy learns as little of singing as a donkey can play the viola."

Nor are the boys always represented in a complimentary light. A novel by the instrumentalist Daniel Speer entitled *Simplicianischer, lustig-politischer Haspel-Hannss* (The Simplician, Merry and Political Bobbin Jack, 1684) features a hunchback orphan who makes his way in the world as a musician. He succeeds in making money by pretending to be a member of the *Kurrende,* the choirs of poor boys who sang for alms on the streets. Surviving records from Leipzig indicate that it was common for beggars to pretend to be students at the St. Thomas School. Bach, although orphaned at age ten, faced no such ordeal: his fine soprano voice won him a scholarship to St. Michael's Partikularschule, the nonresidential school for commoners, in the city of Lüneberg. Although Bach's economic and social class required him to attend the school for commoner boys, he nonetheless had the opportunity to study with many of the same instructors who taught at St. Michael's Ritterschule (knight's school), the boarding school where the sons of noblemen received their education.

LEARNING TO SING

Most young musicians of the period received daily musical training. As is apparent in the numerous primers and treatises written by seventeenth-century voice teachers and choirmasters, this usually involved a mixture of traditional and new styles of singing. Beginning students learned the monophonic repertory (chants, psalm tones, chorales) and then progressed to polyphony, much like their counterparts in the Renaissance. As late as 1672, Lorenzo Penna's *Li primi albori musicali per li principianti della musica figurata* (Musical Daybreaks for Beginners in Measured Music) discussed the fundamentals of music in many of the same terms that Thomas Morley had in *A Plaine and Easie Introduction to Practicall Musicke* (1597). Penna includes a discussion of the modes, rhythms, and proportions, and teaches the same solmization method (a system of designating notes by sol-fa syllable) put forth by Guido d'Arezzo in the eleventh century.

Penna, like other music teachers and writers throughout the 1600s, provided practical instructions for singing *canto figurato*, which required that students learn the many embellishments not explicitly called for in the notation. In this regard, Caccini's *Le nuove musiche* remained an authoritative text. Caccini provided quite precise instructions on the kinds of expressive liberties that students should and should not take in their singing. In the pairs of excerpts shown in Example 9.1, for instance, he first indicates how a passage was likely to be notated, and then beneath shows an alternate way to render the rhythms (with added trills) that is "more graceful than the first" (SR 100:614; 4/20:106). Indeed, as noted above, Playford's edition of Caccini might have been used by the Chapel Royal boys.

Italian-style ornaments in the manner of Caccini are also included in *Von der Singe-Kunst* (The Art of Singing, 1649) by Christoph Bernhard, who served as choirmaster in Dresden during Heinrich Schütz's tenure (see Chapter 5). Example 9.2, for instance, shows how to realize an ornament known as "antici-pazione della nota" (anticipation of the note), where a note borrows part of the value of the previous one. Example 9.3 shows one of many ways to perform "cercar

Example 9.1: *Giulio Caccini, Preface to* Le nuove musiche *(1614): comparison of non-ornamented and ornamented passages*

Example 9.2: *Christoph Bernhard, example of "anticipazione della nota" from* Von der Singe-Kunst *(1649)*

I will praise the Lord

Example 9.3: *Christoph Bernhard, example of "cercar della nota" from* Von der Singe-Kunst *(1649)*

My heart is ready, O God

della nota" (the searching out of the note), an embellishment that later became known as the "portamento della voce" or the carrying of the voice. Bernhard instructs students to sing the initial note briefly and softly, and then to "glide" to the next note "imperceptibly."

Many treatises hint at the challenges faced by students just learning to sing *canto figurato.* After giving instructions for singing ornaments and producing various vowel sounds, Penna advises pupils to follow the words: "sing happily if the words are happy . . . if they are about grief, pain, and torment, etc., sing mournfully and slowly." Finally, he advises them to go to concerts as often as possible to hear good singers: "if nothing else, you will learn the style, the sweetness, the *accenti*, the graces, etc. of good singing." Penna, like many other authors, also provides an extensive discussion of how to accompany compositions for solo voice, where "the organist must be accurate and ready of hand, eye, and ear as well as of spirit." His practical suggestions for keyboardists include practicing "a lot . . . as much with the right as with the left hand," using a lot of arpeggios so as "not to leave the instrument empty," and going "often to academies and concerts" to observe the techniques of other players (SR 105:639–44; 4/25:131–36; see also Chapter 10).

In discussing pitfalls to be avoided, Bernhard advises the singer not to "raise his voice in connection with the affect of humility or love; nor let it fall several tones when anger is to be shown." In recitative, he continues, "pain makes [the voice] pause; impatience hastens it. Desire emboldens it. Love renders it alert. Bashfulness holds it back. Hope strengthens it. Despair diminishes it. Fear keeps it down. Danger is fled with screams." A singer should not "close his teeth together, nor open his mouth too wide, nor stretch his tongue over his lips, nor thrust his lips upward." He concludes by admonishing the singer not to "disfigure his cheeks and nose like the long-tailed monkey," crumple his brows, roll his eyes, or even wink. Evidently, seventeenth-century children, like those of later eras, found ways to get into trouble.

CONVENTS

While young boys were gaining professional experience in choir schools that prepared many for illustrious musical careers, thousands of young Catholic girls received their basic musical training at convents. Convents played a critical role in managing female sexuality among Catholic women in early modern Europe. In a society in which unmarried women were morally suspect and families could not always afford expensive dowries for all their daughters, many girls were destined to spend some or all of their lives in a convent, regardless of whether they had a true religious vocation.

Although ostensibly forbidden by the Church, forced monachization—sending girls to a convent against their will—was a reality of early modern life. The Venetian nun Arcangela Tarabotti, a published author well known in Venetian literary and operatic circles, decried the fate of young girls who were deceived by their parents and forcibly locked away from the world. Yet many girls had become familiar with cloistered life in convent schools or spent time visiting their aunts or cousins at a convent patronized by their family. For them, as for those with musical talent that would otherwise languish, the decision to enter a convent may have seemed natural and even desirable.

Nuns' musical training and exposure to music were necessarily shaped by the rules concerning *clausura* (absolute separation from the outside world), enforced with new rigor in the aftermath of the Council of Trent (see Chapters 1 and 5). Not all residents of convents were subject to these rules. Many convents had tuition-paying students, some of whom might reside at the convent and learn to sing while studying religious doctrine and domestic skills. Novices, who were essentially nuns in training, could also participate more fully in life outside the walls of the cloister while preparing to become "professed nuns."

However, once a woman went through the elaborate ceremony in which she vowed to live in perpetual chastity, poverty, and obedience, she could not leave the convent for any reason. All visitors, including priests, needed written permission from Church authorities to enter. Visitors spoke with nuns through the iron grating of the *parlatorio* (parlor), as shown in Francesco Guardi's painting of a Venetian convent (Fig. 9.1), and although some convents allowed male musicians to teach nuns through the grating, others had rules strictly forbidding any contact between nuns and male instructors. That is not to say that such rules were always followed; in many instances the regulations were devised in an attempt to control behavior. Indeed, there is ample evidence that friends and family found all kinds of ways to work around the many restrictions on the books, clothing, and food nuns could receive from the outside. Convents usually had a *ruota*, or wheel, in the wall that allowed visitors to pass packages to the nuns; this was often used to smuggle in special treats or forbidden books. (In one instance, a diminutive nun managed to sneak out at night by means of the *ruota*.)

Convent architecture was designed to support this system. Churches were divided into two parts: an internal section in which the nuns sang and an external section where the priests performed the liturgy and the public gathered for the service. The nuns listened to the liturgy through iron gratings, which also permitted the disembodied sounds of their voices to be heard by the many visitors and tourists who flocked to hear them sing. The fact that the women could

Figure 9.1: *Francesco Guardi,* Parlatorio of the San Zaccharia Nunnery *(detail) (1745–50)*

not be seen gave their voices a certain mystique (and explains why nuns were often the objects of romantic fantasies in early modern poetry). More important, this was one of the few opportunities to hear adult women sing sacred music. Their voices were richer and more developed than those of boys and falsettists, and had a different quality than those of castrati. Moreover, since nuns' voices didn't change at adolescence and these closed communities experienced less turnover, convent choirs had the opportunity to build their technique and create a tight ensemble sound over time.

NUN MUSICIANS

Because male music instructors were only rarely allowed to teach nuns, musical knowledge was often passed to young girls through a combination of mentoring and apprenticeship. The Bolognese nun Lucrezia Orsina Vizzana (1590–1662), composer of a printed collection of sacred music entitled *Componimenti musicali de motetti concertati a una e più voci* (Musical Compositions of Concerted Motets for One and More Voices, 1623), likely began her musical education at the age of eight with her aunt Camilla Bombacci, who was organist at Santa Cristina, one of the most musically sophisticated of the Bolognese convents. Lucrezia went on to train one of her own gifted cousins Teresa Pompea Vizzana.

Convents with strong commitments to music might recruit a nun specifically for her musical skills, reducing or even waiving the dowry, the fee paid
by the family when the daughter was married into the Church as a "bride" of
Christ. Some families provided private musical instruction for their young
daughters in the hope of gaining this special sort of scholarship. The investment in musical training seems to have paid off particularly well in Spain,
where a substantial number of nuns earned money by teaching and performing; girls trained in this system thus achieved a professional status that would
have been impossible outside the convent. Outside of Spain, however, compen-
sation was less generous: a group of Sienese nuns who sang complex polyphony
for the Feast of the Nativity of the Virgin in 1663 received only a modest reward
of six watermelons.

One of the most prolific and gifted nun composers of the period was Chiara
Margarita Cozzolani (1602–1676-78). The youngest daughter of a wealthy
Milanese family, she followed the example of an older sister and took her vows
at the Benedictine convent of Santa Radegonda at age eight, adopting Chiara as
her religious name. We know nothing about Cozzolani's education, though the
Milanese convents—and Santa Radegonda in particular—were renowned for
their music in the mid-seventeenth century. Her four volumes of printed music,
published between 1640 and 1650 (of which only three survive), reveal not only
Cozzolani's considerable talent and fine training, but also something of the
uniquely female perspective that nuns brought to prayer and spirituality.

Cozzolani's duet for sopranos, *O quam bonus es* (Oh, how good you are), deals
with the blood of Christ and Mary's milk, two bodily fluids linked to salvation.
Like other mid-seventeenth-century motets, it contains numerous sections,
defined by changes of meter, texture, and vocal style. The passionate nature of
Cozzolani's motet is apparent in her setting of three lines of text: "O how kind
you are, O how sweet, O how delicious, Mary." Over a walking bass that propels
the music forward, the solo vocal line luxuriously expands on the word "O" with
extravagant offbeat melismas, while the mention of the Virgin Mary in measure
34 inspires a brief rush of *stile concitato* (Ex. 9.4). The fervent effect is heightened in the next section (not shown in the example) with a shift to triple meter
and the entrance of a second soprano voice for an imitative duet, once again on
the syllable "O."

How aware were Cozzolani and her colleagues of musical innovations and
events in the outside world? There is ample evidence that, despite the best
efforts of Church authorities, even the sights and sounds of Carnival found their
way into convents. It may well have been the glowing report of a performance
at Bologna's Teatro Formagliari that inspired Christina Cavazza, a young nun
at the convent of Santa Cristina, to sneak out four times to hear the opera. The
consequences of this seemingly minor act of rebellion reverberated through the
walls of two convents for some 30 years, monopolizing the attention of a number of ecclesiastical authorities and even leading to the life imprisonment of the
priest who was her accomplice.

Example 9.4: *Chiara Margarita Cozzolani, "O quam bonus es" from* Concerti sacri *(1642), mm. 28–35*

ORPHANS AND FOUNDLINGS

Convents were not the only option for listeners who wished to hear superb female musicians. Of the numerous tourists who flocked to Venice for the opera and Carnival (Chapter 6), many took the opportunity to hear concerts performed by the girls housed in the four large orphanages, or *ospedali grandi*, charitable organizations overseen by the Venetian Republic. The Ospedale di San Lazzaro Mendicanti took in beggars; those with chronic illnesses went to Gesù Salvatore degli Incurabili; Santa Maria dei Derelitti cared for poor children. Santa Maria della Pietà, famous for its music program, accepted foundlings—unwanted newborn infants, who were left anonymously in a niche on the south wall. The number of children housed by these charitable organizations is astounding. It has been estimated, for instance, that in 1727 alone as many as 500 infants were entrusted to the Pietà. Many died in infancy; those who survived lived with wet nurses who served as foster parents, beginning their education in earnest by the age of nine or ten.

That musical training at the *ospedali* was taken seriously is evident from their impressive roster of teachers and music directors. For Giovanni Legrenzi (1626–1690), known for his operas, instrumental works, and sacred compositions, employment at the *ospedali* was a stepping stone to the most prestigious position in the city of Venice, that of *maestro di cappella* at St. Mark's Basilica, a post held earlier in the century by Gabrieli, Monteverdi, and Cavalli. The opera composer Francesco Gasparini (1661–1727), who became *maestro di coro* (chorus master) at the Pietà in 1701, had the good sense to hire no less a musician than Antonio Vivaldi as violinist in 1703. Despite trips as far away as Vienna, Vivaldi—about whom we'll learn more below—would remain associated with the Pietà for the rest of his life.

As in convents, girls and women in the *ospedali* often took responsibility for teaching one another. Only those girls designated as *figlie di coro* (girls of the chorus) served in a musical capacity; the *figlie di comun* (common girls) concentrated on needlework and other feminine occupations. The most talented of the *figlie di coro* performed vocal or instrumental solos; they also had the opportunity to rise within the ranks and be appointed one of the 20 *maestre di coro*. A *figlia privilegiata* (privileged girl) had the honor of serving as tutor to the *figlie in educazione*, the daughters of nobles or Venetian citizens who boarded at the *ospedali* to receive a musical education. Some women asked for and received permission to marry, though the vast majority remained at the *ospedali* for their entire lives.

Since these women were known only by their first names and the instruments on which they excelled, archival records only hint at the lives they led: their rewards and occasional punishments, their versatility, and the trajectory of their often remarkably long careers. (Their longevity may well have been a result of having good nutrition and not being subjected to the dangers of childbearing.) One of the most famous musicians at the Pietà was Anna Maria (1696–1782), who was known for her skills not only on the violin but also on the viola d'amore, cello, lute, theorbo, mandolin, and harpsichord. Despite her exceptional talent, however, we know little more about her life than that she was allowed a special chicken diet in January 1728, awarded extra measures of oil weekly in October 1729, and elected *maestra di coro* at the age of 41.

The performances at the *ospedali* on Sundays and feast days, in which the women (who played behind a screen) were heard but not seen, captivated Venetians and travelers alike. In 1730, the Englishman Edward Wright found the singers' performance "still more amusing, in that their Persons are concealed from view" behind a "Lattice of Ironwork." Jean-Jacques Rousseau was both intrigued by the practice and "riled by the cursed screens which allowed only the sounds to pass and hid me from those angels whose beauty was equal to their voices." One peculiarity of the female choirs at the Pietà—and also in many convents—was that the bass and tenor parts were either sung at pitch by women with low voices or transposed up an octave. After hearing the women at the Pietà sing Latin psalms, the German theorist and composer Johann Mattheson was particularly disconcerted to hear an alto sing the bass part, thus creating the parallel octaves that had so long been forbidden by the rules of counterpoint.

VIVALDI'S CONCERTOS AND ORATORIOS

Among the many talented girls and women at the Venetian ospedali, the Pietà boasted the most accomplished instrumentalists, who displayed their skills in the numerous concertos for one or more solo instruments written by Antonio Vivaldi (1678–1741) that were widely disseminated in print and manuscript throughout Europe. We can only speculate as to whether the talented instrumentalists at the Pietà deserve credit for Vivaldi's innovative approach to the concerto, or if they were merely the beneficiaries of his enormous creativity. Nonetheless, Vivaldi's concertos were an ideal way to show off the individual talents of the women and the quality of the ensemble playing. Thus, it is not surprising that Anna Maria was a featured soloist in Vivaldi's Concerto for Viola d'amore and Lute, RV 540, which was performed at the Pietà in honor of the visit of Friedrich Christian, the crown prince of Saxony-Poland, on March 21, 1740 (see Anthology 15).

This concerto, like many others, demonstrates one of Vivaldi's most notable contributions to the genre: the standardization of the outer movements of the three-movement Baroque concerto into what is usually referred to as ritornello form. Adopted by countless Baroque composers in arias and instrumental works, ritornello form is built around an orchestral ritornello, or refrain. The ritornello, heard in its entirety at the beginning and end of the movement, firmly establishes the home key; sections of it are repeated internally, often confirming the modulation to a new key area. These ritornelli are the structural pillars that unify the movement, linking (and contrasting with) the intervening episodes played by one or more soloists. Although this might sound formulaic, in practice the manner of constructing a movement or aria allowed for enormous dramatic tensions. The ways of constructing a ritornello and contrasting this with the virtuosity or timbral variety of solo instruments are endless.

Vivaldi's concertos also show his penchant for playing with novel sonorities and exploiting the idiomatic capabilities of the instruments. Some of his most remarkable effects are achieved in the (usually slower) middle movements, which are typically not in ritornello form. In the second movement of RV 540, for example, the entire continuo group (cellos, basses, and harpsichord) drops out and its role is taken over by the least likely members of the ensemble, the violins, accompanied by arpeggiated chords in the lute. Meanwhile, the viola d'amore takes the lead with its ornate melodic line. The result is a buoyant, shimmering texture, unfettered by the conventional grounding of the continuo in the bass register (Ex. 9.5). Occasionally Vivaldi's sound effects have extramusical implications. In the set of concertos titled *Le quattro staggioni* (The Four Seasons), his most famous and frequently performed works, Vivaldi uses ordinary violins to mimic the chattering of teeth during a Venetian winter and the singing of birds in summertime.

Perhaps the most telling evidence of the musical prowess of the female performers and the esteem in which they were held can be gleaned from the numerous oratorios featuring biblical heroines that were written specifically for the Pietà and the other ospedali. Vivaldi's *Juditha triumphans* (Judith Triumphant), a "military oratorio" performed at the Pietà in March 1716, was composed when Venetian anxiety about the Turkish siege of Corfu was at its height. The biblical tale—which inspired a number of oratorios and paintings—concerns the chaste Jewish widow

Example 9.5: *Antonio Vivaldi, Concerto for Viola d'amore and Lute in D Minor, RV 540 (1740), Largo, mm. 1–3*

Judith, who fends off the amorous advances of her enemy, the Assyrian general Holofernes, plying him with drink and ultimately beheading him, as depicted with such violence in the painting by Artemisia Gentileschi. (Fig. 9.2). To celebrate the triumph of this remarkable heroine, whose power was seen as analogous to Venice's own, Vivaldi exploited the full orchestral resources of the Pietà by scoring the work for a large and colorful orchestra: in addition to full complement of strings and continuo, Vivaldi included two recorders, two oboes, soprano chalumeau (a high reed instrument, similar to a clarinet), two clarinets, two trumpets, timpani, mandolin, four theorbos, five viole da gamba, and a viola d'amore. The brilliant arias he composed for Judith employ warlike flourishes and fierce coloratura usually reserved for the heroic castrati on the operatic stage.

NEAPOLITAN CONSERVATORIES

Venice was not the only city to transform a charitable civic institution into a music school. As John Rice discusses in *Music in the Eighteenth Century*, the four major orphanages in Naples also provided high-quality and intensive musical training to orphaned, illegitimate, and abandoned children, ultimately accepting tuition-paying students as well. In fact, the term *conservatory*, still used to describe schools that focus exclusively on musical training, is derived from the "conserved" orphans and foundlings in Naples.

In addition to what must have been superb instruction on voice and instruments, Neapolitan students benefited from a unique pedagogical system for the teaching of composition based on *partimenti*. These were bass lines that could be realized at the keyboard, supplying students with a ready vocabulary of musical

Figure 9.2: *Artemisia Gentileschi,* Judith and Holofernes *(1612–21)*

gestures and typical voice-leading patterns that were literally at their fingertips. Boasting some of the most distinguished *maestri di cappella* of the period, such as Franz Joseph Haydn's teacher Nicola Porpora (1686–1768), the Neapolitan conservatories produced a host of accomplished singers, players, and composers, who worked both in the city's many musical institutions and throughout Europe.

———

There is perhaps no better way to grasp the importance that music had in daily life in the seventeenth and eighteenth centuries than to consider the enormous resources and efforts that were dedicated to developing musical skills in girls and boys, including those from the lowest levels of society. For many, music would remain an avocation; but for others, musical skills provided sustenance and shelter, the hope of financial stability, a path to a lucrative career, an opportunity to travel, and even access to the highest echelons of power in the major courts of Europe. Audiences, too, reaped the benefits of music education, for, as we will see in Chapter 10, these talented and well-trained students would satisfy a growing public who eagerly sought new opportunities to hear and play music.

FOR FURTHER READING

Freitas, Roger, *Portrait of a Castrato: Politics, Patronage, and Music in the Life of Atto Melani* (Cambridge: Cambridge University Press, 2009)

Kendrick, Robert, *Nuns and Their Music in Early Modern Milan* (Oxford and New York: Oxford University Press, 1996)

Monson, Craig, *Nuns Behaving Badly: Tales of Magic, Art, and Arson in the Convents of Italy* (Chicago: University of Chicago Press, 2010)

Mould, Alan, *The English Chorister: A History* (London and New York: Hambledon Continuum, 2007)

O'Regan, Noel, "Choirboys in Early Modern Rome," in Susan Boynton and Eric Rice, eds., *Young Choristers, 650–1750* (Woodbridge, UK: Boydell Press, 2008)

Reardon, Colleen, "*Cantando tutte insieme*: Training Girl Singers in Early Modern Sienese Convents," in Susan Boynton and Eric Rice, eds., *Young Choristers, 650–1750* (Woodbridge, UK: Boydell Press, 2008)

Rosand, Ellen, "Vivaldi's Stage," *Journal of Musicology* 18 (2001): 8–30

Rose, Stephen, *The Musician in Literature in the Age of Bach* (Cambridge: Cambridge University Press, 2011)

Talbot, Michael, "Sacred Music at the Ospedale della Pietà in Venice in the Time of Handel," *Händel Jahrbuch* 24 (2002): 125–56

CHAPTER TEN

Academies, Salons, and Music Societies

Some of the most adventurous and sophisticated music was heard outside of the traditional court and ecclesiastical patronage systems, in the numerous academies, salons, and musical clubs that flourished in early modern Europe. These associations, such as the Florentine Camerata considered in Chapter 2, attracted musicians and music lovers, amateurs and professionals, who spent leisure time performing, listening to, and discussing music. For some associations, music was an ancillary activity, supplementing poetry readings, debates, philosophical discussions, and conversation. Others focused almost entirely on music, providing participants with professional support, an arena in which to explore compositional techniques and aesthetics, and opportunities for public performance.

Although many such organizations were established by and for men, during this period women became increasingly active in these groups both as patrons and performers. While earlier female patrons such as Isabella d'Este of Ferrara (discussed by Richard Freedman in *Music in the Renaissance*) had cultivated music in the courts, in the seventeenth and eighteenth centuries an increasing number of women took on active roles in organizations that produced music. Some women capitalized on their high social standing, transforming the conventional role of the hostess into that of patron and supporting musicians both artistically and financially. In other instances, female musicians (usually singers) used their talent to infiltrate masculine musical circles. In so doing, they often put themselves in the vulnerable position of being admired for their talent and beauty and condemned for the danger of their sexual appeal.

In this chapter we explore several organizations in which men and women established spaces for collaborative and creative music-making. While such associations may have comprised only a portion of a professional musician's activities, they had an enormous impact not only on the careers of performers and composers but also on musical culture in general. As such, they were central to the shift in audience demographics and the economics of the musical marketplace that ultimately led to the development of the public concert in the eighteenth century.

SINGING AT THE ITALIAN ACADEMIES

The numerous academies devoted to science, literature, art, and music that gained popularity in the sixteenth and seventeenth centuries were, for the most part, masculine preserves. The Accademia degli Invaghiti in Mantua (which sponsored Monteverdi's *L'Orfeo*) and the Incogniti in Venice (which contributed to the development of public opera), along with other extravagantly named groups such as the Gelati (Frozen Ones) in Bologna, primarily served the intellectual and social needs of men, rarely according women the same rights and privileges. The rules for the Accademia Filarmonica in Verona (not to be confused with the one in Bologna discussed later), founded in 1548 for the performance of music, stipulated that male guests could be brought in without restriction; women, however, needed the approval of the membership to enter. Any member who invited a gentlewoman without permission was fined accordingly; expulsion was the punishment for introducing a woman of ill repute.

THE VOICE OF BARBARA STROZZI

When the Venetian Accademia degli Unisoni (Sonorous Ones), a subgroup of the Republic's renowned Accademia degli Incogniti, welcomed the singer and composer Barbara Strozzi (1619–1677) into their meetings, they may well have sought both to explore intersections between music and poetry and to revel in her beauty and talent in an intimate setting. Strozzi was the adopted (and perhaps illegitimate) daughter of the poet and librettist Giulio Strozzi. The author of eight volumes of printed music, Barbara was also renowned for her singing, though she never appeared on the Venetian operatic stage. She was evidently an object of desire among Giulio's friends and colleagues involved in the Venetian opera industry (one of them likely fathered three of her four children). Archival records show that Strozzi enjoyed financial independence, lending money to several prominent Venetians, and counted the duke of Mantua among her admirers. Some historians hypothesize that she could have been a *cortigiana onesta* (honest courtesan), the term used to describe well-educated, intellectual, and talented women who included sex among their many services. Her portrait by Bernardo Strozzi (no relation), in which the composer is pictured with an open songbook by her side, holding a viol and with one breast exposed, has been interpreted by some as evidence that she might have sold her sexual favors (Fig. 10.1).

We have two contradictory accounts of Strozzi's appearances at the meetings of the Unisoni: a printed volume of discourses dedicated to the composer presents her in a highly complimentary light, while a satirical description in a manuscript, probably intended for an intimate circle, playfully criticizes her lack of chastity. We learn from these writings that Strozzi not only sang—"stealing the souls of the listeners through their ears with sweetness"—but also served as the mistress of ceremonies, participating fully in the conversations. These were not concerts in any conventional sense but rather collaborative enterprises, in which Strozzi's performances were interspersed with debates, poetry readings, and academic discourses, many of which focused on love, desire, and female sexuality—as did her own cantatas and arias. Occasionally the poems she set adopt a female point of view, but the majority present decidedly masculine notions about women's desirability, their unwillingness to love, or their lack of veracity, as in the

Figure 10.1: *Bernardo Strozzi,*
The Singer Barbara Strozzi
with a Viola da Gamba
(ca. 1640)

humorous duet for soprano and bass entitled "Donna non sa che dice, non dice che sa" (A woman doesn't know what she says and doesn't say what she knows).

An intriguing aspect of Strozzi's music is the fact that many of the poems she set condemned female beauty as dangerous, while she herself was so renowned for the seductive nature of her performances, in which her own voice and body gave credence to the poets' ambivalence toward female sexuality. To what extent did Strozzi's musical choices in her compositions confirm or contradict the anti-female tone of the poetry? A close look at her compositions shows that she brilliantly captured the essence of the poetry written by her male colleagues, while interjecting her own female perspective. This is particularly evident in some of her longer works, in which a sudden change in affect—accomplished through alterations in tempo, meter, or harmonic rhythm—undermines or even contradicts the point of view expressed by the poet.

One of Strozzi's favorite devices is the use of long, melismatic, wordless vocalises. As the listeners lose themselves in the pure sound of the voice, the implicit anti-female discourse often seems to evaporate. In the aria "Ardo in tacito foco" (I burn in silent fire), from Strozzi's *Cantate, ariette, a una, due, e tre voce, opera terza* (Cantatas, Ariettas, for One, Two, and Three Voices, Opus 3, 1654), the poet laments his inability to express his passion to his beloved (Ex. 10.1). The poet may be tongue-tied at the outset, but the two melismas on the word "ardo" burst forth like tiny sparks, which are then briefly extinguished with a return to sustained Ds in measures 5–6. There is a sense of resignation with the descending quarter-note bass and the addition of B♭ in measure 5; yet the fire erupts again in measures 7–8 on the word "foco," as the phrase comes to rest momentarily on a Phrygian cadence (a half cadence in which the bass descends by half step). Thus, the extravagant singing by Strozzi—herself an object of desire in this academic setting—paradoxically illustrates the poet's inability to even utter the name of his beloved. Later in the same work, when Strozzi's vocal line bursts

Example 10.1: *Barbara Strozzi, "Ardo in tacito foco" from* Cantate, ariette, *Op. 3 (1654), mm. 1–9*

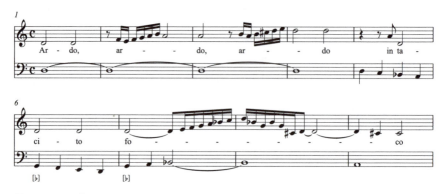

I burn in silent fire

forth in a joyful, dancelike triple meter, all the while singing of the poet's failure to express his emotions, it is hard not to suspect that she is gently mocking his pain.

Despite the often harsh misogynistic rhetoric associated with the Unisoni and their colleagues in the Accademia degli Incogniti, the playful nature of Strozzi's musical settings and the humor that she so often displays make it unlikely that she was an unwilling participant in the jokes and games about female sexuality. For instance, the duet "Begli occhi" (Beautiful eyes), with a text by Incogniti founder Giovanni Francesco Loredano, employs the familiar poetic conceit of eyes so beautiful that they wound and kill the lover (see Anthology 16). The concluding passage features an extensive melismatic section on the first syllable of the word "aspetta" (wait) that leaves little doubt as to the kind of death (sexual release) anticipated by the lovers. What is particularly striking about Strozzi's setting, however, is the vivacious exchange between the two soprano voices: they begin in parallel thirds, then break away from each other as the first voice and then the second initiate sixteenth-note flourishes, finally joining together in thirds for the conclusion. In this instance, Strozzi seems to imply that the male and female partners could share sexual pleasure equally.

Strozzi's *Sacri musicali affetti* (Sacred Musical Passions, 1655), dedicated to Anne of Austria, the archduchess of Innsbruck, including such works as "Mater Anna" (Mother Anna) and "O Maria," provides us with a glimpse into another side of Strozzi's character: her intense spirituality and devotion to the Virgin as a model for her own motherhood. Thus, while we may never know whether Strozzi was actually a courtesan, her music provides ample evidence that she was a complex woman and a gifted composer, whose image is inevitably obscured by the ambivalence toward women that was integral to seventeenth-century life.

TO INSTRUCT AND DELIGHT:

SINGERS IN THE ROMAN ACADEMIES

In Rome, singers were welcomed into the formal and informal academies sponsored by the city's many nobles and cardinals, including not only those with Roman roots but also foreign dignitaries (from the Italian peninsula and elsewhere) who were part of the papacy's diplomatic court. Among the singers were accomplished choirboys such as the young Giovanni Sances and celebrated Roman castrati such as Atto Melani (see Chapter 9) and Marc'Antonio Pasqualini (1614–1691), who sang in the papal choir.

Women, too, sang in Rome, albeit only in private, owing to ecclesiastical prohibitions. As we recall from Chapter 2, Adriana Basile and her daughter Leonora Baroni sang at the households of connoisseurs such as Vincenzo Giustiniani. Like Barbara Strozzi, Basile and the renowned Francesca Caccini (see Chapter 3) both sang for the Roman Accademia degli Umoristi (Academy of the Humorous Ones), the most important of the literary academies to flourish under the patronage of Pope Urban VIII and his cardinal nephews. Female singers had careers that necessarily differed from those of their male colleagues. They did not sing in the city's churches, nor could they perform in the large—or even small-scale operas presented in many of the noble homes. However, women were not only highly prized in Rome for their vocal ability, but must have been the beneficiaries of superb training, since so many of the singers who established opera careers elsewhere, such as Anna Renzi (see Chapter 6), trained in Rome.

A lighthearted dialogue penned by Grazioso Uberti, a lawyer to the papal Curia (court) in Rome, captures the ambivalence with which women singers were regarded. A character named Severo (which means strict) argues that singing has the unfortunate effect of exposing a woman to "admiring gazes, to the desire of each person." Severo's companion Giocondo (smiling or cheerful) defends female music-making. "If a woman be tired of sewing, of spinning, of household duties, what can she do for a little recreation?" He extols the pleasure to be had when "a young hand touches the harpsichord, imitating the garrulous bird with melodious voice." In response to Severo's claim that "singing is not appropriate to the female sex," Giocondo argues that the Muses are not male, that many believe this is the derivation of the word *music*, and that even Harmony is a woman. The problem, Giocondo notes, is not that men shouldn't hear women sing, but rather that they shouldn't give in to their base desires (SR 96:594–95; 4/16: 86–87).

The best evidence that we have about academy performances in Rome is from the extant music—the hundreds of cantatas on devotional and secular themes by composers that survive primarily in manuscript. In a cantata by the gifted castrato Marc'Antonio Pasqualini, for instance, a chromatic descending bass underpins a recitative-like passage (Ex. 10.2, mm. 1–6). The half cadence on an E-major sonority at the conclusion of the example, however, is delayed in a remarkable fashion: the voice first lands on high E, an unprepared dissonance, and then cascades down the scale in a flourish, landing on a low D♯ marked with a trill (mm. 5–6). Since the F in the bass resolves by moving down a half step and the D♯ by moving up a half step, what Pasqualini has given us is a surprisingly modern augmented-sixth chord (for another example see mm. 20–21 of Anthology 12 for the words "o crudele"). The cantata includes many other musical details that would have been especially appreciated by experienced listeners, such as a skillful modulation from A minor to the distant key of B minor, and a challenging melodic skip of a major tenth. For elite patrons, presenting performances of such sophisticated works in their homes by admired singers was akin to showing off their precious collections of antiquities and artworks or serving exotic food and drink.

Apart from musical sources, an additional clue to the esteem in which Pasqualini was held is apparent in a painting by the Roman artist Andrea Sacchi: *Marcantonio Pasqualini (1614–1691) Crowned by Apollo* (Fig. 10.2). The castrato, playing an ornate keyboard instrument called the clavicytherium, is crowned with a laurel wreath by Apollo, while the satyr Marsyas looks on with envy,

Example 10.2: *Marc'Antonio Pasqualini, "Non temo di morte, m'impiaghi, m'uccida,"*
mm. 1–6

I adore the threats, I idolize the hand that stretches the bow

Figure 10.2: *Andrea Sacchi,* Marcantonio Pasqualini (1614–1691) Crowned by Apollo *(1641)*

his bagpipes by his side. The mythological allusions here are somewhat enigmatic. Sacchi makes reference to the musical contest between these two ancient antagonists, in which Apollo, having triumphed over the pipe-playing Marsyas, skins his audacious opponent alive. Does Marsyas, as some commentators have suggested, refer to Pasqualini's castrated body, which differs from the perfection of the naked Apollo? Or are we to see Pasqualini, draped in leopard skins, as the new Apollo, who easily conquers his opponents as both singer and composer? Regardless, the subtle nature of the images in the painting reflects the deep appreciation that Pasqualini's listeners had for his considerable skills, and the respect accorded him and other castrati.

WOMEN PATRONS: THE SALONS

For men and women in seventeenth- and eighteenth-century France who wanted to discuss poetry and literature, have witty conversation, and enjoy a bit of music away from the politics, discipline, and hierarchies of court, salons provided an ideal escape. Salons were sponsored primarily by intellectually inclined women who were known as *les précieuses* (precious ones), a term adopted in mid-seventeenth-century France to describe the women who participated in the Parisian salons, particularly those known for their intellectual pursuits (or pretensions, in the eyes of their critics) and proto-feminist beliefs. Many *précieuses* were highly accomplished and widely admired; however, a somewhat derogatory connotation of the word arose from the widespread perception that "truly refined women have led others into ridiculous attitudes of affected refinement."

The character of French salon culture was established during the reign of Louis XIII by the Italian-born Catherine de Vivonne (1588–1665), the marquise de Rambouillet, who beginning in 1607 welcomed guests to the "chambre bleue" (blue room) in her Paris residence. The Saturday afternoon salons initiated in 1653 by the writer Madeleine de Scudéry (1607–1701) at her house in the Marais district also attracted a number of musicians. The fad for sponsoring music in the home at times became associated with pretentious and snobbish individuals who aspired to be noble; the Music Master in Act 2, scene 1 of Molière's *Le bourgeois gentilhomme* (1670), which we considered in Chapter 7, tells M. Jourdain that it is not enough to have guests for dinner: "a person like you, a lavish host with a leaning toward finer things, should give a concert at home every Wednesday or Thursday."

The art of conversation was at the core of salon culture; politeness and civility mattered above all in an environment where every gesture and social interaction was carefully choreographed. To be considered one of the *honnêtes gens*—a person of good breeding and excellent taste—was a high honor, and could be achieved through the thoughtful appreciation of the best literature, music, and art. Among the musicians who frequented Scudéry's salon were the composer Michel Lambert and his sister-in-law Hilaire Dupuy, and Lully's collaborator

Philippe Quinault. Salons did not just provide entertainment for musical amateurs; since they gave aspiring musicians regular exposure to noble consumers
of music, they were essential for establishing and maintaining one's reputation
as a teacher or performer. They also provided an opportunity for opera enthusiasts to enjoy their favorite airs and dances outside of the theater, as attested to
by the numerous arrangements of excerpts from *tragédies en musique* and *opéras-
ballets* for solo harpsichord or small ensembles that were copied into manuscripts or published throughout the late seventeenth and eighteenth centuries.

Within this rarefied realm, French *airs sérieux*, such as Lambert's "Par mes
chants" (see Chapter 7), published in large numbers in anthologies in the second
half of the century, were particularly well suited to accompany the ubiquitous conversations about love, desire, seduction, and the benefits or liabilities of marriage,
while allowing singers to retain the *politesse* (politeness) so valued in the salon.
Conversely, the inordinately popular *airs à boire*, or drinking songs, often focused
on comic or satirical topics, providing a different sort of listening experience.
As Scudéry discussed in her popular *Conversations morales* (Moral Conversations,
1686), salon participants might present one or more airs as part of a debate, thus
providing an eloquent means of offering opposing perspectives on a given topic.
Scudéry and her colleagues emphasized the collaborative aspect of song composition, and she described instances in which one participant might write the poetry,
another set it to music, and still others, take on the task of singing and playing.
Performing thus was part of a broad social experience where tastes were determined not by the monarch, but rather by a community with shared aesthetic values.

Molière parodied women like Scudéry and their penchant for songs in his
one-act play *Les précieuses ridicules* (The Ridiculous Précieuses, 1659), inventing
a character who boasts that he has created hundreds of songs and over a thousand madrigals, which he has sung in all the most fashionable homes in Paris
and from which he is crafting an entire history of Rome. While Molière's satire
may have captured some of the pretensions of salon enthusiasts, the social gatherings hosted by Scudéry and other salon leaders nonetheless nurtured many of
the stylistic innovations that shaped French music in the eighteenth century.

SALON CULTURE BEYOND FRANCE

French salons established a model for artistic and intellectual communities
that was adopted and emulated by women elsewhere in Europe. In Rome, Maria
Mancini, the niece of Cardinal Mazarin, was one of a number of noblewomen
who sponsored musical entertainments (operas, oratorios, serenades, and cantatas) and gatherings known as *conversazioni* (conversations). After her marriage
to Lorenzo Onofrio Colonna, a nobleman from a distinguished Roman family,
Mancini sought to recapture the freedom and pleasures that she had enjoyed at
the French court (as the youthful lover of Louis XIV) and in the Parisian salons.
Her enthusiasm for musical theater and public entertainments (which included

her personal appearance on a parade float dressed as the enchantress Circe and surrounded by young men) certainly pushed the boundaries of acceptable behavior for women in Rome. Yet Mancini and her colleagues succeeded in creating a forum in which women could exchange ideas with one another, cultivate social networks, and exercise their power and creativity as patrons.

While Mancini was criticized for her "French habits" and improprieties, no such condemnations were directed at another important woman who organized academies and patronized music in Rome: Queen Christina of Sweden (1626–1689). The artistically and intellectually gifted queen had endeared herself to Catholic Europe (and the papacy in particular) by abdicating her throne and converting from Lutheranism to Catholicism. Upon her arrival in Rome in 1655, she was welcomed by Pope Alexander VII amid much splendor—as if she were still queen—at a grand festival presented at the Palazzo Barberini (Fig. 10.3).

Christina eschewed the seductive, distinctly feminine approach to clothing and entertainment that were part of Mancini's French legacy, opting instead to ingratiate herself to cardinals and high-ranking Church officials by assuming a somewhat masculine persona, even in her dress. She quickly became a magnet for Rome's cultural elite, gaining access to ecclesiastical circles that were closed to other women. She sponsored public and private performances, and established academies for which she sought out the best young musicians in the city, such as Alessandro Scarlatti and Arcangelo Corelli. As we will see in Chapter 11, Christina's influence would continue well into the eighteenth century,

Figure 10.3: *Filippo Lauri and F. Gagliari,* Festival at the Palazzo Barberini in Honor of Christina of Sweden *(ca. 1656)*

manifest, after her death, in the founding of the Accademia degli Arcadi (Arcadian Academy) by her devoted followers.

The influence of the French salons was also felt in eighteenth-century Germany, where many intellectuals felt that French culture provided the path to enlightenment. In Leipzig, for example, Christiane Mariane von Ziegler, a poet who would write a number of librettos for Bach's cantatas, held a regular salon in the 1720s and 1730s that included food, drink, literary games, and concerts. Ziegler was an accomplished amateur musician, and it is likely that Bach attended these gatherings after he became cantor at St. Thomas's Church in 1723 (see Chapter 15).

PROFESSIONALISM: THE ACCADEMIA FILARMONICA OF BOLOGNA

The Accademia Filarmonica of Bologna (which literally means "sons of harmony") is perhaps the most important of the academies established specifically to support and promote professional musicians. Founded on May 26, 1666 in the home of the nobleman Vincenzo Maria Carrati, the Filarmonica—which still survives today—boasted a charter membership that included 50 of the city's most distinguished musicians.

Bologna enjoyed a vibrant musical life. Although the city was nominally ruled by the pope (through his representative, a cardinal legate), much of the power was exercised by the Senate, made up of Bolognese nobles who, like their counterparts elsewhere, had occasion to support musicians. Bologna's two central musical institutions likewise had venerable traditions. The Concerto Palatino, a wind band whose roots go back at least to the twelfth century, supplied the ceremonial music for civic festivities, including the Festa della Porchetta (Festival of the Suckling Pig), a Carnival-like celebration held in August. The music, dance, and games culminated in the throwing of a roast pig off the balcony of the Palazzo Maggiore.

The extensive musical establishment maintained by Bologna's central church, San Petronio, was expanded and improved after the election in 1656 of Maurizio Cazzati as *maestro di cappella*, although he would be dismissed in 1671 after being embroiled in a dispute over the presumed faults in one of his masses (echoing the controversy between Monteverdi and Artusi described in Chapter 2). By the mid-1650s, the Bolognese were supporting two public opera theaters. The city's numerous ecclesiastical institutions, including the convent that we considered in Chapter 9, likewise employed many musicians. Moreover, musical life in Bologna had been enriched by the existence of a university since the eleventh century, which nurtured intellectual exchange and created a cosmopolitan atmosphere.

The Filarmonica was founded both to promote its members' welfare and to establish standards for musical composition in the city, as reflected in its motto "Unitate melos" (From unity comes song). The annual dues paid by members went into a fund that was used for their funeral services, eventually offering support to the families of impoverished or deceased members. A governing board oversaw the academy's operations and maintained standards. All members had to go through a trial period before they were officially accepted. Except during Carnival, when the musicians were often otherwise occupied, members devoted two evenings a week to sharing their composition exercises, which were performed, discussed, and analyzed in a weekly *conferenza*. The statutes also stipulated that members treat one other with respect, be virtuous, and display good habits. Lest we imagine that the Filarmonica was all serious business, meetings were also pleasurable social occasions where good food, pastries, and wine were served.

CHAMBER AND CHURCH SONATAS

Bolognese composers in the Filarmonica benefited from and were strongly influenced by the nature of their city's musical culture, which offered opportunities for compositional experimentation and led to the formation of a definitive set of musical stylistic standards. The breadth of their accomplishments is particularly evident in the enormous amount of music for small instrumental ensembles and continuo published by Bolognese printers in the second half of the seventeenth century, usually referred to as sonatas. These included works for various solo instruments and continuo, as well as those in the popular trio sonata format (*sonate a 3*), featuring two treble instruments and continuo. (Trio sonatas that featured a bass line that was independent from the continuo were designated *sonate a 4*.)

Sonatas can be further differentiated by their style and, to some degree, their function. Not surprisingly, Bolognese composers—like their colleagues in other cities—wrote a great deal of chamber music that was used for actual dancing in private homes, colleges, or the theater. Other works, such as the Corrente by Giovanni Maria Bononcini (1642–1678), were dances for the "ears rather than the feet" (Ex. 10.3). Bononcini captures the essence of the lively corrente, but it nonetheless would have been very awkward to dance. Not only is the texture contrapuntal, but the asymmetry of the opening two phrases (made up of four plus three measures) are highlighted by Bononcini's use of hemiola. While measure 1 is in a straightforward $\frac{3}{4}$ meter, measures 2 and 3 comprise one large $\frac{3}{2}$ measure, as do measures 5 and 6. Compositions that were either used for or influenced by dance were frequently labeled *sonate da camera* (chamber sonatas).

A substantial body of chamber works show a preference for fantasia style over dance. The opening movement of the Sonata Op. 1, No. 12 by Tomaso Antonio Vitali (1673–1745) begins with a highly expressive duet between the two violins over a sustained G-minor sonority (Ex. 10.4). Note, for instance, the tension on the downbeat of the second measure, as the violins play an F♯ and C against the G in the bass. After the thirty-second-note flourish in measure 3, release comes in the form of an imitative Allegro.

Example 10.3: *Giovanni Maria Bononcini, Corrente No. 4 from* Primi frutti del giardino musicale, *Op. 1 (1666), mm. 1–7*

Example 10.4: *Tomaso Antonio Vitali, Sonata Op. 1, No. 12 (1693), mm. 1–4*

These more abstract, serious works were sometimes labeled *sonate da chiesa* (church sonatas), since many featured *stile antico* polyphony and thus were sufficiently solemn to be suitable for use as part of the liturgy. They were also played at academy meetings and civic ceremonies, and in the homes of musicians. Some collections reveal a close connection to liturgical practices, since they were published in the order of the so-called church keys (*tuoni ecclesiastici*), tonalities similar to modes that had developed primarily in association with the (usually monophonic) chanting of the psalm tones. Thus, for instance, the sonatas in Bononcini's *Sonate da chiesa*, Op. 6 (1672) could easily be inserted into the service and linked smoothly to the singing of the psalms. Compositions simply labeled "sonata," with no other indication, often exemplified the "church style."

Bolognese composers also experimented with ensembles that featured two contrasting groups of instruments. Some scholars have suggested that these concerto-like works might have been inspired by the architecture of San Petronio, where two organs faced one another and musicians played from separate balconies. Giuseppe Torelli (1658–1709), who began and finished his career as a member of the Filarmonica, wrote a number of works featuring contrasts between one or more soloists (often known as the *concertino* group and sometimes marked *solo* or *soli*) and the orchestra (known as the *ripieno* and often marked *tutti*). These works were variously labeled concerto, sinfonia, or sonata, but were essentially prototypes of the baroque instrumental concerto. Among Torelli's most novel works are his concertos for trumpet, an instrument that was particularly well suited to the unusually live acoustics of San Petronio. What is perhaps most surprising is the extent to which the types of musical motives used in trumpet concertos—fanfares, scales, and arpeggios (associated with the trumpet's role on the battlefield)—would become part of the conventional musical language of Baroque string playing, particularly in the ritornelli in concertos by Vivaldi and Corelli (see Chapters 9 and 11).

MUSICAL ENTREPRENEURS AND THE RISE OF PUBLIC CONCERTS

On December 30, 1672, the *London Gazette* printed an advertisement for a series of concerts with "music performed by excellent masters" to be presented each day at 4 p.m. at the home of the composer and violinist John Banister (see SR 94:587; 4/14:79). Such notices, which would soon appear regularly in London newspapers, show the fundamental changes in the production and consumption of music that occurred in the late seventeenth and eighteenth centuries.

Although London may have been somewhat ahead of the curve in the commercialization of the arts, similar shifts were happening elsewhere. Music societies and clubs sponsored concerts in spaces accessible to a broad segment of the population: pleasure gardens, taverns, shops, and particularly coffeehouses, where the newly popular caffeinated beverage readied patrons for artistic and intellectual stimulation. The control of music that had long been almost exclusively in the hands of noble or ecclesiastical authorities was now shared by enthusiasts and entrepreneurs who produced music for a diverse audience, including a thriving merchant middle class that would give rise to some of the most important consumers of music in the eighteenth century.

Some of these concert series were commercial ventures, launched by investors or performers in the hope of making money, while others functioned as nonprofit organizations. One of the earliest English musical entrepreneurs was the small coal merchant Thomas Britton. His popular concerts, which began in 1678 were later criticized by the eighteenth-century music historian Sir John Hawkins for having been presented in circumstances that "tended rather to degrade than recommend such an entertainment," since the out-of-the-way location was "unfit for the resort of persons of fashion." In fact, however, Britton's "music meetings" were enthusiastically attended by listeners of all classes.

Some public concert series sought to compensate for the relative cultural isolation experienced by the majority of people at this time; those who lived in small cities or towns did not necessarily have access to professional performances. In France during the 1670s and 1680s, the cities of Lyon and Marseilles developed their own music "academies" modeled after the Parisian Académie Royale de Musique. In Britain, the residents of Edinburgh, Newcastle, and Durham formed associations that promoted concerts in which gentleman amateurs and professionals participated, nurturing the enthusiasm for Italian music that would soon take England by storm. In other instances, the customs from one country spread to another. The Concert Spirituel (1725) was established in Paris to provide alternative entertainment during Lent and on other religious holidays, and was imitated in other cities including Vienna and Berlin.

Concerts were also a regular feature of spa towns (such as Bath in England), where visitors with ample leisure time indulged in the tradition of "taking the waters," thought to cure a variety of ills. According to the *Daily Courant* of April 17, 1712, the town of Epsom (famous for the salts that still bear its name) boasted a "variety of Raffling-Shops, Billiard Tables, and the New Bowling Green," as well as the "Consort of Musick," which could be heard each day, "with one performance in the morning beginning at eight and ending at noon, with a second beginning at five and continuing until nine or ten." Outdoor performances flourished in pleasure gardens, the most famous of which was London's Vauxhall Gardens (see Chapter 14), where diverse classes enjoyed food, drink, music (famously that of Handel), and a host of licit and illicit pleasures.

Music societies also filled the artistic needs of players—particularly university students—who wanted to experiment with new repertory. The collegium musicum was popular in northern Europe, particularly in Germany. Typically run by students, this type of organization gave them, as well as gifted amateurs and aspiring professional musicians, the opportunity to meet either to play together for their own edification or to perform occasional concerts in coffeehouses and taverns. Many collegia were begun during the Thirty Years' War, providing a musical outlet for middle-class German musicians during a period in which the exigencies of war had suppressed many cultural activities.

By the middle of the seventeenth century, collegia took on a greater role in the musical life of many cities and towns; they often played for civic festivals and even the nobility. They also became bastions of new musical styles, perhaps as a result of the large number of young musicians who participated in them. This was the case in eighteenth-century Leipzig, when Georg Philipp Telemann founded a collegium musicum that Bach would later direct (see Chapters 13 and 15). Telemann and his collegium, however, faced opposition from Bach's predecessor, Johann Kuhnau, who complained that the student musicians no longer wished to play in the major Leipzig churches since Telemann, with his penchant for opera and modern music, had lured them away.

CANON FORMATION: THE ACADEMY OF ANTIENT MUSIC

While the collegia musica sought to play the most up-to-date music, other groups were more conservative, choosing repertory that consisted of what we might regard today as musical classics—that is, enduring works from earlier periods, in particular the sixteenth and early seventeenth centuries. A knowledge of and interest in "antient music," as it was called, provided a special way to demonstrate musical sophistication and taste that came only with good breeding and an upper-class education. A prime example of this trend is the Academy of Vocal Music, founded in 1726 as a professional society for London musicians. Modeled on the Bolognese Accademia Filarmonica, it included singers from the Chapel Royal and London churches and also welcomed some of the foreign musicians who had made London their home.

The Academy of Vocal Music's first concert was decidedly retrospective. It included a motet by the sixteenth-century composer Luca Marenzio and a psalm by Thomas Morley. To represent two renowned modern Italian composers, Alessandro Stradella and Agostino Steffani, the members chose madrigals, an old-fashioned genre. After much squabbling and infighting, in 1731 the group was reconfigured under the name Academy of Antient Music, led by the German-born composer Johann Christoph Pepusch (1667–1752). Although Pepusch was best known for his stylistically modern theatrical compositions, including *The Beggar's Opera*, the repertory of the Academy remained conservative under his leadership. The view of what constituted a classic also changed over the course of the eighteenth century. While at first Handel belonged to the camp of the moderns, by the latter part of the eighteenth century he would become the most revered of all "antient" English musicians (see Chapter 14).

Although the Academy's concerts were extremely popular, some commentators criticized its backward-looking philosophy. One skeptic, a member of Parliament, saw fit to satirize the "Hummers of Madrigals" who "swoon at the sight of any modern pieces," and preferred works that "when dress'd up in Cobwebs and powdered with Dust, the Philharmonick Spider could dwell on them, and in them, to Eternity." Nonetheless, the urge to canonize a collection of classic works as masterpieces that would retain their intrinsic value regardless of changing fashions or commercial considerations was to become an essential element in concert life by the nineteenth century.

The comments of the cranky parliamentarian remind us of music's political and ideological dimension, which played a critical role in the activities of the societies, salons, and academies considered in this chapter. Whether forming a canon of historical works, cultivating musical innovations, or nurturing new audiences and patrons that included the noblewomen, burgeoning merchant classes, and talented students, these societies and academies created communities and collaborative enterprises that led the way for the development of the rich concert life that would be enjoyed by eighteenth century musicians and their audiences.

FOR FURTHER READING

Barnett, Gregory, *Bolognese Instrumental Music, 1660–1719: Comfort, Courtly Delight, and Commercial Triumph* (Aldershot, UK, and Burlington, VT: Ashgate, 2008)

De Lucca, Valeria, "Strategies of Women Patrons of Music and Theatre in Rome: Maria Mancini, Queen Christina of Sweden, and Women of Their Circles," *Renaissance Studies* 25 (2011): 374–92

Glixon, Beth, "More on the Life and Death of Barbara Strozzi," *Musical Quarterly* 83 (1999): 131–41

Gordon-Seiffert, Catherine, *Music and the Language of Love: Seventeenth-Century Airs* (Bloomington: Indiana University Press, 2011)

Heller, Wendy, "Usurping the Place of the Muses: Barbara Strozzi and the Female Composer in Seventeenth-Century Italy," in George B. Stauffer, ed., *The World of Baroque Music: New Perspectives* (Bloomington: Indiana University Press, 2006)

Kevorkian, Tanya, "Changing Times, Changing Music: 'New Church' Music and Musicians in Leipzig, 1699–1750," in William Weber, ed., *The Musician as Entrepreneur, 1700-1914: Managers, Charlatans, and Idealists* (Bloomington: Indiana University Press, 2004)

Rosand, Ellen, "Barbara Strozzi, *Virtuosissima cantatrice:* The Composer's Voice," *Journal of the American Musicological Society* 31 (1978): 241–81

Weber, William, *The Rise of Musical Classics in Eighteenth-Century England: A Study in Canon, Ritual, and Ideology* (Oxford and New York: Oxford University Press, 1992)

PART III

Musical Synthesis in the Capitals of Europe

I n the final section of the book, we consider the composition and performance of music in several major European capitals in the late seventeenth and early eighteenth centuries, focusing on some of the most renowned composers of the period: Bach, Handel, Vivaldi, Telemann, and Rameau.

The success of these brilliant composer-performers—and the continuing popularity of late Baroque music—are a result of several underlying historical processes. First, this was a period of consolidation in arts and society, despite the fact that the eighteenth century, like the seventeenth, began on a note of political discord. In the War of the Spanish Succession (1702–13), the Austrian and French factions of the Habsburg Empire fought over the Spanish territories left after Charles II of Spain died without an heir. At the same time, this was a period in which the major genres, forms, and expressive language of the Baroque were standardized. Although many works composed during this period were of a longer duration or used a larger orchestra or a more modern tonal language than those considered earlier in this book, composers wrote in all the established genres of the seventeenth century—opera, oratorio, concerto, sonata, motet, mass, and cantata. These followed familiar conventions and were heard in many of the same contexts, including church, chamber, theater, home, and the streets.

Second, the late Baroque (sometimes called the high Baroque) is an era in which national styles crossed political borders with greater frequency. That this was stimulated to some degree by the very political discord that threatened to disrupt European society (including major shifts in dynastic alliances that sometimes resulted from these tensions) is perhaps not surprising. Since the importation of foreign culture—be it music, literature, art, or architecture—was one way for courts both large and small to gain prestige and promote an absolutist program, the best artists, poets, musicians, and stage designers became savvy marketers of their skills and reputations. In order to take advantage of career opportunities, artists not only were required to be mobile but became adept at negotiating with patrons who had different political views, artistic concerns, or religious preferences.

Language was less of a barrier than we might imagine. At the Munich court, for instance, French was the preferred language, while in Vienna, Italian was the standard language not only for opera and oratorio, but for much of the court business. This applied to musical styles as well. Indeed, at the height of the War of the Spanish Succession, the two contenders for the Spanish throne—the Austrian Habsburg candidate Charles III (younger brother of Joseph I, who later became the Holy Roman Emperor Charles VI) and the French candidate Philip V, grandson of Louis XIV—each built different types of musical establishments on the Iberian peninsula: in Barcelona, Charles favored the Italian-style music so beloved in his native Vienna, while Philip sought to transform Madrid into a miniature Versailles with a band of French musicians. As we will see, some courts continued to prefer Italian music and musicians, while other monarchs sought to model their courts on that of Louis XIV, adopting aspects of French musical style in the process. In the public opera theater in the city of Hamburg (Chapter 13), we find operas that juxtaposed French, German, and Italian texts and styles in the same work.

Finally, it is largely as a result of this synthesis and internationalization that a new musical language developed, often referred to as the *style galant*, or galant style. The term refers to a different approach to composition and musical expression characterized by elegant melodies, symmetrical phrasing, preference for homophony or two-part textures as opposed to dense counterpoint, and a reduced harmonic vocabulary. Many view the *galant* style as an antidote to Baroque complexity, embodying a kind of grace, refinement, and cheerful restraint, though in practice we find composers such as François Couperin (for example, in his *Pièces de clavecin*, Chapter 12) moving readily back and forth between these styles with relative ease.

This tension between Baroque intricacy and *galant* elegance is one of the salient features of early-eighteenth-century music. Indeed, they existed side by side. As the *style galant* enticed European listeners in the 1720s and 1730s, a number of major composers born in the late seventeenth century—notably, Handel, Rameau, and Bach—crafted (in their own unique fashions) some of the most quintessentially "Baroque" compositions of the entire era, while nonetheless absorbing elements of the *galant* style into their works. As we delve deeply into the music of these esteemed masters so often viewed as representatives of the musical past rather than the future, we may come to see them as progressive figures who exemplify one of the immutable laws of music history: that the innovations of one age become the conventions of another.

CHAPTER ELEVEN

Rome in the Age of the Arcadian Academy

In 1690, as we recall from Chapter 6, Giovanni Crescimbeni published a review of Francesco Cavalli's *Giasone* that, while appreciative, placed much of the blame for the downfall of musical theater on this inordinately popular work. Crescimbeni was not a musician; but as a critic and one of the founding members of Rome's Accademia degli Arcadi (Arcadian Academy), his words—and those of his colleagues—would have a profound influence on the aesthetics of music and drama in the eighteenth century. Much like Bardi, Peri, Galilei, and Rinuccini in late sixteenth-century Florence (see Chapter 2), Crescimbeni and his fellow Arcadians sought to reconfigure the relationship between music and poetry, self-consciously invoking the ancients as their model.

As in any era, it is difficult to assess the link between the idealism of critics and the practical concerns of musicians and listeners in eighteenth-century Rome. Does speculation about the nature of music inspire creativity? Or is such speculation an inevitable product of an innovative musical environment? Regardless, the poets, critics, and musicians who attended meetings of the Arcadian Academy did so in a remarkably fertile and inventive atmosphere for music-making. Although opera, Italy's most prized export, was often suppressed by the papacy, the city's ecclesiastical institutions and numerous noble patrons supported a sumptuous flowering of musical culture in the early eighteenth century through the efforts of such composers as Arcangelo Corelli, Alessandro Scarlatti and his son Domenico, and George Frideric Handel.

PATRONS AND COMPOSERS
IN EIGHTEENTH-CENTURY ROME

A number of factors conspired to make Rome a vibrant musical center in the early 1700s. It was inevitable that the papal city, centrally located and with so many important ecclesiastical institutions, diplomats at the papal court, and competing patrons, would attract the best musicians from Italy and abroad. Although born in Sicily, Alessandro Scarlatti (1660–1725) received his initial training in Rome and was sufficiently well connected to the artistic world to have been a tenant in the house of the sculptor Gian Lorenzo Bernini before being hired in 1682 as *maestro di cappella* to Queen Christina (whom we met in Chapter 10). Arcangelo Corelli (1653–1713), a violinist from the central Italian town of Fusignano, near Bologna, began his career in Rome as a freelance musician at age 22. By 1679 Corelli, like Scarlatti, had entered the service of Queen Christina. Thus, in 1687, when the queen's academy presented a gala honoring the reign of James II—a Catholic—in England, Corelli led a "grand symphony comprising one hundred and fifty musicians of all sorts," followed by the "most beautiful music ever heard," in which the violinist's music alternated with that of the composer Bernardo Pasquini, renowned as a keyboard player.

Rome also proved a fruitful stop for the 21-year-old George Frideric Handel (1685–1759). Fresh from composing and playing harpsichord for the Theater am Gänsemarkt (goose market), Hamburg's public opera theater (see Chapter 13), Handel made the voyage to Italy "on his own bottom" (meaning at his own expense), as reported to his biographer John Mainwaring. Despite his Lutheran upbringing, he was warmly welcomed into the musical life of the papal city, negotiating religious differences with apparent ease. He also made trips to other Italian cities during his three-year sojourn, composing his first Italian opera, *Vincer se stesso è il maggior vittoria* (To Conquer Oneself Is the Greatest Victory, 1707), for Florence; writing the *serenata* (serenade) *Aci, Galatea, e Polifemo* (Acis, Galatea, and Polyphemus, 1708) for the wedding of a Neapolitan nobleman; and enjoying one of his greatest triumphs in Venice with his opera *Agrippina* (1709). However, it was in Rome that Handel was most prolific, composing two major oratorios and over 100 cantatas, from which he would borrow musical material throughout his career.

The experiences of all these musicians were shaped by the special way in which patronage operated in early-eighteenth-century Rome. Since the election of a new pope meant that outsiders—families that did not have ancient ties to the city—could gain access to the highest echelons of society, virtually all the major families in Italy who could boast a pope in their lineage or had aspirations to do so maintained palaces in Rome. The city was also full of foreign diplomats—particularly from the major Catholic powers, Spain and France—all of whom consumed and produced music. Patronage was thus a sport in which cardinals and nobles competed either for the prize of the papacy or for power and prestige commensurate with their families' position.

When Queen Christina died in 1689, other patrons filled the sizable gap she left in Rome's intellectual and artistic life. Another exiled queen, Maria Casimira of Poland, supported both Alessandro and Domenico Scarlatti, and followed contemporary fashion by building a theater in her house, where several of Domenico's operas were performed. Handel also composed music for a Carmelite feast, likely commissioned by Cardinal Carlo Colonna, the son of Maria Mancini (whom we met in Chapter 10). He also wrote dozens of Italian cantatas while in the employ of Marchese (later Prince) Francesco Maria Ruspoli; they were performed on Sunday evenings at Ruspoli's Palazzo Bonelli, where Handel resided in 1707–08. (Documents that survive from Ruspoli's household include a remarkably large bill for Handel's food during this period, evidence of the voracious appetite that led to his corpulence later in life.) Ruspoli also produced the first performance of Handel's Easter oratorio *La resurrezione*, HWV 47 (The Resurrection), as discussed later.

CARDINALS PAMPHILI AND OTTOBONI

Among the chief inheritors of Christina's dominant role in Roman patronage were Cardinals Benedetto Pamphili and Pietro Ottoboni, both of whom penned numerous librettos for cantatas, operas, and oratorios. Pamphili wrote the poetry for the libretto of Handel's *Il trionfo del tempo e del disinganno* (The Triumph of Time and Disillusion), which was premiered in 1707 at the Palazzo Pamphili, which from its central position in the Piazza Navona, guarded Bernini's famous fountains. Among Pamphili's cantata texts is one intended expressly for and set by Handel, *Hendel, non può mia musa* (Handel, my muse cannot, 1708), in which Pamphili declares Handel a greater musician than Orpheus: Orpheus could merely stop birds in flight and animate rocks; Handel could even coax Pamphili's reluctant muse into song. Thus, all should be inspired by the harmony of the new Orpheus. This would be the first of many instances in which Handel was compared to the legendary bard.

Details about Cardinal Ottoboni's life and activities as a patron reveal a complex picture of the moral ambiguities and occasional hypocrisies that shaped social interactions in such exalted circles. The scion of a great Venetian family, Ottoboni was appointed vice chancellor of the Church when his great-uncle became Pope Alexander VIII. His palace, the Palazzo della Cancelleria, or Chancellery, was the social headquarters for the Ottoboni papacy. Money from the Vatican treasury flowed freely into his coffers and thence into the pockets of some of the greatest artists and musicians of the day, including Corelli, Pasquini, the painter Francesco Trevisani, and the architect and set designer Filippo Juvarra. (The fact that Ottoboni commissioned Trevisani to decorate Corelli's apartments attests to the esteem in which the composer was held.) A serious and accomplished poet, Ottoboni wrote librettos set by leading composers, as well as poetry for Alessandro Scarlatti's first version of the oratorio *Giuditta* (Judith, 1693) and the opera *La Statira* (Stateira, a Persian princess), presented for the grand reopening of the Tordinona Theater in 1690 (see below). Ottoboni's ambitions as a theatrical entrepreneur are reflected in the theater that he commissioned Juvarra to design in the Cancelleria (Fig. 11.1).

Figure 11.1: *Filippo Juvarra, drawing of Ottoboni Theater (1712)*

Ottoboni was as notorious for his decadence as he was famed for his refined taste in art and music. Surviving love letters between the cardinal and a certain Margherita Pio Zeno of Savoy over a 20-year period give credence to his reputation as a man torn between piety and passion. He is also said to have maintained a close, perhaps intimate, relationship with the castrato Andrea Adami, who for a time was *maestro di cappella* at the Sistine Chapel.

While it is uncertain how seriously we should take such rumors, the production of music in the palaces of nobles was associated with social situations in which the love of art, music, and food stimulated other sensual pleasures. It is in the context of these primarily male social groups, as in the Venetian academies, that same-sex relationships were tolerated and even flourished. Evidence about the sexual activity of patrons may or may not be relevant in our consideration of composers' lives. Corelli, for example, was close to the violinist Matteo Fornari throughout his years in Rome, and it was Fornari who ultimately inherited Corelli's considerable estate and the rights to his publications. Scholars have speculated about Handel's sexual inclinations, though there is no definitive evidence to support or refute the hypothesis that he had a preference for same-sex relationships. In an era in which men and women did not define themselves by their sexuality, as we saw in Chapter 1, and friendship between members of the same sex was often expressed in passionate terms, the secrets of the past are apt to remain hidden.

ALTERNATIVES TO OPERA

While there was an apparent tolerance for personal improprieties among high-ranking figures in the Roman ecclesiastical establishment, musical life in the papal city was governed by strict standards concerning public performance. Papal attitudes toward opera vacillated between outright support and complete disapproval, as Church authorities grappled with the potential moral liabilities of allowing the public to enjoy so secular an entertainment.

During the reign of Urban VIII, as we saw in Chapter 3, operas such as *Sant'Alessio* were deemed an ideal way to champion both Rome and the power of the Barberini family. Giulio Rospigliosi, the librettist for *Sant'Alessio*, supported opera during the two years (1667–69) that he served as Pope Clement IX, and his successor, Pope Clement X, supported Queen Christina's efforts to establish Rome's first public opera theater, the Tordinona, in a former prison. After presenting a series of mostly Venetian operas, including Stradella's *Il novello Giasone* (see Chapter 6), the theater was closed down in 1676 by Pope Innocent XI. (Stradella left for Venice, his brilliant career subsequently tainted by scandal and cut short by an assassin's knife in a public square in Genoa.)

There was a brief respite from the ban on opera during the 16-month reign of Pope Alexander VIII, the great-uncle of Cardinal Ottoboni, when Scarlatti's *La Statira* was produced to great acclaim at the Tordinona; Alexander also permitted two other theaters to open. The pendulum swung back as Innocent XII, who ruled from 1691 to 1700, once again put the brakes on public opera in Rome. And while his successor, Pope Clement XI, at first seemed willing to tolerate public opera, a pair of earthquakes in 1703 inspired a fear of divine retribution—and with it a new wave of piety. Thus, came the announcement on February 14, 1703, that "for the next five years there will be totally prohibited from the City of Rome at any time, even in Carnival, Masking, Horse races, Banquets, Dances, and Performances, of Comedies as well as Tragedies, Representations, and the like, even though in music, and also in the Colleges, Seminaries, Monasteries, and Sacred and Profane Palaces."

The ongoing uncertainty about the status of opera had consequences for composers, singers, patrons, and audiences. It was a particularly difficult period for Alessandro Scarlatti, who was trying to control his two badly behaved sisters (both singers) while at the same time finding commissions for himself and his talented son Domenico. Writing to Ferdinando de' Medici about Domenico in 1706, Scarlatti complained: "I now send him away from Rome, because Rome has no roof to welcome Music, who lives here as a beggar. This son who is an Eagle, whose Wings are grown, must not remain at ease in the nest, and I must not impede his flight."

Scarlatti's complaints aside, the sporadic bans on opera may have had the unintended result of inspiring musical creativity, as patrons looked for other ways to enjoy musical theater while circumventing papal restrictions. The closing of public theaters led to the innovative use of private spaces: almost any room, garden, or piazza could be transformed into a theater, rendering the performers and composers who lived and worked in one's palace even more valuable commodities.

ROMAN ORATORIO

This shift from public performance to private entertainment would have a profound influence on the Italian oratorio, as illustrated by the performance of Handel's *La resurrezione* at Ruspoli's Palazzo Bonelli on Easter Sunday 1708. Unlike Giacomo Carissimi's *Jephte* (see Chapter 5) and similar works sponsored by the Roman confraternities, which were intended as spiritual exercises for lay audiences, *La resurrezione* was one of numerous Italian oratorios presented in palaces and court theaters as entertainment, albeit of a spiritually uplifting nature. *La resurrezione* uses the musical language of Italian opera—arias and recitatives—to tell the story of the events between Good Friday and Easter, featuring Lucifer, an Angel, Mary Magdalene, and Mary Cleophas (one of the other women present at the crucifixion).

The splendor of the occasion may have been inspired by Ruspoli's desire to outdo Cardinal Ottoboni, who had produced an oratorio by Alessandro Scarlatti on the subject of the Passion at the Cancelleria on Ash Wednesday. Because Ruspoli anticipated a large audience for the performance of *La resurrezione*, he had constructed—in just five days—an elaborate temporary theater in the Sala Grande of the Palazzo Bonelli. The orchestra, placed on a series of risers, was hidden by a barrier so the audience could not see them. A raised platform in the center presented the *concertino* players, including Corelli, first violinist and conductor of the ensemble, the second violinist, and the vocal soloists. Handel was at one of the two harpsichords. Surviving account books tell of the elaborate decorations that (in the absence of staging) provided the audience with visual imagery to complement the action. Among the decorations commissioned for the occasion was a large painted mural approximately 12 feet square bearing an image of the Angel seated on the tomb of Christ, announcing the resurrection to Mary Magdalene and Mary Cleophas. St. John was pictured nearby on the mountain, and the painter also depicted the demons' fall into the abyss, colored, the documents tell us, in a manner that was entirely natural.

The true drama of *La resurrezione*, however, was created by Handel's varied affects and colorful orchestration. In the brilliant D-major aria "Disserratevi, o porte d'Averno" (Open wide, you gates of Avernus), sung by the Angel at the outset of the oratorio, the resurrection is signaled by vigorous ascending arpeggios in the trumpets, answered by ornamented descending scales in the oboes and strings. As shown in Example 11.1, the Angel enters on the offbeat with a scalar passage that descends a full twelfth from the high A like a beam of light dispelling the darkness of hell only to rise immediately thereafter with a gravity-defying melisma (mm. 15–16). Fearlessly, the angel will go on to conquer

Example 11.1: *George Frideric Handel, "Disserratevi, o porte d'Averno" from* La resurrezione, *HWV 47 (1708), mm. 11–17*

Open wide, you gates of Avernus

the upper register with triumphant, sustained notes and trumpet-like flourishes, joining in celebratory duets with the oboes.

The sacred theme of *La resurrezione* was not enough to overcome the pope's disapproval of the participation of female singers. When Clement XI discovered that Margherita Durastanti, a female soprano, had sung the role of Mary Magdalene, he insisted that Ruspoli substitute a castrato for the repeat performance on Easter Monday. As would become his habit, Handel would reuse much of this material in some later compositions, most conspicuously the opera *Agrippina*, which was performed a year later in Venice with Durastanti transformed from Mary Magdalene into the title role—the mother of Emperor Nero. The Roman oratorio may have been the antithesis of opera in terms of performance context and subject matter; but this example shows that the basic ingredients of early-eighteenth-century music were surprisingly pliable.

THE ARCADIAN ACADEMY

While the production of oratorios was often an elaborate and expensive affair, the secular cantatas and instrumental works that were heard in the palaces of Ottoboni, Pamphili, Ruspoli, and their colleagues were briefer and involved fewer performers. Like oratorios, cantatas were made up of arias and recitatives (and occasional duets or trios); yet it was precisely because of their smaller scale that they were suitable for so many different kinds of social, intellectual, or diplomatic occasions, in particular the academy to which virtually all of the major Roman patrons belonged: the Accademia degli Arcadi.

Born in 1690, in the aftermath of the death of Queen Christina, the Arcadian Academy was the brainchild of various poets and artists who had been members of her inner circle and were seeking a new outlet for their creative energy. They took the name Arcadian from the pastoral poetry of ancient authors such as Virgil and Theocritus, and from Renaissance poets who imagined a golden age in which shepherds and nymphs were inspired by the music and poetry of Apollo, Pan, and the Muses. Under the leadership of Giovanni Crescimbeni, the 14 founding members adopted the panpipes as their symbol and the infant Jesus as their patron. Each member took an Arcadian pseudonym; when possible, meetings were held in garden spaces that brought to mind the idyllic Arcadian world that they were attempting to recover (Fig. 11.2).

The Academy's members included not only nobles but also poets, some musicians, and a smattering of other intellectuals, both men and women. (The latter achieved a measure of equality among the Arcadians that was unusual in Italian academies.) Even the future pope Clement XI joined while still a cardinal. It was probably through the support of Cardinal Ottoboni that Alessandro Scarlatti, Arcangelo Corelli, and Bernardo Pasquini were admitted as members in 1706. Each was given a pastoral name; Scarlatti, for instance, was called Terpander,

Figure 11.2: *Plan of Bosco Parrasio, headquarters of the Accademia degli Arcadi in Rome, from Giovanni Mario Crescimbeni*, Storia dell'Accademia degli Arcadi istituita in Roma *(1690; London, 1804)*

after a Greek poet from the seventh century BCE who played the cithara. The Arcadian movement became so popular that by 1728 there were 2,619 members. Crescimbeni oversaw the development of 40 satellite organizations throughout the Italian peninsula.

Like several academies we have considered, the Arcadians were not directly concerned with music. Rather, their interest was in the reformation of Baroque art more generally, and they wished to substitute rationalism and *buon senso* (good sense) for extravagance, and *buon gusto* (good taste) for wantonness and fantasy. They sought a balance between art that was verisimilar (true to nature) and art that demonstrated poetic invention. At the center of their philosophy was the notion that the arts should be unified and express a common idea of truth. Arcadians embraced the concept popularized by the ancient Roman poet Horace: *ut pictura poesis* (as is painting, so is poetry). They not only viewed painting and poetry as sister arts, but added architecture and theater (and at times music) into the mix. Like the inventors of opera in the late sixteenth century, the Arcadians also looked to antiquity. However, while the members of the so-called Florentine Camerata sought to reclaim the emotional intensity of the ancients, the Arcadians looked to antiquity for formal elegance, symmetry, and simplicity. This they expressed by producing pastoral painting, poetry, and theater—all the while assuming pastoral identities.

A hint of the Arcadians' attitudes toward music is found in an account of a contest between music and poetry in Crescimbeni's *L'Arcadia* (1708), which contains fictionalized descriptions of Arcadian gatherings. The festivities began, Crescimbeni writes, "with one of the most beautiful *sinfonie* made in the noble hut of the acclaimed Crateo [Ottoboni] and later published to the world with such glory for him." Crescimbeni then describes how Tirsi (a poet named Giovanni Battista Zappi), having invented an aria text on the spot, asked Terpander (Scarlatti) to set it to music spontaneously. "Everyone was overwhelmed to see how these two so excellent masters, one of poetry and the other of music, would compete." Crescimbeni marvelled at the collaboration, observing that "just as one finished the last verse of the new aria, the other completed the last line of music." Although there is no record that such a contest ever took place, Crescimbeni presents an idealistic vision of cantata composition as a unified artistic enterprise, in which the joining of music and poetry is a natural and even instinctive act, the results of which will necessarily please an elite, discerning audience.

PASTORAL CANTATAS AND SERENADES

The cantatas and serenades composed by Handel, Scarlatti, and their colleagues provide ample evidence of the ways in which vocal music might have served the Arcadians' desire for truth, poetic invention, and good taste. Scarlatti wrote over 800 cantatas, many of which were intended for listeners in the Arcadian Academy. As with opera (see Chapter 2), cantatas featured alternating arias and recitatives, differentiated by poetic style. The recitatives were written in *versi sciolti* (blank verse) consisting of 7- and 11-syllable lines, while the arias typically had two strophes with an even number of syllables and regular rhyme schemes. Some arias featured two or more stock pastoral characters, such as Tirsi, Fileno, or Clori, and might include duets; others were monologues in which unnamed lovers lamented their unrequited passion. Indeed, we see something of how the pastoral realm of the cantatas might have been visualized from one of the illustrations by Pier Leone Ghezzi that accompany a manuscript of Scarlatti cantatas copied for the castrato Andrea Adami for use at Ottoboni's *conversazioni* (Fig. 11.3).

Lovesick shepherds and hard-hearted nymphs may seem all too stylized and conventional from a twenty-first-century perspective, but they provided the Arcadians with a means of expressing private passions in a socially acceptable manner. Since each member could pretend that his or her desire was that of the simple shepherd, love could be dissected and criticized, and the battle between reason and passion could be played out over and over again. In Scarlatti's cantata *Bella dama di nome santa* (Beautiful Woman with a Holy Name), for instance, the underlying contradiction is set out in the opening recitative. The beloved appears to be fair, blessed by the gods with all perfections; how is it, then, that she should be so cruel? Scarlatti drives home the message by setting the words "tormenti, pene, e cordogli acerbi" (torments, pains, and bitter sorrows) with an equally cruel harmonic thrust: after a couple of marked dissonances in measures 9–10, the passage

Figure 11.3: *Illustration by Pier Leone Ghezzi from a manuscript of cantatas by Alessandro Scarlatti*

cadences on the unusual key of F♯ major (Ex. 11.2). This is typical of the bold modulations and emotional intensity that Scarlatti's elite listeners found particularly desirable.

Other cantatas featured mythological or historical figures, many of whom are familiar from contemporary operas. A more serious, quasi-operatic tone is invoked in Handel's brilliant cantata *O numi eterni* (O Eternal Spirits, 1709), with a libretto by Benedetto Pamphili. It presents the lament of the famous Roman patron Lucretia, described in Livy's *History of Rome* (written in the first century CE), who, having been raped, chooses to kill herself rather than live without chastity. The cantata was composed for Ruspoli and was likely first performed by Margherita Durastanti. Handel's heroine expresses her pride, sorrow, and desire for vengeance in a series of recitatives and arias. Unexpectedly, the cantata ends not with an aria but with an arioso (a lyrical recitative), followed by a recitative passage marked "furioso." Handel's disregard for musical convention evokes the abruptness and violence of Lucretia's suicide.

Another eighteenth-century Italian genre embraced by the Arcadians and discussed by Crescimbeni was the serenata. Serenatas were long cantata-like vocal works, usually performed outdoors, often at night, and typically intended for a special event, such as a birthday, coronation, or military victory. Among the

Example 11.2: *Alessandro Scarlatti, "E come bella," from* Bella dama di nome santa *(1706), mm. 6–10*

And how is it, O beauty, that at every turn of your eyes, you give only torments, pain, and bitter sorrows?

serenatas composed specifically for the Arcadians is Scarlatti's *Venere, Amore, e Ragione* (Venus, Love, and Reason, ca. 1706). As was typical of the genre, the poetry (probably by Silvio Stampiglia, one of the founding members of the Arcadian Academy) does not present a plot per se but rather a moral discussion among allegorical figures, much like the prologues that open many Baroque operas. In this case, the allegory concerns the taming of love. The goddess Venus discovers that Reason has taken away Cupid's dart and blindfold, crowning him with laurels, like Apollo. The nature of love is explored in arias, duets, and trios, and the pastoral mood is imparted by the frequent use of lilting compound-triple meters, unison violins, and obbligato winds. The final trio conveys the moral message of the Arcadians, as Venus, Cupid, and Reason proclaim that one should learn to love well, since that is the true path to appreciating beauty.

OPERA AND THE ARCADIANS

The Arcadians also had a profound influence on opera, as we might surmise from Crescimbeni's passionate criticisms of *Giasone*. A number of Arcadians compared Italian opera unfavorably with the French neoclassical drama, which seemed to them closer to the ideal of the ancients that had inspired the invention of the genre. In order to restore good taste to opera, they favored librettos that were less complex and more dramatically coherent. Allegorical references should be unambiguous; moderation and structural clarity were of primary importance. While imagination and fantasy were still prized, those who ascribed to Arcadian aesthetics believed truth and realism could be achieved by having characters behave in a dignified manner and express themselves in an appropriately elevated poetic style, while also maintaining the purity of the tragic and comic genres, as had been achieved in the operas of Lully and Quinault (see Chapter 7).

It was precisely these principles that were adopted by two of the most important librettists of the period, both of whom would eventually become court poets to the Holy Roman Emperor in Vienna (see Chapter 13): Apostolo Zeno (1668–1750) and Pietro Trapassi (1698–1782), better known as Pietro Metastasio. Zeno was a literary critic and scholar who took up libretto writing because of his interest in improving literature. Although not a member of the Arcadian Academy, in 1691 he founded a Venetian academy that also sought to restore good taste in literature. As the godson of Pietro Ottoboni, Metastasio had more-direct connections to the Arcadians. By the time he came of age, opera was no longer forbidden in Rome, and after achieving successes in Naples, Venice, and Rome, he was hired as court poet in Vienna to replace Zeno, who by then had returned to his native Venice.

The librettos penned by Zeno and Metastasio belong to the genre usually described as *opera seria*, or serious opera. Like the Venetian operas we encountered in Chapter 6, they almost always had happy endings, one notable exception being Metastasio's *Didone abbandonata* (Dido Abandoned), which concludes with the Virgilian heroine's suicide. However, Metastasio and Zeno sought to rid opera of the juxtaposition of comedy and tragedy that had been so essential to Venetian opera. Their poetry was formal, elegant, and concise. Metastasio was particularly gifted at crafting poetic texts well suited to the da capo aria form, in which the poetry for the **A** and **B** sections expressed well-defined, complementary affects, using expressive and metaphoric language that lent itself to musical expansion and the kind of florid singing favored by the *prime donne* and *primi uomini* (first, or leading, women and men).

Metastasio and Zeno also advocated changes in opera's musico-dramatic organization. Throughout much of the seventeenth century, arias could occur at any point in a given scene. However, in the settings of librettos by Metastasio and Zeno, da capo arias were much longer (particularly with the highly ornamented repeat of the **A** section); they were also almost always placed at the end of the scene, to be sung just before the character exited the stage. Thus, the recitative dialogue culminated in a moment of lyricism, which was felt to be more true to life than if a character burst into song in the middle of the scene. (We will have more to say about the so-called "exit arias" in Chapter 14.)

In *opera seria*, the Carnivalesque conventions of Venetian opera—the play with same-sex desire, the effeminate heroes and warrior women—gave way to more standardized representations of virtuous women and heroic men. As John Rice shows in *Music in the Eighteenth Century*, Metastasio's dignified librettos would dominate much of Europe in the eighteenth and nineteenth centuries, particularly in absolutist regimes where unambiguous representations of virtuous monarchs were politically expedient. Reform, however, did not happen all at once, as a number of librettists and composers continued to embrace the pleasurable excesses of the seventeenth century, thus maintaining at least a hint of the Carnival sensibilities disdained by the Arcadians.

CORELLI AND THE CULT OF INSTRUMENTAL MUSIC

In a culture where poetry was highly valued and vocal music was regarded by many as the most significant form of music, there arose a figure who gained international fame exclusively in the realm of instrumental music: Arcangelo Corelli. Corelli's genius, lauded by contemporaries and acknowledged by critics today, manifested itself in several arenas. To begin with, as described in Roman documents, he reigned for over three decades as the leader of virtually every Roman performance involving large instrumental ensembles, serving all the major Roman patrons. Along with Lully, he is one of the most important figures in the development of the modern orchestra.

By the time Corelli arrived in Rome in 1675, the nature of instrumental ensembles was undergoing a transformation. Rather than being arranged into multiple choruses with full complements of voices and instruments, as was typical in polychoral works by Monteverdi and Schütz, voices and instruments were separated and the instruments were arranged by section (violins, violas, cellos, and so on).

CORELLI AND THE CULT OF INSTRUMENTAL MUSIC

The full ensemble, which might contain as many as 80 to 100 players, came to be known as the *concerto grosso* (large concert) or *ripieno* (full, marked "tutti" in the score), while a smaller group (labeled "soli"), which might consist of only two violins, was known as the *concertino* (little concert).

Typically, Corelli's *concertino* group at this time consisted of two players, himself and his colleague Matteo Fornari, who were often set apart from the orchestra in a position of prominence. This arrangement gave Corelli an opportunity not only to explore the contrast between the *ripieno and concertino* (as Giuseppe Torelli does in the works discussed in Chapter 10), but also to supervise the performance and the ensemble blend. He seems to have succeeded. Crescimbeni marveled that Corelli had introduced to Rome "*sinfonie* of so large a number of instruments and of such diversity that it was almost impossible to believe that he could get them to play together without fear of discord, especially since wind instruments were combined with string, and the total very often exceeding one hundred." Corelli achieved this by uncommon musical discipline; he acquired a reputation as a strict task master and is also credited (along with Lully) with being one of the first to insist on uniform bowings for all the members of a string section. Crescimbeni also reminds us that Corelli's published works—which contain no parts for wind instruments— must have indeed differed from what was actually heard in performance.

Corelli was also praised for his virtuoso solo playing and his expertise as a violin teacher, attracting students from all over Europe. An anonymous English eyewitness to one of his performances commented that he "never met with any man that suffer'd his passions to hurry him away so much whilst he was playing on the violin as the famous Arcangelo Corelli, whose Eyes will sometimes turn as red as Fire; his countenance will be distorted, his eyeballs as in an agony, and he gives in so much to what he is doing that he doth not look like the same man."

The other image of Corelli and his music is one that in many respects resonates with the aims of the Arcadian Academy—a composer who attained classical perfection, simplicity, and order in his works. This image, however, is based not on descriptions of his performances but on his publications, which through their wide dissemination and championing by influential players throughout Europe were held up as models for Baroque instrumental genres. Corelli's Opus 1 (1681) and Opus 3 (1689) collections contain *sonate da chiesa* (church sonatas), often arranged in four movements in the pattern slow-fast-slow-fast. The *sonate da camera* (chamber sonatas) in his Opus 2 (1685) and Opus 4 (1694), on the other hand, are essentially suites of dances in binary form.

All of Corelli's sonatas owe a debt to Torelli and his predecessors in the Bolognese Accademia Filarmonica (to which Corelli might have belonged). Corelli's violin sonatas (Opus 5, 1700) started a trend for lyrical and idiomatic violin compositions that could be played by amateurs, but when ornamented were sufficiently challenging for professionals, as is apparent in his Sonata in A Major, Op. 5, No. 9 (see Anthology 17).

Corelli also made an impact with the Op. 6 Concerti Grossi (1716, published posthumously), which likewise are indebted to Torelli's experiments with the concerto. With this single set of concertos, Corelli demonstrates numerous ways in which the *concertino* and *ripieno* can relate to one another, utilizing elements of both the chamber and church styles. The countless concerti grossi composed and published in England in the early eighteenth century reflected Corelli's considerable influence.

These facts, as important as they are, fail to explain the universal appeal of Corelli's music, which critics have long recognized, but often have difficulty describing. This is in part because the aspects of his style that sounded novel in the late seventeenth and early eighteenth centuries became so much a part of later Baroque practice that in the hands of other composers they sound almost like clichés. Unlike the music of early instrumental composers such as Dario Castello or Corelli's contemporary Heinrich Biber (see Chapters 4 and 13), Corelli's works almost always gravitate toward closely related keys, the dominant and relative minor. This would become common practice in the eighteenth century, but Corelli's harmonic motion toward these goals is distinguished by its drive and energy. He frequently uses sequences and pairs of contrasting motives, controlling the pace in a manner that makes the arrival in the new key (or return to the tonic) seem inevitable and satisfying. He takes advantage of the so-called walking or running bass, often in eighth or quarter notes. This regular pattern allowed the composer to dwell on a given harmony without losing a sense of forward motion, setting the contrapuntal activities of the other voices into relief. There is also a smoothness to Corelli's voice-leading: the bass typically moves by step, using first-inversion chords, or by fourths and fifths. Some of the most emotion-laden passages in his works are the series of suspensions that appear not only in slow movements—which sound much richer than they look on paper—but in fast movements as well.

Many of these features can be seen in the second movement of the Concerto Grosso Op. 6, No. 6 (Ex. 11.3). In the *concertino* section that opens the movement, a walking eighth-note bass line (m. 2) and contrapuntal interplay between the first and second violins lead to a series of suspensions in measure 3. With the entrance of the *ripieno*, or *tutti*, in measure 7, the additional violins amplify the *concertino*, while the cello maintains its independence from the basso continuo, with the viola enriching the texture. Corelli uses this larger ensemble to initiate a sequential pattern that thrusts the energy forward, moving away from the tonic only to return to it some 12 bars later.

After spending time with some of the highly expressive but admittedly idiosyncratic instrumental works of composers such as Castello or Girolamo Frescobaldi (see Chapter 4), or with the gentle melancholy of consort music by William Lawes or Henry Purcell (see Chapter 8), many students of the Baroque may well find in Corelli's music a familiar friend.

Although Corelli never left his adopted city of Rome, his music was disseminated well into the eighteenth century as far afield as Amsterdam, Paris,

Example 11.3: *Arcangelo Corelli, Concerto Grosso in F Major, Op. 6, No. 6 (1714), Allegro, mm. 1–8*

London, Philadelphia, and even China and Bolivia. The impact of his music through the medium of print can hardly be overestimated; many composers who had never set foot in Rome regarded Corelli as their teacher. Roger North, who wrote about the state of music in England in the late seventeenth century, credited the "coming over of the works of the great Corelli" with the predominance of the "Italian taste": It became "the only musick relished for a long time," for "if musick can be immortal, Corelli's consorts will be so." North tells us that Corelli's Op. 1 sonatas "cleared the ground of all other sorts of music whatsoever," and that his works were to musicians "like the bread of life."

In France, too, Corelli's influence was so strong that no less a musician than François Couperin composed a trio sonata entitled *Le Parnasse, ou L'apothéose de Corelli* (Parnassus, or The Apotheosis of Corelli) and confessed that he would revere the works of Corelli, along with those of Lully, as long as he lived. It is to France and the impact of the Italian style that we now turn.

FOR FURTHER READING

Allsop, Peter, *Arcangelo Corelli: New Orpheus of Our Times* (Oxford: Oxford University Press, 1999)

Dixon, Susan, *Between the Real and the Ideal: The Accademia degli Arcadi and Its Garden in Eighteenth-Century Rome* (Newark, NJ: University of Delaware Press, 2006)

Harris, Ellen, *Handel as Orpheus: Voice and Desire in the Chamber Cantatas* (Cambridge, MA: Harvard University Press, 2004)

Joncus, Berta, "Private Music in Public Spheres: Chamber Cantata and Song," in Simon O'Keefe, ed., *Cambridge History of Eighteenth-Century Music* (Cambridge: Cambridge University Press, 2009)

Pagano, Roberto, *Alessandro Scarlatti and Domenico Scarlatti: Two Lives in One*, trans. Frederick Hammond (Hillsdale, NY: Pendragon Press, 2006)

Rosand, Ellen, "Handel Paints the Resurrection," in T. J. Mathiesen and B. V. Rivera, eds., *Festa musicologica: Essays in Honor of George J. Buelow* (Stuyvesant, NY: Pendragon Press, 1995)

Spitzer, John, and Neal Zaslow, *The Birth of the Orchestra: History of an Institution, 1650–1815* (Oxford and New York: Oxford University Press, 2004)

Tcharos, Stefanie, *Opera's Orbit: Music Drama and the Influence of Opera in Arcadian Rome* (Cambridge: Cambridge University Press, 2011)

CHAPTER TWELVE

Parisians and Their Music in the Eighteenth Century

At the end of Chapter 7, we left King Louis XIV and his court in a moment of relative decline, at least from the point of view of music and spectacle. Burdened by the cost of foreign wars and under the influence of the devout Madame de Maintenon, Louis was not the adventurous patron of the arts he had been in previous decades.

Maintenon and her pious supporters disapproved of the *tragédie en musique*, with its pagan topics and celebration of love. At her urging, the king substituted religious devotion for hunting, dancing, spectacles, and the popular masked balls, allowing his son, the grand dauphin, to become the host of the *jours d'appartements* (although he expected the nobles to attend just as if he were present). Music continued to be important to Louis XIV, but he idealized the ostensibly pure style of Lully and several of his successors, such as Michel-Richard de Lalande (1657–1726), whose grand motets and instrumental works eschewed Italian influence.

The king's newfound piety created a dilemma for the nobles at Versailles and the royal family. Versailles remained, of course, the heart of the monarchy. In the early eighteenth century, it boasted some 20,000 residents, including nobles and servants who lived either in the palace or in the town, and whose primary function was to glorify the king. Nonetheless, after being entertained for

decades by court amusements, orbiting about the Sun King like so many plan-
ets, the courtiers now found themselves obliged to feign piety.

There was, however, resistance to the monarchy and its religiosity. Libertine
elements that had been suppressed since the early days of his reign emerged
with new insistence, and crude parodies of *tragédies en musique* appeared with
increasing frequency. Most damaging were the antics of the Comédie Italienne
and its popular characters Harlequin, Mezzetin, Scaramouche, and Pierrot, who
outwitted their masters and mocked the operatic heroes that had so long served
the propagandistic goals of the monarchy, even directing their barbs at Madame
de Maintenon and the king's ministers. It is thus not surprising, as we noted in
Chapter 7, that Louis ordered their theater closed in 1697, although a new Italian
troupe would be invited to Paris upon his death in 1715.

These tensions were symptomatic of a shift in aesthetics and audience
tastes that marked French music in the first half of the eighteenth century.
In this chapter we explore these changes and the musical consequences of
Louis XIV's retreat from the pleasures that had characterized the earlier years
of his reign. We follow the gaze of the courtiers who, rejecting the king's new
austerity, focused their attention away from Versailles and onto the theaters and
fairgrounds of Paris, the châteaux of the nobility (including those belonging to
the king's children and grandchildren), salons, and other venues where Italian
music—an alternative to the state style—was so often cultivated. Parisians not
only came to embrace a host of hedonistic pleasures, but also enjoyed a new
synthesis of styles—what Couperin would refer to as the *goûts réunis* (reunion of
tastes)—in which a blend of French *politesse* (politeness) and Italian exuberance
inspired a generation of musicians.

RESISTING THE MONARCHY: THE POLITICS OF THE ITALIAN STYLE

Despite the banishment of the Italian actors and the elderly Louis XIV's disdain
of musical innovation and Italian influence, a number of enclaves for Italian
music survived in Paris. Between 1681 and 1706, for instance, Nicolas Mathieu,
a parish priest at the church of St. André des Arts, produced a series of concerts that included a somewhat retrospective repertory of Italian instrumental
and vocal works by composers such as Francesco Cavalli and Luigi Rossi as well
as more-recent works by Alessandro Stradella and by Giovanni Battista Bononcini, whose cantatas and sonatas were particularly popular in France. The
music of Arcangelo Corelli and other Italian composers was heard by the young
François Couperin at the Château of Saint-Germain-en-Laye, about ten miles
west of Paris, where the exiled James II of England and his Italian wife, Mary of
Modena, supported a substantial musical establishment. Couperin pays tribute

to the Stuart court in the lilting, tender *Les plaisirs de Saint-Germain-en-Laye* (The Pleasures of Saint-Germain-en-Laye), which was published in 1713 in the first of his four volumes of *Pièces de clavecin* (Harpsichord Pieces).

Ironically, many of the leaders of the resistance to French stylistic hegemony came from Louis's own family. Among the most enthusiastic supporters of Italian music were the grand dauphin, Louis de Bourbon, and Louis XIV's nephew, Philippe II d'Orléans (who would become the regent of the king's great-grandson, Louis XV). Having had a superb musical education at the urging of the king, and repelled by the new austerity at court, these young men and women established their own musical circles where they could enjoy the latest fashions in Italian music—and other pleasures—with complete freedom. Their knowledge of music was indeed comprehensive, since it came from the best possible instructors. The three children of Louis XIV began their studies with Couperin in 1693, while Philippe II d'Orléans received his training from Marc-Antoine Charpentier. Philippe's mother complained about their habit of discussing music at length: "I often tell my son that he will go mad when I hear him talking endlessly of minor, major, flats and sharps, and other things of this type of which I understand nothing."

Nevertheless, the grand dauphin's expertise bore fruit in private performances by and for the sophisticated amateurs of his circle, notably a production of Lully's *Alceste* organized by the Princesse de Conti (another member of the king's extended family) at her home. Many activities took place at the dauphin's country château at Meudon, forcing courtiers to choose between it and Versailles, much to the displeasure of Louis XIV. An important consequence of the friction between father and son was that the dauphin took up the patronage activities abandoned by Louis XIV. In addition to supporting the Opéra, he championed Lully's operas at a time when the king had cooled toward the composer; the dauphin also patronized André Campra (1660–1744) and his *opéras-ballets*, considered below.

Philippe II d'Orléans went still further in his support of the Italian style: he hired an ensemble of musicians trained in Italy, including two castrati, two violinists, a cellist, and a bassist. Several of these musicians even had direct connections to Cardinal Ottoboni and the Arcadians in Rome (see Chapter 11), such as the alto castrato Pasqualino Betto, who sang the role of Mary Cleophas in Handel's *La resurrezione*, and the violinist Jean-Baptiste Anet II, who studied with Corelli. The ensemble's repertory included Italian cantatas and instrumental works, some of which were likely direct imports from the Arcadian Academy.

The waning of court entertainments provided the impetus for the wealthiest nobles to stage their own entertainments, which often drew vast crowds. One of the most intriguing hostesses was the Duchesse du Maine, Louise Bénédicte de Bourbon, a legitimate relation to the king of France and thus considered a "princess of the blood." It may well have been her marriage to one of Louis XIV's illegitimate sons, the Duc du Maine, that motivated her desire to establish a splendid court of her own at her château in Sceaux, eight miles southwest of Paris.

At one of the duchess's parties in 1702, 33 top musicians—one of whom may have been François Couperin—reportedly dressed up as sylvans (forest creatures) and satyrs. The evening began with singing and a dinner for 45, followed by cards, a huge supper, party games, fireworks, and dancing. The duchess was particularly fond of impromptu entertainments that blurred fantasy and reality. The most lavish were a series of *grandes nuits* (great nights) in 1714–15, which featured all kinds of entertainment—both rehearsed and impromptu—and in which the duchess and her guests would assume the roles of shepherds and shepherdesses. The duchess once even challenged Louis XIV's authority by daring to play the role of Apollo.

Despite the apparent frivolity of these escapades, the duchess was quite serious in her political ambitions. After the death of Louis XIV, her attempts to have her husband replace Philippe II d'Orléans as regent to the young Louis XV landed both duke and duchess in prison, forcing them to give up the château and all its delights.

PLEASURES IN PARIS

All of these developments meant that Paris, by the end of the seventeenth century, had become a magnet for a diverse audience who readily consumed a host of musical and theatrical spectacles. This had some unintended consequences, especially for those courtiers celebrating at one of the late night parties hosted by the Duchesse du Maine or attending an infamous soirée sponsored by the Duc d'Orléans, since the nobles would face the inevitable traffic jam of carriages as they sped back to Versailles in the wee hours of the morning to resume their faithful attendance on the king.

Despite Louis XIV's efforts to consolidate and control the arts (see Chapter 7), among the most successful theatrical enterprises of the late seventeenth and early eighteenth centuries were seen and heard at the *théâtres de la foire*, or fair theaters, the most famous of which were at Saint-Germain and Saint-Laurent. Established as early as the fifteenth century, these annual fairs were circus-like entertainments featuring magic tricks, tightrope dancers and acrobats, animal shows, dwarves, giants, and other carnival oddities. After Louis XIV banished the Italian actors in 1696, the fair theaters took on much of their repertory and style of performing, drawing audiences with the burlesque and low comedy. The Dutch traveler Johann Christoph Nemeitz was astonished to see "ladies of quality hearing and seeing these obscenities without blushing. Moreover they cannot hide the satisfaction they derive from the spectacle since they laugh with all their hearts. But, why worry? C'est la mode de Paris [It's the Paris way]. The more earthy and grotesque a joke is, the more it amuses." Despite conflicts with the Opéra, by 1716 the fair theaters gained permission to put on musical plays as the Opéra-Comique.

In the musical plays at the fairgrounds, high drama was turned into low comedy. The stock characters originating from the Italian improvisational theater, known as the commedia dell'arte, were transformed into mock heroes and heroines thrust into mythological tales and exotic climes, who often parodied the *tragédie en musique*. A good example is *Arlequin roi de Serendib* (Harlequin, King of Serendib), presented at the Saint-Germain Fair in 1713, in which the object of satire was likely André Campra's *Iphigénie en Tauride* (Iphigenia in Tauris, 1704). Here the plot of the opera (and the ancient Greek tragedy by Euripides on which it is based) is inverted. Instead of the high priestess Iphigenia being compelled to sacrifice a young man whom she discovers is her brother Orestes, Mezzetin (disguised as a high priestess) and Pierrot (also in female garb) are forced to sacrifice a newly crowned king every month, only to discover that their next victim is their old friend Harlequin (Fig. 12.1). After joyfully embracing one another, the three plunder the temple—even taking the statue of the foreign idol

Figure 12.1: *Engraving of Pierrot, Harlequin, and Mezzetin from* Arlequin roi de Serendib *(1713), in* Le théâtre de la foire ou L'opéra comique *(Paris, 1731)*

with them—and plot their escape to Paris, where they plan to drink champagne. "Now the opera is ended," Harlequin sings in the final air, "lon-lan-la, deriri."

Songs such as this were not newly composed; instead, words were fitted to familiar tunes—in this case one known as "Lon lan-la, derirette." Often referred to as vaudevilles, they would have been well known to the audience (who often sang along) and were recycled from one play to another. By the middle of the eighteenth century, as composers began writing original music for these comic plays, a new genre called *opéra comique* (comic opera) (as opposed to the theatrical institution known as Opéra-Comique) would come into its own, as John Rice discusses in *Music in the Eighteenth Century*.

THE *OPÉRA-BALLET*

The plays at Saint-Germain and Saint-Laurent also provided considerable competition for the official French theaters, particularly after the Italians were banished. The theaters, in turn, won back audiences by incorporating Italian elements into their performances. In the 1720s, for instance, the Comédie Française, which had been founded by Louis XIV in 1680, presented plays by Pierre de Marivaux featuring characters and plots inspired by the Italians. The *tragédie en musique* lived on through revivals of Lully's operas and novelties such as Campra's *Iphigénie en Tauride*, the work that may have inspired such parodies as *Arlequin roi de Serendib*. Meanwhile, as noted in Chapter 7, Venice and its Carnival were re-created at the Opéra in the new genre that became known as *opéra-ballet*.

Opéras-ballets typically included a prologue and several entrées or acts, which were usually independent of one another, although some *opéras-ballets* with continuous plots are often referred to simply as ballets. Whereas the *tragédie en musique* was bound up in the propaganda associated with Louis XIV, *opéras-ballets* celebrated an audience of nobles and upper bourgeois (the most prominent and wealthy members of the middle class) who were finally able to bask in the limelight vacated by the king in his old age, often staging parties, festivals, and the "operas within operas" that the public craved. Instead of heroes torn by duty and love or pathetic situations requiring grand eloquence, the *opéra-ballet*, as Rémond de Saint-Mard noted in 1741, was "all laughs." Saint-Mard shrugged off the possibility that such frivolity might not reflect well on the audience: "You will find there also the portrait of our mores. They are to be sure rather unpleasant, but they are, nonetheless, ours."

We see many of these features in works such as Campra's *Le carnaval de Venise* (Venetian Carnival, 1699) and *Les fêtes vénitiennes* (Venetian Festival, 1710), two of six *opéras-ballets* featuring Venetian settings that were premiered at the Opéra between 1697 and 1744. The point was not merely to entice viewers with the temptations of Venice and its famous Carnival. Rather, the city's libertine atmosphere provided a context in which to invoke the Italian style with both humor and music. In the prologue to *Les fêtes vénitiennes*, for instance, instead of the

tragédie en musique's typical celebration of Louis XIV's military feats, the audience is welcomed by La Folie (Folly) the goddess of Carnival madness: "Come
quickly, hasten, sample the delights of life; I dispense them all; there is nothing
·without folly" (Ex. 12.1).

Folly sings in the French style—that is, her vocal line includes French ornamentation and phrase structure, set syllabically and following the accentual
patterns of the French language. However, the Italian atmosphere is manifest in
the relationship between the voice and ritornello. The first ritornello introduces
a "head motif" (the main melodic idea of the aria) and then joins the voice in a

Example 12.1: *André Campra, "Accourez, hâtez-vous" from* Les fêtes vénitiennes (1710),
Prologue, scene 2, mm. 24–29

Step up, hurry, sample the delights of life; I dispense them all; there is nothing without folly

contrapuntal duet, while the subsequent ritornello punctuates the vocal line, using the vocabulary of the Italian concerto: sequences and scales known to us from the music of Torelli, Corelli, and Vivaldi. Implicitly, then, Folly beckons listeners to an entertainment in which she may speak French, but celebrates Italian pleasures.

Further Italianisms are invoked in the entertainments frequently staged within the *opéra-ballet*. *Le carnaval de Venise*, for instance, includes a mini-opera entitled *Orfeo nell'inferi* (Orpheus in the Underworld), sung entirely in Italian. With their substantial ritornelli, melismatic writing, and da capo form, arias such as Orpheus's "La vittoria" (Victory) might well have been composed for a Venetian opera.

FRANÇOIS COUPERIN AND *LES GOÛTS RÉUNIS*

The theater was not the only place where the intersection of French and Italian tastes had significant repercussions. It was felt in the harpsichord, church, and chamber music of the era, in particular the music of François Couperin (1668–1733).

Perhaps more than any of his contemporaries, Couperin was at home in several different worlds. He was well situated at the court of Louis XIV, serving as organist, court composer, and harpsichord teacher to the king's children. But, as we have seen, he was also comfortable in the châteaux of the rebellious nobles and with the public entertainments at the fairs.

Since Couperin's early career coincided with the final decades of Louis XIV's life, his impact was not in the theatrical realm. He never wrote an opera of any kind, devoting his energies instead to music for the church and chamber. He was often called upon to console and entertain the increasingly melancholic king with his harpsichord and chamber compositions. As an organist, particularly at the Church of St. Gervais in Paris, where the Couperin family maintained a musical dynasty lasting until the early years of the nineteenth century, he composed sacred masterpieces of great intensity for both the organ and vocal ensembles. His setting of the *Leçons de ténèbres* (Tenebrae Lessons, 1713–17), for example, was intended for the Tenebrae service during Holy Week, to be sung in growing darkness as the candles were slowly extinguished. The text comes from the lamentations of Jeremiah over the destruction of the first Temple of Jerusalem in the sixth century BCE. Couperin sets the Hebrew letters that open each verse with a luxurious, haunting vocalise, suggestive of Gregorian or even Hebrew chant, albeit with poignant dissonances, thus marrying the florid vocal writing associated with the Italians to the elegant text setting typical of French music (Fig. 12.2).

On the other hand, Couperin's *Pièces de clavecin*, his masterful set of harpsichord works published in four books between 1713 and 1730, tells us a great deal about Couperin's life and friends, as well as his deep familiarity with and

Figure 12.2: *François Couperin,* Leçons de ténèbres, *Wednesday, Lesson 1, facsimile of printed edition (Paris, ca. 1714)*

appreciation for theatrical music. Its 27 suites or *ordres* (orders), as Couperin names them, contain a variety of genres: standard dance movements, dedicatory works with the names of specific individuals, and character pieces with titles that are often enigmatic or obscure, some intentionally so.

Couperin's harpsichord music is thus full of extramusical ideas, as he tells us in the preface to the first book: "I have always had a subject when composing all these pieces: different occasions provided it. Thus the titles refer to ideas that have occurred to me." Some of the pieces are "musical portraits" of individual people, which "under my fingers have, on occasion, been found to be tolerable likenesses."

Many of the references in Couperin's titles remain elusive. The gloom of the Tenebrae service may have been the inspiration for the opening allemande in the "tombeau" key of C minor, titled *La ténébreuse* (Order 3), which exploits the darkness of the harpsichord's lowest register. This could not be more different from *Les moissonneurs* (The Reapers, Order 6), whose purposeful, steady rhythm (with the persistent two-note pickup characteristic of the gavotte) and sharp upbeat articulation seem to portray the cutting of wheat stalks (see Anthology 18). This is one of numerous examples from the music and art of eighteenth-century France that reflects the aristocratic fascination with the pastoral.

L'arlequine (Harlequin, Order 23) is one of a number of works in the *Pièces de clavecin* that reflects Couperin's apparent interest in the fair theaters. With the curious tempo marking "grotesquement" (grotesquely), it features a sly, oscillating neighbor-note figure and syncopations that conjure the character's famous agility. *Le tic-toc-choc, ou Les maillotins* (Order 18) also provides strong evidence that Couperin was an enthusiastic patron of the popular Parisian fairs. The subtitle *Pièce croisée* (literally, crossed piece) is Couperin's instruction to the harpsichordist to play one part on the upper keyboard and the other on the lower. Here Couperin gives us two insistent repetitive figures, one in the left hand and the other in the right, which may well invoke the ticking clock, as the title suggests (Ex. 12.2). The word *maillotins* is a bit more mysterious. It may be the diminutive of *maillot*, which means hammer, but more likely it refers to the Maillot family, a group of tightrope dancers who performed at the Parisian fairs, the two oscillating figures perhaps representing the balance required by the acrobats.

Couperin's most definitive endorsement of the blending of French and Italian styles is found in his chamber music. As early as 1692 he composed a set of Italian-style trio sonatas under a pseudonym—an Italian anagram of his name—indicating that it was not quite politic to endorse the Italian style during this period of Louis XIV's reign. When Couperin revised and published the sonatas 34 years later, after the king's death, he added a long suite of dances and retitled the entire collection *Les nations* (The Nations, 1726). In the preface, he felt free to acknowledge that "I was much taken by the sonatas of Corelli, whose works I shall love until the day I die, just as I do the French works of Monsieur de Lully."

Couperin's reverence for both the Italian and French traditions, and his ability to combine them without stylistic discord, are reflected in the titles of other chamber music collections, most notably *Le Parnasse, ou L'apothéose de Corelli* (Parnassus, or The Apotheosis of Corelli), in which Corelli and Lully are treated as equals as they are brought to Mount Parnassus to meet Apollo. Even more dramatic in its advocacy of the *goûts réunis* is the *Concert instrumental sous le titre d'Apothéose composé à la mémoire immortelle de l'incomparable Monsieur de Lully* (Instrumental Concert Entitled Apotheosis, Composed in Immortal Memory of the Incomparable Monsieur de Lully, 1725), another chamber work in which Apollo reigns as arbiter of taste. In it, Lully ascends Parnassus and is met by Corelli and Apollo, who persuades both composers that the marriage of the French and Italian styles will lead to the perfection of music. Among the movements they play together is a set of airs; in the first Lully plays the subject and Corelli the accompaniment, and in the second their roles are reversed (Fig. 12.3). Lully's theme is in G major,

Example 12.2: *François Couperin,* Le tic-toc-choc, ou Les maillotins, *from* Pièces de clavecin, *Book 3 (1722), Order 18, mm. 1–3*

Figure 12.3: *François Couperin,* Lully Plays the Subject and Corelli Accompanies Him; Corelli Plays the Subject in His Turn, While Lully Accompanies. *From* Concert instrumental sous le titre d'Apothéose composé à la mémoire immortelle de l'incomparable Monsieur de Lully *(Paris, 1725)*

with French-style ornamentation and relatively little dissonance, while Corelli's, in G minor, is full of Italianate chromaticism, sigh motives, and arpeggios. In Couperin's reunion of tastes, both styles retain their identities while coexisting in perfect stylistic harmony.

THE FRENCH CANTATA

The melding of French and Italian styles gave birth to a new genre known as the French cantata. Particularly popular in salons, at court, and in other chamber settings, its development was in part stimulated by the performances of Italian cantatas under the auspices of Philippe II d'Orléans. While French cantata composers were attracted to many features of Italian music—its use of virtuosity, melismas, sequential patterns, and dissonance—they nevertheless sought to retain much of the restraint and color of their own style.

The special features of the French cantata are apparent in *Le sommeil d'Ulisse* (The Sleep of Ulysses, 1715) by Elisabeth Jacquet de la Guerre (1665–1729). Having come to public attention as a child prodigy playing harpsichord and organ at the court of Louis XIV, Jacquet published a number of works including her *Pièces de clavecin* (1687), a *tragédie en musique* called *Céphale et Procris* (Cephalis and Procris, 1694), and two sets of cantatas on Old Testament themes (1708 and 1711, respectively). *Le sommeil d'Ulisse*, published with several other secular cantatas, depicts an episode from Homer's *Odyssey*. On his way home to Ithaca after fighting the Trojan War, Ulysses's voyage is interrupted by a tempest caused by Neptune. The boat capsizes, but the goddess Minerva protects the hero by sending him into a deep sleep. The cantata ends as Ulysses enjoys the favor and entertainment of Alcinous, king of the Phaecians.

What differentiates this and other French cantatas from those produced by Italian composers is that the entire drama is conveyed by a single singer, who not only expresses the feelings of all the characters, but also narrates the action. In *Le sommeil d'Ulisse*, moreover, Jacquet exploited the resources of an ensemble that included strings and winds, which both accompany the soprano and help create the atmosphere for the cantata's two most potent scenes. The tempest is represented by rushing sixteenth and thirty-second notes, sudden dynamic contrasts, and the repeated notes associated with the *stile concitato* (Ex. 12.3). In the sleep aria, the mood is enhanced by the voice's duet with the flute; the gentle rocking of the dotted quarter and eighth notes create a sense of calm, while the singer's unusually long notes bring time to a halt (Ex. 12.4). By annexing elements of the Italian style in the service of a uniquely French narrative ideal, Jacquet and her fellow cantata composers created dramatic miniatures in which voices and instruments constructed a theater in the listener's mind.

Example 12.3: *Elisabeth Jacquet de la Guerre,* Le sommeil d'Ulisse *(1715), tempest aria, mm. 88–92*

To destroy this warrior, he gives in to rage

Example 12.4: *Elisabeth Jacquet de la Guerre,* Le sommeil d'Ulisse *(1715), sleep aria, mm. 200–203*

Sleep

PARIS DURING THE REGENCY

With the death of Louis XIV in 1715, Versailles receded still further into the background of musical life as the regent, Philippe II d'Orléans, moved the entire court back to Paris. During the Regency (1715–23), public balls were held three times a week at the Opéra. The theater was sumptuously decorated, often with operatic sets that transported dancers into the fictional realms of the *opéra-ballets.* (In order to make room for all the masked guests, machines were required to level the floors.) Although the regent himself was less interested in dance than Louis XIV, he encouraged the young Louis XV to participate in spectacles. In 1721, for instance, the 11-year-old king danced in the prologue of the *opéra-ballet* entitled *Les élémens* (The Elements), with music by André Cardinal Destouches and Michel-Richard de Lalande and poetry by Pierre-Charles Roy.

As we recall from Chapter 10, Paris was also home to the Concert Spirituel, the concert series established in 1725 to provide entertainment during Lent, when the Parisian theaters were closed. Significantly, the first concert featured motets by Lalande alongside Corelli's Concerto Grosso Op. 6, No. 8, known as the Christmas Concerto. Meanwhile, salons and private musical establishments continued to thrive at the behest of noble or wealthy patrons. The Hôtel des Soissons, the home of the Prince de Carignan, was renowned for gambling and debauchery, as well as for trial runs of works to be presented at the Opéra. At the influential salon run by Alexandre Jean Josephe Le Riche de La Pouplinière, cantatas and airs were sung, and composers often made their reputations and careers playing not only original harpsichord pieces but also transcriptions of popular operatic excerpts, consumed by an opera-hungry public.

JEAN-PHILIPPE RAMEAU

Both the Prince de Carignan and La Pouplinière would become patrons of the most important and controversial composer of the Regency and the reign of Louis XV: Jean-Philippe Rameau (1683–1764). That Rameau achieved his greatest fame in his own day late in life as an opera composer is remarkable, given that his intellectual innovations were primarily in music theory. Previously, most authors of figured bass treatises had taught that chord and harmonic progressions were vertical manifestations of a primarily horizontal process. Rameau, by contrast, was interested in describing how chords (particularly the tonic, dominant, and subdominant) related to one another, arguing that all musical parameters derive from these basic harmonic functions. This theory, codified in Rameau's pathbreaking *Traité de l'harmonie* (Treatise on Harmony, 1722), underlies the modern practice of identifying chords by Roman numerals. While both his contemporaries and modern scholars agree that his theories are not entirely consistent, Rameau's search for knowledge and unity aligns him with Enlightenment thinkers such as Immanuel Kant and Voltaire. (See the extract from the *Treatise on Harmony* in SR 115:691–96; 4/35:183–88.)

Rameau spent the early part of his career primarily as a composer of keyboard and chamber music on the model of Couperin acquiring some firsthand knowledge of Italian music as a young man. Indeed, later in life he regretted not having had the opportunity to refine his taste with another Italian sojourn. Shortly after his fiftieth birthday he set out on a new path when he presented his first opera, *Hippolyte et Aricie* (Hippolytus and Aricia, 1733), at the Opéra. Rameau regarded his previous study of music as an essential part of his qualifications as an opera composer. Six years before the premiere of *Hippolyte,* he wrote to the librettist Antoine Houdar de La Motte that it was "desirable that there should be found for the stage a musician who has studied nature before painting her and who, through his learning, knows how to choose the colours and shades which his mind and his taste make him feel to be related with the required expressions."

Rameau's sense of color is reflected in the richness of his harmonic language, which shocked listeners accustomed to the relative blandness of Lully's style. He uses more-complex chords, with added sevenths and ninths, utilizing extreme keys on both the sharp and flat sides of the harmonic spectrum. In the second Trio of the Fates, in Act 2 of *Hippolyte et Aricie,* Rameau depicts the horrors of the underworld with a series of half-step modulations that descend chromatically from G minor to D minor (Ex. 12.5). Rameau also achieves spectacular effects as an orchestrator, creating timbres and textures that vividly enhance the dramatic action.

Not surprisingly, one finds Italianate melismas and occasional da capo arias in Rameau's operas. Indeed, he strayed sufficiently from the Lullian model in his *tragédies en musique* that he found himself embroiled in a controversy during the 1730s that almost led to a duel with Pierre-Charles Roy, the librettist of *Les élémens.* The complaints offered by the *lullistes,* who for the most part were not professional musicians, were that Rameau's operas were too learned, that "nothing flowed naturally," that there was too much dissonance and noise, and that once a pleasing tune started, it quickly ended. In fact, Lully's partisans used the word *Baroque* to condemn Rameau's style, as we recall from Chapter 1. Meanwhile, the *ramistes* took aim at the revivals of Lully's operas, which they described as boring and staid, without the color and virtuosity of Rameau's works.

There is ample reason to believe that Rameau did not relish his role as the inheritor of Lully's mantle. Only seven of his 28 works are *tragédies en musique* in the Lullian mold (one was never performed). He contributed to a number of other genres of theatrical music, including not only *opéras-ballets* but also *pastorales héroïques* (heroic pastorals) and *comédies lyriques* (lyric comedies). An example of the latter is *Platée* (Plataea, 1745), with poetry by Adrien Joseph

Example 12.5: *Jean-Philippe Rameau, Trio of the Fates from* Hippolyte et Aricie *(1733), Act 2, scene 5, mm. 16–22: chord progressions with enharmonic equivalents*

Le Valois d'Orville, based on a play by Jacques Autreau that owes much to the fairground tradition. The story involves the libidinous god Jupiter, who is forever getting himself involved with earthly women and thus inspiring jealousy in his wife Juno. To fool her, Jupiter pretends to be in love with an ugly water nymph—played by a cross-dressed counter-tenor—who nonetheless believes herself to be quite beautiful and deserving of the god's love.

Rameau's score plays with the boundaries between humor and pathos, creating for the nymph Plataea an exaggerated tragic rhetoric that emphasizes the inherent ridiculousness of the situation: the swamp creature—sung by Pierre de Jélyotte, who was known for his serious romantic leads—could not possibly be an object of desire for Jupiter. The incongruity of the match is highlighted in the extended monologue sung by Plataea in Act 2 (see Anthology 19), as Jupiter descends to the earth, presumably to court the deluded nymph. The colorful orchestral writing and bold harmonic progressions dramatize the supernatural feats of Jupiter, who, descending in a cloud to meet his beloved, transforms himself into a donkey and then finally into an owl that flies around the stage, frightening Plataea.

Despite his innovative compositional style and the comedic skill displayed in works like *Platée*, Rameau was once again put on the defensive in 1754, when an Italian company arrived in Paris to perform Giovanni Battista Pergolesi's *La serva padrona* (The Servant Turned Mistress) taking Paris by storm. Having begun his career as a progressive composer rallying against the strictures of Lully's style, he found himself cast in the role of a conservative when confronted with *opera buffa*, the comic opera style that arose in Italy and swept across Europe in the mid-eighteenth century. A new era had begun, and Rameau, despite his many innovations, was regarded as a product of the Baroque.

We conclude our overview of Parisian pleasures in the early eighteenth century with a brief glimpse back at Versailles, where the young Louis XV would take up residence in 1722. Under his rule, the court kept up many of the artistic traditions that his great-grandfather had observed, but with one crucial difference: rather than leading Parisian fashions, as it had under Louis XIV, the court became a follower and imitator. Moreover, some of the most novel artistic ventures of Louis XV's reign were initiated not by the king, but by his mistress, Madame de Pompadour. A gifted singer and actress, she planned a number of operas and entertainments—including those by Rameau—for the private theater that she maintained in her apartments at Versailles. Indeed, it is telling that when Madame de Pompadour revived *Les élémens* in the late 1740s, a statue took the place of the role previously danced by the young Louis XV. By midcentury, the artistic glory of the French court was in the hands of the royal mistress, and the *ancien régime* and the king who represented it were reduced to an inanimate stone image.

FOR FURTHER READING

Anderson, Nicholas, "Rameau's *Platée*: Burlesque or Grotesque?" *Early Music* 11 (1983): 505–8

Cabrini, Michele, "Breaking Form through Sound: Instrumental Aesthetics, Tempête, and Temporality in the French Baroque Cantata," *Journal of Musicology* 26 (2009): 327–78

Cowart, Georgia, "Carnival in Venice or Protest in Paris? Louis XIV and the Politics of Subversion at the Paris Opéra," *Journal of the American Musicological Association* 54 (2001): 265–302

Dill, Charles, *Monstrous Opera: Rameau and the Tragic Tradition* (Princeton, NJ: Princeton University Press, 1998)

Fader, Don, "The 'Cabale du Dauphin,' Campra, and Italian Comedy: The Courtly Politics of French Musical Patronage around 1700," *Music and Letters* 86 (2005): 380–413

Fader, Don, "Philippe II d'Orléans's 'Chanteurs Italiens,' the Italian Cantata and the *Goûts-réunis* under Louis XIV," *Early Music* 35 (2007): 237–49

Harris-Warrick, Rebecca, "Staging Venice," *Cambridge Opera Journal* 15 (2003): 297–316

Mellers, Wilfred, *François Couperin and the French Classical Tradition* (London and Boston: Faber, 1987)

Sadler, Graham, "Patrons and Pasquinades: Rameau in the 1730s," *Journal of the Royal Musical Association* 113 (1988): 314–37

Semmens, Richard Templer, *The Bals Publics at the Paris Opéra in the Eighteenth Century* (Hillsdale, NY: Pendragon Press, 2004)

CHAPTER THIRTEEN

Music in City, Court, and Church in the Holy Roman Empire

On September 12, 1683, an army of Poles, Austrians, and Germans defeated the Turkish forces that had laid siege to Vienna since mid-July. This was a momentous turning point for the Holy Roman Emperor Leopold I. The Turks had tried to conquer Vienna unsuccessfully once before, in 1529. By 1699 they had been completely expelled from Hungary, ending, at least for the time being, the Ottoman incursions into the Holy Roman Empire.

In the aftermath of this critical conflict between East and West, Leopold and his successors, Joseph I and Charles VI, devoted themselves to transforming Vienna into Europe's foremost capital city, one that could compete with and even surpass the splendor of Versailles. Among the bold architectural projects initiated by Charles VI was the magnificent St. Charles Church, begun at the emperor's orders in 1713 in gratitude for the end of the plague; it would not be completed until 1737, just three years before Charles's death.

That the Habsburg emperor and his family would wish to surround themselves with sumptuous architecture, art, and music is by no means surprising. As the seat of the symbolic power of the Holy Roman Empire and the residence for the ruler of the Austrian realms, Vienna was a city in which ceremony mattered. Much of this was a result of the multifaceted role of the Habsburg emperor, whose power was largely derived from his direct rule over the lands long controlled by the Austrian branch of the Habsburg family. This included the regions now known as Austria, the Czech Republic (then the kingdoms of Moravia and Bohemia), Slovakia, Slovenia, Croatia, parts of Poland and northern Italy, and Hungary.

The Habsburg emperor was also the symbolic head of the Holy Roman Empire, the loose confederacy of German-speaking territories spread over a vast area of northern and central Europe. By tradition, the emperor was chosen by a select group of rulers of the various principalities, who were known as electors. Although maintaining a degree of loyalty to the emperor, the electors were essentially absolute monarchs of their own realms. In addition, the Holy Roman Empire encompassed "free" imperial cities—nominally under the rule of the emperor, but essentially self-governing. These included Hamburg and Lübeck, which were part of a network of trading partners on the North Sea known since the Middle Ages as the Hanseatic League. The Holy Roman Emperor also had jurisdiction over ecclesiastical states such as Salzburg, which was ruled by an archbishop-prince who exercised both religious and temporal authority over his own territories. The fact that some of these principalities were Protestant placed even more pressure on the militantly Catholic Habsburg emperor to maintain an image of invincibility and piety.

In this chapter we look at music in several corners of the Holy Roman Empire, where profoundly different modes of government, worship, and patronage influenced musical styles and production. We begin on the western and northern edges of the empire in the free imperial cities of Lübeck and Hamburg, where Dieterich Buxtehude and later Georg Philipp Telemann enjoyed the support of affluent merchants and city officials in presenting music in the Lutheran churches and for increasingly popular public concerts. We then stop in Salzburg, where the violinist Heinrich Ignaz Franz Biber flourished under the patronage of the Catholic archbishop-prince. Finally, we return to the Vienna of Charles VI, where Metastasio's opera librettos (see Chapter 11) dominated the stage, and masses, oratorios, concertos, and chamber music—musical manifestations of the Austrian Baroque—would become central to the rituals of court life and the representation of Vienna to the world.

A DOMESTIC MUSIC SCENE IN NORTH GERMANY

We gain some insights into music in the North German cities of Hamburg and Lübeck from a painting by Johannes Voorhout entitled *Domestic Music Scene* (Fig. 13.1). On the surface, this is a conventional representation of well-dressed, upper-middle-class musicians playing for one another at home. Yet there are

Figure 13.1: *Johannes Voorhout,* Domestic Music Scene *(1674)*

some fascinating contradictions in this painting. On the right-hand side, Voorhout emphasizes exoticism and sensuality: an alluring female singer, with loose hair and a revealing gown, her bosom discreetly hidden by her lute, glances seductively at the attentive young man to her right, while just behind in the center a couple extend their hands to one another, as if they might be about to dance. The costumed African boy and the silk dressing gown worn by the harpsichordist remind the viewer of the mysterious pleasures of the eastern and southern hemispheres, and perhaps the trade with those far away climes that filled the coffers of bankers in Hamburg and Lübeck.

The painting's left side depicts serious music-making and musicians. The harpsichordist who faces the viewer has been identified as Johann Adam Reincken (ca. 1643–1722), who served for much of his long life as organist at St. Catherine's Church in Hamburg. The cheerful viola da gamba player is believed to be the Lübeck-based composer of vocal and keyboard music Dieterich Buxtehude (ca. 1637–1707). The two sides of the painting are mediated by the image of a listener, who looks longingly at the singer, while under his elbow sits a canon for eight voices, dedicated to Buxtehude and Reincken: "Behold how good and pleasant it is for brethren to dwell together in unity."

Intended to be understood allegorically rather than as a realistic representation of a specific event, the painting touches on all the major elements of music-making in Hamburg and Lübeck in the late seventeenth and early eighteenth centuries. First, there are the political implications. As a group, these musicians epitomize the independence from the strictures of royal patronage that were enjoyed by musicians in these two free imperial cities. Hamburg's government resembled Venice's in that power was shared by a small group of patricians: its governing bodies included the city council, with representatives from 20 of the city's wealthiest families, a citizens' assembly made up of landowners, admiralty, and a council of ministers that oversaw church matters. The somewhat more conservative Lübeck was ruled by a city council, which frequently conducted city business in the pews of Buxtehude's church, St. Mary's. In both cities groups of citizens shared the responsibility of supporting music, motivated by artistic or spiritual ambitions, a desire for prestige, or hope of commercial profit.

The details of Voorhout's painting also tell us about musical tastes in Hamburg and its environs. The prominence of Reincken underscores the importance of keyboard and organ music in Hamburg and northern European culture in general, music in which counterpoint (evoked by the canon) played a vital role. The presence of the female singer and dancing couple reminds us that this was a musical culture that encompassed high and low, sacred and secular, including the public opera that would take hold in Hamburg. Finally, the sympathetic portrait of the young Buxtehude invokes the musical riches to be heard in nearby Lübeck, where the composer, like his Hamburg friends, established his own public concert series.

BUXTEHUDE IN LÜBECK

By the time Buxtehude took the oath of citizenship in Lübeck in 1668, the city was no longer the center of power in the Hanseatic League, as it had been for centuries. Nonetheless, Lübeck still boasted a citizenry that derived its considerable wealth from shipbuilding and trade. The city's ten churches were highly valued, none more than St. Mary's, the official church of the city council, whose two towers stood proudly in the city's center. Buxtehude, who had received a solid Lutheran education at the Latin School in the Danish city of Elsinore (best known from Shakespeare's *Hamlet*), would spend 40 years as organist at St. Mary's, the most prestigious and highly paid musical position in the city. Buxtehude also had at his disposal the municipal musicians (employed by the city) and other members of the musicians' guild (the city's freelance players), which even in the first half of the century had possessed a tradition of fine string playing.

ORGAN MUSIC IN LÜBECK

Civic pride and religious fervor were certainly factors motivating the mastery of organ building and organ music in both Lübeck and Hamburg, where the great builder Arp Schnitger established his reputation (see Chapter 4). At St. Mary's, Buxtehude had two organs, which were sometimes used together. The Grand Organ, originally built in the early sixteenth century, was restored in the mid-seventeenth century by Friederich Stellwagen, another famous builder of the period. (Buxtehude tried but failed to enlist Arp Schnitger to do further restoration of the Grand Organ.) There was also a smaller organ referred to as the Totentanz (dance of death) Organ, situated near a side chapel where masses for the dead were often recited. Both organs were destroyed by Allied bombs in 1942.

Unlike his Hamburg colleague Reincken, from whom relatively few organ works survive, Buxtehude left a large repertory encompassing virtually every genre of organ music: toccatas, preludes, chorale settings, canzonas, suites, and variations, as well as two chaconnes and a passacaglia based on a ground bass. Some of Buxtehude's most masterful works for keyboard are those in the fantasia style, such as the Toccata in F Major, BuxWV 156. With its juxtaposition of freely improvisatory and imitative sections, the Toccata in F Major is reminiscent of the Frescobaldi toccata we considered in Chapter 4. Buxtehude, however, places greater demands on the player's pedal technique. The drama of the work derives in no small part from Buxtehude's utter command of counterpoint and the fluidity with which he moves from one texture to another, careening from moments of tonal stability to distant sonorities, accelerating and decelerating the tempo at will.

The opening of the toccata is in pure fantasia style, with virtuosic scalar passages and seemingly spontaneous exchanges between the right and left hands, grounded by pedal points (sustained notes in the pedals). After playing with a number of different textures and rhythmic ideas, occasionally shifting meter, Buxtehude introduces a quite sober four-voice fugal section, marked by a fanfare motive in the subject (Ex. 13.1). He draws upon the fanfare in a subsequent episode (a section in a fugue in which the main theme or subject is not present), quickening the pace, until in measures 65–66 an arpeggio in the pedal inspires a thirty-second-note scalar flourish in the right hand, interrupted by a dissonant F♯ against the G in the pedal (Ex. 13.2). Toward the end of the toccata, Buxtehude demonstrates his technical mastery of the instrument, as the feet are required to play broken tenths in sixteenth notes (Ex. 13.3).

Buxtehude's reputation as an organ virtuoso would inspire the 20-year-old Johann Sebastian Bach to take an extended leave from his position in Arnstadt and walk all the way to Lübeck—a distance of more than 250 miles—to hear the master play (see Chapter 15).

Example 13.1: *Dieterich Buxtehude, Toccata in F Major, BuxWV 156, mm. 32–33*

Example 13.2: *Dieterich Buxtehude, Toccata in F Major, BuxWV 156, mm. 65–67*

Example 13.3: *Dieterich Buxtehude, Toccata in F Major, BuxWV 156, mm. 120–123*

LUTHERAN SPIRITUALITY: *MEMBRA JESU NOSTRI*

Buxtehude was also an accomplished composer of vocal music in both German and Latin, utilizing a broad range of styles and genres, and observing many of the stylistic conventions with which we are now familiar. Like Claudio Monteverdi, Lodovico Viadana, and Heinrich Schütz, Buxtehude composed settings of biblical texts as sacred concertos for one or more voices (see Chapter 5). By the mid- to late seventeenth century, however, Buxtehude and his colleagues increasingly began to experiment with integrating sacred concertos into multisectioned vocal works that might contain arias (settings of rhymed strophic poetry), recitatives, and even familiar German hymns or chorales. These composite works are often referred to as cantatas, since in some respects they resemble the Italian secular cantatas, though Buxtehude himself never used the term.

One example is *Ad cor: Vulnerasti cor meum* (To the heart: You have wounded my heart), the sixth in a cycle of seven cantatas entitled *Membra Jesu nostri* (The Limbs of Our Jesus), BuxWV 75. The aria texts were drawn from a thirteenth-century Latin poem entitled *Salve mundi salutare* (Long Live the Salvation of the World), each section of which is addressed to part of the crucified Christ's body. The cantatas open with an instrumental sinfonia and a sacred concerto setting of an appropriate biblical text. However, only in this cantata does Buxtehude use viole da gamba, rather than violins, violas, and cellos, thus creating a somber mood for the sacred concerto that begins and ends with one of the most poignant verses of the Song of Songs 4:9: "You have wounded my heart, my sister, my bride" (see Anthology 20).

Example 13.4: *Dieterich Buxtehude,* Jubilate Domino, *BuxWV 64, mm. 60–63*

Sing

Buxtehude uses a different technique in the sacred concerto *Jubilate Domino* (Shout Joyfully to the Lord), BuxWV 64, a setting of the celebratory Psalm 98:4–6: the viol is an equal partner with the solo alto voice. The two are in the same register and present similarly virtuosic lines that explore their full ranges. Indeed, Buxtehude blurs the line between voice and instrument: in measures 60–63 the viol's extravagant melisma is imitated by the voice, which crosses into the upper register (Ex. 13.4). It is as if Buxtehude were staging a competition to see who is better able to sing in praise of God. If *Jubilate Domino* was written for a visiting castrato, as scholars have suggested, a striking feature of the first performance may have been the contrast in timbre between the mellow viol and the brilliant sound of the castrato voice.

PUBLIC CONCERTS IN HAMBURG AND LÜBECK

Voorhout's painting reminds us that the wealthy merchants of Hamburg and Lübeck also promoted music outside of the church, both as players (amateur and professional) and as audiences. Buxtehude, for instance, established a public concert venture in Lübeck known as Abendmusik (evening music), in which he served as composer, impresario, and chief fund-raiser, garnering support from the Lübeck business community. Like the leaders of nonprofit arts organizations today, Buxtehude recognized that businessmen who supported the arts would not only enjoy the fruits of their contributions, but also gain prestige.

Buxtehude's programming for these concerts was also unusual. As the extant librettos attest (little actual music survives), he presented oratorio-like dramatic works consisting of choruses, instrumental excerpts, recitatives, and arias. While he experimented with different formats, one of his most innovative moves was to divide the works into five-part serial dramas, presented on successive Sunday afternoons.

The Abendmusik tradition was to continue until the French occupation and annexation of Lübeck in the early nineteenth century during the course of the Napoleonic Wars.

PUBLIC OPERA IN HAMBURG

Hamburg's wealthy merchants provided even more support for music outside the church than did those in Lübeck. The German traveler Johann Friedrich von Uffenbach was impressed that the "most prominent men in the city—including the city council—do not absent themselves from public concerts," and credited as well the "many connoisseurs and intelligent people" of Hamburg, where opera "is now at its greatest flowering." The Theater am Gänsemarkt, which opened in 1678, was the first public opera theater to flourish outside of Italy, where Handel composed his first operas (see Chapter 11). Although Hamburg opera producers had to deal with the objections of Pietist ministers, whose anxieties about the negative influence of the Italian style were a factor in the Lutheran Church (see Chapter 5), public opera in Hamburg enjoyed considerable success for 50 years, particularly through the efforts of two outstanding composers: Reinhard Keiser (1674–1739), who composed some 66 operas after assuming the directorship of the theater in 1696 or 1697; and Georg Philipp Telemann (1681–1767), whose association with the Hamburg opera began shortly after his appointment as cantor of the Johanneum Latin School in 1721, which required him to direct music in all five of the city's churches. Telemann would write for the Hamburg opera until the enterprise went bankrupt in 1738.

Unlike the many Italian *opere serie* that were heard in the absolutist courts in Dresden, Munich, and Vienna, operas produced in Hamburg reflected that city's cosmopolitan leanings in both their languages and their styles. The majority of Keiser's operas, for instance, were in German, though many included some arias in Italian. His *Carneval von Venedig* (Carnival of Venice, 1707), an adaptation of Campra's *opéra-ballet* (see Chapter 12), is one of a number of works presented at the Theater am Gänsemarkt that was inspired by French models.

Telemann's charming *Orpheus* (1726), based on *L'Orphée* (1690) by Louis Lully (son of Jean-Baptiste), is mostly in German, but also contains Italian and French texts borrowed from librettos set by Handel and the elder Lully. This was by no means an unusual practice. An opera in which the text was pieced together from different sources or in which different composers contributed acts or sections was known as a *pasticcio*—literally, a pastry. The villainess Orasia, who (in this odd version of the tale) plots the demise of Orpheus, sings in German; Orpheus's entreaties to Pluto are in Italian; and the pastoral choruses are in French, invoking the *tragédie en musique*.

This international style appealed to the diverse audience in Hamburg, where opera and the arts fueled the city's economy. Johann Mattheson, one of the city's most prominent native musicians and a violinist in the opera orchestra (alongside Handel) under Keiser's direction, likened the pleasure and instruction audiences received in the opera house to the service and security that banks supplied to their customers. Taking the comparison one step further, he noted that "it is almost always true that where the best banks are found so too are the best opera houses."

TELEMANN'S ORCHESTRAL AND CHAMBER MUSIC

In addition to composing operas and sacred vocal music as required for his position as director of the city's five churches, Telemann presented numerous public concerts of both sacred and secular music in Hamburg. We recall from Chapter 10 that he had established a collegium musicum in Leipzig during his student years; he would do the same in his subsequent position in Frankfurt. In Hamburg, where a collegium musicum had been founded by Matthias Weckmann as early as 1660, Telemann would find an eager audience for such concerts, although he initially faced opposition from church authorities, who took a dim view of the ease with which he moved from the sacred to the secular realm.

Many of Telemann's orchestral and chamber works, such as his overture-suites (suites that begin with a French overture, often with extramusical associations), were likely composed for collegia and heard in public concerts. A good example is Telemann's *Ouverture burlesque de Quixotte*, TWV 55: G10, likely composed in Hamburg between 1725 and 1730. The swirling sixteenth-note violin passages and impressive *stile concitato* in the third movement aptly represent Don Quixote's famous joust with the windmills, as described in Miguel de Cervantes's classic novel (see Anthology 21).

It may have been the cosmopolitan atmosphere of Hamburg, coupled with his desire to appeal to a public that paid to hear concerts, that led Telemann, in the latter decades of his life, to cultivate the pleasing symmetrical phrases and somewhat less complex textures associated with the *galant* style, which John Rice discusses in *Music in the Eighteenth Century.*

HEINRICH BIBER IN SALZBURG

Unlike his near contemporary Buxtehude, Heinrich Ignaz Franz Biber (1644–1704) did not have the opportunity to become a musical entrepreneur. Rather, his creativity was nurtured in the ecclesiastical city of Salzburg. A tradition of musical excellence had been established there early in the seventeenth century by Archbishop Wolf Dietrich, who had developed a love of Italian music during his studies at the Collegio Germanico in Rome. When Biber, a violinist from northern Bohemia, arrived in Salzburg in 1671 to serve another musically enlightened archbishop-prince, Maximilian Gandolph von Khuenburgh, he found himself in a city in which Italian architecture had replaced the medieval buildings, and in which the musical institutions at court and in the cathedral were organized according to Italian practices. There were ample resources to perform large polychoral works, plays with music, and court operas. Biber had access to trumpeters and timpanists for ceremonial occasions, as well as musicians for chamber performances and to accompany meals at court.

The talented violinist rose quickly through the ranks. Having begun his employment on the lowest rung of the musical ladder as a musically inclined servant, he was appointed vice-Kapellmeister in 1679, Kapellmeister in 1684, and finally lord high steward in 1692. On his second and successful petition for a knighthood from Emperor Leopold I in 1690, he self-deprecatingly referred to his fame in a great many courts as the result of "slight application in music." "Slight application" is indeed an understatement, for Biber was one of the most original composers of the period—a point no doubt recognized by Leopold I, who ennobled him under the courtly title of Biber von Bibern.

Despite the fact that the majority of his dramatic music is lost—only one opera survives—Biber left a large and impressive legacy of both vocal and instrumental music, ranging from intimate chamber music, such as his works for unaccompanied violin, to large-scale sacred vocal works. Biber's massive *Missa salisburgensis* (Salzburg Mass), likely composed in 1682 for the celebration of the eleven-hundredth anniversary of the archdiocese, gives a sense of the grandeur and ceremony associated with the Salzburg Cathedral. The mass is scored for 52 vocal and instrumental parts: there are four SATB choruses, two string choirs, a choir of oboes and recorders, a choir of cornetti and trombones, two choirs of timpani and trumpets, and parts for two organs and basso continuo. A sense of how all these singers and players might have been accommodated can be seen in Melchior Küsel's 1682 engraving of a celebration at the cathedral, which shows singers and instrumentalists spread throughout the choir area in the front of the church, as well as in all of the organ galleries or balconies (Fig. 13.2).

The splendor of the *Missa salisburgensis* results in part from the sheer size of the performing forces, typical of the "colossal" Baroque style that we considered in Chapter 5. Biber took full advantage of the myriad sonic possibilities created by contrasting vocal and instrumental groups. Expressing the grand architecture with his music, Biber used a dizzying array of textures and sonorities, overwhelming the listener with monumental walls of sound, rapid shifts between large and small forces, imitative polyphony, and virtuosic solo writing. There is variety too in the work's tonal styles, as static sections of primarily tonic and dominant sonorities are juxtaposed with more harmonically adventurous passages.

BIBER'S INSTRUMENTAL MUSIC

Perhaps the most ingenious of the many Renaissance and Baroque pieces intended to convey the sounds of battle, Biber's *Battalia* (1673) vividly demonstrates his eagerness to experiment with unusual harmonies and instrumental sonorities. The work is unmistakably programmatic, as the complete title indicates: *The Battle. The dissolute swarm of the musketeers. Mars, the fight, and the lament of the wounded, imitated with arias, and dedicated to Bacchus.* Biber represents the "dissolute swarm" of the presumably drunken warriors in the second movement

Figure 13.2: *Melchior Küsel, engraving of the interior of Salzburg Cathedral (1682)*

Example 13.5: *Heinrich Ignaz Franz von Biber, "Die liederliche Gesellschafft von allerley Humor" (The Dissolute Company of All Humors), from* Battalia *(1673), mm. 28–31*

by having each instrument play a well-known popular song in a different key and meter; according to a Latin note in the score, "here all voices are at variance, as different songs are being roared out simultaneously." Example 13.5, which shows the entrance of the first four voices, provides a hint of the chaos that will ensue when all ten voices join in. Note, for instance, the C, G, and F on the second beat of measure 30 and the F, D, and E on the third beat of measure 31. The result is a remarkably dissonant movement that could easily be mistaken for a composition written in the early twentieth century.

Biber is best known for his compositions for violin, in particular those involving *scordatura*. *Scordatura*, which literally means "mistuning," refers to the practice of using an alternative to the violin's normal tuning, allowing the player to produce different sonorities and timbres, as well as otherwise impossible double- and triple-stops (two- and three-note chords). Biber was by no means the only composer of the Baroque to use this technique, but he employed it to great effect throughout his career, nowhere more memorably than in the so-called *Mystery* Sonatas, a set of 15 multimovement works for violin and continuo collected in an elaborate manuscript dedicated to Archbishop Khuenburgh. Each sonata is accompanied by an engraving that links it to one of the 15 Mysteries of the Rosary associated with the Virgin Mary: five joyous events (the Annunciation, the Visitation, the Nativity, the Presentation of the Infant Jesus in the Temple, the 12-Year-Old Jesus in the Temple), five sorrowful events (the Agony in the Garden, the Scourging, the Crown of Thorns, Jesus Carries the Cross, the Crucifixion), and five miraculous events (the Resurrection, the Ascension, Pentecost, the Assumption of the Virgin, the Beatification of the Virgin).

To achieve maximum effect and heighten the music's distinctive character, Biber prescribed a different tuning scheme for each sonata, indicated by the notes just to the left of the clef at the beginning of the piece. In the *Resurrection* Sonata (No. 11), where the engraving shows Christ's ascension (Fig. 13.3), Biber prescribes the most novel tuning, which includes the "crossing" of the middle strings, so that the second string is tuned lower than the third. Specifically, the

Figure 13.3: *Engraving of the Resurrection from the manuscript of Heinrich Ignaz Franz von Biber, Sonata No. 11 (Resurrection) from the* Mystery Sonatas *(ca. 1676)*

E string, the highest, is tuned down to D; the A string, the second highest, is tuned down a fifth to D; the D string is tuned up a fourth to G, so that it is now higher than the A string, and the lowest string, the G string, remains at pitch. The resulting tuning pattern (top down), D–C–D–G, rather than the usual E–A–D–G, creates a brilliant unearthly sound appropriate to the notion of resurrection, while the "crossed" strings themselves are symbolically significant. Biber also incorporates an Easter chorale, *Surrexit Christus hodie* (Today Christ Is Risen), which—because of the *scordatura*—the violinist can play in octaves.

In the *Crucifixion* Sonata (No. 10), by contrast, the top two strings are tuned as a fourth rather than a fifth, lending the movement a darker timbre (see Anthology 22). The *Mystery* Sonatas conclude with an entirely abstract work, a passacaglia for solo violin (tuned in the normal fashion). Although there is evidence that some of the sonatas may have been written earlier and were not expressly associated with the mysteries of the rosary, there is sufficient connection between them in terms of style, form, and affect to lend the set a deep sense of spirituality and mysticism.

VIENNA AND THE IMPERIAL STYLE

The composers that we have considered thus far in this chapter had opportunities and relative freedom to explore their creative options and develop highly original compositional voices. Buxtehude and Telemann, working in the free imperial cities of the Hanseatic League, broke down the conventional barriers between sacred and secular realms to promote public concerts that included both types of music. In Salzburg, Biber may have had less autonomy—later in the century Mozart would find it a remarkably stifling place to work—but his music provides evidence that his employer nurtured or at least tolerated his innovative style.

The composers who served in the courts of the various absolute monarchs of the Holy Roman Empire—Munich, Dresden, and Vienna—were no less talented.

However, circumstances required that their compositions not only support the rituals of court life, but also conform to the tastes of the monarch, who more often than not valued uniformity of style in music as well as in the other arts. In Dresden, for instance, Friedrich Augustus I the Elector of Saxony (also known as Augustus II the Strong) converted from Lutheranism to Catholicism so that he might also become king of Poland and Grand Duke of Lithuania. Augustus self-consciously emulated Louis XIV's notion of using cultural display to suppress potential political unrest. Having acquired a passion for French music while at Versailles in the 1680s, Augustus replaced many of the Italians at court with French actors, dancers, and musicians. Italian *opera seria* was still presented in Dresden, including Johann Adolf Hasse's *Cleofide,* likely one of the operatic "ditties" that Bach noted hearing with his eldest son Wilhelm Friedmann Bach. But it was only after the elector's death in 1733 that his son Friedrich Augustus II, who had become a devotee of Italian music during his own grand tour of the Continent, nurtured the Dresden opera and its star composer, Hasse.

Perhaps nowhere was uniformity of style more valued than in Vienna, the capital city of the Holy Roman Empire and the Habsburg lands. Emperor Charles VI, who ruled from 1711 to 1740, was musically sophisticated, like his father Leopold I (who also composed) and his older brother Joseph I. Charles had already had an opportunity to build a musical establishment during his residency in Barcelona, where he spent five years as the Habsburg contender to the Spanish throne. The fact that he brought ten trumpeters from Barcelona for his coronation in 1712, augmenting his brother's already impressive ensemble, tells us something about his penchant for ceremony. Trumpets and drums became musical symbols of his personal motto, "Constancy and fortitude," and would be heard at the most important court feasts. The motto provided the title for *Costanza e fortezza* (1723), an opera by Johann Joseph Fux (1660–1741) presented at an outdoor theater in Prague in celebration of the coronation of Charles VI as king of Bohemia.

ITALIANS IN VIENNA

Like his predecessors, Charles VI was able to attract a superb team of musicians and artists, a large proportion of whom were Italians. Imperial employment, which offered steady work, good pay, and acceptable living conditions, was an attractive option for many artists, and likely a welcome relief from the constant travel associated with opera. Antonio Caldara (ca. 1671–1736), who like Alessandro Scarlatti (see Chapter 11) had been frustrated by the vagaries of opera in early-eighteenth-century Rome, sought a position in Vienna as vice-Kapellmeister. He had previously served Charles in Barcelona, but had to wait for the death of his competitor, Marc'Antonio Ziani, before being called to the imperial capital. There he remained in the shadow of Fux, the long-term Kapellmeister.

Among the many Italians who came to Vienna was Antonio Vivaldi (see Chapter 9); he sought a position at Charles's court, but the emperor's death just prior to Vivaldi's arrival in 1740 eliminated that possibility, and he died impoverished the following year. The demand for grand spectacle at the Viennese court also attracted the Italian theater architect (stage designer) Giuseppe Galli-Bibiena, who was appointed official engineer to the court in 1723. Along with his father, Francesco Galli-Bibiena, and brother, Antonio Galli-Bibiena, Giuseppe belonged to the foremost family of stage designers. When Apostolo Zeno and later Pietro Metastasio became court poets, serving from 1718 to 1730 and from 1730 to 1786 respectively, they were benefiting from a long Viennese tradition of hiring Italian poets, stretching back to the mid-seventeenth century.

Thanks to these talented individuals, Charles VI created what scholars have referred to as an "Austro-Italian Baroque" musical culture. Operas, cantatas, oratorios, and other liturgical works each had their place in the court's musical calendar. Programming and commissioning of works followed a strict set of protocols. The most elaborate music—whether sacred or secular—was used to celebrate special occasions honoring the royal family. Major feasts, particularly those honoring saints' days associated with the emperor or his family, called for concerted music with trumpets and timpani. During lesser holidays and Lent, the Viennese opted for the simplicity of unaccompanied vocal music. Birthdays called for operas and oratorios. For example, Fux's *Angelica, vincitrice di Alcina* (Angelica, Conqueror of Alcina, 1716), another opera based on Ariosto's *Orlando furioso*, was performed in the gardens of the Favorita, a palace near Vienna, for the birth of his son Leopold, with elaborate stage designs by Giuseppe Galli-Bibiena (Fig. 13.4).

It was not unusual to hear the music of Palestrina at the Viennese court, but the development of a uniquely Viennese style of counterpoint for the church can be credited to both Caldara and Fux. The latter's *Gradus ad Parnassum* (Steps to Parnassus, 1725) became the standard counterpoint textbook for the next two centuries.

It was in the realm of opera that the marriage between Italian music and imperial policies and politics proved most significant. *Opera seria*, the style of opera that grew out of the Arcadian Academy (see Chapter 11), was well suited to the needs of the Viennese court. The streamlining of dramatic structure, the elimination of comic elements, the endorsement of appropriate virtues for male and female characters, the equal distribution of arias that both shaped and conformed to the expectations of singers and audiences, and, particularly in the case of Metastasio, elegant poetry presenting clearly defined emotional states that lent themselves well to musical setting—all served the dignified sensibilities of the Habsburg monarchy. Its system of imperial patronage, which allowed for continued collaborations between poets, designers, and musicians, proved both highly successful and useful to the monarchy. These artists, and in particular composers such as Caldara and Fux, were able to produce works of consistently high quality and originality while still embracing a uniform set of

Figure 13.4: *F. Dietell, after Giuseppe Galli-Bibiena, proscenium for* Angelica, vincitrice di Alcina *(1716)*

stylistic features: vocal virtuosity, contrapuntal richness, and a colorful orchestration that maintained a certain studied, ceremonial formality.

After his death in 1782, Metastasio was honored with a monument in St. Michael's Church, the beloved family parish of the Habsburg family, located adjacent to the palace. The political power of the Habsburgs and the Holy Roman Empire would wane after their defeat at the hands of Napoleon in 1806. But through Metastasio's 27 *opera seria* librettos, set by as many as 400 composers and adored by audiences throughout Europe, and as far east as Russia, the artistic sensibilities of the Viennese imperial court and the Holy Roman Empire would be exported throughout the world.

FOR FURTHER READING

Brewer, Charles E., *The Instrumental Music of Schmeltzer, Biber, Muffat, and Their Contemporaries* (Farnham, UK, and Burlington, VT: Ashgate, 2011)

Buelow, George, "Hamburg and Lübeck," in George Buelow, ed., *The Late Baroque Era: From the 1680s to 1740* (Englewood Cliffs, NJ: Prentice Hall, 1993)

Chafe, Eric Thomas, *The Church Music of Heinrich Biber* (Ann Arbor: University of Michigan Research Press, 1987)

Heller, Wendy, "Reforming Achilles: Gender, 'Opera Seria,' and the Rhetoric of the Enlightened Hero," *Early Music* 26 (1998): 562–81

Neville, Don, "Metastasio and the Image of Majesty in the Austro-Italian Baroque," in Shearer West, ed., *Italian Culture in Northern Europe in the Eighteenth Century* (Cambridge: Cambridge University Press, 1999)

Snyder, Kerala, *Dieterich Buxtehude: Organist in Lübeck,* rev. ed. (Rochester, NY: University of Rochester Press, 2007)

Wollenberg, Susan, "Vienna under Joseph I and Charles VI," in George Buelow, ed., *The Late Baroque Era: From the 1680s to 1740* (Englewood Cliffs, NJ: Prentice Hall, 1993

Zohn, Stephen David, *Music for a Mixed Taste: Style, Genre, and Meaning in Telemann's Instrumental Works* (New York and Oxford: Oxford University Press, 2008)

CHAPTER FOURTEEN

The London of Handel and Hogarth

We begin this chapter with two very different images of music and musicians in eighteenth-century London. *Apotheosis of Handel* (Fig. 14.1) was printed in 1787 on the occasion of a Handel commemoration held in Westminster Abbey and distributed along with *Messiah* to all who subscribed to Samuel Arnold's printed edition of Handel's music. With a quill in one hand and scroll of music in the other, Handel is honored by two angels: one, brandishing the trumpet of fame, places a laurel wreath on Handel's head, while the other bears a torch signifying immortality. Beneath the billowing clouds lies the city of London in the distance, readily identified by two of the most enduring symbols of England's civic and religious power, the towers of Westminster Abbey and the dome of St. Paul's Cathedral.

An engraving by the English artist William Hogarth entitled *The Enraged Musician* (1741) presents an equally fantastic view of music in London, this time from the streets rather than the heavens (Fig. 14.2). The title refers to the fashionably dressed violinist in the window, believed to be an Italian (likely the violinist Pietro Castrucci), who clamps down his ears to shut out the confusion and cacophony outside. A pregnant ballad singer clutches a crying baby, a boy in military uniform beats on a drum, and an oboist dressed in rags (whose swarthy skin, beard, and large nose might mark him as one of the many Jews in London) unabashedly directs his sound toward the violinist, while to the far right a soldier blows a horn.

Figure 14.1: *Rebecca Biagio,* Apotheosis of Handel, *after George Frederick Handel, engraved by James Heath (1787)*

Figure 14.2: *William Hogarth,* The Enraged Musician *(1741)*

Hogarth also allows the viewer to imagine the cries of the fish seller, the barking of the dog, and the scraping of a knife being sharpened, not to mention the sounds of the little boy urinating outside the violinist's window, while a little girl shakes a rattle. Even the elegant milkmaid, who might easily have wandered in from a pastoral play, seems to be singing. Significantly, Hogarth makes reference to a musical event that is not audible: to the violinist's left is a broadside advertising an upcoming performance of *The Beggar's Opera* (1728), which, as we will see later, became so popular that contemporaries would blame it for forcing Handel's first opera company, the Royal Academy of Music, to close.

In this chapter, we consider the competing visions embodied in these engravings, one in which George Frideric Handel (1685–1759) dominates the musical firmament, and another in which the tensions between high and low, rich and poor, foreign and native, and even music and noise are palpable, as are the contrasts between the various audiences that are part of this variegated soundscape. Neither of these depictions of musical life is particularly realistic. But they convey something of the richness and complexity of music-making in London, and the ethical issues that music so often engages.

COMMERCE AND POLITICS IN EIGHTEENTH-CENTURY LONDON

In the autumn of 1710, the 25-year-old Handel, fresh from his Italian voyage (see Chapter 11) and having just been appointed Kapellmeister at the Hanoverian court in Germany, arrived in London, a city that presented economic opportunities and political complexities in equal measure. When Scotland and England were united to form Great Britain in 1707, the power of the monarchy was consolidated. Britain's wealth was enhanced by its domination of international trade routes, thanks in no small part to slave labor in the British colonies, particularly the West Indies, where the sugar trade offered high profits.

The Peace of Utrecht (1713), the set of treaties that ended the War of the Spanish Succession, would also prove advantageous to the English economy. Although Great Britain and its allies had suffered significant losses in the decade-long conflict, they were no longer threatened by French territorial expansion or by a unified Bourbon monarchy in France and Spain. For individual investors, too, the growth of commercial interests opened new paths to prosperity. Handel was one of many Londoners who earned sizable profits by investing in joint-stock companies, which allowed those with spare capital to fund new enterprises.

For musicians in particular, London offered unparalleled opportunities. The twin branches of the court music establishment, the sacred Chapel Royal and the secular King's Musick (see Chapter 8), continued to provide music for the royal family; both institutions were revitalized during the reign of Queen

Anne (1702–14). Nonetheless, as nobles, doctors, and bankers made their homes in the West End of London—along with artists, musicians, and immigrants—the city's cultural center also shifted. This increasingly diverse population supported theater, opera, and the publication of music through ticket fees and subscriptions. Music was heard in taverns, coffeehouses, concert rooms, and many competing theaters.

All of this commercial and economic activity might suggest that England had achieved political stability since the Civil War and the Glorious Revolution of 1688 that had brought William and Mary to the throne, but this was not the case. Conflicts over whether England should be a constitutional monarchy (as supported by the Whig party) or adhere to absolute rule (as supported by the Tories) continued to dominate the political discourse. Some objected to the Act of Settlement in 1701 that had secured the throne for the German Elector George I and the Hanoverian (German) line. The perennial fear of Catholicism, which was exacerbated by the so-called Jacobites' attempts first to restore the Catholic James II and later his grandson Charles Edward Stuart to the English throne, even extended to Italian singers. In 1745—the same year in which "Bonnie Prince Charlie," as he was known, attempted to gain the English throne, a satirical English poem refers to an Italian castrato as a "Popish capon." When in 1695 parliament refused to extend the censorship law, the resulting proliferation of polemical political pamphlets from Tories and Whigs further increased political tensions.

HANDEL'S "UTRECHT" *TE DEUM* AND *JUBILATE*

London musicians, who depended upon the aristocracy for their livelihoods, did their best to navigate these rough waters. Handel's success was a direct result of his ability to accommodate the various factions, serve up entertainments that were satisfying both financially and artistically, ultimately tapping into the consciousness of his adopted country so thoroughly that his music created a new common ground between various factions of the English public. On the way to accomplishing this, Handel followed two paths: one as composer of foreign and thus exotic Italian operas, the other as master—and some might say inventor—of a quintessentially English style. Remarkably, he scored successes in both realms within three years after his arrival in London, with the premiere of his opera *Rinaldo* in 1711 and the music celebrating the Peace of Utrecht two years later.

On July 7, 1713, for the General Thanksgiving that marked the end of the War of the Spanish Succession, Handel's "Utrecht" *Te Deum* and *Jubilate* were performed at St. Paul's Cathedral. That he accepted this commission at all is surprising; Handel, who was still employed by the future George I at the Hanoverian court and in London only with his employer's permission, found himself in the delicate situation of writing music to celebrate the signing of a treaty that the Hanoverians in fact opposed. In fact, the composer's eagerness to write the celebratory music for the service of thanksgiving—which was rehearsed multiple times in public before the end of the peace negotiations—led to his abrupt dismissal from his post in Germany. Perhaps that was what Handel had in mind all along, for in the process he garnered the support of Queen Anne and the English court. Nonetheless, by the time George I ascended the throne in 1714, fences had been mended and Handel found a strong supporter in his former patron. Eventually, Handel would become the chief composer for all the major political events and occasions relating to the Hanoverian royal family, such as the coronation of George II in 1727 and the funeral service for Queen Caroline in 1737.

Handel could not have accomplished this with political savvy alone; his music was at the core of his success. Although the "Utrecht" *Te Deum*, HWV 278, and *Jubilate*, HWV 279 may betray a certain debt to Henry Purcell's oft-performed settings of these texts (see Chapter 8), Handel established a far grander, more expansive style of writing for chorus, orchestra, and soloists. From the very first measures of the opening chorus in the *Te Deum*, English audiences must have known that something special was in the offing (Ex. 14.1). Handel commands the listener's attention with three powerful chords (I, V^6, and VI); but then, with the unexpected shift to *piano* in the middle of measure 2 (marking the arrival on a first-inversion tonic chord), the orchestra begins to tiptoe, quieting all the way down to *pianissimo* in measure 3 (with a reduction in the orchestration) leading to a cadence in the middle of measure 4. Just when the ear becomes accustomed to listening that much harder, Handel surprises us by changing the pace and giving us yet another V–I cadence, which brings in the full orchestra for the fugal Allegro. By the time the chorus enters singing "We praise thee, O God," their bold homophonic proclamations set in relief against a rapidly moving orchestra, the listener is prepared for the heightened drama that ensues when the chorus embarks on its own imitative adventures.

Through the juxtaposition and layering of different textures, and by placing the large orchestra in opposition to (rather than merely accompanying or

Example 14.1: *George Frideric Handel, "Utrecht" Te Deum, HWV 278 (1713), mm. 1–6*

imitating) the chorus, Handel creates choral music that is formal and dignified. Enlivened with shifts between polyphony and homophony, varied orchestral colors, and bursts of vocal virtuosity, it is also highly expressive and emotionally compelling. It is precisely this grand, dramatic style that he would employ in his English oratorios, to be considered later in this chapter.

ITALIAN MUSIC IN LONDON

At the time that Handel's *Rinaldo* premiered at the Queen's Theatre in the Haymarket on February 24, 1711, the London audience had a passionate, if sometimes ambivalent, attitude toward foreign music, particularly that of the Italians. The Italian diaspora in England had begun in the late seventeenth century with the arrival of Nicola Matteis, a Neapolitan violinist whom John Evelyn praised for his ability to make the violin "speak like the voice of a man" and sound "like a consort of several instruments." Among the flock of Italians that followed was the cellist Nicola Haym, who made his living teaching and playing in noble homes, giving public benefit concerts, and performing between the acts of plays; he also revised a number of Italian opera librettos for the London stage.

As we noted in Chapter 11, the trio sonatas, violin sonatas, and concerti grossi of Arcangelo Corelli were hot commodities in the British market and were quickly followed by new editions from the English printer John Walsh. The composer Francesco Geminiani, who arrived in London in 1714, was one of any number of Italian musicians who made a career in London by marketing the Italian style in a steady stream of publications, including transcriptions of Corelli's Op. 5 violin sonatas for a concerto grosso ensemble.

An interesting case study is Pietro Castrucci (1679–1752), the likely model for the "enraged musician" in Hogarth's engraving (see Fig. 14.2). When the 22-year-old Richard Boyle, the third earl of Burlington, went to Rome on his Grand Tour in 1714–15, he brought back some unusual souvenirs: Castrucci, Pietro's young brother Prospero, and the cellist Filippo Amadei. Handel had worked with all three during his time in Rome. Since Handel spent some time living in Burlington's palatial Venetian-style house, he had ample opportunity to renew his working relationship with these fine musicians.

Castrucci made his first appearance in London in 1715, playing his own music on what was known then as a benefit concert. (In the eighteenth century such concerts were not charitable events; rather, the profits were for the "benefit" of the players.) He became the concertmaster of Handel's opera orchestra in 1720, serving in that position for over 20 years, and published two sets of solo sonatas for violin and one set of string concertos. Like many Italian émigrés during this period, Castrucci was reduced to relative poverty by the time he died in Dublin in 1752, but he nevertheless received a grand funeral befitting his considerable reputation.

ENGLISH AND ITALIAN OPERA

Italian opera, though popular in London, did not enjoy the same unambiguously enthusiastic reception as instrumental music. As we recall from our consideration of Purcell's *King Arthur* in Chapter 8, the English had their own notions about opera and musical theater. The use of spoken dialogue, which had been central to the masque tradition, was regarded as not only acceptable but preferable to an entirely sung drama. Even after the death of Purcell, Christopher Rich, director of the Theatre Royal, Drury Lane, and the Dorset Garden Theatre, continued to produce quintessentially English "Dramatick"operas.

The English flirtation with Italian opera began in 1705 at Drury Lane with Thomas Clayton's *Arsinoe*, the first of several operas based on Italian librettos but sung in English in the "Italian Manner of Music." Clayton's preface to the score offers a hint of the problems the newly imported genre faced: for instance, he apologizes for the quality of the English singers, who, despite his diligence in training them, were not equal to their Italian counterparts. Nevertheless, *Arsinoe* was a commercial success.

John Vanbrugh, who designed and managed the brand-new Queen's Theatre (which would be renamed the King's Theatre under George I), attempted unsuccessfully to beat this competition by presenting his own Italian-style opera for the opening of his new theater in April of 1705. Nonetheless, it was Drury Lane that had the smash success with *Camilla* by Giovanni Bononcini (the son of Giovanni Maria Bononcini, whom we met in Chapter 10). London audiences were in fact captivated by the English version of Bononcini's popular *Il trionfo di Camilla* (The Triumph of Camilla), translated and adapted by Nicola Haym from the version that had premiered in Naples in 1696. Both theaters continued to produce English operas that occasionally poked fun at the Italian competition. At one point in Thomas D'Urfey's pasticcio *Wonders in the Sun* (Queen's Theatre, 1706), for instance, the stage directions call for a character to mimic the Italians.

The separate paths of English and Italian opera became institutionalized in 1707 when Vanbrugh persuaded the Lord Chamberlain, who controlled theatrical licenses in London, to give him a monopoly on Italian opera. This was not a wise decision. Italian opera was less profitable than other forms of theater, since not only were the singers more expensive, but the necessity of resting their voices meant that fewer performances could be held in a given week. The Queen's Theatre became the home of Italian opera in London: Handel would spend most of his career there, except for the period between 1734 and 1737, when it was occupied by a competing company, the Opera of the Nobility. Plays, musical theater, and later ballad operas (discussed later) were presented at Drury Lane. The competitive soup was thickened when the theater owner and director John Rich (Christopher's son) obtained royal permission to reopen the old Lincoln's Inn Fields Theatre in 1714; in 1732 he moved operations to the Theatre Royal, Covent Garden, which would later feature Handel's operas and oratorios.

HANDEL'S *RINALDO*

As the first Italian opera written specifically for the English stage, *Rinaldo*, HWV 7, was carefully designed to show the best the genre had to offer while also appealing to English audiences. The poet Aaron Hill (briefly in charge of the Queen's Theatre) and the impresario J. J. Heidegger (who would become Handel's long-term business partner) recognized the potential of marrying the English taste for plots with witches, magic, and special effects, known from works such as *King Arthur*, to the new fashion for Italian music. The plot of *Rinaldo* was borrowed from Tasso's *Gerusalemme liberata*, the same epic that inspired, among others, Lully's *Armide* (see Chapter 7). The librettist Giacomo Rossi, hailing Handel as "the Orpheus of our century," noted the speed at which the composer worked: "to my great wonder I saw an entire Opera put to music by that surprising genius, with the greatest degree of perfection, in only two weeks."

Rossi, like the London audience, could not have known that Handel had "borrowed" much of the music for *Rinaldo* from his earlier compositions. The practice of borrowing, whether from oneself or others, was not unique to Handel, though he seems to have done it more frequently than many of his contemporaries. Some nineteenth-century music historians criticized Handel's frequent reuse of musical themes or even whole sections of music taken from other pieces, seeing it as a form of plagiarism—even when the "stolen" music was Handel's own. (Bach, on the other hand, was rarely criticized for recycling his own music, although he did so frequently; large sections of the famous Mass in B minor, for instance, were taken from Bach's earlier compositions [see Chapter 15]). Johann Mattheson, Handel's old friend from the Hamburg Opera, put the issue succinctly, at least as it was understood in Handel's time: it was perfectly acceptable to borrow as long as one "did so with interest"—that is, as long as one improved upon the original work.

Rinaldo was a tremendous success, playing to full houses for ten consecutive nights and establishing both Handel's fame and the place of Italian *opera seria* in London's cultural life for the next several decades. In addition to Handel's evocative and varied orchestration, the opera featured a cast of accomplished Italian singers, including Nicolo Grimaldi (known as Nicolini), the first of several castrati to take London by storm. The writer Richard Steele praised Nicolini's acting as highly as his singing: "Every Limb, every Finger, contributes to the Part he acts in so much that a deaf man might go along with the sense of it."

Among the production's many special effects were aerial feats for the sorceress Armida and monsters that came up from a trapdoor in the stage. The essayist Joseph Addison even claimed that a flocks of live birds were released on the stage to accompany Almirena's aria "Augelletti che cantate" (You little birds who sing). Addison may well have been exaggerating when he wrote of having purchased the libretto to *Rinaldo* after meeting the purveyor of the birds on the streets of London. Nonetheless, he wrote eloquently about how he found absurd the whole notion of bringing nature into the opera house—be it live sparrows, horses, or fountains spewing actual water—as "shadows and realities ought not to be mixed together in the same piece" (SR 113:684; 4/33:176). Real birds, Addison went on to declare, also presented a practical problem: having been let loose in the theater, they were unwilling to leave, and even made entrances in scenes where they did not belong.

DRAMATIC PACING, REALISM, AND THE DA CAPO ARIA

Addison's concerns about the relationship between realism and fantasy in opera might well have extended to the special pacing of the operas of Handel and his contemporaries, engendered through the use of the da capo aria. Handel's operas followed the same formulas that characterized the *opere serie* we examined in Chapter 11. They were composed primarily of recitatives and da capo arias, with an occasional duet or trio, and maybe a celebratory chorus at the end of an act. By the end of the seventeenth century, the "exit aria," after which the singer would usually leave the stage, had become a standard feature of the musico-dramatic design. Thus the end of the scene always carried the greatest lyric weight.

This episodic and highly stylized mode of presenting a drama has long inspired complaints from critics accustomed to the lively ensembles of a Mozart *opera buffa* or the continuous flow of a Wagner opera. The problem for many is the stasis of the da capo aria: how can characters progress or change if they are required to repeat both the same music and the text with which they began? However, it is important to recognize that with da capo arias composers and librettists were not attempting to create a "realistic" dramatic experience in which time flowed in a natural way. Instead, these arias allow listeners to reflect upon the emotion or affect being represented and also appreciate the skills of the individual singers, which came to the fore in the repeat of the **A** section.

Consider, for example, Rinaldo's aria in Act 1, scene 7, one of Nicolini's great hits from the opera (see Anthology 23). In the aftermath of Rinaldo's love duet with his beloved Almirena (a character added to Tasso's tale by the librettist), Armida arrives to challenge Rinaldo. The sorceress contrives for a black cloud to descend with fire-breathing monsters and furies, which she uses to abduct Almirena. Rinaldo's heartfelt response, "Cara sposa," is realistic only within the fantastic realm of opera, as operatic time slows to a stop while he contemplates the horror of his situation. In the **A** section of the aria, the hero laments the loss of Almirena ("Dear bride, dearest lover, where are you? Ah, return to my tears"). The opening ritornello features the first and second violins in an imitative duet, replete with sigh motives, supported by ascending chromatic quarter notes in the viola. The continuo is silent. When Rinaldo finally sings a sustained B♮, followed by a simple melody that descends stepwise, his voice,

Example 14.2: *George Frideric Handel, Rinaldo, HWV 7a (1711), Act 1, scene 6, "Cara sposa," mm. 1–18. (The bass continuo, silent in this passage, is omitted.)*

Dear bride, dearest lover, where are you?

like his emotions, is enveloped by the contrapuntal intensity of the orchestra (Ex. 14.2). Handel delays the entrance of the basso continuo until after the end of Rinaldo's first phrase, creating a musical representation of the very ground being pulled out from beneath the hero's feet.

In the **B** section, Rinaldo turns from contemplation of his unhappiness to a spirit of resolve about the future. As he proposes to defy the evil spirits, the pace quickens with a series of syllabic passages in sixteenth notes against a brisk *stile concitato* accompaniment in the orchestra. Instead of sustaining long notes, Rinaldo is unable to catch his breath. The magic of the da capo aria, however, is the effect of the repeat of the **A** section. Now that the listener knows of Rinaldo's courageous resolve, the return to the initial pathos—the ascending chromatic lines, sigh motives, and falling fifths—is that much more moving, particularly when the singer adds his own embellishment to Handel's melodic line. Rinaldo's confidence—and virtuosity—are completely restored by Act 1, scene 9: in the aria "Venti, turbini," the fiery coloratura that represents the turbulent winds shows off the singer's skill and reflects Rinaldo's tortured emotions.

HANDEL AND THE "ACADEMY" YEARS

Despite the success of *Rinaldo* and other works produced over several subsequent seasons, London's first Italian opera company disbanded in 1717, the victim not only of competition and mismanagement but also of the fracturing of the patronage base in the wake of a feud between George I and his son, the prince of Wales (see below). Just three years later, Italian opera would return to the King's Theatre under the auspices of the Royal Academy of Music, a venture in which Handel played a leading role. While its name might have been borrowed from France, the mode of financing the new company was typically English: the Royal Academy was organized as a joint-stock company, supported by a £1,000 pledge from George I and subscriptions from 50 members. The repertory included operas not only by Handel but also by Bononcini and Attilio Ariosti.

These were boom times for Handel, who brought from Italy such singers as the soprano Margherita Durastanti (with whom he had worked in Rome and Venice) and the castrato Senesino, as well as two sopranos who became known for their presumed on- and offstage battles, Francesca Cuzzoni and Faustina Bordoni. Although 20 seasons were planned, the "First Academy" folded after eight years, and only the first year was truly profitable for the investors. Handel then began a Second Academy in partnership with the impresario Heidegger, which succeeded for a time. By the late 1730s, however, the attempt to operate two competing opera companies in London—the Royal Academy, led by Handel and supported by George II, and the Opera of the Nobility, patronized by the prince of Wales—proved untenable.

Financial failure is not, however, the same as artistic failure. Between 1720 and 1733, before the Opera of the Nobility opened in 1734, Handel had produced 18 new operas and contributed to a number of pasticcios. To judge by the comments of Pierre-Jacques Fougeroux, who saw three of Handel's operas during the 1727 season, the quality of the singing and playing was high. "Faustina," he wrote, "has a charming voice, with quite a big sound, though a little rough; her face and her looks are very ordinary," while Cuzzoni's weaker voice "has an enchanting sweetness, with divine coloratura," and "Senesino is the very best they have ever had, is a good musician, and is a reasonably good actor." The orchestra, which consisted of 24 violins, led by the Castrucci brothers (and presumably including violas), three cellos, three basses, three bassoons, occasional trumpets and flutes, archlute, and two harpsichords, made "a very loud noise." Fougeroux commended the "arias with string accompaniment and the wonderfully rich harmony, which leave nothing to be desired."

Although the basic musico-dramatic formula of Handel's later operas remained the same as in *Rinaldo*—arias and recitatives, expressing varied affects and characters, combined with stage spectacle—they were never formulaic in terms of subject, style, or tone. Some, such as *Rinaldo* and *Orlando* (1733, based on Ariosto's *Orlando furioso*), deal in magic and special effects. Others, such as *Rodelinda* (1725) *and Ariodante* (1735), are entirely serious; despite the happy endings, the ordeals endured by the characters are of tragic proportions. Unlike the Arcadians, who rejected comedy, Handel integrated comic elements quite successfully into a few of his operas, such as *Admeto* (Admetus, 1727) and *Serse* (Xerxes, 1739), both based on librettos from mid-seventeenth-century Venice.

DUELING DIVAS, DUELING COMPANIES

What went wrong with so great an enterprise? Finances, of course, were always a problem; commercial opera, as we have seen throughout this book, rarely earned profits for its investors. Another factor was the very element that made London such an attractive option for Handel and other musicians: competition, for both singers and audiences. Some blamed the public feud that erupted at the Royal Academy of Music between the supporters of Cuzzoni and Bordoni during a performance of Bononcini's opera *Astianatte* in 1727. "Those costly Canary-Birds," wrote the actor and director Colley Cibber, "have sometimes infested the whole Body of our dignified Lovers of Music, with the same childish animosities: Ladies have been known to decline their visits, upon account of their being of a different musical party." Scholars, however, have suggested that the actual competition between the divas may have been far more in the minds of the spectators, fueled in part by their onstage rivalries.

Others attributed Italian opera's problems to competition from a new genre called ballad opera, which combined spoken dialogue with popular songs of the day. In 1728, Lincoln's Inn Fields scored a run-away success with 62 performances of *The Beggar's Opera*, with words by John Gay set to music arranged by Johann Christoph Pepusch, whose involvement with the Academy of Antient Music we considered in Chapter 10. Where the operas of Handel and his colleagues were concerned with ancient myth and history, this first ballad opera presented episodes inspired by the life of a real thief, Jack Shepherd, whose public hanging created a sensation in 1724. (John Rice discusses *The Beggar's Opera* in detail in *Music in the Eighteenth Century*.)

Yet it would be misleading to say that the popularity of ballad operas was directly responsible for the failure of Handel's Royal Academy and the Opera of the Nobility. The new satirical genre certainly provided competition for Italian opera, but by presenting songs based on tunes from Handel's operas, it also helped disseminate his music to a broader audience. In fact, the actress and singer Kitty Clive, known for her renditions of Handelian tunes in ballad operas, was later cast by Handel himself as the first Dalila in his oratorio *Samson* (1745).

We gain some understanding of the artistic and political issues at stake in English musical theater from another satirical engraving by William Hogarth, *Masquerades and Operas, Burlington Gate*, also known as *Bad Taste of the Town* (1724, Fig. 14.3). From the opera theater pictured on the left-hand side hangs a copy of another Hogarth engraving showing three of Handel's singers being offered

Figure 14.3: *William Hogarth,* Masquerades and Operas, Burlington Gate, *also known as* Bad Taste of the Town *(1724)*

bags of money. The impresario Heidegger leans out of the window, welcoming the crowd to a masquerade. Across the street is Lincoln's Inn Fields, where the audience is gathering to see a popular pantomime based on the story of Doctor Faustus. The Italianate "Academy of Arts" in the background represents the estate of Lord Burlington, the patron of Handel, Castrucci, and others. In the center of the print, a street merchant is selling the works of the great English dramatists—John Dryden, William Congreve, and William Shakespeare—as scrap.

Hogarth's satire spares neither the English nor the Italian theatrical ventures (nor, for that matter, patrons such as Burlington, who were besotted by Italian architecture); all of London, instead of embracing the works of Shakespeare and Dryden, is portrayed as afflicted with bad taste. Printed more than a decade before Handel turned to oratorio, the engraving captures something of the competition, partisanship, and contrasting artistic values that characterized London's theatrical scene. As the rival companies divided the opera-loving public in the 1730s, audiences, particularly those from the middle and lower classes, were drawn to less expensive entertainments—ballad operas, pantomimes, and masquerades—that some regarded as more natural, more patriotic, and even more masculine than opera. Nonetheless, while Handel would withdraw from opera completely by 1741, Italian operas and singers remained an integral, albeit contested feature of English cultural life through the *opere serie* of such composers as Johann Adolf Hasse and Johann Christian Bach.

ORATORIO AND THE APOTHEOSIS OF HANDEL

The cultivation of the English oratorio was perhaps the most logical step for the composer who had impressed English audiences in 1713 with his "Utrecht" *Te Deum* and *Jubilate*. Even as Handel dealt with the vagaries of the opera business in London, he was intent upon developing both a reputation and a voice as a quintessentially English composer. Just before his death in 1727, George I signed an act making Handel a naturalized British citizen. Handel's next official commission was to write four anthems for the coronation of King George II and Queen Caroline on October 11, 1727. One of these, *Zadok the Priest*, with large orchestra (including timpani and trumpets) and chorus, has been sung at every subsequent British coronation.

Like their continental counterparts, English oratorios were sacred music dramas, without staging or costumes. However, in crafting their oratorios, Handel—and lesser-known colleagues such as Maurice Greene (1696–1755), Willem de Fesch (1687–1761), and William Boyce (1711–1779)—looked less to opera than to the English church-music tradition and ceremonial works written for the monarchy. This point is clearly made in the postscript to the advertisement for Handel's oratorio *Esther* in the *Daily Journal* on April 19, 1732, which emphasizes that "there will be no Action on the Stage, but the House will be fitted up in a decent Manner, for the Audience. The Musick to be disposed after the Manner of the Coronation Service."

Esther was not a new work; the first version had been performed for James Brydges, the earl of Carnavon and future duke of Chandos, who maintained a literary and artistic salon at his grandiose house near Cannons, where Handel served as composer in residence in 1717–18. However, the version presented at the King's Theatre in May 1732—while Handel was still deeply involved in producing operas—had all the ingredients that made oratorio such a success in England. Sung in English and including excerpts from the 1727 coronation anthems, *Esther* also succeeded in attracting the attention of the royal family: King George II and Queen Caroline attended all six performances.

Subject matter also accounted for the popularity of oratorio in England. A substantial number of Handel's oratorios presented the victories and misfortunes of the Israelites as described in the Old Testament, such as *Israel in Egypt* (1739), *Judas Maccabeus* (1746), and Handel's final oratorio, *Jephtha* (1751). Such stories were not as distant for Handel's Christian audiences as one might imagine. Handel's librettists transformed the Israelites into symbols of the modern British nation, and through them portrayed the courage, virtue, religious fervor, and greatness of the English people. By combining the solo aria and recitative from opera with the dynamic style of his English choral works, Handel created a morally uplifting genre in which the expression of individual valor and suffering was juxtaposed with the stirring collective expression that had long been part of the English church-music tradition.

The contrast between public and private modes of expression is particularly evident in another Handel oratorio, *Saul*, HWV 53, composed in 1738 and premiered at the King's Theatre in January of 1739. It was the first of four collaborations between Handel and the librettist Charles Jennens, which include Handel's most famous oratorio, *Messiah* (1741). The story, taken from the First Book of Samuel, deals with a military victory, in this case David's triumph over the giant Goliath. However, the core of the drama is the tragic tale of Saul's gradual descent into madness as he is consumed by jealousy of David, who will eventually succeed him as king of the Israelites.

In Act 1, scene 3 (see Anthology 24), Handel juxtaposes the joyful cries of the victorious Israelites ("Welcome, welcome mighty king"), accompanied by the exotic bells of a miniature carillon, with the anguished utterances of Saul, driven to madness by his envy of David. Saul emerges in Handel's music as a flawed tragic hero: his jealousy drives him to break Jewish law and consult the Witch of Endor, who conjures up the ghost of Samuel in a terrifying incantation aria in Act 3 (Ex. 14.3). The sustained oboes and bassoons establish an eerie atmosphere, while the violins—in an unsettling duet with the Witch—obsessively repeat a jagged, two-measure descending sequential pattern, with gravity-defying skips followed by precipitous drops.

Whether in an oratorio such as *Saul* or in the popular *Messiah*, which eschews a dramatic presentation in favor of a more abstract meditation on the prophecy, birth, and resurrection of Christ, Handel found a voice in his oratorios that seemed to speak with equal passion and eloquence to listeners of differing social classes and political inclinations. As a result, this foreign-born musician, like the Italian-born Jean-Baptiste Lully in France (see Chapter 7), had the privilege of creating a national style for the country that had welcomed and adopted him as its own.

We began this chapter with a depiction of Handel at his grandest: the hero of English music receiving inspiration from the angels as he hovers over the city of

Example 14.3: *George Frideric Handel,* Saul, *HWV 53 (1738), Act 3, scene 1, "Infernal spirits," mm. 9–14*

London. While we will never know whether Handel would have been amused or touched by this extravagant compliment, he did have the rare opportunity to see himself immortalized during his own lifetime. In 1738, as Handel's oratorios were gaining ground and opera was on the wane, a life-size statue of the composer by Louis-François Roubiliac was erected in Vauxhall Gardens (Fig. 14.4).

Under the management (1729–1767) of the resourceful entrepreneur Jonathan Tyers, a close friend to both Handel and Hogarth, Vauxhall Gardens was a popular haunt not only for London's elite but also for a diverse population (the entrance fee was only a shilling) who took delight in the reputedly terrible food (it was said the ham was sliced so thinly that it resembled cobwebs) and the superb entertainments in an idyllic outdoor setting. By day a respectable outing for a family, the pleasure gardens at night were illuminated by oil lamps, casting shadows on visitors who indulged in dancing, eating, and other, decidedly impious activities.

Music by Handel and colleagues, such as the British composer Thomas Arne, was frequently heard at Vauxhall Gardens, which boasted an outdoor bandstand and even an organ. Programs included concertos, overtures, dances, military music, and songs of all sorts; many were written specifically for Vauxhall and other pleasure gardens (such as Vauxhall's rival Ranelagh) rather than for the concert hall or theater. In 1749 Vauxhall was also the site of a rehearsal for

Figure 14.4: *Louis-François Roubiliac, Handel (1738)*

Handel's *Music for the Royal Fireworks* that reportedly attracted 12,000 spectators, causing a huge traffic jam on London Bridge.

It is significant that Tyers chose Handel—a living man who was frequently seen at Vauxhall in the flesh—as the model for a marble effigy to watch over his patrons, casually plucking a harp, charming London much like Orpheus, as a *putto* nestles at his feet. In this newly democratized realm, the chaos of London's noisy streets, as evoked in Hogarth's *The Enraged Musician*, found a home in the pleasure gardens where Handel's statue stood as a proud symbol of the music that united the British people. In the next and final chapter, as we turn to the music of Johann Sebastian Bach, we will encounter another great composer memorialized in stone, who, unlike Handel, did not receive great acclaim until long after his death.

FOR FURTHER READING

Aspden, Suzanne, "'Fam'd Handel Breathing, tho' Transformed to Stone': The Composer as Monument," *Journal of the American Musicological Society* 55 (2002): 39–90

Burrows, Donald, *Handel,* rev. ed. (Oxford: Oxford University Press, 2012)

Burrows, Donald, *Handel and the Chapel Royal* (Oxford: Oxford University Press, 2008)

Dean, Winton, and John Merrill Knapp, *Handel's Operas, 1704–1726* (London: Boydell and Brewer, 2009)

Harris, Ellen T., "Handel the Investor," *Music and Letters* 84 (2004): 521–75

Joncus, Berta, "Handel at Drury Lane: Ballad Opera and the Production of Kitty Clive," *Journal of the Royal Musical Association* 131 (2006): 179–228

Joncus, Berta and Jeremy Barlow, eds., *The Stage's Glory: John Rich (1692–1761)* (Newark, DE: University of Delaware Press, 2011)

McVeigh, Simon, "Italian Violinists in Eighteenth-Century London," in Reinhard Strohm, ed., *Eighteenth-Century Diaspora of Italian Music* (Turnhout, Belgium: Brepols, 2001)

Roberts, John, "Why Did Handel Borrow?" in Stanley Sadie and Anthony Hicks, eds., *Handel Tercentenary Collection* (Baskingstoke, Hampshire: Royal Musical Association, 1987)

Smith, Ruth, "Early Music's Dramatic Significance in *Saul*," *Early Music* 35 (2007): 173–90

Smith, Ruth, *Handel's Oratorios and Eighteenth-Century Thought* (Cambridge: Cambridge University Press, 1995)

CHAPTER FIFTEEN

Postlude and Prelude
Bach and the Baroque

In 1985, in honor of the 300th anniversary of Bach's birth, the German sculptor Bernd Göbel created a statue of the composer for the market square of Arnstadt, the town in which Bach served from 1703 to 1707 as organist of the New Church (Neukirche), his first appointment in such a position. In contrast to the formal, paternal statue of Bach at the organ that has stood outside St. Thomas's Church (Thomaskirche) in Leipzig since 1908 (Fig. 15.1), visitors to Arnstadt see a brash and arrogant young man, boldly reclining in his shirtsleeves, unabashedly aware of his own talent and virility (Fig. 15.2).

The contrast between these two statues reflects the often contradictory notions about Johann Sebastian Bach (1685–1750) that have emerged since the composer's death. For most readers, Bach is likely to be the best known among Baroque composers. Yet, although his music is universally revered, he is in some respects an enigmatic figure whose shadow threatens to obscure the very musical context this book has set out to explore. Many critics view Bach as the culmination of the Baroque, the brilliance of his compositions and playing far outshining that of any of his contemporaries. A few even take the extreme position that the story of Baroque music is but a preface to the arrival of Bach on the scene, that each new genre or style—be it a concerto, a fugue, a passion, or a cantata—did not become fully formed or realized until the perfect hand of Bach was laid upon it.

Figure 15.1: *Johann Sebastian Bach, monument by Carl Seffner outside St. Thomas's Church, Leipzig (1908)*

Figure 15.2: *Bernd Göbel, Bach statue in market square, Arnstadt (1985)*

There is, admittedly, more than a grain of truth to that version of the tale, even as it ignores much of the richness and variety of the period on which we have focused in the preceding chapters. There are relatively few aspects of Baroque musical style that Bach did not absorb, refine, synthesize, and ultimately make his own, and the level of profundity he achieves with this material is only occasionally glimpsed in the works of other Baroque composers.

It was precisely this depth and complexity that made Bach's works inaccessible to some of his contemporaries, particularly in a period in which listeners were captivated by the elegance of the *galant* style. The young Johann Adolph Scheibe (1708–1776), for instance, famously criticized Bach for writing music that was too intricate and technically difficult. And many commentators, even those who were some of Bach's most enthusiastic admirers, saw him as representing the end rather than the beginning of an era. One was the twentieth-century German physician, philosopher, and musician Albert Schweitzer, who called Bach's music a "terminal point" to which all music from the previous century had led. Indeed, many critics have viewed Bach as an "old-fashioned" master who had little if any immediate influence on the subsequent generation.

Moreover, unlike the vast majority of the best-known musicians of the period, Bach hardly left home, spending all of his life in a tiny corner of the Holy Roman Empire, in the area in central Germany known as Thuringia. His most adventurous voyage was a trip on foot to Lübeck to hear Dieterich Buxtehude play the organ (see Chapter 13). The fact that Bach traveled so little means there is less of a trail for historians to follow, and the documents that have been handed down, including the relatively small number of letters, shed little light on his personal life and character. As one Bach scholar notes, his life was "notoriously and frustratingly uneventful." Much of what we know about his childhood and his relationship with his two wives and many children comes to us obliquely through official documents or through the obituary written by his son Carl Philipp Emanuel and a former student, Johann Friedrich Agricola.

We thus approach Bach in the final chapter of this book with a number of questions. Was he a great intellectual whose profound knowledge of music can be compared with the scientific inquiries of his contemporary Isaac Newton, or a master craftsman endowed with a rare combination of perseverance and inborn talent? Was he an old-fashioned representative of the end of the Baroque Era or a progressive innovator with an eye on the latest musical techniques? To put the question another way, are Bach's works a postlude to the Baroque or a prelude to modernity?

THE ROAD TO LEIPZIG

By the time Bach arrived in Leipzig in 1723 to begin his 27-year tenure as cantor (director of music) at St. Thomas's Church, he had held a series of positions in various courts and churches not far from his birthplace in Eisenach. After serving first as a court violinist in Weimar and then as organist in Arnstadt, where he met and married his first wife, Maria Barbara, he moved to the free imperial city of Mühlhausen in 1707—the same year Handel arrived in Italy (see Chapter 14).

A year later he returned to Weimar to accept a prestigious appointment as court organist (and later, concertmaster) at Weimar (1708–17), the ducal court of the ruler of Saxe-Weimar.

Bach's next position as Kapellmeister for the Calvinist court at Cöthen (1717–23), the home of the ruler of the Anhalt-Cöthen region, represents his longest break from a Lutheran environment and the duties of a church organist. It was in Cöthen that Bach, after the death of Maria Barbara, would meet his second wife, the young court singer Anna Magdalena Wilcke, daughter of the court trumpeter.

Despite the fact that he traveled relatively little, particularly as compared with so many of his colleagues, during the early part of his career Bach nonetheless acquired full fluency in the various national styles. In this he was certainly aided by the tastes of his musically knowledgeable and well-traveled patrons. From the young Duke Ernst August of Weimar, only three years Bach's junior, he might have gained access to a copy of Vivaldi's set of twelve concertos entitled *L'estro armonico* (Harmonic Inspiration), Op. 3 (1711), which the young duke would have purchased in Amsterdam. In fact, during his Weimar years, Bach arranged some nine works by Vivaldi (along with music by other Italian composers, such as Corelli). Certain elements of Vivaldi's concerto style—in particular the contrast between the tonal and motivic clarity of the ritornello and the potential for contrapuntal and thematic development in the solo sections—seem to have been particularly useful for Bach.

In Cöthen he would have benefited from the musical interests of the young Prince Leopold, who at age 16 had embarked upon a three-year grand tour through Holland, England, Germany, France, and Italy. Bach's compositions at Cöthen—which include the six sonatas and partitas for solo violin, the six suites for solo cello, and the six concerti grossi known as the Brandenburg concertos—reveal the cosmopolitan tastes of a world-traveling connoisseur. Bach's journey from Weimar to Cöthen was thus much longer than the 280 miles mere geography would suggest.

MUSIC IN LEIPZIG

Early in 1723 Bach auditioned for and accepted the position of cantor and municipal music director in Leipzig, assuming charge of music at the city's two principal churches, St. Thomas and St. Nicholas. On the one hand, he was returning to the Bach family business—playing the organ for the Lutheran church. On the other hand, his new duties were of a scale which neither he nor his many musical forebears had previously enjoyed. Leipzig, moreover, had a good deal more to offer the organist-Kapellmeister above and beyond his professional situation. An international center of commerce, the city hosted trade fairs where luxuries

Figure 15.3: *Leipzig in the eighteenth century*

such as books, tobacco, and coffee, along with more basic commodities, were bought and sold. Its famed university attracted scholars and theologians from throughout Germany (Fig. 15.3). Bach's employment at the St. Thomas School insured that his children would have the kind of advanced education that he himself had not experienced.

Bach arrived in Leipzig at age 38 with many of his most renowned compositions under his belt. It is unclear whether he envisioned from the start of his time in Leipzig that he would live out his remaining years as the "Thomascantor." He continued to develop relationships with nobles at neighboring courts, earning the honorary title of Kapellmeister from Duke Christian of Weissenfels in 1729 and performing at the courts of Dresden and Potsdam. However, Bach never won an illustrious court appointment in Dresden, as did his friend Johann Adolf Hasse. Nor did he ever compose an opera. (He did, however, attend opera in Dresden in the company of his eldest son Wilhelm Friedemann; Bach's use of *opera seria*–style arias in his Passions and cantatas attests to his interest in dramatic music.) Nor did he achieve the commercial success that his friend Telemann, godfather to Carl Philipp Emanuel, enjoyed in Hamburg. A few surviving documents allude to his frustrations with Leipzig officials and the sometimes stifling atmosphere in the city. However, with its students, visitors, and growing population of artisans, tradesmen, and merchants who flocked to hear music in the churches and coffeehouses, Leipzig provided Bach with a stable and fertile environment in which to absorb and experiment with the latest innovations and developments in musical style.

MUSIC FOR THE CHURCH

When the 23-year-old Bach resigned from Mühlhausen to take up his position at the court of Weimar, he observed, in a rare self-revelatory moment, that God had brought about the possibility of his earning "a more adequate living" and the "achievement of his goal of a well-regulated church music without further vexation."

Bach might well have had similar hopes upon his arrival in Leipzig. The notion of a "well-regulated" church music was not only tied to having the necessary musical forces, a subject he discussed in a well-known petition to the Leipzig town council in 1730 (SR 88:565–69: 4/8:57–61). He seems also to have been interested in systematically building a repertory that would, in accordance with the liturgical calendar, appropriately express Lutheran theological principles. Bach's lifelong interest in theology was personal as well as professional. He owned an extensive theological library of at least 80 volumes (some scholars estimate as many as 112) and his Bible, translated by Luther with commentary by the theologian Abraham Calov, survives with Bach's own annotations.

CHURCH CANTATAS

Although Bach composed organ music for the liturgy throughout his career, one of the central ways in which he realized his goals as a church composer was by providing sacred cantatas for the Lutheran service. He wrote cantatas for all seasons and feasts of the liturgical year (with the exception of Lent, during which elaborate instrumental or vocal works were prohibited), throughout his career, though with particular concentration in Leipzig; of the several hundred alluded to in his obituary, a little over 200 survive.

Perhaps more than any other works we have considered in this book, Bach's cantatas pose something of a puzzle to the modern listener, who is likely not to be familiar with their function and meaning within the Lutheran service. Cantatas by Bach and his colleagues were not merely ornaments to the service; they represented an additional layer of interpretation, explicating the significance of the Gospel, psalms, and readings, as well as the general concerns of the congregation during each season of the liturgical year. The musical language may be familiar—one finds, for instance, lament gestures in references to death, and love duets depicting Jesus's union with the soul. Bach's choral and instrumental writing uses the techniques that we have studied earlier in this book: imitation, *stile antico*, *stile concertato*, chorales as cantus firmi, and the like. But grasping the meaning of the cantatas depends on recognizing the significance of the chosen excerpts from scripture, linked to the Gospel of the day, and understanding the complex theological concepts and obscure allegories that were taught as part of the traditional Lutheran education.

We can see how this might work by considering one of Bach's earliest cantatas, *Gottes Zeit ist die allerbeste Zeit* (God's Time Is the Best Time), BWV 106, also known as *Actus Tragicus* (A Tragic Performance). Like the other cantatas composed in Arnstadt and Mühlhausen, *Gottes Zeit* reveals its debt to the sacred concertos of Johann Hermann Schein and Heinrich Schütz (see Chapter 5) and the cantata arias of Buxtehude (Chapter 13). Possibly composed for the funeral of Bach's uncle, Tobias Lämmerhirt, in 1707, the cantata's text combines biblical verses from the Old and New Testaments with selections from chorale texts that take the believer on a journey from the acceptance of the inevitability of death to the promise of redemption through the Gospel of Christ.

Bach uses a number of musical strategies to express the central concerns of the cantata. The opening sinfonia, scored for recorders, bass viols, and continuo, conveys a sense of "God's time" in the steady eighth notes in the continuo and viols and the oscillating imitative figures in the recorders; the orchestration lends a somber, introspective character to the movement. Bach dramatizes the contrast between the expectation of death and the hope of redemption in the chorus that comes in the center of the cantata. The lower three voices join in an F-minor chromatic fugue (the beginning of which is shown in Example 15.1), marked by a half-step ascent and falling diminished fifth, as they mournfully intone the text from Ecclesiastes: "This is the ancient law: Man, you must die."

Over this somber fugue, the soprano unexpectedly enters with a joyful affect like a beam of light, singing, "Ja, komm, Herr Jesu, komm" (Come, Lord Jesus, come). Written in a free and florid style, the soprano line, as it has come down to us in a later manuscript, ascends into the upper register, the diatonic melodic line briefly veering toward the major, the plea becoming increasingly insistent as the passage continues. A third musical—and theological—idea is introduced by the recorders and viols, which play a chorale: "In you I have placed my trust, O God." Although the lower voices persist in the dire fugue, the soprano gets the final word in the movement: a ravishing, ornamented cadential passage with sixteenth-note triplets that lands with tentative optimism on a plagal cadence on F (with a Picardy third) that even silences the continuo (Ex. 15.2).

The sense of spiritual transformation is also conveyed by the sequence of keys throughout the cantata: it moves from the initial E♭ major as far to the flat side of

Example 15.1: *J. S. Bach,* Gottes Zeit ist die allerbeste Zeit, *BWV 106, movement 2, alto and tenor at beginning of choral fugue, mm. 1–3*

This is the ancient law: Man, you must die

Example 15.2: *J. S. Bach,* Gottes Zeit ist die allerbeste Zeit, *BWV 106, movement 2, mm. 51–55*

Come, Jesus, come

the tonal spectrum as Bb minor for the alto aria that follows the central chorus, ultimately returning to Eb for the concluding chorus in praise of the Trinity. Bach's listeners may not have been aware of the impact of the tonal journey, but the basic substance of this voyage in time—from the inevitability of death put forth in the Old Testament to the New Testament's promise of redemption through the death and resurrection of Christ—would nonetheless have been deeply meaningful to them.

The church cantatas that Bach composed later in Weimar and Leipzig differ considerably from such earlier works, particularly in their inclusion of the recitatives and da capo arias that were so much a part of contemporary Italian vocal music. In this regard, Bach and his colleagues were aided by the publication of cantata poetry by such authors as the theologian-poet Erdmann Neumeister and the Weimar court poet Salomo Franck. In many instances, however, we do not know who was responsible for the writing and compilation of Bach's cantata texts.

This is the case with *Wachet auf, ruft uns die Stimme* (Awake, the voice calls to us), BWV 140, first performed during the Advent season in Leipzig on November 25, 1731. This is one of Bach's many chorale cantatas that use a familiar Lutheran hymn as a unifying feature. The cantata concerns the parable of the wise and foolish virgins, the first of whom prepares to meet the heavenly bridegroom. Bach integrates Philipp Nicolai's "Wachet auf," a popular hymn on the same topic, into movements 1, 4, and 7. In the first movement, the chorale, sung by the sopranos and doubled by the horn, is presented in line-by-line fashion, while the chorus and orchestra perform independent material in what is usually referred to as a chorale fantasia.

Movement 4 uses the chorale in what is essentially a trio-sonata texture (Ex. 15.3). The chorale is sung by the tenors, while the violins and violas, also in unison, present an intricate countermelody that teasingly dips down into the tenor range. Both parts are set over an independent continuo line. The duets in the third and sixth movements, each preceded by a recitative, illustrate one of Bach's favorite strategies of vocal casting: the bass sings the role of Jesus, while the soprano represents the soul. Their union is celebrated in the penultimate movement as the two voices joyously intertwine, much as in an operatic love duet, to a text drawn from the Song of Songs.

COMPOSING THE CANTATAS

During Bach's first two years in Leipzig, when he composed two full cycles of cantatas (there were approximately 60 cantatas in each annual cycle), the weekly routine must have been grueling. He would likely begin by selecting a cantata text relating to the Gospel of the day. It might be by Franck or Neumeister, or by one of his local collaborators, such as Christian Friedrich Henrici (known as Picander) or Christiane Mariane von Ziegler, the only known female poet whose works were sung in Lutheran churches during this period, who hosted the salons in the French style at her home (Chapter 10). Taking into account the dramatic and theological implications of the text, and the abilities of the available singers and instrumentalists, Bach then composed the cantata. Before writing out the music, he even had to prepare the music paper, with the appropriate layout and scoring. The most frantic part of the process must have been copying the parts. For this all available competent hands were pressed into service, including Bach's wife Anna Magdalena, his children, and his students. The performance materials would then be proofread and corrected, with expression marks (dynamics,

Example 15.3: *J. S. Bach, Cantata No. 140 (Wachet auf), BWV 140, movement 4, mm. 13–15*

Zion hears the watchman singing . . .

tempos, articulations) added as necessary. Finally, Bach gathered the musicians for a single rehearsal on Sunday morning, likely while the ink on the parts was still wet. Young singers from the St. Thomas School performed alongside instrumentalists from the town and, occasionally, university students.

Bach took care to parcel out the more difficult music over the liturgical year, so as not to overtax his players, his listeners, or, presumably, himself. For the young boys who sang in Bach's choir, the challenges must have been considerable, particularly in the winter, when they would have been called to church in the dark to perform huddled together in an unheated organ loft. (Unlike Catholics, Protestants had removed the choir stalls from the front of the church, so the choir usually sang from the organ loft in the back.) Moreover, the choristers were required to sing both morning and afternoon services, one at St. Thomas's Church and the other at St. Nicholas's. Additional concerted music—sometimes another brief cantata or the second part of a lengthier one—would be heard after the sermon during communion.

PASSIONS

The multimovement cantata, with its shifts in mood, affect, and poetic styles, reinforced the message of the Gospel and comforted listeners with familiar hymn tunes, while using arias and recitatives to dramatize the fundamental mysteries of the Lutheran faith. Bach used these same elements—choruses, chorales, recitatives, and arias—in his musical settings of the Passion, the story of Christ's trial and crucifixion, which was performed on Good Friday in alternate years at each of Leipzig's two principal churches. While Bach's obituary mentions five Passions, only two have survived in their entirety: the *St. John Passion* (1724; revised in 1725 and several times thereafter) and the *St. Matthew Passion* (1727).

Although the Passions remain a staple of concert repertory today, they too present challenges to modern listeners arising from their liturgical content and context. Especially in the Gospel according to St. John, on which the *St. John Passion* is based, the story is presented in a way that holds the Jews responsible for the decision to crucify Jesus. While historians now recognize that the situation was far more complicated and that the Romans could be held directly responsible for the death of Jesus, dramatic performances of the Passion at Easter time since the Middle Ages have traditionally evoked strong anti-Semitic feelings, and occasionally incited violence against Jews.

Nonetheless, what makes Bach's Passions so dramatically compelling is that they depict not only actions but also reactions. In Part 2 of the *St. John Passion*, for instance, the listeners and performers are time travelers, witnessing the trial and death of Christ and learning from the arias how the true believer might interpret them centuries later (see Anthology 25). The role of the chorus in this process is multifaceted. The chorus represents both the Jews, who call

Example 15.4: *J. S. Bach*, St. John Passion, *BWV 245, conclusion of No. 29 and beginning of No. 30*

It is accomplished

for the crucifixion with merciless intensity, and the Roman soldiers, who take irreverent pleasure in drawing lots for Jesus's clothing in the immediate aftermath of the crucifixion. In the subsequent recitative, in which the Evangelist describes the action and Jesus presents his mother Mary, the chorus sings a chorale, thus taking on the role of the future believers, meditating on the significance of these seminal events even as they are happening.

The death of Jesus is presented somewhat obliquely, albeit powerfully, in the *St. John Passion*. Jesus utters the words "Es ist vollbracht" (It is accomplished) in recitative on a stepwise descent of a sixth, marked with an appoggiatura. This motive furnishes the material for the subsequent aria for alto and obbligato viola da gamba, in which the alto cries out for comport, but as we see in the opening ritornello, the tune here is highly ornamented (Ex. 15.4). The middle section of the aria, with its reference to battle and victory (set by Bach in the appropriate *stile concitato*), may seem curious to the modern listener, but it captures an almost militant quality of John's Gospel that would have been completely recognizable to Bach and his listeners.

The next movement, the bass aria "Mein teurer Heiland" (My precious Savior), and its accompanying chorale, provides yet another interpretation of Jesus's words "Es ist vollbracht," one that offers comfort and even resolution. In this D-major aria, however, the viola da gamba is replaced by an obbligato cello, which not only has a brighter sound but also conveys the suggestion of modernity. Instead of the intricate ornamentation and duple meter of the previous movement, the aria is characterized by a flowing, pastoral melodic line and rocking motion in $\frac{12}{8}$ meter. As the bass soloist asks if he has achieved freedom from death, lingering doubts are silenced by the firm reassurance of the chorale.

Example 15.5: *J. S. Bach Cantata No. 211 (Schweigt stille, plaudert nicht), BWV 211, movement 3 (Lieschen), mm. 22–28*

Ah! How sweet coffee tastes, lovelier than a thousand kisses

THE COFFEEHOUSE COMPOSER

Customers of Gottfried Zimmermann's popular coffeehouse in Leipzig during the early 1730s had the unusual pleasure of listening to an advertisement—by none other than Bach—for the very beverage that they were drinking. "Mm! How sweet the coffee tastes, more delicious than a thousand kisses, mellower than muscatel wine," sings Lieschen to her father in the third movement of the cantata *Schweigt stille, plaudert nicht*, BWV 211 (Be still, stop chattering; Ex. 15.5), often referred to as the "Coffee Cantata."

The Coffee Cantata was one of a number of secular vocal and chamber works that Bach wrote in conjunction with his duties as director of one of Leipzig's two collegia musica. His decision in 1729 to take over the leadership of the ensemble that Telemann had founded in 1702 seems to mark a change of direction for the composer. Over the next 12 years, Bach either became increasingly uninterested in the regular production of sacred cantatas, or perhaps had accumulated a large enough reusable repertory to turn his attention elsewhere. (It was during this period that he unsuccessfully petitioned August II [The Strong] for a position at the Dresden court that would free him from the various "unmerited affronts" he had suffered in Leipzig.) The collegium gave Bach access to some of the best instrumentalists in town (many of whom he also hired for the church) and an opportunity to compose and perform music in the newest styles—keyboard and chamber works of the sort that might have been heard in Berlin, Vienna, or Paris.

Zimmermann's coffeehouse, located in Leipzig's main market square, presented regular concerts by Bach's collegium musicum. It also attracted select guest performers, such as the soprano Faustina Bordoni (who sang for Handel in London) and her husband, Johann Adolf Hasse, who rose to prominence as an opera composer in Dresden. During the winter, weekly concerts were held in Zimmermann's establishment, which could accommodate as many as 150 auditors. Summer concerts were held in the afternoon in a "coffee garden" outside the city walls. In Leipzig, as elsewhere, women were discouraged from partaking of either coffee or tobacco, two stimulants associated with "French" intellectual pretensions, or even patronizing coffeehouses at all, though it is likely their presence was more acceptable in the summer, when they could sit outside.

Although no programs have survived, we assume that Bach's collegium performed a wide variety of chamber and vocal music, including works by Handel, Alessandro Scarlatti, and Telemann, as well as his own compositions, which included the so-called Coffee Cantata. Indeed, this charming work provides intriguing hints of Bach's sense of humor and appreciation of earthly pleasures—and perhaps a glimpse into Leipzig's gender wars as well.

When Lieschen's father, Schlendrian, asks her to stop drinking coffee, she refuses and extols the virtues of the beverage in the aria shown in Example 15.5. The **B** section of the aria becomes increasingly impassioned, as Lieschen exclaims, "Coffee, coffee, I must have it." The link between the desire for coffee and the pleasures of the marriage bed is unmistakable. Finally, her father insists that he will forbid her to marry if she does not give up coffee, and she acquiesces—or so it appears in Picander's original text. However, the version set by Bach includes two strophes at the end of the cantata, in which we learn that Lieschen has told her suitors that they must let her drink coffee or else she will not marry them. A trio featuring the narrator, father, and daughter concludes with the moral of the story: "Drinking coffee is natural."

Bach's customary stylistic complexities mesh in intriguing ways with the lighter style that suits the witty scenario. Lieschen's aria, for instance, is a lively minuet, with largely syllabic writing requiring little in the way of virtuosity from the singer. The obbligato part for flute, on the other hand, is unaccountably intricate, with sixteenth-note triplets, suspensions over the barlines, and thirty-second-note flourishes. In the father's aria, "Mädchen, die von harten Sinnen" (Girls with obstinate minds), the continuo and vocal lines, with their persistent angularity and chromaticism, convey a sense of paternal rigidity and the daughter's resistance; nonetheless, they seem at first glance to be at odds with the humor of the situation. Are we to imagine that Bach, so able to penetrate the meaning of his sacred texts, fails to get the point here? Or could it be that it is precisely this incongruity that Bach was interested in conveying with a dry sense of comedy? In his version it is the daughter—and the pleasures of coffee drinking—that ultimately triumph.

BEYOND GENRE: THE UNIVERSAL BACH

Bach's cantatas and passions, and even lighter works such as the Coffee Cantata, seem to belong to particular times and places. Other of his compositions, in particular the instrumental works, transcend not only the specific circumstances in which they were performed, but also the genres they represent. This is particularly apparent in a number of the collections that he assembled, either in print or for special dedicatees, that seem in one way or another to make a statement about a particular type of Baroque composition or style: either to explore every imaginable version of a single type of work or to go beyond the conventional definition of a single genre.

INSTRUMENTAL WORKS

Bach's accomplishments as a keyboard composer, virtuoso, and pedagogue are manifest in his massive *Clavier-Übung* (Keyboard Practice). Published in four parts between 1726 and 1735, the *Clavier-Übung* is a compendium of virtually every genre and style of music for harpsichord and organ. Bach demonstrates his mastery of dance forms in the first volume, which contains the Six Partitas (that is, suites). His fluency in the French and Italian styles is displayed in the second volume, in which we find the *Italian Concerto* and *French Overture*. Part 3 contains a variety of organ works, while part 4 includes the *Goldberg Variations*, the longest and most elaborate set of keyboard variations before Beethoven.

Bach's penchant for transcending conventional genre boundaries is particularly evident in Part 2 of the *Clavier-Übung*. Despite their misleading titles, the *Italian Concerto* and *French Overture* are for keyboard rather than orchestra. The opening ritornello of the *Italian Concerto*, the beginning of which is shown in Example 15.6, follows the Vivaldian model by establishing the key of F major in a strong declamatory style, with clearly delineated segments and the usual triadic motives. At the cadence in measure 30 (Ex. 15.7), the change in dynamics and texture in the keyboard signals the beginning of the first "solo" section. Thus Bach has grasped the essence of the concerto—the contrast between the *ripieno* and solo sections—and is able to express it without using the separate forces and shifts in orchestral color that normally define the genre. The *French Overture*,

Example 15.6: *J. S. Bach,* Italian Concerto, *BWV 971, opening ritornello, mm. 1–8*

Example 15.7: *J. S. Bach,* Italian Concerto, *BWV 971, beginning of first "solo" section, mm. 29–32*

which consists of a model three-part overture in the French style (followed by a suite of French dances), likewise translates this grand relic of the French court (see Chapter 7) to the keyboard medium.

Bach is similarly unconventional in his six *Brandenburg* Concertos, which feature an unusually rich variety of instrumental colors in novel combinations. In the first movement of the Fifth Concerto, for instance, Bach elevates the harpsichord from its accustomed role as continuo support for the *ripieno* by also placing it in the *concertino* group, on an equal footing with the solo violin and flute. The harpsichord—whose part is fully written out, except when functioning as the continuo—seems to lose all sense of propriety about two-thirds of the way through the movement: After supporting the other instruments with virtuosic passagework, often consisting of extensive thirty-second-note runs and arpeggios, it goes off on its own for an unexpected solo cadenza that lasts over 60 measures—more than a fourth of the entire movement. In stretching the boundaries of the concerto grosso, Bach provided a model for the solo keyboard concerto, of which he would be an important early proponent.

In his works for unaccompanied cello and violin, Bach also transcends convention. He was by no means the first composer to write for unaccompanied string instruments; Heinrich Ignaz Franz Biber, for example, concluded his *Mystery* Sonatas with a passacaglia for solo violin (see Chapter 13). However, even for the seemingly most lighthearted dance movements, Bach achieves in his unaccompanied works a level of profundity that seems to go beyond many of his contemporaries. In the Gigue from the C-Major Suite for solo cello (Fig. 15.4), for instance, Bach transforms this "dance for the ears" into a highly virtuosic work, in which the challenging skips between the upper and lower registers, double-stops, and *style brisé* imply a rich polyphonic texture.

Bach's pedagogical works, such as the two volumes of *Das Wohltemperierte Clavier* (The Well-Tempered Clavier, 1722 and 1742), designed, as he notes on the title page of Book 1, for "the use and profit of the musical youth desirous of learning, as well as for the pastime of those already skilled in their study," are equally original and unlocked a wide range of stylistic possibilities. As his son Carl Philipp Emanuel observed, Bach "composed his most instructive pieces for the clavier" and "brought up his pupils on them." These pupils included Carl Philipp Emanuel and his brothers Wilhelm Friedemann and Johann Christian Bach.

The novelty of *The Well-Tempered Clavier* lay not in the pairing of preludes and fugues in each of the 24 major and minor keys, for which there were a few precedents, but in their tremendous stylistic variety. The D-major Prelude in Book 2 is one of several in which Bach eschews the improvisatory fantasia style in favor of binary form and uses symmetrical antecedent-consequent phrasing and slower harmonic rhythm suggestive of the *galant* style. Fugues like the stately one in E-major in Book 2 invoke the learned *stile antico*, but Bach shows no such restraint in the C♯-minor Fugue from Book 2, with its Italianate triplet sixteenth-note figuration (Ex. 15.8).

Figure 15.4: *Manuscript of Gigue from the Suite for Cello in C Major, BWV 1009, copied by Anna Magdalena Bach*

Example 15.8: *J. S. Bach,* The Well-Tempered Clavier: *(a) Book 2, Fugue No. 9 in E Major, BWV 878, mm. 1–3; (b) Book 2, Fugue No. 4 in C♯ Minor, BWV 873, mm. 1–3*

Bach displayed an even greater mastery of fugal techniques in the early 1740s when he began composing the monumental *Kunst der Fuge* (Art of Fugue), BWV 1080, which was not published until after his death. Here he focuses exclusively on one contrapuntal genre, exploring every possible fugal and canonic treatment of a single theme (see Anthology 26). For the printed edition, Bach insisted on using the Latin word *contrapunctus* instead of fugue. This term, according to Bach's contemporaries, denoted contrapuntal part-writing in general—"the adroit combination of several melodies sounding simultaneously, whereby manifold euphony arises conjointly"—rather than the specific genre of the fugue. Indeed, part of the joy of these works—and of Bach's compositions in general—is the way in which contrapuntal technique and harmony are woven together.

MASS IN B MINOR

If *The Art of Fugue* is a summary of Bach's accomplishments in the contrapuntal idiom and the *Clavier-Übung* explores the varieties of keyboard music in the late Baroque, then the Mass in B minor, compiled in 1748–49 with some original and some previously composed works, served a similar purpose in the realm of vocal music. Bach's Mass differs from much of his sacred output in that it was not intended for Lutheran services; nor, given its extraordinary length, was it practical for any actual liturgical occasion. (Bach divides the main sections of the Latin mass—Kyrie, Gloria, Credo, Sanctus, and Agnus Dei—into 27 separate movements lasting nearly two hours.) Indeed, there is no evidence that it was ever performed in its entirety while the composer was alive.

The Mass in B minor reflects Bach's changing interests, both professional and musical, in the latter decades of his life. Much of what would become the Kyrie and Gloria had been presented to the elector of Saxony in 1733, when Bach was vying for a position at the Catholic court in Dresden. As he became increasingly dissatisfied with the resources in Leipzig in the 1730s and began devoting more time to the collegium musicum, he began exploring Latin church music of his predecessors, in particular Palestrina, as well as that of his contemporaries, including Caldara and Fux in Vienna and Hasse and Jan Dismas Zelenka in nearby Dresden. It may be that it was through the universal message of the Christian mass that Bach felt most comfortable summarizing and synthesizing the wide range of styles that he had employed throughout his career. Encompassing both the *stile antico* and the *stile moderno*, the Mass in B minor looks back to the Renaissance and forward to the *galant* style of the later eighteenth century.

The seamless way in which Bach shifts from one style to another is apparent in the opening Kyrie. It begins with an extended choral fugue with an independent, obbligato orchestra. The *galant* soprano duet that follows in the "Christe eleison," with its parallel sixths and thirds and Italianate violin ritornello, contrasts with the solemn *stile antico* of the second Kyrie. The opening of the Credo—one of the movements composed expressly for the Mass rather than being adapted from one of his earlier compositions—was built on a cantus firmus borrowed from plainchant, a procedure often used by Renaissance composers. (Monteverdi, as we recall from Chapter 5, used the same technique in his Vespers of 1610.) The dramatic climax of the Credo, in which the crucifixion is described (a recycling of some early compositions), is a lament for choir in which the throbbing

Example 15.9: *J. S. Bach, Mass in B Minor, BWV 232, Crucifixus, mm. 5–9*

He was crucified . . .

half-note sighs in the vocal part are supported by a chromatic descending ground bass (Ex. 15.9). The ensuing "Et resurrexit" celebrates Christ's resurrection in jubilant D major, replete with flutes, oboes, trumpets, and timpani.

In the poignant concluding chorus, "Dona nobis pacem" (Grant us peace), Bach reprises music heard in the Gloria to the words "Gratias agimus tibi" (We give thanks to Thee). This movement is basically a motet with more than a touch of Palestrina-style polyphony. The choral fugue, for instance, begins with a simple stepwise theme that might well have been borrowed from plainchant. Yet, lest we imagine that we are still in the Renaissance, Bach enriches the sonorities with the typically Baroque sounds of timpani and trumpets; the latter relinquish their customary role of doubling the chorus in order to shine above the ensemble in a triumphant celebration of peace.

In his preface to the 1752 edition of *The Art of Fugue*, published just after Bach's death, the editor Friedrich Wilhelm Marpurg wrote: "No one has surpassed him [Bach] in knowledge of the theory and practice of harmony." He praised the composer for his execution "of ingenious ideas, far removed from the ordinary run, and yet spontaneous and natural." For Marpurg, Bach's musical ideas, by virtue of their profundity, their connection to one another, and their means of organization, "should meet with the acclaim of taste, [in] no matter what country."

Marpurg was right, but it would be some time before many others agreed with his assessment. While Handel's music, particularly his oratorios, remained part of the concert repertory throughout much of the eighteenth and nineteenth centuries, the revival of Bach's vocal music did not begin in earnest until its "rediscovery" by Felix Mendelssohn and others in the early nineteenth century. (Bach's keyboard music had never entirely gone out of fashion, at least with teachers and students.) Bach became the most prominent Baroque composer in the twentieth-century concert repertory, his works continuing to influence composers of even the most modern bent.

As much as Bach can justly be viewed as a postlude to the Baroque, building ingeniously on the accomplishments of his predecessors, he is and for many will remain a prelude to modernity. Indeed, interest in Bach's music should be given much of the credit for stimulating the early music movement that led to the wholesale revival of many of the works considered in this book, and the search for historically informed ways to play and sing them. Nevertheless, the music of the past remains elusive. We can build replicas of Baroque instruments and edit and record music that has languished in libraries and archives. Players and singers, armed with historical knowledge, can do their best to uncover the performance practices of a long-lost time. Yet, in modern concert halls and in a noisier era in which audiences are saturated with so many different kinds of music, we can never truly re-create the essence of a Baroque performance.

We can, however—as we have tried to do in this book—listen as if this music were new, fresh, and dangerous, with the ears of our seventeenth- and eighteenth-century counterparts. We can picture ourselves having supper near Handel at the Vauxhall Gardens, listening through the grating to the nuns in Milan, marveling at the virtuosity of the orphans in Venice, singing an *air sérieux* at a fashionable Parisian salon, or catching a glimpse of Louis XIV as Apollo in *Ballet de la nuit*. We can even imagine what it must have been like to be in the audience in Mantua for the premiere of *L'Orfeo*, as Music boldly declared her newfound ability to calm troubled hearts and kindle the most frigid minds with anger and love. In this most theatrical and passionate age, Music kept her promise.

FOR FURTHER READING

Chafe, Eric, *Analyzing Bach Cantatas* (Oxford and New York: Oxford University Press, 2004)

David, Hans T., Arthur Mendel, and Christoph Wolff, eds., *The New Bach Reader: A Life of Johann Sebastian Bach in Letters and Documents* (New York: W. W. Norton, 1998)

Erickson, Raymond, ed., *The Worlds of Johann Sebastian Bach* (New York: Amadeus Press, 2009)

Goodman, Katherine R., "From Salon to *Kaffeekranz*: Gender Wars and the Coffee Cantata in Bach's Leipzig," in Carol Baron, ed., *Bach's Changing World: Voices in the Community* (Rochester, NY: University of Rochester Press, 2006)

Marshall, Robert, "Towards a Twenty-First Century Bach Biography," *Musical Quarterly* 84 (2000): 497–525

Marshall, Robert, "Bach the Progressive: Observations on His Later Works," *Musical Quarterly* 62 (1976): 313–57

Rose, Stephen, *The Musician in Literature in the Age of Bach* (Cambridge: Cambridge University Press, 2011)

Williams, Peter, *J. S. Bach: A Life in Music* (Cambridge: Cambridge University Press, 2007)

Wolff, Christoph, *Johann Sebastian Bach: The Learned Musician* (New York: W. W. Norton, 2001)

academy (French, *académie*; Italian, *academia*) Society to promote artistic or scholarly activities and goals. In France, organizations established by the monarch, often monopolistic, to regulate intellectual and artistic life. In Italy, organizations, often under the patronage of the nobility or intellectuals, where amateurs and professionals met to support, perform, and discuss literary, scientific, and artistic endeavors.

accompanied recitative RECITATIVE with orchestral accompaniment, often used in opera and oratorio for highly dramatic moments. Compare *SECCO* RECITATIVE.

agrément (French, "charm") French Baroque term for melodic embellishments that were obligatory for the correct performance of the music, often of a formulaic nature and indicated by signs above or below the staff.

air French and English name for a song or aria, sometimes referring to a verse-refrain or strophic setting with instrumental accompaniment.

air de cour (French, "court air") French Baroque term for accompanied strophic songs, especially those composed for performance in court.

airs à boire (French, "drinking song") Term used to describe a popular style of drinking song in mid-seventeenth- and early-eighteenth-century France, typically with a simple melody, a syllabic text setting, and in strophic form.

airs sérieux (French, "serious song") French Baroque term used to describe the most sophisticated among the genres of French songs, usually dealing with serious topics such as love, despair, absence, and desire, in which the irregular melodic contours and shifting meetings followed the speech patterns of the poetry.

alexandrine A line of verse with twelve syllables that became the standard for French neoclassical tragedy.

allemande (French, "German") A somewhat stately dance in duple meter and in binary form; one of the standard movements of the Baroque suite, often the opening movement.

anthem English choral composition, generally for liturgical or ceremonial performance.

anticipation Melodic figure or ornament in which an arrival pitch is anticipated by a short note at the end of the preceding beat.

aria Lyrical setting of poetic text for solo voice and instrumental accompaniment, especially in an opera, oratorio, cantata, or similar vocal work.

arioso Term used to describe a florid and less syllabic setting of a poetic text that normally would be set as recitative.

A1

arpeggio (Italian *arpa*, "harp") Melodic or accompaniment figure in which the pitches of a chord are sounded in succession instead of simultaneously.

ballad opera English comic play of the eighteenth century consisting of spoken dialogue alternating with songs in which new words are set to borrowed tunes.

ballet de cour (French, "court ballet") Courtly entertainment danced by members of the court, with verse, music, scenery, and costumes.

basso continuo Continuous instrumental bass line with improvised harmonies underlying other melodic lines, integral to most instrumental and vocal music of the Baroque. Harmonies were often indicated by figures written above or below the bass notes (FIGURED BASS), to be "realized" extemporaneously at the keyboard or lute; the bass line itself was generally played as well by a bass instrument such as cello or BASS VIOL. Also known as "continuo" or "thoroughbass."

basso ostinato (Italian, "persistent bass") See GROUND BASS; OSTINATO.

bass viol The most popular member of the VIOL family, similar in range to a cello and used extensively for both solo music and BASSO CONTINUO throughout the Baroque.

beat Unit of regular pulsation in musical time.

binary form Compositional structure of most Baroque dance suite movements, with two sections, each repeated, AABB; by the later Baroque, the harmonic structure was defined by an A section concluding on the dominant or the relative major, and a B section effecting a return to the tonic. When the first part is repeated, AABBAA, it is often referred to as "rounded binary."

broadside ballad Narrative song for which lyrics, often on a current topic, are printed on sheets (broadsides) and sold at a low price to the public, to be sung to familiar tunes.

broken consort An instrumental CONSORT consisting of instruments from different families—for example, mixing flutes and viols (compare WHOLE CONSORT).

cadence Close of a musical phrase, in different eras often marked by a particular melodic figure or harmonic motion; see FULL CADENCE, HALF CADENCE, PLAGAL CADENCE.

cadenza A highly embellished passage improvised or performed in a virtuosic, improvisatory manner by a soloist, typically near the end of an aria or concerto movement; its placement is traditionally indicated by the composer by a fermata or, in the Baroque, by the indication *adagio*.

canon (Latin, "rule") A polyphonic compositional technique in which contrapuntal voices enter successively on the same melody, but according to specific rules of transformation by which the whole piece is derived; such "rules" might include singing or playing the melody backward, in mirror form, at different pitch, or at different speeds.

cantar recitando (Italian, "reciting in song") Term used to describe a tuneful, more arialike style of recitation in early opera. Compare with STILE RECITATIVO.

cantata (Italian *cantare*, "to sing") Generic term for a work for voice and instruments, on secular or sacred texts, set as movements such as arias, duets, and choruses, interspersed with recitatives.

canto figurato (Italian, "figured song") Term used to differentiate a florid, ornate style of sacred vocal music from plainchant, usually accompanied by basso continuo in the Baroque.

cantor Solo singer, generally one trained in church music; the term is sometimes used for a church music director.

cantus firmus (Latin, "fixed melody") Plainchant, chorale, or other preexisting melody that is used as the basis of a polyphonic movement or work, often by being presented in long time values.

canzonetta (Italian, "little song") A light, secular vocal work, set syllabically. In the seventeenth century, canzonettas were usually strophic solo songs with accompaniment, set to a poem with lines of regular lengths but shifting accentual patterns that made for a rhythmically energetic musical setting.

canzona (Italian, "song") In the Baroque, a type of solo keyboard work with roots in Renaissance vocal polyphony. Also, a type of ensemble composition, especially popular in Venice in the early Baroque, exploiting the architecture of, e.g., the Basilica of San Marco by featuring CORI SPEZZATI.

castrato Male singer castrated before puberty to preserve a high vocal range (soprano or alto), but achieving full vocal power as an adult; castrati were featured prominently as soloists and ensemble members in sacred and secular music, particularly in Italy, but also in other major European centers such as Vienna and London.

cembalo Italian word that generally means harpsichord, but was sometimes used to refer to any stringed keyboard instrument.

chaconne Instrumental composition much like a PASSACAGLIA, consisting of a series of variations on a harmonic progression, usually in triple meter.

chamber music Music written for performance in intimate settings for small instrumental and vocal forces.

chamber sonata See SONATA DA CAMERA.

character pieces Term used to describe instrumental works or single movements that express extra-musical ideas, depicting narrative ideas, specific people, animals, or actions. See PROGRAMMATIC.

chittarone Bass LUTE, often used as a basso continuo instrument.

chorale German Protestant hymn.

chorale cantata A sacred cantata that was performed as part of the Lutheran liturgy in the eighteenth century, usually in German, in which a single chorale or hymn tune is used prominently in some or all of the movements.

chromaticism The use of several notes of the chromatic scale in a composition or passage.

chromatic scale Scale built of all twelve pitches in the octave.

church sonata See SONATA DA CHIESA.

ciaccona See CHACONNE.

clavecin French word that in the Baroque usually referred to the harpsichord, but could mean any stringed keyboard instrument.

clavier (also spelled "Klavier") German word used in the seventeenth and eighteenth centuries to refer to any stringed keyboard instrument.

collegium musicum (plural, collegia musica) Music society, particularly in Germany, typically for students, amateurs, and professionals to discuss and perform music, often in an informal setting such as a coffeehouse.

coloratura Highly ornamented singing, with fast, generally MELISMATIC passagework.

colossal baroque Term used to describe a style of choral composition in the seventeenth and eighteenth centuries usually featuring multiple choruses and large instrumental ensembles with a grand, opulent style.

comédie-**ballet** Comic play or spectacle incorporating music and dance.

commedia dell'arte Italian improvised comedy involving stock characters and plotlines.

common practice tonality General term to describe widely shared conventions of tonal practice in Western music from the late seventeenth century to the late nineteenth century, creating expectations for which chords were likely to follow one another in a chord progression and how a given key or tonic could be established.

concertato style Baroque musical style or texture in which two or more groups of instruments or voices interact or compete with one another.

concertino (Italian, "little concert") The solo group of instruments in a Baroque CONCERTO GROSSO.

concerto In general, three-movement (fast-slow-fast) instrumental work in which a solo instrument or group of instruments is contrasted with a full orchestra; the outer movements often employ an orchestral RITORNELLO.

concerto grosso (Italian, "large concert") Baroque concerto in which a group of solo instruments (*concertino*) is used in contrast with a large ensemble (*ripieno*).

consort Term used in England for a small instrumental ensemble, either of all one family of instrument (*whole consort*) or of different families (*broken consort*). Also, a work for consort.

continuo See BASSO CONTINUO.

contrafactum (Latin, "imitations" or "counterfeit"; plural, *contrafacta*) A vocal work in which one text replaces another, as when the melody of a popular song is used as the basis for a hymn.

cori spezzati (Italian *coro spezzato*, "split choir") Musical texture created by placing two or more ensembles of instruments or voices at a distance in a large space such as a cathedral and having them sound in alternation and together.

cornett, cornetto Family of cone-shaped wind instruments with a cupped mouthpiece like a trumpet but finger holes like a woodwind; often used in Baroque church and chamber music.

corrente. See COURANTE.

counterpoint The practice of combining melodic lines to create polyphony.

courante (French, "running") Baroque BINARY FORM dance in triple meter; one of the standard movements of dance suites in the seventeenth and eighteenth centuries, more stately and often more contrapuntally complex than its Italian counterpart, the *corrente*.

cross-relation The occurrence, simultaneous or in quick succession, of two different chromatic forms of a note (e.g., F and F-sharp) in two different voices.

da capo aria Popular ARIA form of the Baroque, in ABA form; the return of the A section, frequently not written out but indicated by the notation *da capo* (Italian, "from the top"), was an occasion for vocal ornamentation.

dance suite See SUITE.

descending minor tetrachord Melodically descending fourth with a semitone between the two lowest notes; also known as a Phrygian tetrachord.

diatonic Built from the seven pitches of a major or minor scale.

diminutions See DIVISIONS.

dissonance Interval or sonority that is considered unstable or harsh, usually requiring resolution to a consonance.

diva (Italian, "goddess") Female vocal star; more formally, PRIMA DONNA.

divisions Method of improvising on or ornamenting a melody by subdividing the notes into successively smaller time values or adding quicker melodic figures; a form of VARIATIONS popular in late Renaissance and early Baroque instrumental music. Also known as *diminutions*.

double-stop On a violin or other bowed string instrument, the playing of two pitches simultaneously.

Dramatick opera The name given by the poet John Dryden to a style of English opera that featured both singing and spoken dialogue; later called SEMI-OPERA.

dramma per musica (Italian, "drama through music") The generic title applied to Italian sung drama (opera) during much of the seventeenth century, regardless of whether it was serious or comic.

dynamics Elements of musical expression relating to the degree of loudness or softness, or volume, of a sound.

episode An intermediate, subsidiary passage of music, as between the theme statements in a rondo; in a FUGUE, a section in which the main theme or subject is not present in full.

falsetto High, lighter vocal register of a male voice, used by noncastrated males to sing in the alto or soprano range.

fantasia Instrumental composition that is improvisatory in style; in the Baroque, the term is sometimes used for works that incorporate imitative counterpoint.

fantastic style (Latin, *stylus phantasticus*) Term used to describe a style of composition that is free and unbridled, highly expressive, often incorporating both virtuosic, improvisatory passages and sophisticated use of counterpoint, thereby displaying the practitioner's skill.

favola in musica (Italian, "fable in music") One of a number of genre designations for early opera based on mythological themes.

figured bass Shorthand method of notating harmony and voice leading for BASSO CONTINUO by means of numbers ("figures") and accidentals.

French overture Overture type developed in seventeenth-century France and popular in the late Baroque, generally consisting of a slow duple section with dotted rhythms, followed by a lively fugal section, sometimes closing with a brief return of the opening material.

fugue Complex polyphonic form in which one or more themes or subjects are treated in imitative counterpoint; between *expositions* (in which the subject is stated successively in all voices), there are *episodes* in which the subject may be fragmented, inverted, or otherwise manipulated.

galant style See STYLE GALANT.

galliard Lively dance of the late Renaissance, usually in compound duple meter and often employing hemiola rhythmic patterns, and sometimes paired with the PAVAN; in its mature form in early-seventeenth-century England, generally in three repeated sections, AABBCC.

gigue Lively dance of the Baroque, generally in triple or compound meter and BINARY FORM, often the concluding movement of the standard Baroque SUITE.

grand motet (French, "large") Term used in France for a large MOTET for double choir and orchestra, composed for festivals and other celebrations.

ground bass Repeating bass line over which melodic lines are varied, forming the basis of a type of variation form. Also called *basso ostinato*.

guilds Associations of craftsmen and artisans, which by the seventeenth century included instrument builders.

half cadence Musical CADENCE ending on the dominant and giving a sense of incompleteness.

harmony Aspect of music that pertains to the simultaneous combinations of notes, the intervals and chords that result, the sucession of chords, and the underlying principles.

harpsichord Keyboard instrument in wide use from the fifteenth through the eighteenth centuries, in which strings are plucked by quills.

head motif Musical motive introduced at the beginning of movement, often as part of a RITORNELLO, and recurring throughout.

hemiola (Greek, "ratio of 3:2") In triple meter, shift of rhythmic accentuation so that two groups of three beats sound as one group of three larger beats; common in GALLIARDS and COURANTES, and used to signal a CADENCE in many Baroque pieces.

homophony Musical texture in which all the voices move at the same pace.

imitative counterpoint COUNTERPOINT built from imitation between the voices or instrumental parts.

impresario Musical producer, especially one who manages a theater and oversees the production of operas.

inégalité (French, "inequality") Baroque performance practice according to which the duple subdivisions of a beat are performed unequally, with the strong note of the subdivision lengthened to some degree, at the discretion of the performer; akin to "swing" in jazz.

intermedio (Italian, "intermezzo," plural *intermedi*) Musical interludes with song, dance, and spectacle, usually on mythological topics, performed between the acts of plays.

just intonation Tuning of pitches according to their natural harmonic ratios; according to this system, some thirds and fifths in a given scale are perfectly in tune, while others are somewhat or even extremely out of tune.

Kantorei (German, "church choir") The professional or semi-professional choir connected with church, court, city, or university, directed by the cantor.

Kapellmeister (German, "master of the chapel") Originally, a church music director, but eventually a term for a conductor or other leader of a musical organization.

kit See POCHETTE.

Lent In Roman Catholicism, the penitential period of forty days before Easter during which time the theaters were traditionally closed, encouraging the production of oratorios and important series of public concerts.

libretto (Italian, "little book"; French, *livret*) The text of an opera or oratorio, often printed and sold separately to the public.

lute Plucked string instrument, usually pear-shaped with a rounded back, with a wide-fretted neck, a single highest treble string, and five or more unison pairs of lower strings, popular in the Renaissance and Baroque and often used for performing polyphonic music.

madrigal (Italian *madrigale,* "song of the modern tongue") Setting of (usually) secular Italian (and, in the late sixteenth century, English) poetry as a polyphonic vocal work, often featuring elaborate musical depictions of the text; seventeenth-century madrigals were also composed for small vocal ensembles with continuo; the name was occasionally given to settings of sacred vernacular poetry composed in the style of madrigals.

madrigalism Term used to describe the kind of word painting associated with madrigals.

maestro di cappella (Italian, "master of the chapel") See KAPELLMEISTER.

masque In England, a staged entertainment, frequently mythological in subject, created for a special occasion, and often with the participation of courtiers and other revelers; by the later seventeenth century; masques were performed in theaters or as part of an opera.

mass Central service of the Roman Catholic Church; in music, a setting for voices, with or without instruments, of the texts from the Ordinary (that part of the service that does not change with the Church calendar), consisting of the Kyrie, Gloria, Credo, Sanctus, and Agnus Dei.

melisma Portion of a melody in which many notes are sung to a single syllable of text.

melismatic Style of setting text with many notes per syllable.

mode A scale or melody type, identified by the particular intervallic relationships among the pitches; in particular, one of the twelve (earlier eight) scale or melody types recognized by church musicians beginning in the Middle Ages (and often termed "church mode"), distinguished by the arrangement of whole and half steps in relation to the final tone.

monody Term applied to an innovative style of the early Baroque period in which solo singers perform with continuo, often in a dramatic, declamatory style.

motet (from French *mot,* "word") In the Renaissance, a term used generally for polyphonic settings of sacred texts (other than the mass); in the Baroque could refer to a variety of settings of sacred texts, both small and large scale, in Latin and the vernacular. See also PETITS MOTETS, GRANDES MOTETS, SACRED CONCERTOS.

motive Short melodic or rhythmic idea; the smallest fragment of a theme that forms a recognizable unit.

musette Bagpipe-like instrument in which air is supplied by a small bellows; popular in French courts for its evocation of the pastoral.

musique mesurée (French, "measured music") Vocal music in late-sixteenthth-century France in which note durations followed the stress of poetic verse in imitation of quantitative stresses of Greek and Latin poetry.

opera Large-scale dramatic musical stage work in which the actors sing throughout, accompanied by instruments, and generally consisting of a succession of arias, recitatives, and ensembles.

opéra-ballet Genre of French Baroque stage work with AIRS and other sung numbers interspersed with dances and purely instrumental movements, loosely linked by a plot.

opera buffa (Italian, "comic opera") Genre of Italian opera of the mid-eighteenth through the nineteenth centuries, including ensembles in addition to arias and recitatives and featuring tenors and basses rather than castrati.

opéra comique (French, "comic opera") Genre of French opera that in the eighteenth century treated comic and romantic themes and had spoken dialogue.

opera seria (Italian, "serious opera") Genre of Italian opera of the late Baroque and Classical periods, generally in three acts, with serious, often historical, subject matter and usually lacking comedic characters; in the late Baroque, dominated by the DA CAPO ARIA.

oratorios (1) Latin sacred dramas, usually on biblical themes, that were performed in prayer halls known as oratories in early-seventeenth-century Rome; (2) large-scale sacred music dramas, generally without staging or costumes, but with arias, recitatives, and choruses as in an opera.

orchestra Performing group generally consisting of groups of "sections" of string instruments, combined with single, paired, or multiple woodwind, brass, and percussion instruments.

ornament Brief elaboration of a melodic instrumental or vocal line, whether notated or improvised.

ornamentation The practice of embellishing an instrumental or vocal part, integral to the performance of Baroque music.

ostinato (Italian, "obstinate") A continuously repeating melodic pattern; in the bass, known as a *basso ostinato* or GROUND BASS.

ouverture-suite A type of orchestral SUITE that became popular particularly in early eighteenth-century Germany, beginning with a FRENCH OVERTURE and often with explicitly programmatic or extra-musical associations.

overture Orchestral piece introducing an opera or other long vocal work. See also FRENCH OVERTURE.

partbook The standard format for vocal or instrumental parts in the late Renaissance and Baroque in which each part was bound separately, so that singers and players read from their own parts rather than from a full score.

partimento In eighteenth-century Italy, a keyboard bass line devised for study purposes to practice improvisation and voice leading.

partita See SUITE.

passacaglia Instrumental composition consisting of a series of variations on a harmonic progression or a BASSO OSTINATO.

Passion The story of Jesus's sufferings and death, often performed with musical setting during Holy Week.

pasticcio (Italian, "pastry") Opera in which the text is pieced together from different sources or in which arias and ensembles are contributed by different composers.

pastorale héroïque (French, "heroic pastorale") Form of OPÉRA-BALLET, generally in three acts and based on classical pastoral characters and plots.

pavan Slow processional dance in duple meter, popular in the late Renaissance, often followed by a GALLIARD; in its mature form in early-seventeenth-century England, generally in three sections, ABC.

pedal point Sustained bass note over which harmonies change, with sonorities that are in part dissonant with the bass; the name is derived from its use in organ music, where foot pedals allow bass notes to be sustained for extended passages.

perfect cadence CADENCE in which the arrival chord is preceded by its dominant, providing strong reinforcement for a tonality.

petit motet (French, "small") Term used in France for a small-scale sacred work for solo voices and BASSO CONTINUO.

Picardy third In a minor key, the raised third of the final tonic chord to make it major, extremely common in the Renaissance and Baroque periods.

plagal cadence CADENCE in which final tonic chord is preceded by the subdominant, essentially as an elaboration of the tonic.

pochette (French, "little pocket") Miniature violinlike instrument used by dance masters to accompany dancers; called in English *kit*.

polyphony Musical texture consisting of two or more independent melodic lines, combined according to the practice of counterpoint.

portamento Expressive glide from one pitch to another, particularly in the performance of vocal and string music.

prelude General name for an instrumental work used as an introduction, but often a free-standing composition; the title is also used for solo compositions for a keyboard instrument.

prima donna (Italian, "first lady") Lead female singer or role in an opera.

prima prattica (Italian, "first practice") Claudio Monteverdi's term for the style and practice of sixteenth-century polyphony, characterized by strict adherence to contrapuntal rules for approaching and leaving dissonances. Compare with *SECONDA PRATTICA*.

programmatic Depicting a nonmusical narrative or idea through instrumental music.

recitative Speechlike singing that follows the natural rhythms of the text; used in opera and oratorio. See also ACCOMPANIED RECITATIVE, ARIOSO, and SECCO RECITATIVE.

regal Small reed organ, having a nasal tone quality.

ricercar (Italian, "to look for") In the sixteenth and seventeenth centuries, name sometimes used for an instrumental composition characterized by imitative counterpoint; precursor to the fugue.

ripieno (Italian, "full") Designation of the full ensemble or *tutti* in a concerto grosso, in contrast to the CONCERTINO or solo group.

ritornello (Italian, "little return"; plural, ritornelli) A musical refrain.

ritornello form A form typically used in arias and the opening and closing movements of concertos, in which the entire ritornello is presented initially by the full orchestra (*tutti*), recurring in part throughout the movement, in alternation with solo passages, and usually heard in its entirety at the end.

sacred concerto Term used in the seventeenth century for a setting of a biblical text for voices (usually solo or small ensemble), continuo, and sometimes other instruments. See also MOTET.

salon A gathering in a private home for intellectual discussion and the performance of musical or literary works; salons often provided creative and intellectual opportunities to women and members of the bourgeoisie.

sarabande BINARY-FORM dance in slow triple meter, with a characteristic accent on the second beat of the measure; one of the standard dances of the Baroque SUITE.

scordatura (Italian, "mistuning") The practice of using an alternative to the normal tuning of a violin or other string instrument to create a different timbre and enable particular chords and other figuration.

secco recitative (Italian *secco*, "dry") Recitative that is accompanied only by keyboard or a BASSO CONTINUO group and is close to the rhythm and speed of natural speech.

seconda prattica (Italian, "second practice") Term adopted by Monteverdi and his brother to refer to the new style in which it was permissible to break the rules of counterpoint in the interest of expressivity. See STILE MODERNO.

semi-opera See DRAMATICK OPERA.

serenata (Italian *sera*, "evening") In the Baroque, an extended cantatalike vocal work, composed for a special occasion and usually performed outdoors, often at night.

sigh motive An expressive melodic gesture in which a stressed, dissonant note resolves smoothly by step to an unstressed chord tone, suggesting a sigh.

sinfonia General term for an instrumental overture or other instrumental movement within an opera or other vocal work.

sonata (Italian *suonare*, "to sound, play") Composition for an instrumental ensemble (see especially TRIO SONATA), generally in several movements; later, the term was also applied to works for solo instruments.

sonata da camera (Italian, "chamber sonata") Sonata composed of BINARY-FORM dance movements; see SUITE.

sonata da chiesa (Italian, "church sonata") Term often used for a sonata in four movements, slow-fast-slow-fast, and often featuring STILE ANTICO, in contrast with the SONATA DA CAMERA.

stile antico (Italian, "ancient style") Style of composition or texture imitating the equal-voiced polyphonic style of the late Renaissance, in contrast with the STILE MODERNO and later Baroque styles using a basso continuo and favoring the polarity between melody and bass.

stile concertato (Italian, "concerted style") See CONCERTATO.

stile concitato (Italian, "excited style") Used first by Claudio Monteverdi, the term describes a texture characterized by rapidly repeating short notes, to convey agitation, anger, or battle.

stile moderno Term used in the early Baroque period to describe both vocal and instrumental music usually featuring soloist(s) and basso continuo (as opposed to the equal-voiced polphony of STILE ANTICO), in which virtuosity, dissonance, and unusual harmonies were used for expressive purposes.

stile recitativo One of the terms used in the early seventeenth century to describe the new style of speech song that was more generically termed RECITATIVE.

strophic Written with repeating poetic meter and rhyme scheme; in music, with all poetic verses set to the same music.

style brisé (French, "broken style") Musical texture for keyboard imitating the arpeggiated texture of lute music.

style galant In the mid- and late eighteenth century, an approach to composition and musical expression characterized by relatively simple textures, symmetrical phrasing, and a reduced harmonic vocabulary.

style luthé See STYLE BRISÉ.

suite Instrumental work composed of a collection of contrasting movements, most commonly BINARY-FORM dances (DANCE SUITES) and all in the same key.

syllabic Style of setting text with one note per syllable; compare MELISMATIC.

temperament Any system of tuning that compromises (tempers) just intonation in order to avoid extremely out-of-tune intervals; the result is that most intervals are to a lesser or greater extent out of tune.

tento See TIENTOS.

tetrachord (Greek *tetrachordos*, "four-stringed") Term used in music theory for a series of four pitches arranged by step and spanning a perfect fourth.

thoroughbass See BASSO CONTINUO; also, specifically, FIGURED BASS.

tiento (Spanish; Portuguese, *tento*) Solo instrumental genre of the Iberian Baroque, for keyboard or plucked string instrument, with roots in imitative Renaissance vocal music style.

toccata (Italian, "touch") Virtuosic solo instrumental piece for keyboard or plucked string instrument.

tragédie en musique Extended operatic form of the French Baroque, incorporating stylized social dancing or ballet and serious dramatic text.

tragédie lyrique See TRAGÉDIE EN MUSIQUE.

trio sonata Sonata genre featuring two treble instruments and basso continuo, widely popular in the Baroque; because the basso continuo was generally played by two instruments, the trio sonata was actually likely to be played by four players.

triple-stop Three-note chord played with the bow of a violin or other string instrument, generally sounding as a broken chord.

tutti (Italian, "all") Designation in the score for RIPIENO.

unprepared dissonance A dissonance arrived at by melodic leap.

variation form, variations Type of compositional form structured by multiple repetitions of a melody, harmonic progression (see CHACONNE, PASSACAGLIA), GROUND BASS, or other material, with each repetition undergoing different transformations or elaborations but maintaining the length and phrasing of the varied unit. See also *divisions*.

verse anthem Seventeeth-century English genre of sacred work for chorus and soloists with instruments; sections for full chorus alternate with solo verses.

villancico (Spanish, diminutive of *villano*, "peasant") A Spanish poetic form with strophes and refrains; also, the settings of popular songs based on them. In the seventeenth century, the name *villancico* was given to a large body of sacred songs in the vernacular that were a central part of liturgy and devotional practices on the Iberian peninsula and especially in New Spain, often mixing characters from popular theater and contemporary life with religious themes.

viol Bowed instrument with a fretted fingerboard and six or seven strings, resting on or between the legs (*gamba*, leg), in wide use in the Renaissance and Baroque; while the viol family consisted of different sizes, from treble to double-bass or violone, by the Baroque the term is often used to signify the BASS VIOL.

viola da gamba See VIOL.

vocalise Vocal melody sung without text.

whole consort Instrumental ensemble of all one type of instrument, especially viol.

ENDNOTES

CHAPTER 1

4. "harmony is confused, charged with modulations and dissonances": Cited in Georgia Cowart, ed., *French Musical Thought, 1600–1800* (Ann Arbor: UMI Research Press, 1989), 13.

8. "I must altogether abandon the false opinion that the sun is the center of the world": Giorgio di Santillana, *The Crime of Galileo* (Chicago: University of Chicago Press, 1955), 312.

CHAPTER 3

40. "It should be most unusual": Angelo Solerti, *Gli albori del melodramma* (Hildesheim: Georg Olms Verlag, 1969), 1: 69; cited in Paolo Fabbri, *Monteverdi*, trans. Tim Carter (Cambridge: Cambridge University Press, 1994), 63.

44. "so much emotion and in so piteous a way": Cited by Fabbri, *Monteverdi*, 85–86.

CHAPTER 4

58. "that one man can produce by himself more beautiful inventions": André Maugars, *Response faite à un curieux sur le sentiment de la musique d'Italie* (Rome, 1639); cited by Alexander Silbiger, "Fantasy and Craft: The Solo Instrumentalist," in John Butt and Tim Carter, eds., *A Cambridge History of Seventeenth-* *Century Music* (Cambridge: Cambridge University Press, 2005), 426.

59. "all musical instruments old and new": Michael Praetorius, *Theatrum instrumentorum* (Wolfenbüttel, 1619 and 1620), frontispiece.

63. "ready to hang themselves in their strings": Cited in Christopher Marsh, *Music and Society in Early Modern England* (Cambridge: Cambridge University Press, 2010), 108.

64. "imitate the voice in all its modulations": Marin Mersenne, *Harmonie Universelle: The Book on Instruments*, trans. Roger E. Chapman (The Hague: M. Nijhoff, 1957), 254.

64. "many Pathetical Stories, Rhetorical and Sublime Discourses": Thomas Mace, *Musick's monument, or, A remembrancer of the best practical musick, both divine and civil, that has ever been known to have been in the world* (London, 1676), 234.

66. "the most free and unrestrained method of composing": Athanasius Kircher, *Musurgia universalis* (Rome, 1650); cited by Paul Collins, *The Stylus Fantasticus and Free Keyboard Music of the North German Baroque* (Aldershot, UK, and Burlington, VT: Ashgate, 2005), 29.

70. "more for the ears" than "for the feet": Johann Hermann Schein, *Suite XIII aus "Banchetto Musicale,"* ed. Ferdinand Conrad (Celle: Moeck Verlag, 1969); cited by Barbara

Sparti, "Irregular and Asymmetric Galliards: The Case of Salamone Rossi," in Maureen Epp and Brian E. Power, eds., *The Sights and Sounds of Performance in Early Music: Essays in Honor of Timothy J. McGee* (Farnham, UK, and Burlington, VT: Ashgate, 2009), 220.

72. "piece of music resembles a piece of rhetoric": Michel de Saint Lambert, *Principles of the Harpsichord*, trans. and ed. Rebecca Harris Warrick (Cambridge: Cambridge University Press, 1984), 32.

CHAPTER 5

88. "not with a sober, distinct, and orderly reading": Thomas Coryat, *Coryat's Crudities* (London: Stansby, 1611). 231.

90. "special, nightly procession with great pomp and apparatus": Alexander Fisher, *Music and Religious Identity in Counter Reformation Augsburg* (Aldershot, UK, and Burlington, VT: Ashgate, 2004), 238–39.

91. "represented a personage of the story and expressed perfectly the force of the words": Ernest Thoinon, *Maugars, célèbre joueur de Viole, Musicien du Cardinal Richlieu . . . : Sa biographie suivi de sa "Response faite à un curieux sur le sentiment de la musique d'Italie"* (Paris: Claudin, 1865), 29; cited by Howard E. Smither, *A History of the Oratorio*, vol. 1: *The Oratorio in the Baroque Era: Italy, Vienna, and Paris* (Chapel Hill: University of North Carolina Press, 1977), 211.

CHAPTER 6

95. "magnificent and expensive diversions the wit": *Memoires of John Evelyn*, ed. W. Bray (London, 1819); cited by Ellen Rosand, *Opera in Seventeenth-Century Venice: The Creation of a Genre* (Berkeley and Los Angeles: University of California Press, 1991), 9.

105. "breadth of the heavenly gyrations": Maiolino Bisaccioni, *Apparati scenici per lo teatro novissimo di Venetia* (Venice: G. Vecellio and M. Leni, 1644), 34.

110. "the first and the most perfect drama": Cited by Rosand, *Opera in Seventeenth-Century Venice*, 275.

CHAPTER 7

126. "make Christians pray excellently": Jean Laurent Lecerf de La Viéville, *Comparaison de la musique italienne et de la musique françoise*, 2d ed. (Brussels: François Foppens, 1705; repr. Geneva: Minkoff, 1972), part 3, 78–79; cited by Jean-Paul C. Montagnier, "French Grand Motets and Their Use at the Chapelle Royale from Louis XIV to Louis XVI," *Musical Times* 146 (2005): 50.

CHAPTER 8

138. "made the addition of some necessary plain Rules": John Playford, *A Breefe Introduction to the Skill of Musick for Song and Violl* (London, 1654), Preface.

141. "Instead of the antient grave and solemn wind musique": Cited by Donald Burrows, *Handel and the Chapel Royal* (Oxford: Oxford University Press, 2005), 21.

CHAPTER 9

151. "the subject and dogma themselves go deeply and far more pleasantly": Erasmus Gruber, *Synopsis musica* (Regensburg, 1673); cited by John Butt, *Music Education and the Art of Performance in the German Baroque* (Cambridge: Cambridge University Press, 1994), 15.

152. "with such a teacher, a boy learns as little of singing": Johann Beer, *Des abentheurlichen . . . . Ritten Hopffen-Sack* (1678); cited by Stephen Rose, *The Musician in Literature in the Age of Bach* (Cambridge: Cambridge University Press, 2011), 121–22.

154. "raise his voice in connection with the affect of humility or love": Walter Hilse, "The Treatises of Christoph Bernhard," *Music Forum* 3 (1973): 24–25.

159. "still more amusing, in that their Persons": Edward Wright, *Some Observations Made in Travelling through France, Italy . . . in the Years 1720, 1721, 1722*, 2 vols. (London, 1730), 1: 79; cited by Daniel Heartz, *Music in European Capitals: The Galant Style, 1720–1780* (New York: Norton, 2003), 180.

159. "riled by the cursed screens": Jean Jacques Rousseau, *Les confessions* (Paris: Garnier, 1964); cited and translated by Daniel Heartz, *Music in European Capitals*, 183.

CHAPTER 10

165. "stealing the souls of the listeners": *Le veglie de' signori academici Unisoni*, vol. 1 (Venice: Sarzina, 1638), 10.

170. "truly refined women have led others": Charles Saint-Évremond, "Sur les Précieuses," in *Oeuvres*, ed. René de Planhol, 3 vols. (Paris: La Cité des Livres, 1927), 1: 45; cited by Benedetta Craveri, *The Art of Conversation*, trans. Teresa Waugh (New York: New York Review Books, 2005), 171.

170. "a person like you": Molière, *Tartuffe and The Bourgeois Gentleman / Tartuffe et le Bourgeois Gentilhomme: A Dual Language Book*, trans. Stanley Applebaum (Mineola, NY: Dover Publications, 1998), 203.

176. "unfit for the resort of persons of fashion": John Hawkins, *A General History of the Science and Practice of Music*, vol. 2 (London: J. Alfred Novello, 1853), 700.

178. "Hummers of Madrigals": William Weber, *The Rise of Musical Classics in Eighteenth-Century England: A Study in Canon, Ritual, and Ideology* (Oxford and New York: Oxford University Press, 1992), 66.

CHAPTER 11

185. "grand symphony comprising one hundred and fifty musicians": Cited in John Spitzer and Neal Zaslow, *The Birth of the Orchestra: History of an Institution, 1650–1815* (Oxford and New York: Oxford University Press, 2004), 118.

189. "for the next five years there will be totally prohibited": Francesco Valesio, *Diario di Roma*, ed. Gaetano Scano with Giuseppe Graglia (Milan: Longanesi, 1977–79), 2: 546; cited by Roberto Pagano, *Alessandro Scarlatti and Domenico Scarlatti: Two Lives in One*, trans. Frederick Hammond (Hillsdale, NY: Pendragon Press, 2006), 147.

189. "I now send him away from Rome": Cited by Roberto Pagano, *Alessandro Scarlatti and Domenico Scarlatti: Two Lives in One*, trans. Frederick Hammond (Hillsdale, NY: Pergamon Press, 2006), 164.

193. "with one of the most beautiful *sinfonie*": Giovanni Maria Crescimbeni, *L'Arcadia* (Rome: Rossi, 1708), 288.

193. "just as one finished the last verse of the new aria": ibid., 293.

197. "*sinfonie* of so large a number of instruments": Crescimbeni, *Notizie istoriche degli Arcadi morti* (Rome, 1720), 1: 250; cited in Spitzer and Zaslow, *Birth of the Orchestra*, 115.

197. "never met with any man that suffer'd his passions": Cited by Peter Allsop, *Arcangelo Corelli: New Orpheus of Our Times* (Oxford: Oxford University Press, 1999), 53.

199. "if musick can be immortal": Roger North, *Memoirs of Musick*, ed. Edward F. Rimbault (London: Bell, 1846), 128–29.

199. "cleared the ground of all other sorts of music": Roger North, *On Music, being a Selection from His Essays Written during the Years c. 1695–1728*, ed. John Wilson (London: Novello, 1959), 310–11.

CHAPTER 12

203. "I often tell my son that he will go mad": Letter of March 24, 1695, in *Lettres de Madame duchesse d'Orléans née Princesse de Palatine*, ed. Olivier Amiel (Paris, 1981); cited by Don Fader, "The 'Cabale du Dauphin,' Campra, and Italian Comedy: The Courtly Politics of French Musical Patronage around 1700," *Music and Letters* 86 (2005): 392.

204. "ladies of quality hearing and seeing these obscenities": Johann Christoph Nemeitz, *La vie de Paris sous la régence* (Paris: Plon, Nourrit, 1897), 103.

206. "You will find there also the portrait of our mores": Rémond de Saint-Mard, *Réflexions sur l'opéra* (Paris, 1741); cited by James R. Anthony in the introduction to André Campra, *Carnaval de Venise*, vol. 17 of *Comédie Lyrique: French Opera in the 17th and 18th Centuries* (Stuyvesant, NY: Pendragon Press, 1989), x.

209. "I have always had a subject": François Couperin, *Pièces de clavessin composées par Monsieur Couperin* (Paris, 1713).

215. "desirable that there should be found for the stage": Cited in Cuthbert Girdlestone, *Jean Philippe Rameau: His Life and Work* (New York: Dover Publications, 1969), 10.

CHAPTER 13

225. "most prominent men in the city": *Georg Philipp Telemann Briefwechsel*, ed. H. Grosse and H. R. Jung (Leipzig, 1972), 213; cited by George Buelow, "Hamburg and Lübeck," in George Buelow, ed., *The Late Baroque Era: From the 1680s to 1740* (Englewood Cliffs, NJ: Prentice Hall, 1993), 206.

225. "it is almost always true that where the best banks are": Johann Mattheson, *Der musicalische Patriot* (Hamburg, 1728); cited by George Buelow, "Hamburg and Lübeck," in Buelow, *The Late Baroque Era*, 194.

227. "slight application in music": Cited and translated by Eric Thomas Chafe, *The Church Music of Heinrich Biber* (Ann Arbor: University of Michigan Research Press, 1987), 21.

CHAPTER 14

240. "speak like the voice of a man": *The Diary of John Evelyn, Esq., FRS from 1641 to 1705–6, with memoir*, ed. John Bray (London and New York: Fredrick Warne, 1889), 381.

242. "to my great wonder I saw an entire Opera": Giacomo Rossi, *Rinaldo, an Opera* (London, 1711), From the Poet to the Reader.

242. "Every Limb, every Finger": *The Tatler*, ed. Alexander Chalmer, vol. 3 (London, 1822), 6.

245. "Faustina . . . has a charming voice": Cited by Donald Burrows, *Handel*, rev. ed. (Oxford: Oxford University Press, 2012), 610.

246. "Those costly Canary-Birds": Colley Cibber, *An Apology for the Life of Colley Cibber, Comedian* (London: 1750), 343.

248. "there will be no Action on the Stage": Burrows, *Handel*, 215.

CHAPTER 15

254. "notoriously and frustratingly uneventful": Robert Marshall, "Towards a Twenty-First Century Bach Biography," *Musical Quarterly* 84 (2000): 499.

257. "a more adequate living": "Bach's Request for His Dismissal" (letter of June 25, 1708), in Hans T. David and Arthur Mendel, eds., *The New Bach Reader*, revised and enlarged by Christoph Wolff (New York: Norton, 1998), 57.

266. "composed his most instructive pieces": Carl Philipp Emanuel Bach, "Letter Answering Questions about Bach," in David and Mendel, *New Bach Reader*, 399.

268. "the adroit combination of several melodies": Christoph Wolff, "The Compositional History of the Art of Fugue," in *Bach: Essays on His Life and Music* (Cambridge: Cambridge University Press, 1991), 277.

270. "No one has surpassed him": Friedrich Wilhelm Marpurg, "Preface to the 1752 Edition of *Art of Fugue*," in David and Mendel, *New Bach Reader*, 375–76.

CREDITS

MUSICAL EXAMPLES

134 William Lawes: Pavan and Divisions, Harp Consort, Lefkowitz edition 1971, Stainer and Bell. Reprinted by permission. **166** Barbara Strozzi: "Ardo in tacito" by Barbara Strozzi is published in *Barbara Strozzi: Cantate, ariete a una, due e tre voci, Opus 3,* edited by Gail Archer, Recent Researches in the Music of the Baroque Era, vol. 83. Middleton, WI: A-R Editions, Inc., 1997. Used with permission. All rights reserved. **213** (top) Élisabeth-Claude Jacquet de la Guerre: *Le sommeil d'Ulisse* (1715), Tempest Aria. Edited by Mary Cyr. © 2005 by The Broude Trust for the Publication of Musicological Editions. Reproduced with the permission of the publisher; (bottom) Élisabeth-Claude Jacquet de la Guerre, *Le sommeil d'Ulisse* (1715), Sleep Aria. Edited by Mary Cyr. © 2005 by The Broude Trust for the Publication of Musicological Editions. Reproduced with the permission of the publisher. **222** Dieterich Buxtehude: Toccata in F Major, BuxWV 157. Edited by Michael Belotti. Copyright © 1998, 2001 by The Broude Trust for the Publication of Musicological Editions. Reproduced by permission of the publisher. **223** (top) Dieterich Buxtehude, Toccata in F Major, BuxWV 157. Edited by Michael Belotti. Copyright © 1998, 2001 by The Broude Trust for the Publication of Musicological Editions. Reproduced by permission of the publisher; (bottom) Dieterich Buxtehude, Toccata in F Major, BuxWV 157. Edited by Michael Belotti. Copyright © 1998, 2001 by The Broude Trust for the Publication of Musicological Editions. Reproduced by permission of the publisher.

PHOTOGRAPHS AND FIGURES

2 The Metropolitan Museum of Art. Image source: Art Resource, NY. **5** (both) Scala/Art Resource, NY. **6** Bridgeman Art Library. **24** V&A Images, London/Art Resource, NY. **27** The Metropolitan Museum of Art/Art Resource, NY. **36** © Folger Shakespeare Library ®. **48** Bayerische Staatsbibliothek. **53** Chatsworth House, Derbyshire, UK/The Bridgeman Art Library. **59** National Gallery, London/Art Resource, NY. **61** Photo by Ulf Celander/Used with permission from GOArt (www.goart.gu.se). **62** © The Metropolitan Museum of Art/Art Resource, NY. **69** Ms. Parville 79, US-BEM 778/University of California, Berkeley. **73** Reproduced by permission of the Osterreichische Nationalbibliothek. **77** Courtesy of the Pitts Theology Library, Candler School of Theology,

INDEX

Note: Page numbers in *italics* indicate illustrations or musical examples.

academic institutions. *See* education, music
academies
  French, 94, 114–15, 177
  Italian, 22–23, 41, 96, 100, 115, 163, 164–70, 172–73, 188, 191–96
Academy of Antient Music, 178
Academy of Vocal Music (London), 178
Accademia degli Arcadi (Rome), 173, 184, 191–96, 203, 232
Accademia degli Incogniti (Venice), 96, 100, 102, 164, 167
Accademia degli Invaghiti (Mantua), 41, 164
Accademia degli Umoristi (Rome), 167
Accademia degli Unisoni (Venice), 164–67
Accademia di San Luca (Rome), 115
Accademia Filarmonica (Bologna), 164, 173–76, 197
Aci, Galatea, e Polifemo (Handel), 185
Act of Settlement (1701), 238
Adami, Andrea, 188, 193
Ad cor: Vulnerasti cor meum (Buxtehude), 223–24

Addison, Joseph, 242–43
Adelaide of Savoy, 47
Admeto (Handel), 246
Aeneid (Virgil), 33, 145
aesthetics
  ancients, 7
  Baroque in art, 4–5
  affections doctrine, 64
  Aristotelian unities, 7
  Artusi–Monteverdi controversy, 29–30
  French, 116–21, 202
  opera, 110, 184, 196–97
  patronage and, 64–65
Affetti musicali (Marini), 72
Africans portrayed in theatrical works, 53
agréments, 119. *See also* embellishment
Agricola, Johann Friedrich, 254
Agrippina (Handel), 185, 191
air de cour, 117
airs à boire, 171
airs sérieux, 117, 125, 171, 270
Alceste (Lully), 203
Alexander III, Pope, 88
Alexander VII, Pope, 172
Alexander VIII, Pope, 186, 188–89
Allegory of Music (de La Hyre), *1, 2,* 14
allemande, 71, 209

alternatim practice, 121
Amadei, Filippo, 240
amateur musicians, 66, 94, 203
Amati family, 9, 60
Americas
  African slaves in, 52
  broadside ballads in, 140
  Corpus Christi festival in, 90
  missionaries to, 13
  Puritans in, 11, 76–77
  villancicos in, 78, 81
Amsterdam, 63, 66, 77
ancien régime, 115
Andreini, Giovanni, 40, 43
Anet, Jean-Baptiste, II, 203
Angelica, vincitrice di Alcina (Fux), 232, *233*
Anglebert, Jean Henry d', *Pièces de clavessin,* 119, *120*
Anglican music, 11, 76–77, 135–36, 141, 146, 150–51
Anna Maria (Venetian orphan and musician), 159
Anne of Austria, 150, 167
Anne of Denmark, 49–50, 53, 132
Anne, Queen of England, 237–38, 239
anthems, 135–36, 146
antimasque, 49, 54
antiphonal music, 175–76

anti-Semitism, 88
  in the St. John Passion, 261
Antwerp, 60–61, 66
Apollo and Daphne (Bernini),
  4, *5*, 6
Apollo's Banquet (Playford),
  141–42
Apotheosis of Handel (Biagio),
  235, *236*, 250
*Apotheosis sive consecratio SS.
  Ignatii et Francisci Xaverii*
  (Kapsberger), 91
Arcadia, L' (Crescimbeni), 193
Arcadians. *See* Accademia degli
  Arcadi
Archilei, Vittoria, 23, 31
architecture, Baroque, 4
"Ardo in tacito foco" (Strozzi),
  166, 166–67
Arezzo, Guido d', 153
Ariane ou Le Marriage de Bacchus
  (Cambert), 143
Arianna (Monteverdi), 40, 43,
  44–45, *45*, 117
arias, 25, 106
  da capo, 109–10, 196, 215,
    243–44
  exit, 196, 243
Ariodante (Handel), 246
Ariosti, Attilio, 245
Ariosto, Ludovico, *Orlando
  furioso*, 7, 47, 232, 245
Aristotle, 7, 13, 22
Arlequin Roi de Serendib, 205,
  205–6
Armida (Handel), 125
Armide (Lully), 124–25, 126–27,
  127, 242
  "Enfin il est en ma
    puissance," 124–25, *125*
Arne, Thomas, 250
Arnold, Samuel, 235
Arsinoe (Clayton), 241
art
  academies for, 115
  Baroque compared with
    Renaissance, 4, 6
  patronage of, 27, 31, 61, 133
  sexuality in, 8–9
Artusi, Giovanni Maria,
  29–30, 81
Ashkenazic Jews, 86, 88
Asia, missionaries to, 13
Astianatte (Bononcini), 246
astrology, 7–8

astronomy, 7–8
Attaignant, Pierre, 115
Augsburg, Peace of (1598), 11
Augsburg, processions in, 89–90
  Protestants and Catholics in,
    89–90
Austria, 10, 219. *See also* Holy
  Roman Empire; Vienna
Autreau, Jacques, 216
Ave verum corpus (Byrd), 135

Bach, Anna Magdalena, 255, 260
Bach, Carl Philipp Emanuel,
  254, 256, 266
Bach, Johann Christian, 247, 266
Bach, Johann Sebastian
  Arnstadt, 222, 252, 254, 258
  Brandenburg Concertos,
    265–66
  Buxtehude and, 222
  as cantor, 151–52
  Clavier-Übung, 264–65
  collegium musicum
    directorship, 177,
    263–64, 268
  Cöthen, 255
  death of, 3
  education of, 152
  French musical style and,
    116, 122
  French Overture, 12, 265
  Goldberg Variations, 265
  Gottes Zeit ist die allerbeste Zeit,
    258–59, *258–59*
  Italian Concerto, 12, 265, *265*
  Kunst der Fuge, 266, 270
  in Leipzig, 173, 255–64
  Lutheran church music,
    257–62
  Mass in B minor, 242,
    268–70, *269*
  reputation, 182, 251, 252–54
  St. John Passion, 92, 261–62,
    262
  St. Matthew Passion, 261
  "Schweigt stille, plaudert
    nicht," *263*, 263–64
  Suite for Cello in C Major,
    266, *267*
  *Wachet auf, ruft uns die
    Stimme*, 258–60, *260*
  Weimar, 254–55, 257, 259
  Das Wohltemperierte Clavier,
    15, 266, *268*
Bach, Maria Barbara, 254–55

Bach, Wilhelm Friedemann,
  231, 256, 266
*Baedeker's Central Italy and
  Rome*, 4
Balbi, Giovanni Battista, 104,
  108, 122
ballad operas, 246–47
Ballard family, 115
ballet de cour, 39, 51–52, 54,
  65, 112, 114, 116, 117, 122,
  123, 270
Ballet de la nuit (Lully), 112, *113*,
  114, 115, 270
Ballet des Moscovites, 54
Ballet du Prince de la Chine, 54
balli, 39, 44, 46, 104
Banister, John, 176
Barbados, 52
Barberini, Antonio, 31
Barberini family, 47, 62
Barcelona, court at, 182, 231
Bardi, Giovanni de', 22–23,
  30–31
Bardi, Piero de', 23, 26
Baroni, Leonora, 31, 167
Baroque. *See also specific countries, composers, and topics*
  astronomy and astrology
    in, 7–8
  biology and sexuality in, 8–9,
    31–32, 109, 164
  conflict and crises during,
    18–19
  defining, 3–4, 6, 215
  Enlightenment and, 13–14,
    214
  genres standardized in, 182
  instrumental music in,
    56–73
  literature in, 7, 152
  music and education in,
    148–62
  music and style in, 14–16
  music in civic and religious
    ritual, 75–92
  music in eighteenth-century,
    182–270
  political and religious con-
    flict, 10–13
  politics of music, 11–13, 54
  technology, 9–10, 37, 104–6,
    242–43
  theatrical performances in,
    39–54
  as time period, 3

Bartolini, Nicolò, *Venere gelosa,*
    104–5
Basile, Adriana, 31, 167
basso continuo, 3, 24, 35, 37, 46,
    67, 79, 84, 139, 198, 244
bassoon, 3, 60, 245, 249
Bath, public concerts in, 177
Battalia (Biber), 227, 229, *229*
Bay Psalm Book, The, 76–77, 84
Beauchamps, Pierre, 119, 123
Beer, Johann, 152
Beggar's Opera, The (Pepusch and
    Gay), 178, 237, 246
"Begli occhi" (Strozzi), 167
Bella dama di nome santa
    (Scarlatti), 193–94
"E come bella," *194*
Bella, Gabriele, *Presentation of
    the Doge to the
    Population, 80*
Bembo, Antoina, 115
benefit concerts, 240
Berain, Jean, the elder, *127*
bergamesca, 71
Berlin, public concerts in, 177
Bernhard, Christoph, *Von der
    Singe-Kunst,* 153–54,
    153–54
Bernini, Gian Lorenzo, 47,
    185
    Apollo and Daphne, 4, *5*
    Ecstasy of Saint Teresa, 6, *6*
Betto, Pasqualino, 203
Biagio, Rebecca, *Apotheosis of
    Handel, 235, 236, 250*
Biber, Heinrich Ignaz Franz von,
    198, 219
    Battalia, 227, 229, *229*
    Missa salisburgensis, 227
    Mystery Sonatas, 229–30,
    230, 266
    in Salzburg, 226–30
biology, 8–9
Bissari, Pietro Paolo, *Medea
    vendicativa, 47, 48*
Blow, John, 141, 150–51
    *Ode on the Death of Mr. Henry
    Purcell,* 151
Bologna, 164, 173–76, 197
Bombacci, Camilla, 156
Bononcini, Giovanni Battista,
    202, 245
    Astianatte, 246
    Camilla, 241
    Il trionfo di Camilla, 241

Bononcini, Giovanni Maria, 241
    Corrente no. 4 from *Primi
    frutti del giardino musicale,*
    Op. 1, 174, *175*
    Sonate da chiesa, Op. 6, 175
Bordoni, Faustina, 245, 246, 263
Boscoli, Andrea, *24*
bourgeois gentilhomme, Le (Lully,
    Molière, and Beau-
    champs), 123–24, 170
bourrée, 71
bowed string instruments, 3, 58
bowings, standard, 197
Boyce, William, 151, 248
Brahms, Johannes, 85
Brandenburg Concertos (Bach),
    265–66
*Breefe Introduction to the Skill of
    Musick, A* (Playford), 138
Britton, Thomas, 176
broadside ballads, 131, 140–41
broken consort, 59
Bruno, Giordano, 18
bubonic plague, 18
Bull, John, 63, 132, 148
Buontalenti, Bernardo, *24*
Burckhardt, Jacob, 4
Burlington, Richard Boyle, third
    earl of, 240, 247
Burney, Charles, 88
Busenello, Giovanni Francesco,
    100, 101
Buxtehude, Dieterich, 151, 219,
    220, 254
    Ad cor: Vulnerasti cor meum,
    223–24
    cantata arias, 258
    Jubilate Domino, 224, *224*
    in Lübeck, 221–24, 230
    Membra Jesu nostri, 223–24
    Toccata in F Major (Buxte-
    hude), 222, *222–23*
Byrd, William, 78, 131
    Ave verum corpus, 135

Caccini, Francesca, 167
    *La liberazione di Ruggiero
    dall'isola d'Alcina, 47, 51*
Caccini, Giulio, 22, 23, 24, 47
    "Amor ch'attendi," *32,* 32–33
    "Dovrò dunque morire," 32
    figured bass used by, 35
    Le nuove musiche, 21, 30–31,
    32–33, 34, 79, 151, 153, *153*
Cadmus et Hermione (Lully), 124

Caldara, Antonio, 231, 232–33,
    268
Calov, Abraham, 257
Calvinists, 11, 76–77
Calvin, John, 76
Cambert, Robert, 124
    *Ariane ou Le Marriage de
    Bacchus, 143*
Camerata, Florentine, 30–31,
    163, 192
Camilla (Bononcini), 241
Campra, André
    Le carnaval de Venise, 129,
    206, 208, 225
    Les fêtes vénitiennes, 206–8
    Iphigénie en Tauride, 205, 206
    opéras-ballets, 203
cantar recitando, 24–25
cantatas
    eighteenth-century, 182
    French, 212–13
    Italian, 186
    Lutheran, 78, 223–24,
    257–61
    pastoral, 193–95
    in Rome, 168, 170
    sacred, 78, 79–88
    virtuosity in, 14
Cantate, ariette, op. 3 (Strozzi),
    166
Canterbury Cathedral, 135
cantillation, 86
canto figurato, 154
cantors, 151–52
cantus firmus, 81
canzonas, 68
canzonettas, 32–33, 41, 42
Capriccio stravagante
    (Farina), 72
Caravaggio, Michelangelo Merisi
    da, *The Musicians,* 31
Carignan, Prince de, 214
Carissimi, Giacomo, 127, 149
    Jephte, 91, 189
carnaval de Venise, Le (Campra),
    129, 206, 208, 225
Carneval von Venedig (Keiser),
    225
Caroline, Queen of England,
    248
Carracci, Agostino, *24*
Carrati, Vincenzo Maria, 173
Castello, Dario, 22, 198
    *Sonate concertate in stil mod-
    erno,* 21, 67–68

castrati, 9, 31, 47, 95, 99, 103, 122, 150, 167, 168, 170, 188, 193, 224, 242, 245
Castrucci, Pietro, 235, 240, 245
Castrucci, Prospero, 240, 245
catches, 139–40
Catholicism and Catholic church, 10, 18
England's break with, 76, 135, 238
in Holy Roman Empire, 23
music in, 12, 18, 78–79, 142, 182, 227, 268–70
nun musicians, 9, 154–57, 270
recusant Catholics in England, 11, 78, 135
Cavalcanti, Rafaello, 20–21, 23, 31, 148
Cavalieri, Emilio de', 23
"Dalle più alte sfere," from *La pellegrina*, 25
Rappresentazione di anima et di corpo, 27–28
Cavalli, Francesco, 158, 202
Ercole amante, 122
in France, 108
Giasone, 100, 106–8, 110, 127–28, 184, 195
Le nozze di Teti e di Peleo, 106
Il Xerse, 122
Cavazza, Christina, 157
Céphale et Procris (Jacquet de la Guerre), 212
Cervantes, Miguel de, 226
Cesti, Antonio, *La Semirami*, 109
chaconne, 71, 119–20, 144, 222
Champmeslé, Marie, 124
Chandos, James Brydges, duke of, 248
Chapelle Royale (France), 114, 115, 121
Chapel Royal (England), 48, 63, 78, 131, 135, 136, 141, 142, 151, 178, 237–38
character pieces, 72
Charles I, King of England, 11, 49, 130–31, 133–34, 135, 137, 148
Charles II, King of England, 11, 65, 116, 136, 141–44, 151
Charles II, King of Spain, 182
Charles d'Albert, duke of Luynes, 51

Charles III of Austria, 182
Charles VI, Holy Roman Emperor, 218, 231–32
Charpentier, Marc-Antoine, 203
Médée, 127–28
Chiabrera, Gabriello, 23, 43
Child, William, *Mr. William Childs set of Psalms for 3 Voyces*, 139
chittarone, 42
choirboys
Anglican, 150–51
Catholic, 149–50
Lutheran, 151–52
Oxford, 136–37
in Roman academies, 167
training of, 152–54
chorales, 77–78, 84, 152, 222–23, 230, 257–58
chorale cantata, 259–60
chorale fantasia, 260
in the St. John Passion, 261–62
Christian, Duke of Weissenfels, 256
Christian IV, King of Denmark, 34, 132
Christina, Queen of Sweden, 172–73, 185, 186, 188, 191
Christine of Lorraine, 23, 47
Church of England, 77, 78, 131, 135–36, 141. *See also* Anglican music
Ciaccona from *Canzoni overo sonate concertate per chiesa e camera* (Merula), 71, 119
Cibber, Colley, 246
Cicognini, Giacinto, 106, 128
Clavier-Übung (Bach), 264–65
Clayton, Thomas, *Arsinoe*, 241
Clement IX, Pope, 188
Clement X, Pope, 47, 188
Clement XI, Pope, 189, 191
Cleofide (Hasse), 231
Clive, Kitty, 246
collegia musica, 177–78, 225, 263–64, 268
Colonna, Carlo, 186
Colonna, Lorenzo Onofrio, 62, 171
"Come, come away to the Taverne" (catch), 139–40, *140*

comedias nuevas, 52
comédie-ballet, 123–24
Comédie Italienne, 121, 202
comédies lyriques, 215
commedia dell'arte, 121, 202, 204–6
Componimenti musicali (Vizzana), 156
concertato style, 18–19, 79, 81
Concerti ecclesiastici (Viadana), 79
Concerti Grossi, Op. 6 (Corelli), 197, 198, *199*, 214
concertino group, 176, 197–98, 265–66
Concert instrumental . . . d'Apothéose . . . de . . . Lully (Couperin), 210, *211*, 212
Concerto for Viola d'amore and Lute (Vivaldi), 159–60, *160*
concerto grosso, 197–98
Concerto Palatino (Bologna), 173
concertos
early instrumental, 176
eighteenth-century, 182
sacred, 78, 79–80, 83, 84, 92, 115, 223–24, 258
stile concertato in, 14
Concert Spirituel, 177, 214
concerts, public, 13, 176–78, 219, 224–26, 238, 240, 262–64
congregational singing, 76–77, 78
consonance and dissonance, 14
emotion and, 18, 22, 32, 37, 46
in French music, 215
ground bass and, 29, 45–46, 146
in Jewish religious music, 86
Consort No. 8 in G Major (Lawes), 133–34, *134*
Conti, Princesse de, 203
contrafacta, 78
convents, 9, 94, 148, 154–57, 270
conversazioni, 171, 193
Cooke, Henry, 151
Coprario, John, 133
Corelli, Arcangelo, 172, 185, 188, 190, 191, 196–200
Bach's arrangements of, 255
Concerti Grossi, Op. 6, 197, 198, *199*, 214, 240

Corelli, Arcangelo (*continued*)
  Couperin's tribute to, 200, 210
  influence of, 198–200, 202,
    240
  Violin Sonatas, op. 5, 197, 240
cori spezzati, 80
Corneille, Pierre, 124
Corneille, Thomas, 128
cornetti, 56
Corpus Christi, Feast of, 88, 90
Corrente no.4 from *Primi frutti
  del giardino musicale*, Op.1
  (Bononcini), 174, *175*
Corsi, Jacopo, 22–23, 26
Coryat, Thomas, 12, 87–88
cosmopolitanism, 12–13
Costanza e fortezza (Fux), 231
Council of Trent, 12, 78, 155
counterpoint
  dissonance and, 14, 22, 29–30
  in instrumental music,
    66–67, 266, 268
  in Jewish religious music, 86
Couperin, François, 148, 214
  *Concert instrumental...
    d'Apothéose... de... Lully*,
    210, *211*, 212
  goûts réunis, 202, 208–12
  Leçons de ténèbres, 208, *209*
  *Messe à l'usage ordinaire des
    paroisses*, 121
  Les nations, 12, 210
  ornamentation viewed by, 119
  *Le Parnasse, ou L'apothéose de
    Corelli*, 200, 210
  Pièces de clavecin, 183, 203,
    208–10, *210*
  *Les plaisirs de Saint-Germain-
    en-Laye*, 202–3
Couperin, Louis, 148
  Suite in A minor, 68, *69*, 70
Couperin, Marguerite-Antoi-
  nette, 148
courante, 70
Covent Garden (London), 241
Cozzolani, Chiara Margarita, *O
  quam bonus es*, 157, *158*
Cremona, 60
Cremonini, Cesare, 8
Crescimbeni, Giovanni, *192*
  Arcadian Academy and,
    191–93, 194
  L'Arcadia, 193
  opera critiques of, 110, 184,
    195, 197

Cristofori, Bartolomeo, 9
Croatia, 219
Cromwell, Oliver, 11, 131
Cromwell, Richard, 131
"Cruda Amarilli" (Monteverdi),
  29, *29*
Cuzzoni, Francesca, 245, 246
Czech Republic, 219

da capo aria, 109–10, 196, 215,
  243–44
Dafne, La (Schütz and Rinuccini), 47
dance
  ballet de cour, 39, 51–52, 54,
    65, 112, 114, 116, 117, 122,
    123, 270
  ballo (balli), 39, 44, 46, 104
  comédie-ballet, 123–24
  English masque, 49
  English dancing tunes, 139,
    142
  "for the ears," 70–71, 174
  French social, 117, 119
  instrumental accompaniment
    for, 59
  in *King Arthur* (Purcell), 144
  nobles, training in, 20, 146
  opéra-ballet, 129, 203, 206–8,
    213–14
  in seventeenth century, 37
  at the Spanish court, 52
  on tightrope, 210
  in Venetian opera, 104, 109
  dance suites, 70–71, 208–10
David (Michelangelo), 4, *5*, 6
délivrance de Renaud, La, 51–52,
  126
del Monte, Francesco Maria,
  31
Denmark, Protestants in, 10
Descartes, René, 13
descending tetrachords, 34, 46,
  102, 103, 145–46
Destouches, André Cardinal, *Les
  élémens*, 214, 216
*Dialogo della musica antica, et
  della moderna* (Galilei),
  21–22
Dido and Aeneas (Purcell),
  144–46
  "When I am laid in earth,"
  145, 145–46
Didone abbandonata
  (Metastasio), 195

Dietrich, Wolf, 226
dissonance. *See* consonance and
  dissonance
Domestic Music Scene (Voorhout),
  219–21, *220*
Dowland, John
  "Flow, my tears," 34, *36*
  lute songs, 34–35
Draghi, Antonio, 108
Dramatick opera, 142–44, 241.
  See also semi-operas
dramma per musica, 26
Dresden
  court of, 230
  Italian opera in, 47, 108,
    153, 225
  Protestant music in, 81,
    84–85
  sacred concertos in, 80
Drottningholm Court Theater
  (near Stockholm), *105*,
  105–6
Drury Lane Theatre (London),
  143
Dryden, John, 143–44, 151
dulcian, 3
Dumanoir, Guillaume, 114
Dupuy, Hilaire, 170
Durand, Etienne, 51
Durastanti, Margherita, 191,
  194, 245
Durham, public concerts in, 177
D'Urfey, Thomas, *Wonders in the
  Sun*, 241

early modern era, 3, 7, 8, 18
Edinburgh, public concerts
  in, 177
education, music, 148–62
  choir schools, 149–52
  institutions for, 94, 148–49
  nun musicians, 9, 154–57
  in orphanages, 149, 158–62,
    270
  for royalty and nobility, 132,
    148, 203, 208
  singing instruction, 152–54
élémens, Les (Destouches and
  Lalande), 214, 215, 216
Elizabeth I, Queen of England,
  34, 48, 131, 135
embellishment
  in da capo arias, 244
  French-style ornamentation,
    116, 119, *120*, 215

Italian-style ornamentation,
    32, 35, 56, 153–54, 215
    in Jewish religious music, 86
encyclopedias, 13
England. *See also* London
    broadside ballads in, 131,
        140–41
    catches and polyphonic songs
        in, 139–40
    choirboys in, 150–51
    convents and monasteries
        destroyed in, 76, 135
    Interregnum in, 11, 131,
        136–37, 150
    lute songs in, 33–34, 133
    madrigals in, 130, 133
    masques in, 39, 49–50,
        53–54, 123, 131, 132, 241
    music in seventeenth-
        century, 94, 130–46
    music publishing in, 34–35,
        137–41, 146, 240
    opera and semi-opera in,
        143–46, 238, 240,
        241–47
    public concerts in, 176–78
    recusant Catholics in, 11,
        78, 135
    religious conflict in, 10, 11, 78
    religious music in, 78, 81,
        135–36
    theater in, 142–44
English Civil War, 18, 63, 76,
    130–31, 133, 136, 150
English Dancing Master, The
    (Playford collection),
    139, 140
Enlightenment, 13–14, 214
Enraged Musician, The (Hogarth),
    235, *236*, 237, 240, 251
entrées, 51
episodes, 222
Epsom, public concerts in, 177
equal temperament, 15
Ercole amante (Cavalli), 122
Ernst August, Duke of Weimar,
    255
Este family, 28
Este, Isabella d', 163
Esther (Handel), 248
estro armonico, L' (Vivaldi), 255
Euridice (Peri and Rinuccini),
    26–27, 28, 41
    "Lassa! che di spavento,"
        26, *26*

Euripides, 7, 106
Evelyn, John, 12–13, 95, 96, 99,
    104, 141, 240
exit arias, 196, 243
exoticism, 10, 13, 52–54, 123
exploration, 13, 52

falsobordone, 82
Fantasia chromatica (Sweelinck),
    67, *68*
fantasias, 66, 68, 222
Fantasia upon One Note (Purcell),
    142, *143*
Farina, Carlo, *Capriccio strava-*
    gante, 72
Farnese family, 10
Fassler, Margot, *Music in the*
    Medieval West, 90
favola in musica, 26
Fedeli, I, 40
female personifications, 1–2
Ferdinand II, Holy Roman
    Emperor, 12, 65, 81
Ferdinand III, Holy Roman
    Emperor, 12, 72,
    88–89
Ferdinand IV of Hungary, 72
Ferdinand Maria, Elector, 47
Ferrabosco, Alfonso, 132, 133
    "So beautie on the waters
        stood," 50, *50*
Ferrara, 28, 40, 163
Fesch, Willem de, 248
Festa della Porchetta (Bologna),
    173
Festival at the Palazzo Barberini
    in Honor of Christina of
    Sweden (Lauri and
    Gagliari), *172*
fêtes vénitiennes, Les (Campra),
    206–8
    "Accourez, hâtez-vous," *207*
Feuillet, Raoul-Auger, 119
Ficino, Marsilio, 22
figured bass, 35. *See also* basso
    continuo
"Fili mi, Abasalon" (Schütz), 85
Fitzwilliam Virginal Book, 70
flagellants, 90
Florence
    Camerata, 30–31, 163, 192
    court entertainments,
        40, 47
    Handel in, 185
    invention of piano, 9

lute music in, 20–21
    Mantua's competition with,
        40
    Medici rule in, 10, 22, 23
    opera in, 47
    solo singing, 23–28
"Flow my tears" (Dowland),
    34, *36*
flutes, 60, 121
folia, 71
Follino, Federico, 43, 44, 46
form, musical, 15–16
Fornari, Matteo, 188, 197
fortepiano, 9
Fougeroux, Pierre-Jacques,
    245
France. *See also* Paris; Versailles
    ballet de cour, 39, 51–52, 54,
        65, 112, 114, 116, 117, 122,
        123, 270
    cantatas in, 212–13
    Catholics in, 10
    centralization of arts under
        Bourbon rule, 114–15,
        121–22
    comédie-ballet, 123–24
    court musicians in, 58, 65,
        114
    court of Louis XIV, 112–29
    instrument making in, 60,
        65
    Italian musicians in, 51, 108
    Italian theater in, 121, 202,
        204–8
    music in eighteenth-century,
        201–16
    musique mesurée in, 116–17
    national style in, 12, 116–21
    patronage in, 12, 64–65
    seventeenth-century music
        in, 94
    social dances, 117, 119
    theater in, 48
    tragédie en musique, 124–28
Franck, Salomo, 259, 260
Frederick V of the Palatine, 132
Freedman, Richard, *Music in the*
    Renaissance, 6–7, 163
French overture, 122, 226,
    265
French Overture (Bach), 12, 265
Frescobaldi, Girolamo, 62–63,
    198
    expressive performance style,
        63–64

Frescobaldi, Girolamo (*continued*)
  Toccata No. 2, from *Toccate e
    partite d'intavolatura di
    cimbalo*, 67, *67*
  *Toccate e partite d'intavolatura
    di cimbalo*, 63
Friedrich Augustus I, Elector of
  Saxony, 231
Friedrich Christian, crown
  prince of Saxony-Poland,
  159
Frisch, Walter, *Music in the
  Nineteenth Century*, 85
Froberger, Johann Jacob, 62
  Suite in C Major, 70–71,
    72, *73*
  Toccata No. 1, 68, 70
Fronde uprising, 115
Fux, Johann Joseph, 268
  Angelica, vincitrice di Alcina,
    232, *233*
  Costanza e fortezza, 231
  Gradus ad Parnassum, 232

Gabrieli, Giovanni, 84–85,
  158
Gagliano, Marco da, 43
Gagliari, F., *Festival at the Palazzo
  Barberini in Honor of Chris-
  tina of Sweden*, *172*
galant style, 183, 226, 254, 266,
  268–69
Galilei, Galileo, 7–8, 21
Galilei, Vincenzo, 23–24
  *Dialogo della musica antica, et
    della moderna*, 21–22
galliard, 70
Galli-Bibiena, Antonio, 232
Galli-Bibiena, Francesco,
  232
Galli-Bibiena, Giuseppe, 232,
  233
Gasparini, Francesco, 158
Gastoldi, Giovanni, 43
Gay, John, 246
Gelati, Accademia dei, 164
Geminiani, Francesco, 240
gender
  ambiguity, 8–9, 110
  in education, 148–49
  at the French court, 115
  ideology and lament, 46
  vocal casting, 103
  wars in Leipzig, 264
Genoa, 10

Gentileschi, Artemisia, *Judith
  and Holofernes*, 161, *161*
George I, King of England, 238,
  239
George II, King of England,
  239, 248
Germany. *See also specific cities*
  choir schools in, 151–52
  instrument making in, 60, 65
  Protestants in, 11
  salons in, 173
Gerusalemme liberata (Tasso), 7,
  51, 126, 242
Ghezzi, Pier Leone, 193, *194*
Giasone (Cavalli), 100, 106–8,
  110, 127–28, 184, 195
  "Delitie e contenti," *107*
Gibbons, Orlando, 63, 131, 133
  "If ye be risen again with
    Christ," *135*, 135–36
gigue, 70, 71, 266
Girard, Antoine, 48
Giuditta (Scarlatti), 187
Giustiniani, Vincenzo, 64, 167
  *Discorso sopra la musica de'
    suoi tempi*, 31
Göbel, Bernd, Bach statue by,
  252, *253*
Goldberg Variations (Bach),
  265
Gombert, Nicholas, 81
Gonzaga, Eleonora, 65
Gonzaga family, 1–3, 10, 28, 39,
  40–46, 81, 85–88
Gonzaga, Francesco, 40–41, 43
Gonzaga, Vincenzo, 40, 41, 43
Gothenberg, Sweden, organ in,
  60, *61*
Gottes Zeit ist die allerbeste Zeit
  (Bach), 258–59, *258–59*
Grabu, Luis, 143–44
Gradus ad Parnassum (Fux), 232
Grande Écurie, 58, 114
Greek thought, ancient, 7
  early opera and, 22–23, 31
  music theory, 24
Greene, Maurice, 248
Grimani family, 97
ground bass, 46, 102, 103,
  145–46
grounds, 71–72
Gruber, Erasmus, 151
Guardi, Francesco, *Parlatorio of
  the San Zaccharia Nunnery*,
  155, *156*

Guarini, Battista
  Idropica, 43, 44
  Il pastor fido, 28–29, 40
Guarneri family, 9, 60
Guédron, Pierre, 51
guilds, 60–61
guitar, 35
Gwynn, Nell, 142
Gypsies portrayed in theatrical
  works, 53

Haas, Johann Wilhelm, 60
Habsburg monarchy, 10, 12, 65,
  81, 89, 108, 182, 218–19,
  232, 233
Hamburg
  collegium musicum, 177, 226
  as free imperial city, 219–21
  government of, 221
  Handel in, 185
  music-making in, 219–21
  public opera in, 225
  public theater in, 183, 185, 225
Handel, George Frideric
  Aci, Galatea, e Polifemo, 185
  Admeto, 246
  Agrippina, 185, 191
  Ariodante, 246
  Armida, 125
  borrowings, 242
  cantatas of, 186, 194
  cosmopolitanism of, 12
  da capo aria arias, 110
  death of, 3
  Esther, 248
  French musical style and,
    116, 122
  Hendel, non può mia musa, 186
  Israel in Egypt, 248
  Jephtha, 248
  Jubilate, 238–40, 248
  Judas Maccabeus, 248
  Messiah, 235, 249
  Music for the Royal Fireworks,
    251
  O numi eterni, 194
  opera career in London, 146,
    182, 241–46
  Orlando, 245
  oratorios, 240–41, 246, 247,
    248–50
  patrons of, 185–88, 239,
    245, 247
  reception in England, 178,
    239–40

reputation, 182, 235, 248, 251
La resurrezione, 186, 189–90, 190, 203
Rinaldo, 238, 240, 242–44, 244
Rodelinda, 246
in Rome, 185, 186, 254
Royal Academy of Music, 245–47
Samson, 246
Saul, 249, 249
Serse, 246
Il trionfo del tempo e del disinganno, 186
"Utrecht" *Te Deum,* 238–39, 239, 248
Vincer se stesso è il maggior vittoria, 185
Zadok the Priest, 248
Hanseatic League, 219, 221, 230
harmonies of the spheres, 22, 23
Harmonie universelle (Mersenne), 64
Haro y Guzmán, Gaspar de, 108
harps, 3, 35, 56
harpsichord, 3, 35, 58, 61, 62, 62, 121
harpsichord music, 183, 203, 208–10, 212
Hashirim asher leSholomo (Rossi), 86, 86
Hasse, Johann Adolf, 247, 256, 263, 268
Cleofide, 231
Hawkins, Sir John, 176
Haydn, Franz Joseph, 162
Haym, Nicola, 240, 241
Heather, William, 137
Heidegger, J. J., 242, 245, 247
hemiola, 70, 174
Hendel, non può mia musa (Handel), 186
Henrici, Christian Friedrich, 260
Henrietta Maria, Queen of England, 49, 133
Henry II, King of England, 51
Henry II, King of France, 65
Henry IV, King of England, 51
Henry IV, King of France, 26
Henry VIII, King of England, 76, 135
Henry, Prince of England, 130, 132

"Here dwells a pretty Mayd" (catch), 140
Hill, Aaron, 242
Hilton, John, *Catch that Catch Can,* 139, 139–40
Hippolyte et Aricie (Rameau), 214–15, 215
historia, 91–92
Hogarth, William, 140
The Enraged Musician, 235, 236, 237, 240, 251
Masquerades and Operas, Burlington Gate, 246–47, 247
Holland, Protestants in, 10, 11
Holy Roman Empire
ceremonial music, 230–31
free cities in, 219
music in eighteenth-century, 218–33
religion in, 10, 11, 231
territory of, 219
Homer, 7
Odyssey, 212
homosexuality, 8–9, 109, 188
Horace, 192
horns, 60
Hôtel des Soissons (Paris), 214
Hotteterre family, 60
Houdar de La Motte, Antoine, 215
humanism, 6–10, 21–22
Hume, Tobias, "Tobacco is like love," 34
Humphrey, Pelham, 151
Hungary, 219
hurdy-gurdy, 48

Idropica (Guarini), 43, 44
"If ye be risen again with Christ" (Gibbons), 135, 135–36
imperialism, 10, 52–54
improvisation in instrumental music, 66–67
incoronazione di Poppea, L' (Monteverdi), 98–103
impresario and singers for, 99
librettist for, 99–101
"Non morir, Seneca," 102, 103
"Pur ti miro," 103, 103
"Signor, sempre mi vedi," 101, 102

India, Sigismondo d', 145
"Infelice Didone," 33, 33
inégalité, 119
Innocent X, Pope, 13
Innocent XI, Pope, 188
Innocent XII, Pope, 189
Inquisition, 78
instrumental music. *See also specific instrumens and groups*
affections and, 64
character pieces, 72
concertos, 14, 159–60, 175–76, 240, 255, 265
consort music, 133–34
dance suites, 70–71
early seventeenth-century, 56–73
English seventeenth-century, 132–34
expressive performance style, 63–64
fantasy and craft in, 66–70
French eighteenth-century, 208–12
French seventeenth-century, 120–21
genre and style in seventeenth-century, 65–73
German eighteenth-century, 221–23, 226, 264–68
grounds and variations, 71–72, 134
Italian eighteenth-century, 196–98
patronage and audiences for, 61–63
rhetoric and, 72–73
sonatas, 174–75
virtuosity in, 14, 56–58, 66–68
instruments
for basso continuo, 3
building of, 59–61, 65
as possessions, 58–59
used in worship, 79
intermedi, 23, 24, 31, 39, 43, 44
Interregnum (1649–60), 11, 131, 136–37, 150
Iphigénie en Tauride (Campra), 205, 206
Israel in Egypt (Handel), 248
Italian Concerto (Bach), 12, 265, 265

Italy. *See also specific locations*
  academies in, 22–23, 41,
    96, 100, 115, 163, 164–70,
    172–73, 188, 191–96
  cantatas and serenades in,
    193–95
  Catholicism in, 10, 18
  choirboys in, 149–50
  madrigals in, 28–30
  national style, 12
  northern, 219
  opera in, 22–28, 39, 40–47,
    188–89
  oratorios in, 189–91
  solo songs in, 30–34
  violin family making in,
    60, 65

Jacquet de la Guerre, Elisabeth,
  115
  Céphale et Procris, 212
  Pièces de claveçin, 212
  Le sommeil d'Ulisse, 212, *213*
James I, King of England, 11, 48,
  49, 130, 131–32, 135
James II, King of England, 142,
  185, 202–3, 238
Jélyotte, Pierre de, 216
Jenkins, John, 133
Jennens, Charles, 249
Jephte (Carissimi), 91, 189
Jephtha (Handel), 248
Jesuits, 90–91, 149–50
Jewish actors and musicians,
  40, 41
Jewish religious music, 76,
  85–88
Johann Georg I, Elector of
  Saxony, 47
Johann Georg II, Elector of
  Saxony, 81, 84–85, 108
Jones, Inigo, 133
  costumes by, 49, *53*
Jonson, Ben, 49
Joseph I, Holy Roman Emperor,
  218, 231
Jubilate (Handel), 238–40, 248
Jubilate Domino (Buxtehude),
  224, *224*
Judas Maccabeus (Handel),
  248
Judith and Holofernes
  (Gentileschi), 161, *161*
Juditha triumphans (Vivaldi),
  160–61

just intonation, 15
Juvarra, Filippo, 186, 187, *187*

Kant, Immanuel, 214
Kapsberger, Giovanni,
  *Apotheosis sive consecratio
  SS. Ignatii et Francisci
  Xaverii,* 91
Keiser, Reinhard, *Carneval von
  Venedig,* 225
Kepler, Johannes, 7
keyboard instruments, 3,
  9, 58, 62. *See also specific
  instruments*
Khuenburgh, Maximilian
  Gandolph von, 226, 229
King Arthur (Purcell), 142–44,
  241
King's Musick (England), 131,
  133, 136, 141, 237–38
King's Theatre (London), 241,
  242–44, 245, 248, 249.
  See also Queen's Theater
Kircher, Athanasius, 64
  Musurgia universalis, 66
Kleine geistliche Conzerte
  (Schütz), 80
Kuhnau, Johann, 177
Kunst der Fuge (Bach), 266,
  270
Küsel, Melchior, engraving of
  Salzburg Cathedral, 227,
  228

Lachrimae (Dowland), 34
La Hyre, Laurent de, 137
  Allegory of Music, 1, *2,* 14
Lalande, Michel-Richard de, 201
  Les élémens, 214, 216
Lambert, Michel, 170
  "Par mes chants," 117, *118,* 171
Lambranzi, Gregorio, *Neue und
  curieuse teatralische Tantz-
  Schul,* 104, *104*
Lamento della ninfa (Monte-
  verdi), 45–46, 103, 145
laments, 33, 42, 44, 72, 117
Lämmerhirt, Tobias, 258
Landi, Stefano, *Sant'Alessio,*
  46–47, 188
Lappoli, Geronimo, 99
Lauri, Filippi, *Festival at the
  Palazzo Barberini in Honor
  of Christina of Sweden,* 172
Lawes, Henry, 133

Lawes, William, 133, 198
  Consort No. 8 in G Major,
    133–34, *134*
Le Cerf de la Viéville, Jean
  Laurent, 126
Leçons de ténèbres (Couperin),
  208, *209*
Legrenzi, Giovanni, 158
Leipzig, 152, 177, 252, 255–56,
  256, 262–64
Leopold I, Holy Roman Em-
  peror, 12, 218, 227, 231
Leopold, Prince of Cöthen, 255
Le Riche de La Pouplinière, Al-
  exandre Jean Josephe, 214
Lerma, duke of, 54
Le Rochois, Marie, 127, *127,* 128
Le Valois d'Orville, Adrien
  Joseph, 215–16
liberal arts, 21–22
*liberazione di Ruggiero dall'isola
  d'Alcina, La* (Caccini),
  47, 51
lieto fine, 41
Ligon, Richard, 52
Lincoln's Inn Fields (London),
  247
literature in Baroque, 7, 152
liturgical music, 76, 79, 86, 88,
  131, 135, 150, 175, 232,
  257–63. *See also* religion
  and religious music in the
  Baroque
London
  Academy of Antient Music
    in, 178
  amateur music societies, 94
  commerce and politics in,
    237–40
  Italian music in, 240–47
  music in eighteenth-century,
    235–51
  music publishing in, 66
  opera and semi-opera in,
    142–46, 238, 240,
    241–47
  oratorios in, 248–49
  pleasure gardens in, 177,
    250–51, 270
  public concerts in, 176
  theater in, 48, 142
Lope de Vega, Félix Arturo,
  48, 52
Loredano, Giovanni Francesco,
  96, 167

Louis XIII, King of France, 133
  court of, 65, 114, 141
  as dancer, 51–52, 54, 65, 126
  reign of, 116
Louis XIV, King of France
  affair with Maria Mancini,
    171
  court of, 112–29, 141, 171,
    183, 203
  as dancer, 51, 52, 65, 112, *113*,
    114, 270
  death of, 204, 213
  marriage to Madame de
    Maintenon, 126–27, 201
  marriage to Maria Theresa,
    108, 122
  patronage, 12
  propaganda program of, 122,
    126, 231
  reign of, 11
  resistance to, 123–24
Louis XV, King of France, 148,
    214–15, 216
Louis de Bourbon, 203
Louise Bénédicte de Bourbon,
    Duchesse du Maine, 203–4
Loyola, Ignatius, 90–91
Lübeck
  Abendmusik concerts, 224
  as free imperial city, 219–21
  music-making in, 219–24
Lugaro, John Maria, 132
Lully, Jean-Baptiste, 197, 200,
    249
  Alceste, 203
  Armide, 124–25, 126–27, *127*,
    242
  Ballet de la nuit, 112, *113*,
    114, 115
  Le bourgeois gentilhomme,
    123–24, 170
  Cadmus et Hermione, 124
  Couperin's tribute to, 210,
    211, 212
  French overture of, 122
  Italian opera viewed by, 122
  lulliste followers, 215
  Phaëton, 119
  Pomone, 124
  Rameau contrasted with, 4
  Roman opera influenced
    by, 195
  Te Deum, 126
  tragédies lyrique, 124–28, 143,
    201, 203

Lully, Louis, *L'Orphée*, 225
lute, 3, 15, 24, 35, 58, 60, 65, 119,
    121, 133
  in basso continuo, 35, 109
  concerto, 159–60
  making, 60
  pictured in painting, 59, 220
  songs, 20–21, 33–34,
    50, 133
  tablature, 21, 35, 36, 138
Lutherans and Lutheran music,
    11, 76–78, 84, 151–52, 219,
    221–24, 257–62
Luther, Martin, 11, 76, 257
Lyon, public concerts in, 177
lyra viol, 138–39

Macbeth (Shakespeare), 49
Mace, Thomas, *Musick's
    Monument*, 64
Madrid, court at, 182–83
Madrigali guerrieri et amorosi
    (Monteverdi), 45–46, 102
madrigalisms, 24
madrigals
  English, 130, 133
  Italian, 28–30, 40, 41, 45–46
  Italian sacred, 78
Magni, Carlo, 40–41
Maine, Duc du, 203–4
Maintenon, Madame de, 126–27,
    201
Mainwaring, John, 185
Mancini, Maria, 171–72, 186
Mantua
  Jews and Jewish music in, 40,
    41, 85–88
  madrigals in, 28–30, 40
  opera in, 1–3, 10, 39, 40–46
  political power in, 10, 40
  wedding celebration, 43–46,
    98
*Marcantonio Pasqualini
    (1614–1691) Crowned by
    Apollo* (Sacchi), 168, *169*,
    170
Marenzio, Luca, 178
Margaret, Queen of Spain, 52
Margherita of Savoy, 43
Maria Casimira, Queen of
    Poland, 186
Maria Magdalen, Archduchess, 47
Marian devotion, 89
Maria Theresa of Spain, 122,
    124

Marini, Biagio, 62, 63
  Affetti musicali, 72
  instrumental music
    collection, 66
Marivaux, Pierre de, 206
Marpurg, Friedrich Wilhelm, 270
Marseilles, public concerts
    in, 177
Mary II, Queen of England, 142,
    238
Mary of Modena, 202–3
Masaniello, 11
Mascherata dell'ingrate
    (Monteverdi), 43–44, 46
Masque of Blackness, The, 53, *53*
Masque of Flowers, The, 54
Masque of Queens, The, 49, 132
*Masque of the Exspulsion of the
    Moriscos, The*, 54
masquerades, 247
*Masquerades and Operas,
    Burlington Gate* (Hogarth),
    246–47, *247*
masques, 39, 49–50, 53–54, 123,
    131, 132, 241
masses, 242
  eighteenth-century, 182, 227,
    268–70
Mass in B minor (Bach),
    268–70, *269*
Mathieu, Nicolas, 202
Matteis, Nicola, 240
Mattheson, Johann, 64, 225,
    242
Maugars, André, 58, 91
Maximilian II Emanuel,
    Elector, 47
Mazarin, Cardinal, 108, 112,
    121–22, 150, 171
Mazzarini, Giulio. See Mazarin,
    Cardinal
Médée (Charpentier), 127–28
  "Noires filles du Styx," 128,
    128
Medici, Catherine de', 51, 65
Medici family, 10, 20–21, 23,
    26, 132
Medici, Ferdinando de', 47, 189
Medici, Francesco de', 23
Medici, Marie de', 26, 51
Mei, Girolamo, 23–24
melancholy, 34
Melani, Alessandro, 149–52
Melani, Atto, 122, 150, 167
Melani, Domenico, 150

Melani, Jacopo, 150
Membra Jesu nostri (Buxtehude), 223–24
Memoirs of Music (North), 141
Mendelssohn, Felix, 270
Mercure galant, Le (journal), 4, 128
Mersenne, Marin, *Harmonie universelle*, 64
Merula, Tarquinio, Ciaccona from *Canzoni overo sonate concertate per chiesa e camera*, 71, *71*, 119
Messa, Magnificat et Jubilate Deo (Valentini), 81
Messe à l'usage ordinaire des paroisses (Couperin), 121
Messiah (Handel), 235, 249
Metamorphoses (Ovid), 41, 44
Metastasio, Pietro, 195–96, 219, 232, 233
Meudon, Château de, 203
Michelangelo, *David*, 4, *5*, 6
middle-class consumers, 13, 58–59, 238
Milan, 10
military training, 37
Minerva Protects Pax from Mars (Rubens), 133
minuet, 71
Missa salisburgensis (Biber), 227
missionaries, 13, 90
Modena, Leon, 87
modes, 15, 175
Molière, 121, 123
  Le bourgeois gentilhomme, 170
  Les précieuses ridicules, 171
Monmouth, duke of, 144
monody, 24–28, 32
Montagu, Mary Wortley, 53
Montalto, Alessandro Peretti, 31
Monteverdi, Claudio, 21, 22, 39, 158, 223
  Arianna, 40, 43, 44–45, *45*, 117
  Ballo delle ingrate, 43–44, 46
  "Cruda Amarilli," 29, *29*
  L'incoronazione di Poppea, 98–103
  Lamento della ninfa, 45–46, 103, 145
  Madrigali guerrieri et amorosi, 45–46, 102

Missa in illo tempore, 81
L'Orfeo, 1–3, 9, 23, 27, 40–43, 56–57, *57*, 82, 85, 101, 164, 270
  at Saint Mark's Basilica, 63
  Scherzi musicali, 30, 33
  seconda prattica of, 30
  Vespers, 76, 81–83, 85, 269
Monteverdi, Giulio Cesare, 30, 43
Moors, 54
Morley, Thomas, 178
  on fantasies, 66
  A Plaine and Easie Introduction to Practicall Musicke, 153
motets, 79, 84. *See also* concertos, sacred
  eighteenth-century, 182
  French, 81
  grands motets, 115, 121, 201
  petits motets, 115
Mozart, Wolfgang Amadeus, 230
Munich, 65
  court of, 230
  French spoken at court, 182
  Italian opera in, 225
  theatrical spectacles in, 47
musette, 60
Musical Party, A (Olis), 59, *59*
Music for the Royal Fireworks (Handel), 251
Musicians, The (Caravaggio), 31
Musick's Monument (Mace), 64
Musicks Recreation on the lyra viol (Playford collection), 138–39
music publishing, 13, 66
  in Bologna, 174
  broadside ballads, 140–41
  in England, 34–35, 137–41, 146, 240
  in Italy, 21, 28, *87*, 199
  printed music for Protestant services, 83–85
music theory, 214
musique mesurée, 116–17
musique récitatif, 91
Muslims portrayed in theatrical works, 53, 54
Musurgia universalis (Kircher), 66
Mystery Sonatas (Biber), 229–30, *230*, 266

Naples
  conservatories in, 149, 161–62
  political power in, 10
  revolution in, 11
  Venetian opera in, 108
national identity
  national styles and, 12, 116–21, 182
  patronage and, 12
nations, Les (Couperin), 12, 210
Native Americans portrayed in theatrical works, 53, 54
Nemeitz, Johann Christoph, 204
Neo-Platonic philosophy, 22, 23
Neri, Filippo, 91
Nero, Roman emperor, 98
Neue und curieuse teatralische Tantz-Schul (Lambranzi), 104, *104*
Neumeister, Erdmann, 259, 260
Newcastle, public concerts in, 177
Newton, Isaac, 7, 254
Nicolai, Philipp, "Wachet auf," 259–60
Nicolini (Nicolo Grimaldi), 242, 243
"Non temo di morte, m'impiaghi, m'uccida" (Pasqualini), 168, *169*, 170
Noris, Matteo, 109
North, Roger, 199
  Memoirs of Music, 141
Notari, Angelo, 132
notation
  figured bass, 35
  tablature, 21, 35, 138
novello Giasone, Il (Stradella), 108, 188
nozze di Teti e di Peleo, Le (Cavalli), 106
nuns as musicians, 9, 154–57, 270
nuove musiche, Le (Caccini), 21, 30–31, 32–33, 35, 79, 151, 153, *153*
Nuremberg, 60, 66

oboe, 60
Ode on the Death of Mr. Henry Purcell (Blow), 151
odes, musical, 151

Odyssey (Homer), 212

Olis, Jan, *A Musical Party*, 59, *59*

O numi eterni (Handel), 194

opera
  aria–recitative division, 106, 109–10
  ballad operas, 246–47
  beginnings of, 1–3, 22–28, 39
  composers for, 101–3
  conventions in late seventeenth century, 109–10
  eighteenth-century, 182
  English, 143–46
  exoticism in, 13, 123
  French, 115, 124–28, 143, 195, 201, 203, 213–16
  German, 225
  in Hamburg, 221
  Italian, 1–3, 22–28, 39, 40–47, 95–110, 121–22, 225, 232–33, 238, 240, 241–47
  librettists for, 99–101, 195–96, 219, 232, 233
  in London, 238, 240, 241–47
  papal attitudes toward, 46–47, 188
  in Rome, 46–47, 188–89, 195–96
  sacred, 90–91
  set designs and machinery for, 104–6, 122
  in Venice, 94, 95–108
  in Vienna, 232–33
  virtuosity in, 14
opera buffa, 216
Opéra-Comique (Paris), 204
Opera of the Nobility (London), 241
opéras-ballets, 129, 203, 206–8, 215
opéras comique, 206
opere serie, 195–96, 225, 231, 232–33, 242, 247
O quam bonus es (Cozzolani), 157, *158*
oratorios, 14, 25, 109–10, 182, 232
  English, 246–47, 248–50
  Italian, 160–61, 186–87, 189–91
  Latin oratorios, 91–92, 127
  Lutheran, 78
  at the Pietà, 160–61

Orfeo (Rossi), 122, 150
Orfeo, L' (Monteverdi), 1–3, 9, 27, 40–43, 56–57, 101, 164, 270
  "Ahi, caso acerbo," 42, *42*
  embellishments in, 56
  endings of, 41, 42–43
  "Io la musica son," 1–2, *2*, 23, 24
  music reworked for *Vespers*, 82
  orchestration, 56–57, *57*, 85
  "Vi ricorda, o boschi ambrosi," 42, *42*
organ music, 35, 121, 221–23
organs, 3
  Amsterdam recitals, 77
  chamber, 58
  in England, 136–37, 150
  German builders, 60, 65, 221–22
Orlando (Handel), 245
Orlando furioso (Ariosto), 7, 47, 232, 245
Orléans, Duc d', 204
ornamentation. *See* embellishment
orphanages, 94, 148, 149, 158–62, 270
Orphée, L' (Lully), 225
Orpheus (Stati), 27, *27*
Orpheus (Telemann), 225
ospedali grandi, 158–61
ostinato, 34, 46
Ottoboni, Pietro, 186–88, 189, 191, 193, 195, 203
Ottoman Empire, 10, 53, 218
Ouverture burlesque de Quixotte (Telemann), 226
Ovid (Publius Ovidius Naso), 7
  Metamorphoses, 41, 44
Oxford, music during Interregnum, 136–37

Palazzo Barberini (Rome), 172, *172*
Palazzo Bonelli (Rome), 186, 189–90
Palestrina, Giovanni Pierluigi da, 232, 268
Pallavicino, Carlo, 108
Pamphili, Benedetto, 186, 191, 194
pantomimes, 247
Papal States, 10. *See also* Rome

paraliturgical music, 88–92
Paris
  Concert Spirituel in, 177, 214
  grandes nuits and parties, 203–4
  Italian operas in, 108, 121–22
  medicine shows in, 48
  music in eighteenth-century, 201–16
  politics of Italian style in, 202–4, 206–8, 212
  during Regency, 213–16
  salons in, 94, 170–73, 214
  théâtres de la foire, 204–6
Parlatorio of the San Zaccharia Nunnery (Guardi), 155, *156*
Parma, Duchy of, 10
"Par mes chants" (Lambert), 117, *118*, 171
Parnasse, ou L'apothéose de Corelli, Le (Couperin), 200, 210
partbooks, 28, 137
Parthenia (keyboard anthology), 132, *132*
particulares, 52
Pascal, Blaise, *Pensées*, 39
Pasqualini, Marc'Antonio, 167
  "Non temo di morte, m'impiaghi, m'uccida," 168, *169*, 170
Pasquini, Bernardo, 185, 191
passacaglia, 71
passacaille, 71
passepied, 71
Passion plays, 90, 91–92
Passions, 78, 261–62
pastorales héroïques, 215
pastor fido, Il (Guarini), 28–29, 40
patronage
  cosmopolitanism and, 182
  in England, 131–34, 237–38, 245
  as expression of identity, 12
  in Florence, 22–23
  in France, 51–52, 112–29, 201–4
  in Germany, 254–55
  in Holy Roman Empire, 46–47, 218–19, 226–27, 230–33
  of instrumental music, 61–63
  in Italy, 28–30, 31, 47

patronage (*continued*)
  in Rome, 184–88
  royal weddings and, 43–46,
    65, 98
  in seventeenth century, 94
  of spectacles, 39–40, 49
  in Venice, 96, 97–98
Paul V, Pope, 81
pavan, 70
pedal points, 222
pellegrina, La, intermedi for, 23,
    24, 25
Penna, Lorenzo, *Li primi albori
    musicali per li principianti
    della musica figurata,*
    152–53, 154
Pepusch, Johann Christoph, 178,
    237, 246
performers. *See also* women
  academies and societies,
    173–78
  cantors, 151–52
  castrati, 9, 31, 47, 95, 99, 103,
    122, 150, 167, 168, 170, 188,
    193, 224, 242, 245
  choirboys, 149–52
  English court musicians,
    131–34, 146, 151, 237–38
  English court musicians
    exiled to Oxford, 136–37
  French court musicians, 58,
    65, 114
  German court musicians,
    230–31, 254–55
  German municipal
    musicians, 221–22, 226
  instrumentalists'
    employment, 58–62
  Italian female orphans as,
    158–61, 270
  opera singers, 95, 99, 127,
    150, 242, 245–47, 263
  virtuosity and, 14, 23, 35,
    56–58, 61
Pergolesi, Giovanni Battista, *La
    serva padrona,* 216
Peri, Jacopo, 23, 24
  Euridice, 26–27, 28, 41
Perrin, Pierre, 124
Phaëton (Lully), 119
Philidor family, 60
Philip III, King of Spain,
    52, 54
Philip IV, King of Spain, 52
Philip V, King of Spain, 182

Philippe II d'Orléans, 203, 204,
    212, 213–14
Phrygian cadence, 166
Picander (Christian Friedrich
    Henrici), 264
Pièces de clavecin (Couperin),
    183, 203, 208–10, *210*
Pièces de clavecin (Jacquet de la
    Guerre), 212
Pièces de clavessin (Anglebert),
    119, *120*
Piedmont, Duchy of, 10
Pietism, 78, 225
piffari, 58
Pio Zeno, Margherita, 188
Pistoia, 150
*Plaine and Easie Introduction
    to Practicall Musicke, A*
    (Morley), 153
*plaisirs de Saint-Germain-en-Laye,
    Les* (Couperin), 202–3
Platée (Rameau), 215–16
Plato, 22, 31
Playford, John, 137–42, 146, 151
  Apollo's Banquet, 141–42
  *A Breefe Introduction to the
    Skill of Musick,* 138
  *The English Dancing Master,
    The,* 139, 140
  *Musicks Recreation on the lyra
    viol,* 138–39
  Select Ayres and Dialogues,
    137, *138*
pleasure gardens, 177, 250–51,
    270
plucked string instruments, 3,
    58, 71
pochette, 59
Poland, 47, 66, 186, 219, 231
Pomone (Lully), 124
Pompadour, Madame de, 216
Porpora, Nicola, 162
Portugal, villancicos, 78, 81
Praetorius, Michael, *Theatrum
    instrumentorum,* 59, 72
précieuses, 170–71
précieuses ridicules, Les
    (Molière), 171
*Presentation of the Doge to the
    Population* (Bella), *80*
prima prattica, 30, 81
*primi albori musicali per
    li principianti della
    musica figurata, Li*
    (Penna), 152–53, 154

Primi frutti del giardino musicale,
    Op.1 (G. M. Bononcini), *175*
principes du clavecin, Les (Saint
    Lambert), 72–73
Private Musick (England), 131,
    133
processions, 58, 75, 88–90, *89*
program music, 160, 227, 229
  See also character pieces.
Prophetess, The (Purcell), 144
Protestant Reformation and
    Protestant churches, 10,
    11, 78. *See also* specific
    denominations
  in Holy Roman Empire, 219
  impact of, 76
  music in, 11, 18
  printed music for services,
    83–85
Prynne, William, 136
Psalmen Davids (Schütz), 85
psalm settings, 76, 81–85, 139,
    159, 224
Puccitelli, Virgilio, 47
Purcell, Henry, 131, 141, 142–46,
    151, 239
  consort music of, 198
  Dido and Aeneas, 144–46
  Fantasia upon One Note, 142,
    143
  King Arthur, 142–44, 241
  The Prophetess, 144
  Sonnata's of III Parts, 142
Pure, Michel de, 117
Puritans, 11, 76–77, 136, 139, 141
Pythagoras, 15, 22
Pythagorean comma, 15

quattro staggioni, Le (Vivaldi), 160
Queen's Theatre (London), 241,
    242–44, 245, 248, 249
Quinault, Philippe, 124–25,
    171, 195
Quintilian, 13

Racine, Jean, 121, 124
Rameau, Jean-Philippe, 182
  Hippolyte et Aricie, 214–15, *215*
  Platée, 215–16
  term "baroque" used to
    condemn, 4
  Traité de l'harmonie, 214
Ramponi, Virginia, 40, 44, 46
*Rappresentazione di anima et di
    corpo* (Cavalieri), 27–28

Rasi, Francesco, 56
recitatives, 106, 109–10, 154
  in cantatas, 193, 223, 259
  French, 25
  in *opere serie*, 196, 243,
    245
  in *St. John Passion*, 262–63
  types of, 25
recitativo accompagnato, 25
recitativo secco, 25
récits, 124
recorders, 60, 121
Reincken, Johann Adam, 220,
  221, 222
religion and religious music
  in the Baroque. *See also*
    specific denominations
  colossal works, 18, 80–81,
    92, 227
  conflicts, 10–13, 18, 89–90
  congregational singing,
    76–77, 78
  diversity and stylistic
    pluralism, 79–88
  English sacred music,
    135–36, 139
  French sacred music, 121
  German sacred music, 227
  Jewish, 76, 85–88
  music and paraliturgical
    practices, 88–92
  music, faith, and ideology,
    76–79
  printed music for Protestant
    services, 83–85
  psalm settings, 76, 81–85,
    139, 159, 224
  in rituals, 75, 77–79
  sonate da chiesa and, 175
  theatrical devotion, 90–92
Rémond de Saint-Mard,
  Toussaint, 206
Renzi, Anna, 95, 99, 102, 168
resurrezione, La (Handel), 186,
  189–90, 203
  "Disserratevi, o porte
    d'Averno," *190*
rhetoric, 72–73
Rice, John, *Music in the
  Eighteenth Century,* 13, 196,
  206, 226, 246
ricercars, 68
Rich, Christopher, 241
Richelieu, Cardinal, 114–15
Rich, John, 241

Rigaud, Hyacinthe, 112, *113,*
  114, 128
Rinaldo (Handel), 238, 240,
  242–44
  "Cara sposa," *244*
Rinuccini, Ottavio, 23
  Arianna, 43, 44–45, *45*
  La Dafne, 47
  Euridice, 26–27, 28, 41
ripieno, 176, 197, 198, 265
ritornello,
  in the canzonetta, 32
  da capo aria, 109
  in Italian Concerto (Bach), 265
  in *Rinaldo* (Handel), 243–44
  ritornello form in the
    baroque concerto, 160, 255
  use of by Campra, 207–08
Rodelinda (Handel), 246
romanesca, 71
Roman thought, ancient, 7
Rome
  academies in, 167–70, 184,
    191–96, 203
  instrumental ensembles in,
    196–98
  instrumentalists in, 63, 240
  Jesuit choir school in, 149–50
  opera in, 46–47, 108, 110
  sacred operas and drama in,
    27–28, 90–91
  salons in, 171–73
  solo singing, 31
Rospigliosi, Giulio, *Sant'Alessio,*
  46–47, 188
Rossi, Giacomo, 242
Rossi, Luigi, 202
  Orfeo, 122, 150
Rossi, Salamone, 40, 43, 76,
  85–88
  Hashirim asher leSholomo,
    86, *86*
Roubiliac, Louis-François,
  Handel, 250, *250*
Rousseau, Jean-Jacques, 4,
  159
Royal Academy of Music
  (London), 245–46
Roy, Pierre-Charles, 214, 215
Rubens, Peter Paul, *Minerva
  Protects Pax from Mars,* 133
Ruckers studio, 61
ruggiero, 71
running bass, 198
Ruspoli, Francesco Maria, 186

Sacchi, Andrea, *Marcantonio
    Pasqualini (1614–1691)
    Crowned by Apollo,* 168,
    169, 170
Sachs, Curt, 4
sackbut, 3
Sacrati, Francesco, *Venere gelosa,*
    104–5
sacrificio d'Ifigenia, Il (Striggio
    and Gagliano), 44
Sacri musicali affetti (Strozzi),
    167
St. Catherine's Church
    (Hamburg), 220
Saint-Didier (nobleman), 109
Saint-Germain-en-Laye,
    Château de, 202–3
St. Gervais Church (Paris), 208
St. John Passion (Bach), 92,
    261–62, *262*
Saint Lambert, Michel de, *Les
    principes du clavecin,*
    72–73
St Mark's Basilica (Venice), 63,
    80, 81, 88, *89,* 99, 158
St. Mary's Church (Lübeck),
    221–22
St. Matthew Passion (Bach), 261
St. Paul's Cathedral (London),
    48, 78, 135, 136, 238
St. Thomas Church (Leipzig),
    252, 254, 255–56
St. Thomas School (Leipzig),
    152, 260–61
salons, 13
    in Leipzig, 173, 260
    in Paris, 94, 170–73, 214
Salzburg
    Biber in, 226–30
    as free imperial city, 219
Samson (Handel), 246
Sances, Giovanni Felice,
    149–50, 167
San Petronio (Bologna),
    175–76
Sant'Alessio (Landi and
    Rospigliosi), 46–47, 188
Santa Maria della Pietà (Venice),
    158–61
sarabande, 70–71
saraos, 52
Saul (Handel), 249
    "Infernal spirits," *249*
Savoy, Duchy of, 10
Scacchi, Marco, 66

Scarlatti, Alessandro, 108, 172, 185, 186, 189, 191–92, 231
  Bella dama di nome santa, 193–94, *194*
  cantatas, 193
  Giuditta, 187
  La Statira, 187, 188
  Venere, Amore, e Ragione, 194–95
Scarlatti, Domenico, 185, 186, 189
Sceaux, Château de, 203–4
Scheibe, Johann Adolph, 254
Schein, Johann Hermann, 70, 76, 78
  sacred concertos, 258
  "Vom Himmel hoch, da komm ich her," 84, *84*
Scherzi musicali (Monteverdi), 30, 33
Schnitger, Arp, 60, *61*, 221–22
Schütz, Heinrich, 76, 81, 153, 223
  La Dafne, 47
  "Fili mi, Abasalon," 85
  Kleine geistliche Conzerte, 80
  Psalmen Davids, 85
  sacred concertos, 258
  sacred music collections, 84–85
  Symphoniae sacrae, 85
  "Wie lieblich sind deine Wohungen," *85*
"Schweigt stille, plaudert nicht" (Bach), *263*, 263–64
Schweitzer, Albert, 254
scordatura, 229, 230
Scudéry, Madeleine de, 170
  Conversations morales, 171
seconda prattica, 30
Seffner, Carl, Bach statue by, 252, *253*
"Seldome Cleanely" (broadside ballad), 141
Select Ayres and Dialogues (Playford collection), 137, *138*
semi-operas, 144, 241. *See also* Dramatick opera
Semirami, La (Cesti), 109
Senesino (Francesco Bernardi), 245
Sensa celebration, 88
Sephardic Jews, 86

sepulcro, 91
serenades, 193, 194–95
Serse (Handel), 246
serva padrona, La (Pergolesi), 216
sexuality, 8–9, 31–32, 109, 164, 188
Shakespeare, William, 48, 110
  Macbeth, 49
Shepherd, Jack, 246
Simplicianischer (Speer), 152
Simpson, Christopher, 71–72, 134
Singer Barbara Strozzi with a Viola da Gamba, The (Bernardo Strozzi), 165, *165*
singing instruction, 152–54
Slovakia, 219
Slovenia, 219
"So beautie on the waters stood" (Ferrabosco), 50, *50*
societies, music, 94, 177–78
sommeil d'Ulisse, Le (Jacquet de la Guerre), 212, *213*
sonata da camera, 197
sonata da chiesa, 197
Sonata Op. 1, No. 12 (Vitali), 174, *175*
sonatas, 68, 174–75, 182, 229–30, 240
Sonate concertate in stil moderno (Castello), 21, 67–68
sonate da camera, 174
sonate da chiesa, 175
Sonate da chiesa, Op. 6 (Bononcini), 175
songs, solo Italian, 23–28, 30–34
Sonnata's of III Parts (Purcell), 142
Spain
  Catholics in, 10
  French music in, 182–83
  imperial court in, 182, 231
  Italian music in, 182–83
  nun musicians in, 157
  theater in, 39, 48, 52
  villancicos, 78, 81
Speer, Daniel, *Simplicianischer,* 152
spinets, 62
sprezzatura, 35
Stadtpfeifern, 58
Stampiglia, Silvio, 195
Stati, Cristoforo, *Orpheus,* 27, *27*
Statira, La (Scarlatti), 187, 188

Steele, Richard, 242
Steffani, Agostino, 178
Stellwagen, Friederich, 222
stile antico, 121, 257, 266, 268–69
stile concertato, 14, 257
stile concitato, 45, 72, 85, 212, 226, 262
stile moderno, 30, 67, 268
stile rappresentativo, 24–25
stile recitativo, 24–25, 26–27, 33, 41–43
Stradella, Alessandro, 178, 202
  Il novello giasone, 108, 188
Stradivari family, 60
Striggio, Alessandro, the Younger
  L'Orfeo, 41, 43
  Il sacrificio d'Ifigenia, 44
Strozzi, Barbara, 164–67, *165*
  "Ardo in tacito foco," from *Cantate, ariette,* Op. 3, *166*, 166–67
  "Begli occhi," from *Cantate, ariette,* Op. 3, 167
  Sacri musicali affetti, 167
Strozzi, Bernardo, *The Singer Barbara Strozzi with a Viola da Gamba,* 165, *165*
Strozzi, Giulio, 164
Stuart, Charles Edward, 238
Stuart, Elizabeth, 63, 132, 148
style brisé, 65, 119, 266
style galant, 183
style luthé, 119
style luthée, 65
Suite for Cello in C Major (Bach), 266, *267*
Suite in A minor (Couperin), 68, *69*, 70
Suite in C Major (Froberger), 70–71, 72, *73*
Surrexit Christus hodie (chorale), 230
Sweden, Protestants in, 10
Sweelinck, Jan Pieterszoon, 63, 77
  Fantasia chromatica, 67, *68*
Symphoniae sacrae (Schütz), 85

Tabarin, 48
tablature notation, 21, 35, 138
Tacitus (Cornelius), 100
Tarabotti, Arcangela, 155
Tasso, Torquato, *Gerusalemme liberata,* 7, 51, 126, 242

Tate, Nahum, 144
Te Deum (Lully), 126
Telemann, Georg Philipp, 182, 219, 230
   collegium musicum founded by, 177, 225
   French musical style and, 116, 122
   instrumental music, 225
   operas of, 225
   Orpheus, 225
   Ouverture burlesque de Quixotte, 226
text painting, 24, 29, 32, 34, 102, 168, 212, 269
theater
   composer's role in, 54
   court performances, 37, 49
   English Restoration, 142–44
   exoticism in, 52–54
   French spoken, 121, 124
   Greek drama, 26
   medicine shows, 48
   pastoral plays, 28–29, 40
   requisites for, 37
   in Rome, 184
   spoken drama, 48
   technology in, 9–10, 37, 104–6, 242–43
   théâtres de la foire, 204–6
Theater am Gänsemarkt (Hamburg), 225
theaters, public, 13
   in Bologna, 173–76
   in Hamburg, 183, 185, 225
   in Rome, 188, 189
   in Venice, 97–98
theatrical dance, 104
Theatrum instrumentorum (Praetorius), 59, 72
theorbo, 2, 3, 42, 137
Thirty Years' War, 11, 18, 76, 80, 81, 84, 88–89, 177
"Tobacco is like love" (Hume), 34
Toccata in F Major (Buxtehude), 222, *222–23*
Toccata No. 1 (Froberger), *68*, 70
Toccata No. 2 , from *Toccate e partite d'intavolatura di cimbalo* (Frescobaldi), *67, 67*
toccatas, 63, 67, 68, 222
Toccate e partite d'intavolatura di cimbalo, 63, 67

tombeaux, 72
Tordinona theater (Rome), 108, 187, 188
Torelli, Giacomo, 9–10, 104–5, 122, 197
   trumpet concertos, 176
tragédies en musique, 115, 124–28, 143, 195, 201, 203, 215, 225
   parodies of, 121, 202, 205–6
   revivals, 206
Traité de l'harmonie (Rameau), 214
Trevisani, Francesco, 186
trionfo del tempo e del disinganno, Il (Handel), 186
trionfo di Camilla, Il (Bononcini), 241
trio sonatas, 142, 174, 240
trombone, 3, 60
trumpets, 60, 176
tuning systems, 15, 138–39, 229
Turner, William, 151
tutti, 176, 198
24 *Violons du Roi*, 65, 114
Tyers, Jonathan, 250–51

Uberti, Grazioso, 168
Uffenbach, Johann Friedrich von, 225
universities, 148
unmeasured preludes, 68, 70
"Upon a Summer's Time" (ballad), 141
Urban VIII, Pope, 31, 47, 62, 90, 167, 188
Utrecht, Peace of (1713), 237, 238
"Utrecht" *Te Deum* (Handel), 238–39, *239*, 248

Valentini, Giovanni, *Messa, Magnificat et Jubilate Deo*, 81
Valeria, Anna di, 99
Vanbrugh, John, 241
van Dyck, Anthony, 133
variations, 71–72, 78, 119, 134
vaudeville, 206
Vauxhall Gardens (London), 177, 250–51, 270
Venere, Amore, e Ragione (Scarlatti), 194–95
Venere gelosa (Sacrati and Bartolini), 104–5

Venice
   Carnival in, 94, 95, 96, *97*, 129, 157, 158
   colossal Baroque style, 80
   conservatories in orphanages, 149, 158–61, 270
   cosmopolitanism of, 13
   Jewish music in, 87
   music publishing in, 66
   opera in, 94, 95–108
   patronage in, 12
   Piazza San Marco procession, *89*
   political power in, 10, 221
   Saint Mark's Basilica, 63, 80, 81, 88, 99, 158
Versailles, 115–29, 201–2, 216, 231
verse anthems, 81, 135–36
versets, 121
versi sciolti, 25, 101, 193
Vespers (Monteverdi), 76, 81–83, 85, 269
   "Laudate pueri," *82*
   "Nigra sum," *83*
Vetter, Conrad, 90
Viadana, Lodovico, 223
   Concerti ecclesiastici, 79
Vienna
   court poets, 232
   as imperial capital, 218–19, 230–33
   Italian opera in, 108, 225, 232–33
   Italian spoken at court, 182
   Italian style in, 12, 65, 81, 182, 231–33
   public concerts in, 177
   sepulcro performances, 91
   siege of (1683), 10, 89, 218
villancicos, 78, 81
Vincer se stesso è il maggior vittoria (Handel), 185
viola da gamba, 3, 59, 71, 161, 165, 220, 223, 262
viola d'amore, 159–60
viol consorts, 64, 133, 146
viol family, 3, 58, 121, 133, 137
violin family, 58
violin making, 9, 60, 65
violoncello, 3
Virgil (Publius Vergilius Maro), 7
   Aeneid, 33, 145

virginal, 58
virtuosity
in colossal Baroque sacred
music, 81
in French dance, 126
in instrumental music,
56–58, 61, 65, 66–68
in sixteenth century, 14,
23, 35
in vocal music, 45–46, 102,
166–67
Vitali, Tomaso Antonio, Sonata
Op. 1, No. 12, 174, *175*
Vivaldi, Antonio, 158, 182, 232
concertos of, 159–60
death in Vienna, 232
L'estro armonico, 255
influence on Bach, 255, 265
Juditha triumphans, 160–61
Le quattro staggioni, 160
at the Pietà, 158–59
Vivonne, Catherine de,
marquise de
Rambouillet, 170
Vizzana, Lucrezia Orsina, *Componimenti musicali*, 156
Vizzana, Teresa Pompea, 156
Volcius, Melchior, 90
Voltaire, 214
"Vom Himmel hoch, da komm
ich her" (chorale), *77*, 77–78
"Vom Himmel hoch, da komm
ich her" (Schein), 84, *84*
Von der Singe-Kunst (Bernhard),
153–54, *153–54*

Voorhout, Johannes, *Domestic
Music Scene*, 219–21, *220*

Wachet auf, ruft uns die Stimme
(Bach), 258–60, *260*
waites, 58
Walsh, John, 240
Ward, John, "Weep forth your
tears," 130
War of the Spanish Succession,
182, 237, 238–39
Warsaw, Italian opera in, 47
Weckmann, Matthias, 226
"Weep forth your tears" (Ward),
130
Westminster Abbey, 63, 78, 136,
151, 235
"Wie lieblich sind deine
Wohungen" (Schütz), *85*
William III, King of England,
142, 238
wind instruments, 3, 58, 65. *See
also specific instruments*
Władysław, Prince of Poland, 47
Wohltemperierte Clavier, Das
(Bach), 15, 266, *268*
Wölfflin, Heinrich, 4
women. *See also* gender
as academy members, 191
as courtesans, 165
as domestic musicians, 139
Italian orphans as performers, 158–61, 270
music education for, 149
nun musicians, 9, 154–57, 270

as opera singers, 95, 99, 102,
168, 245, 246
as patrons, 47, 163–64,
170–73, 185, 186, 188
as performers and composers
in France, 115, 127, 148,
212
Puritan condemnation of
women musicians, 136
royal musicians, 132
singers in Italy, 31–32, 99,
164–68, 191
wedding laments and,
46
Wonders in the Sun (D'Urfey),
241
Wright, Edward, 159

Xavier, Frances, 90–91
Xerse, Il (Cavalli), 122

York Cathedral, 135

Zadok the Priest (Handel),
248
Zappi, Giovanni Battista, 193
Zarlino, Gioseffo, 22
Zelenka, Jan Dismas, 268
Zeno, Apostolo, 195–96, 232
Ziani, Marc'Antonio, 231
Ziani, Pietro Andrea, 108
Ziegler, Christiane Mariane von,
173, 260
Zimmermann, Gottfried,
262–64